AF333245

Performance and Spanish film

Manchester University Press

Performance and Spanish film

Edited by Dean Allbritton, Alejandro Melero and Tom Whittaker

Manchester University Press

Published by Manchester University Press
Altrincham Street, Manchester M1 7JA
www.manchesteruniversitypress.co.uk

British Library Cataloguing-in-Publication Data
A catalogue record for this book is available from the British Library

Library of Congress Cataloging-in-Publication Data applied for

ISBN 978 0 7190 9772 0 hardback

First published 2016

Typeset by Out of House Publishing
Printed in Great Britain
by TJ International Ltd, Padstow

Contents

Figures

Notes on contributors

Dean Allbritton is an Assistant Professor of Spanish at Colby College, where he teaches courses on Spanish cinema and culture. His work analyses representations of illness and health in contemporary Spanish culture and media as focalising points for larger discourses of national and societal health. More broadly, he has interests in the fields of illness and disability studies, film theory, contemporary Spanish film, and cultural studies. He is currently working on a manuscript that explores the cultural history and legacy of HIV/AIDS in Spain. He has published articles in the *Bulletin of Hispanic Studies*, *Journal of Spanish Cultural Studies*, *Hispanic Research Journal* and in *The Companion to Pedro Almodóvar* (Wiley-Blackwell, 2013).

Carmen Ciller is a Lecturer of Film Studies at University Carlos III of Madrid. She has extensively published on interculturality, femininity and performance, and film production. Her most recent publications study the work of Argentinian actress Cecilia Roth.

Maria M. Delgado is Professor and Director of Research at Royal Central School of Speech and Drama University of London and an Honorary Fellow of the Institute for Modern Languages Research in the School of Advanced Study at the University of London. She has published extensively on Spanish-language performance and film and her work as a film curator and programmer includes work for the BFI and London Spanish Film Festival as well as a programme advisory role at the London Film Festival. She is a member of the Academia Europea.

Brad Epps is Professor of Spanish and Head of the Department of Spanish and Portuguese at the University of Cambridge. He was Professor of Romance Languages and Literatures and Professor and former Chair of the Committee on Degrees in Studies of Women, Gender and Sexuality at Harvard University for over two decades. He has published extensively on modern literature, film, art, architecture, urban theory, queer theory and immigration from Spain, Latin America, Hispanophone Africa and Catalonia, and is the author of *Significant Violence: Oppression and Resistance in the Narratives of Juan Goytisolo* (Oxford University Press, 2006); *Spain Beyond Spain: Modernity, Literary History, and National Identity* (with Luis Fernández Cifuentes, Bucknell University Press, 2005); *Passing Lines: Immigration and Sexuality* (with Bill Johnson-González and Keja Valens, Harvard University Press, 2005); *All About Almodóvar: A Passion for Cinema* (with Despina Kakoudaki, University of Minnesota Press, 2009); a special issue of *Catalan Review* on Barcelona and modernity (2004), and a special issue of *GLQ* (with Jonathan Katz) on lesbian theorist Monique Wittig (2007). His research interests include eighteenth- to twenty-first-century Spanish and Latin American literature, Catalan literature and film, Ibero-American cinema, photography and art, Hispanophone Africa, theories of visuality, modernity, critical theory, gender and sexuality studies, feminist thought, queer theory, urban cultures, immigration and post-colonial studies, among others.

Sally Faulkner is Professor of Hispanic Studies and Film Studies at the University of Exeter, where she is also Founder-Director of the Centre for Translating Cultures. She has published widely on Spanish film, literature and cultural studies, and is the author of *Literary Adaptations in Spanish Cinema* (Tamesis, 2004), *A Cinema of Contradiction: Spanish Film in the 1960s* (Edinburgh University Press, 2006) and *A History of Spanish Film: Cinema and Society 1910–2010* (Bloomsbury Academic, 2013). In 2013 she was awarded the Philip Leverhulme Prize (Modern Languages and Literatures).

Santiago Fouz-Hernández is Reader in Hispanic Studies at Durham University (UK). He is author of *Cuerpos de cine, Masculinidades carnales en el cine y la cultura popular contemporaneous* (Bellaterra, 2013), co-author of *Live Flesh: The Male Body in Contemporary Spanish Cinema* (I. B. Tauris, 2007), editor of *Mysterious Skin: Male Bodies in Contemporary Cinema* (I. B. Tauris, 2009) and co-editor of *Madonna's Drowned Worlds* (Ashgate, 2004) and *Re-thinking 'Identities': Cultural Articulations of Alterity and Resistance in the New Millennium* (Peter Lang, 2014). Currently he is preparing a monograph on the late Bigas Luna for Manchester University Press and an edited collection entitled *Spanish Erotic Cinema* for Edinburgh University Press.

Stuart Green is Senior Lecturer in Spanish at University of Leeds, where he teaches and researches on peninsular culture from the Golden Age to the present day. He is author of *From Silver Screen to Spanish Stage*

(University of Wales Press, 2011), a study of the influence of Hollywood on theatre in Spain. He has published on theatre and film in journals such as *Modern Language Review, Bulletin of Spanish Studies* and *Don Galán*. Since 2011, much of his research has focused on the ways in which contemporary theatre, television, cinema and music engage with the question of ethnic diversity. He is member of the editorial board of journal *Estreno* and co-editor of *New Cinemas*.

Alejandro Melero is Lecturer at University Carlos III de Madrid. He has published several articles dealing with the representation of sex on screen and queer and gender theory, and contributed to *Gender and Spanish Cinema* (Berg, 2004) and *Hispanic and Lusophone Women Filmmakers* (Manchester University Press, 2012). His books *Placeres ocultos: Gays y lesbianas en el cine español de la Transición* and *Guía ilustrada del cine europeo* were both published by Notorious in 2010.

Alberto Mira is Reader in Spanish and Film Studies at Oxford Brookes University. He teaches Film Narrative and Star Studies. His publications include *Miradas insumisas, De Sodoma a chueca* and *Historical Dictionary of Spanish Cinema*. He has worked extensively on gay culture in Spain, particularly on film reception. Currently he is working on a series on essays on autobiographical representation in the work of Spanish gay writers and filmmakers, as well as a long-term project on Spanish Star Sara Montiel.

Rob Stone is Professor of Film Studies at the University of Birmingham, author of *Spanish Cinema* (Longman, 2001), *Flamenco in the Works of Federico García Lorca and Carlos Saura* (Edwin Mellen, 2004), *Julio Medem* (Manchester University Press, 2007) and *Walk, Don't Run: The Cinema of Richard Linklater* (Columbia University Press, 2013). He is co-editor of *The Unsilvered Screen: Surrealism on Film* (Wallflower Press, 2007), *Screening Songs in Hispanic and Lusophone Cinema* (Manchester University Press, 2012) and *A Companion to Luis Buñuel* (Wiley-Blackwell, 2013) and is co-author of *Basque Cinema: a Cultural and Political History* (I. B. Tauris, 2015)

Kathleen Vernon is Associate Professor and Chair of the Department of Hispanic Languages and Literature at the State University of New York at Stony Brook, where she teaches courses on Spanish and Latin American cinema and culture. She has published widely on various aspects of Spanish-language cinema from the 1930s to the present, with special focus on melodrama, film music and sound, and women's cinema. Her most recent publications include *A Companion to Pedro Almodóvar*, co-edited with Marvin D'Lugo (Wiley-Blackwell,

2013). She is currently completing a book on voice, music and sound in film, *Listening to Spanish Cinema*, and two multi-authored books, *The Mediation of Everyday Life: An Oral History of Cinema-Going in 1940s and 1950s Spain* and *Film Magazines, Fashion and Photography in 1940s and 1950s Spain*.

Duncan Wheeler is Associate Professor in Spanish at the University of Leeds, where he is also a member of the Executive Committee of the Centre for World Cinemas. Until recently, he was a Leverhulme Research Fellow working on the role of arts and cultural institutions in Spain's transition to democracy, the subject of his second monograph – following *Golden Age Drama in Contemporary Spain: The Comedia on Page, Stage and Screen* (University of Wales Press/ University of Chicago Press, 2012). A published translator and author of over twenty peer-reviewed articles and book chapters, Duncan is also Reviews Editor for *New Cinemas* and subject editor of *The Literary Encyclopedia*.

Tom Whittaker is Senior Lecturer in Film and Spanish Cultural Studies at the University of Liverpool. He is the author of *The Films of Elías Querejeta: A Producer of Landscapes* (University of Wales Press, 2001), and has published widely on Spanish cinema. He is co-editor of *Locating the Voice in Film: Global Practices and Critical Approaches* (Oxford University Press, 2016) and is currently completing a monograph entitled *Quinquis, Criminality and Sound in Spanish Film*.

Eva Woods Peiró is an Associate Professor at Vassar College in Hispanic Studies. She has taught and mentored in the Media Studies, Latin American and Latino Studies and Women's Studies. Her books include *White Gypsies: Race and Stardom in Spanish Musicals*, (Minnesota University Press, 2012), *Visualizing Spanish Modernity* (Berg, 2005), co-edited with Susan Larson (University of Kentucky), and the forthcoming, collaborative *Cinema and the Mediation of Everyday Life: An Oral History of Cinema-Going in 1940s and 1950s Spain* (Berghahn).

Sarah Wright is Senior Lecturer at Royal Holloway, University of London, where she specialises in Spanish theatre, film and cultural studies. She is the author of *The Trickster-Function in the Theatre of García Lorca* (Tamesis, 2000), *Tales of Seduction: The Figure of Don Juan in Spanish Culture* (I. B. Tauris, 2007) and *The Child in Spanish Cinema* (Manchester University Press, 2013).

Acknowledgements

We would like to thank the department of Modern Languages and Cultures at University of Liverpool, Departamento de Periodismo y Comunicación Audiovisual at Universidad Carlos III de Madrid and the Spanish Department at Colby College for their support during the editing of this book. This book would not have been possible without the help of various institutions which have helped the editors during their research: the Center for the Arts and Humanities, the Humanities Division, and the Office of the Provost at Colby College and Proyecto de investigación 'El Cine y la Televisión en la España de la Post-Transición', CSO2012-31895, Ministerio de Economía y Competitividad. We are particularly indebted to Filmoteca Española and Biblioteca Nacional in Madrid. Thanks also to Matthew Frost and Paul Clarke at Manchester University Press for their cooperation and assistance throughout the project.

Finally, we would like to acknowledge our debt of gratitude to the authors of the chapters for their work.

Introduction: approaching performance in Spanish film

Dean Allbritton, Alejandro Melero and Tom Whittaker

The importance of screen acting has often been overlooked in studies on Spanish film. While several critical works on Spanish cinema have centred on the cultural, social and industrial significance of stars, there has been relatively little critical scholarship on what stars are paid to do: act. This is perhaps surprising, given the central role that acting occupies within a film. In his essay 'Why Study Film Acting?', Paul McDonald argues that acting is not only crucial to understanding the affective charge of movies, but integral to the study of film as a whole (2004: 40). Yet, despite its significance, performance remains one of the most elusive and difficult aspects of film analysis. One of the reasons for this, according to Pamela Robertson Wojcik, is its apparent transparency (2004: 1). A 'good' actor supposedly renders their performance 'invisible', thereby concealing the process of acting from the audience, and engaging us within the emotional universe of the character. To this effect, discussion on acting is all too frequently evaluative: we think in terms of how convincing or naturalistic a given performance is, or are invited to appreciate the actorly skills and techniques that are brought to bear on the film.

Yet, when it comes to writing about performance academically, it can prove altogether more challenging. It requires us to single out and momentarily freeze the flow of specific moments of performance within a film, and to break them down to their tiniest details. We need to pay attention to what Paul McDonald has called the 'micromeanings of the voice and body' (2004: 40), intricately drawing out the ways in which gesture, body, facial expression and vocal delivery work together to create meaning. From the clench of a fist to the faintest curl of a lip, we should be attuned to the repetition and rhythm of the most minute and subtle of gestures. The orchestration of all of these signs – which, crucially, are both visual and aural – not only help the actor to construct their character, but enable us to glean a greater understanding of cinematic practices and politics of Spanish film. Analysing the fine grain of performance enables us to connect the micro to the macro, alerting us to the broader industrial, technological and social-historical contexts in which it is produced.

Breaking a performance down into its constituent parts (or 'micromeanings', to once again follow McDonald) firstly reveals that screen acting cannot be studied in isolation. That is, an actor's performance cannot be examined without considering its interaction with the other formal components of film, such as cinematography (camerawork and framing), editing and sound design. These factors frequently serve to emphasise a performance within a given film, as much as they can work together to delimit its expressivity and stymie its flow. For instance, on the one hand, the energetic and fluid style of acting in the *sainete*-inflected comedies of Berlanga and Ferreri were made possible through protracted long takes and post-synch sound. Compare this, on the other hand, to the performance of Javier Bardem in *Mar adentro/The Sea Inside* (Alejandro Amenábar, 2004) which, through the frequent use of static camera and the closeup, is more finely modulated and minimalist in both gesture and tone. These examples serve to demonstrate that screen acting is always mediated to one degree or another. This process of mediation, moreover, further leads us to challenge an actor's agency or authorship within a given film. To what extent is the final performance determined by the actor, or the filmic apparatus which records her or him? Looking at screen performance from this perspective thus casts a critical light on the broader industrial and technological contexts in which it is produced.

Yet screen acting is of course far more than a passive component of *mise-en-scène* or montage. After all, a performance is vividly brought to life by an actor, whose skill and craftsmanship are most often products of lengthy rehearsals and years of intensive training. An analysis of acting, therefore, also needs to take account of the importance of the actor's labour and craft, and the subsequent lengths to which an actor goes to improve their acting skills. Many of these empirical details draw our attention away from the textual analysis of a given scene or sequence, to a consideration of the pre-production stages of a film. These can often reveal the gruelling regimes and punishing processes of bodily transformation that actors sometimes undertake in order to carry out specific roles. This perhaps found one of its most drastic expressions in Christian Bale's performance in the Spanish-produced film *The Machinist* (Brad Anderson, 2004). The actor famously lost 27 kilograms for the role of Trevor Reznik, a machinist whose insomnia has led to his becoming emaciated.

An exploration of an actor's technique can often lead us back several years to their initial entry into acting school, and the acting methods they were subsequently taught. Several acting techniques taught within

Spain have been influenced and shaped by international practices and methods. According to Elly Konijn (2005: 63), contemporary scholars of performance studies tend to agree that there are three key approaches to acting: Method acting, the detachment approach and the self-expressive approach. If, as Konijn suggests, each of these acting techniques have occupied a prominent place in most Western film industries, then the history of Spanish cinema similarly bears this out. While the Method – a school of acting which draws on the teachings of Stanislavski, and was later modified by the likes of Lee Strasberg and Stella Adler in the US in the 1940s and 1950s – is most famously associated with Hollywood cinema, its influence has also been felt within Spanish cinema. Indeed, several of its techniques were also synthesised and developed by William Layton, an American director and actor who was largely responsible for bringing the Method to Spain. In founding the Teatro Estudio de Madrid in 1960 and the Teatro Experimental Independiente in 1968, Layton trained a generation of Spanish actors, which includes Ana Belén and Julieta Serrano. The subsequent arrivals of the Argentine teachers Cristina Rota in the late 1970s and Juan Carlos Corazza in 1990 further led to the creation of two very influential acting schools in Spain. The Escuela de Interpretación de Cristina Rota trained several contemporary Spanish actors, such as Penélope Cruz (who has also studied with Corazza) and Fernando Tejero. For his part, Corazza has famously coached Javier Bardem for his roles in *Mar adentro* and *Biutiful*, as well as other prominent actors such as Raúl Arévalo and Jordi Mollá. Like the work of William Layton, Corazza and Rota are similarly influenced by Stanslivaski, and they encourage their students to find the emotional truth of their performances through improvisatory techniques.

By way of contrast, the detachment approach refuses to follow the Method's belief that one needs to experience an emotion in order to perform it. Quite on the contrary, it proposes that 'the emotionally detached actor [is] more capable of arousing intense emotional effects on the spectator via a reflection on the character and on situational demands' (Koniijn, 2005: 63). The detachment approach had a particular presence in Spanish acting in the years of the Transition to democracy (1975–82), in the works of very influential stage and screen actors such as José Luis Gómez, Juan Diego, Fernando Guillén and Rafael Álvarez 'El Brujo'. These actors worked with others who came from different schools, first on the stage and later in films of noted directors such as Eloy de la Iglesia (for instance, José Luis Gómez's performance in *La estanquera de Vallecas*, 1987) and Carlos Saura (Juan Diego in *La noche oscura/The Dark Night*, 1989).

The self-expressive approach, the final technique, encompasses a variety of styles developed by different schools which are interested in the actor's self-expression, and which argue that the actor should present his or her most authentic self. Peter Brook, for instance, the British theatre director whose work is inspired by the experimental theatre of Antonin Artaud and Jerzy Grotowski, is perhaps the most influential proponent of this approach. In Spain, evidence of the self-expressive approach has shaped acting schools such as Teatro de La Abadía, in Madrid, which is directed by José Luis Gómez. The legacy of Sanford Meisner (1905–97) is of extreme relevance to this third stream. Meisner was originally exposed to the techniques of Method Acting, but he disagreed (as Stanislavski himself would eventually do) with the use of affective memory, that is, actors searching for emotions in their own memories. The influence of Meisner's techniques is particularly significant for contemporary actors. In Madrid, schools such as La Compañía de Cine have been teaching the Meisner method since the 1990s.

While international methods have dominated much of the teaching of acting in Spain, an older generation of actors also drew on traditions and techniques that are intrinsic to Spanish culture, particularly within the genre of comic performance. Pepe Isbert, Rafaela Aparicio and Gracita Morales, for instance, learned their distinctive modes of physical and vocal performance through the comic theatre. These actors famously drew on the tradition of the *sainete*, a theatrical comic form that centred on farcical situations, everyday locations and large groups of actors. Noticeably expansive and gestural, *sainete* performances were made up of external traits and tics – a style of acting that would appear to be antithetical to the three approaches of acting set out by Konijn. While younger generations of actors are more likely to have been exposed to international methods of performance, the *sainete* still tends to shape several of the acting styles encountered in Spanish comedies. Take, for instance, the 'choral' films of Álex de la Iglesia, whose narratives are structured around large casts of stock characters (Buse, Triana-Toribio and Williams 2007: 127); films like *Ocho apellidos vascos/A Spanish Affair* (Emilio Martínez-Lázaro, 2014), similarly, contain traces of the *sainete* in their use of regional stereotypes and humour vividly conveyed through gesture and voice.

If the study of acting brings into relief performance practices that are specific to a particular nation, it also illuminates the ways in which national or regional identities are in turn performed. Situating an actor's work within a consideration of its broader national and industrial context can bring into play the tension between performance and the performative – that is, the differences or similarities involved in acting for the screen versus the conscious or unconscious repetition of signs that coalesce into an identity. The connections between these concepts are multiple and far-reaching, hence the easy slide from one into another in much work in Performance and Film Studies. Although by no means the first to write about public performance and identity, Judith Butler's coining of 'performativity' (1990) has perhaps had the most influence in the way both are considered today. For Butler, 'performativity' denotes the ways that gender is performed through a series of culturally recognisable signs and actions; her prime example, although later modified slightly, drew on the (often visual) performance of gender amongst drag queens.

By relating the enactment of gender signs to their very construction, Butler's analysis notably correlated action to creation; in doing so, 'performativity' provided another way to reconceptualise how ideals of identity, race and sexuality are constituted and reified. As such, performance and the performativity of identity have long been linked, shared and viewed together. Analyses of screen performance, to that end, have much to teach about the way we perceive identities, as well as our understanding of the cinematic medium. Javier Bardem, for example, became an iconic symbol of Spanish masculinity with his early roles as the bisexual Jimmy in *Las edades de Lulú/The Ages of Lulu* (Bigas Luna, 1990) or the lusty Raúl in *Jamón, jamón* (Bigas Luna, 1992), and has strengthened his Latin lothario image internationally with films like *Vicky Cristina Barcelona* (Woody Allen, 2008) and *Eat Pray Love* (Ryan Murphy, 2010). Although this image is now debated (even in this volume), Bardem's performance of recognisable and approved signs for Spanishness coalesce into an identity that reifies what it means to act – or, critically, *be* – Spanish.

With the crucial exception of James Naremore's brilliant *Acting in the Cinema* (1988), which centres predominantly on performance in Hollywood in its classical period, specific studies on acting in Film Studies were thin on the ground until relatively recently. Naremore's book introduced several critical terms and interpretative frameworks that would be highly influential to the study of acting. While in everyday life people frequently find themselves 'performing' different roles and facets, theatrical performance for Naremore is distinct in so far as it suggests a 'degree of ostensiveness that marks it off from quotidian behavior' (1988: 17). 'Ostensiveness', then, as a term can be used to analyse the scale of the gestures of a performance – a scale which, as he shows, is largely dependent on its 'mode of address' (that is, the size and context of the people the actor is speaking to). Later anthologies on film performance, such as Alan Lovell and Peter Kramer's *Screen Acting* (1999) and Pamela Robertson Wojcik's *Movie Acting: The Film Reader* (2004), have explored screen acting across a more eclectic corpus of films. The anthology *More Than a Method: Trends and*

Traditions in Contemporary Film Performance (Cynthia Baron, Diane Carson and Frank Tomasulo, 2004), which mainly focuses on American cinema, also considers British, French and Cuban practices of acting, while *Reframing Screen Performance* (Cynthia Baron and Sharon Marie Carnicke, 2008) innovatively draws on theatre theory to illuminate acting techniques in film. More recent still is Aaron Taylor's edited collection *Theorizing Film Acting* (2012) and Donna Peberdy's monograph *Masculinity and Film Performance: Male Angst in Contemporary American Cinema* (2011). In addition to these anthologies are textbooks such as Andrew Klevan's *Film Performance: From Achievement to Appreciation* (2005) and Martin Shingler's *Star Studies: A Critical Guide* (2012), which also contains a highly useful overview to the field of performance.

While literature on screen acting has clearly gathered apace since the new millennium, the vast majority of this scholarship has focused squarely on American cinema. In contrast, screen acting in non-Anglophone film industries has received significantly far less attention. Analyses of star performances have been incorporated into monographs on European stardom, such as Guy Austin's *Stars in Modern French Film* (2003), Ginette Vincendeau's *Stars and Stardom in French Cinema* (2000) and Catherine O'Rawe's *Stars and Masculinities in Contemporary Italian Cinema* (2014). Recent anthologies also centre on star performances within global and transnational contexts, such as Andrea Bandhauer's and Michelle Royer's *Stars in World Cinema: Screen Icons and Star Systems Across Cultures* (2015) and Russell Meeuf's and Raphael Raphael's *Transnational Stardom: International Celebrity in Film and Popular Culture* (2013). The focus in these books, however, is more on performers rather than performance *per se*, and to our knowledge there has yet to be a book that addresses screen performance within its specific national context.

In Spain, one of the earlier examples of literature on screen acting is Mainou Pla's *La interpretación cinematográfica: Ensayo sobre su fundamento y su técnica*, first published in 1956. This volume was possibly the first theoretical approach to the techniques of acting in front of the camera, as well as an early attempt to import into Spain perspectives from international cinemas. It also shows how, for decades, the literature of acting was extremely dependent upon the theory of theatre performance. One of the consequences of the scarcity of literature about acting was that the few books that existed had relatively long lives and reached different generations. An example of this is Luis Arana's *El actor: Bosquejo de una sociología del comediante* (1966), which had several editions and was, for decades, one of the few manuals that practitioners, actors and fans of actors alike were able to get hold of. In contrast, the 1990s saw the publication of several new acting manuals such as Assumpta Serna's *El trabajo del actor de cine* (1999), as well as the translation of a range of texts on performance, such as Iain Mackintosh's *Architecture, Actor and Audience* (1993), which was published in Spain in 2000 as *La arquitectura, el actor y el público*. Another relevant example is David Mamet's *True and False: Heresy and Common Sense for the Actor* (1997), published in Spain in 1999 as *Verdadero y falso: herejía y sentido común para el actor*.

Anglophone studies of Spanish film have frequently addressed figurative performance of identity – with several seminal studies subsequently concerned with the 'performance' of nation, region or gender – at the expense of deep analyses of film acting. Notable exceptions here include Isabel Santaolalla's *The cinema of Iciar Bollaín* (2012), in which the author provides an invaluable account of both Bollaín's directorial and acting career, and Chris Perriam's incisive chapter on the performance of Penélope Cruz and Javier Bardem in *Vicky Cristina Barcelona* (2013). Studies on Spanish stardom have similarly provided useful discussion of actors' techniques: Chris Perriam's *Stars and Masculinities in Spanish Cinema: From Banderas to Bardem* (2003) combines a precise study of acting with the theoretical paradigms of Star Studies, as well as research into masculinities and body representations; Ann Davies's eponymously titled book on Penélope Cruz (2014); Duncan Wheeler's chapter 'Acting and Directing in Spain: Historicising Stardom and the Author-Function' (2014) and Rebecca Naughten's article 'Subtle Gestures and Tonsorial Distractions: Javier Bardem as a Travelling Performer' (2014).

About this book

Bringing together a range of scholars that attend carefully to the performances, acting styles and historical influences of Spanish film, this book seeks to place the process of acting centre stage. The chapters that follow look closely at the 'micromeanings' and gestures of Spanish film acting, offering broad-ranging and probing analyses of individual performances and acting styles from the silent period to the present day. Comprising fifteen original chapters by scholars from the United States, the United Kingdom and Spain, this book casts light on the manifold meanings, methods and influences of Spanish screen performance. In each of the chapters, acting serves as a powerful site of meaning through which broader questions around Spanish film practices, culture and society can be explored. The chapters here situate the development of Spanish screen acting in both its national and global contexts, tracing acting techniques that are largely indigenous to Spain, as well as unpicking the ways in which Spanish performance has frequently been shaped by international influences and forces.

In Chapter 1, 'Acting for the camera in Spanish film magazines of the 1920s and 1930s', Eva Woods Peiró locates specific instances in which writers, directors and actors of the 1920s referenced the actual object of the camera in relationship to film acting and performance. She further shows how, contrary to how Spaniards have been represented or have portrayed themselves throughout history, the phenomenology of techno-logical mediation – here, acting – is deeply embedded in Spanish filmic culture. This chapter includes extensive archival work in order to analyse how Spanish critics of silent film regularly theorised on complex ideas concerning the need for actors to physically and psychologically adjust their performances to the requirements of the camera medium, the frag-mentation and monotonisation of acting, and ultimately its commoditi-sation. Woods Peiró's study persuasively documents the ways in which the camera influenced acting styles and performances, and how the con-sciousness of cinemagoers participated in the policing, self-policing and racialisation of subjects as readers of film magazines.

Chapter 2, Sarah Wright's 'Performance and gesture as crisis in *La aldea maldita/The Cursed Village* (Florián Rey, 1930)', examines the sig-nificance of gestures and sonorisation and the politics behind these in order to understand the relationships between body, cinema and ideol-ogy. Through a close analysis of the 1930 version of *La aldea maldita*, Wright reflects on the influences ushered in by Spain's embrace of moder-nity. Touted as 'Spain's last silent film', as well as its 'most important' one, *La aldea maldita* presents a harsh, minimalist beauty that has long been praised by audiences and critics. The acting style is influenced not just by trends of the time but also by the film's relationship to sound: according to Wright, after the disastrous experience with the sonorisation of a pre-vious film, Rey decided to film *La aldea maldita* as if it were silent, when in fact the first showing of the film included sound. Wright studies the performance in the version of this film, questioning the sense of anach-rony that now pervades them and reflecting on attitudes to aesthetics, acting and the cinematic medium itself.

In Chapter 3, 'Exaggeration and nation: the politics of performance in the Spanish sophisticated comedy of the 1940s', Stuart Green explores the acting styles of the decade that followed. In analysing the so-called sophisticated comedies of early Francoism, Green examines how dis-courses of nation in the post-war decade determined the study of the performance of their stars and supporting actors. He explores the per-formance style of both supporting actors, which he sometimes considers to be exaggerated, and romantic leads, which, as Green demonstrates, is largely influenced by the theatre. The problematic combination of these two acting styles, Green argues, is fundamental to understanding the commercial success of the sophisticated comedies of the post-war period. The author analyses in detail the work of prominent actors such as Rafael Durán or Guadalupe Muñoz Sampedro, in order to problematise Susan Hayward's idea that 'gestural codes are deeply rooted in a nation's culture'. Green ultimately shows that it is more appropriate to talk about general performance paradigms rather than national models. If the acting styles of exaggerated secondary characters and theatrical romantic leads are more prominent in Spanish films of the time, it is because of the persistence of a paradigm that transcended the theatre and was appropriated by the cinema.

Chapter 4, 'The voice of comedy: Gracita Morales' by Kathleen Vernon, participates in recent scholarship on Spanish cinema which revalorises the comic performances and personas of a number of well-known actors. Vernon analyses the typification and standardisation of the voice in Spanish cinema, which she argues is the result of a long history of film dubbing, with its strict codification of vocal types according to gender and role. This practice has resulted in a series of unwritten rules and expectations that continue to shape and restrict the kinds of voices that Spanish audiences hear on screen. Under these norms, while non-standard voices may be permitted and are even cultivated for comic and character parts, leading roles continue to demand what Vernon calls the 'phonogenic' expression of unproblematically feminine and masculine identities. With her unmistakable, high-pitched voice, Gracita Morales was inevitably slotted into supporting roles, her childlike affect and lack of verbal inhibition put to classic comic ends as weapons used to skewer the pretensions of a would-be upwardly mobile and modernising middle class. Despite being categorised in this manner, Vernon argues, Gracita Morales become an example of what Kathleen Rowe calls 'unruly women', female comics who by talking back and laughing loudly claim their right to a traditionally male privilege, thereby challenging the notion of comedy as a male-dominated genre.

Tom Whittaker also addresses the importance of sound and the voice in acting in Chapter 5, 'The sounds of José Luis López Vázquez: vocal performance, gesture technology', exploring the transition from post-synch to direct sound in Spanish cinema through a particular emphasis on José Luis López Vázquez's voice. This chapter shows the ways in which sound design marked a shift in register from a gestural and presentational acting style to a more Stanislavskian mode of performance that stressed interiority and the unspoken. Whittaker argues that direct sound shaped and transformed Spanish performance, reconfiguring the relationship between body and space in cinema. His analysis of López Vázquez's vocal performance thus casts a light on the limits between the embodiment and disembodiment of performance and sound, as well as providing a means of tracing the emerging acting styles of the 1970s. The presence (and absence) of his voice in his performances, and how these were determined by the synchronisation of sound in post-production, provide a valuable opportunity to understand how technology and acting are linked in complex ways.

In Chapter 6, 'The influence of Argentinian acting schools in Spain from the 1980s', Carmen Ciller analyses the legacy of Argentinian performers and acting schools in contemporary Spanish cinema. Ciller begins by studying how different waves of migration between Spain and Argentina resulted in rich collaborations, both in terms of industry and familial bonds (which favoured the appearance and continuation of families of actors such as the Alterios and Diosdados). The arrival of these Argentinian actors and actresses during the Transition to democracy contributed to the disappearance of traditional acting styles in Spanish cinema and promoted innovative modes and methods of performance. Thus, for Ciller, the generation led by Cecilia Roth provided Spanish cinema with new ways to represent the body and perform femininity and sexual freedom, in films as influential as Iván Zulueta's *Arrebato/ Rapture* (1979). Ciller concludes with a discussion on how the proliferation of Argentinian schools of acting, such as those of Cristina Rota and Juan Carlos Corazza, has contributed greatly to the success of recent generations of actors such as Penélope Cruz and Javier Bardem.

In Chapter 7, 'Askance, athwart, aside: the queer plays of actors, *auteurs* and machines', Brad Epps sharply juxtaposes the Spanish 'comedia de mariquitas' ['poofter comedy'] *No desearás al vecino de quinto* (Ramón Fernández, 1970) with the Argentine film *La niña santa* (Lucrecia Martel, 2004). By dissecting Alfredo Landa's performance in *No desearás al vecino de quinto*, Epps studies how the actor's on- and off-screen persona as modern-day everyman, and his flamboyant character, highlight the split between actor and his craft; this performance, for Epps, also brings to the fore a queer performance of identity that dovetails with the 'queer sensibility' of Martel's directorial hand. While insisting on the multiple positions available to queerness, particularly in two films that seem to teeter on its edge, this chapter questions what it can mean to perform humanity through utterances, gestures and glances, through objects, positions and gestures.

In Chapter 8, 'The future of nostalgia: revindicating Spanish actors and acting in and through *Cine de barrio*', Duncan Wheeler considers the impact of the television programme *Cine de barrio* on popular discourses surrounding national film and performance styles. First airing in 1995, *Cine de barrio* pairs the viewing of a classic national film (generally made sometime between 1950 and the late 1970s, after the death of Spanish dictator Francisco Franco) with a talk-show segment between a host and an invited guest. By linking discourses on cultural and historical memory with the subsequent revival of classic national cinema brought about by *Cine de barrio*, Wheeler explores the relationship between actors, their films and their audiences; the affective response produced in this encounter, he argues, generates a nostalgia for classic national cinema that also influences contemporary Spanish film. As Wheeler demonstrates the links between the seemingly disparate films of the 1970s and the comedic box office blowouts of the 2010s, he argues for a sustained reflection on nostalgia, memory and their connections to acting and performance.

In Chapter 9, 'Performing the nation: mannerism and mourning in Spanish heritage cinema', Sally Faulkner explores performance and identity in what she terms 'Spanish heritage films', a type of national cinema that operates from within intermedial, intertextual and transnational networks. Faulkner discusses the particular cases of *El perro del hortelano/The Dog in the Manger* (Pilar Miró, 1997) and *Alatriste/Captain Alatriste: The Spanish Musketeer* (Agustín Díaz Yanes, 2006), describing their domestic popularity and international failure. These successes and failures, for Faulkner, ultimately produce a national cultural discourse that (despite the adoption of foreign cinematic aesthetics) fails to be legible to foreign audiences familiar with those very aesthetics. In studying the foreign-influenced performance style of the actors of these two films, Faulkner deftly tracks their attempts to reach local and foreign audiences. The history of these particular acting styles – and in spite of the transnational aesthetics that guide these films – are haunted, Faulkner argues, by earlier performances and roles that ultimately provide a national opportunity for Spanish audiences to experience history, cinema and mourning.

Chapter 10, Alejandro Melero's 'Performing sex in Spanish erotic films of the 1980s', considers the importance of acting and performance in the 'S'-rated sex films that peppered the late 1970s and 1980s in Spain. In this chapter, Melero explores the question of what precisely constitutes 'performance' in films which showcase 'real' sex between its actors; that is, if a lead actor has an erection in a scene, how much of his physical response might be considered acting? Focusing on one film in particular, *Con las bragas en la mano/Panties in the Hands* (Julio Pérez Tabernero, 1981), he argues that the lines between eroticism, pornography and cinema were blurred by the explosion of sex films in Spain at this time. Finally, and turning to the career of the film's lead actor, Emilio Línder, Melero discusses the attempts to legitimise these films and the performances they contain, and whether or not they may have a space in Spanish cinematic history.

Chapter 11, 'Becoming Mario: performance and persona adaptation in Mario Casas's career' by Alberto Mira, looks at the body of work of one of Spain's most ubiquitous young stars. Analysing Casas's on- and off-screen performances of masculinity and the role that his star persona plays in his filmography, Mira argues that the actor's career has revolved around his carefully sculpted physique and behaviour – and that Casas is indicative of a new generation of young male stars in Spain. As 'The Great Hope of Spanish Cinema', therefore, Casas comes to represent a shift in public perceptions of manhood and is evocative of a new type of manufactured, cinematic masculinity. With ties to the work of Susan Bordo and Richard Dyer, this chapter underscores the importance of physicality to Casas's performance of masculinity, as made evident in his iconic roles in films such as *Tres metros sobre el cielo/Three Steps Above Heaven* (Fernando González Molina, 2010) and *Tengo ganas de ti/I Want You* (Fernando González Molina, 2012).

From a body in its theoretically perfect prime, we turn to those bodies that are seen to be outside the realm of the desirable in Chapter 12, 'Performing fatness: oversized male bodies in recent Spanish cinema' by Santiago Fouz-Hernández. This chapter looks at three actors who have gained weight for roles – Javier Bardem, Santiago Segura and Antonio de la Torre – in order to discuss the role of fatness and fat masculinities in their performances. The substantial weight gain of each actor in all three films, for Fouz-Hernández, becomes a metric for understanding the way that their bodies are represented, filmed and discussed. Like Melero, Fouz-Hernández questions the limits of performance and acting, particularly when the body one inhabits is so drastically altered for a role. These physical alterations between the actors' general appearance and their personal appearances, in turn, negatively mark the masculinity of their characters, Fouz-Hernández argues.

In Chapter 13, 'Disabling Bardem's body: the performance of disability and illness', Dean Allbritton questions what it means to 'perform' sickness and disability, and in particular, how common perceptions of the two may be revealed in their cinematic reiteration. Analysing the Corazza-trained Javier Bardem as emblematic of a whole branch of Spanish acting expertise, Allbritton discusses the appearance of disability and illness in *Mar adentro/The Sea Inside* (Alejandro Amenábar, 2004) and *Biutiful* (Alejandro González Iñárritu, 2010). Rather than assume that illness and disability are already understood phenomena, Allbritton instead argues that their threat is kept at bay, that the performance of the two serves to reify the importance of the healthy body. Bardem, for this reason, is emblematic, as his physicality has long been praised and admired in Spanish cinema. For that reason, Allbritton concludes, acting choices, cinematic styles and the artificiality imposed by the camera keep illness and disability at arm's length, constantly eluding audiences and actors alike.

In Chapter 14, 'Body doubles: the performance of Basqueness by Carmelo Gómez and Silvia Munt', Rob Stone examines the reconstruction of regional and national identities through acting. In this chapter, Stone dissects the performances of Gómez and Munt, two actors made famous for their multiple and iconic Basque roles. By closely examining their performances, Stone argues that the actors' false identities articulate a Basqueness that is at once desirable and desiring, seeded with unattainability; that is, the creation of Basque archetypes by non-Basque actors may ultimately render nonexistent whatever potential promise or threat they contain. Going against the presumption that an actor may be able to breach the gap between his or her personal identity and that of the character, Stone argues instead that their performances will always be inauthentic, that audiences assume this fact and that this shades cinematic acting in very important ways.

In the final chapter of the book, 'Los amantes pasajeros/I'm So Excited! (2013): "performing" la crisis', María M. Delgado brings us to the present moment in Spain, and in particular the economic crisis which began in 2008 that provides the backdrop to Almodóvar's film. Describing the shift of director Pedro Almodóvar from melodrama to drawing-room farce made evident in this film, Delgado highlights its theatricality; in so doing, she argues that Los amantes pasajeros owes much to broad traditions of theatre acting that range from vaudeville, to mime to classic Shakespearian. The language of theatrical acting that the film employs, to that end, incorporates gestures and dramatic histrionics in order to make a clear indictment of the current state of Spain in crisis. By making clear the links between the politics of acting and acting out politics, Delgado's account of performance further demonstrates just how nuanced the landscape of Spanish acting can be.

References

Arana, Luis (1966) *El actor: Bosquejo de una sociología del comediante*, Madrid: Taurus.
Austin, Guy (2003) *Stars in Modern French Film*, London: Arnold.

Bandhauer, Andrea and Michelle Royer (2015) *Stars in World Cinema. Screen Icons and Star Systems across Cultures*, London: I. B. Tauris.

Baron, Cynthia, and Sharon Marie Carnicke (2008) *Reframing Screen Performance*. Ann Arbor: University of Michigan.

Baron, Cynthia, Diane Carson and Frank P. Tomasulo (eds) (2004) *More than a Method: Trends and Traditions in Contemporary Film Performance*. Detroit: Wayne State University Press.

Baron, Cynthia and Victoria Lowe (2008) *Reframing Screen Performance*, Ann Arbor: University of Michigan Press.

Buse, P., Triana-Toribio, N. and Willis, A. (2007) *The Cinema of Álex de la Iglesia*, Manchester: Manchester University Press.

Butler, Judith (1990) *Gender Trouble: Feminism and the Subversion of Identity*, London and New York: Routledge.

Davies, Ann (2014) *Penélope Cruz*, Basingstoke: Palgrave Macmillan.

Klevan, Andrew (2005) *Film Performance: From Achievement to Appreciation*, London: Wallflower.

Konijn, Elly (2005) 'The Actor's Emotions Reconsidered', in Phillip B. Zarrilli (ed.), *Acting (Re)Considered: A Theoretical and Practical Guide*, London and New York: Routledge, pp. 62–84.

Lovell, Alan and Peter Krämer (1999) *Screen Acting*, London: Routledge.

McDonald, Paul (2004) 'Why Study Film Acting?: Some Opening Reflections', in Cynthia Baron, Diane Carson and Frank P. Tomasulo (eds), *More than a Method: Trends and Traditions in Contemporary Film Performance*, Detroit: Wayne State University Press, pp. 23–41.

Mackintosh, Iain (1993) *Architecture, Actor and Audience*, London: Routledge.

Mackintosh, Iain (2000) *La arquitectura, el actor y el público*, trans. Ana Elena Ruiz Reyes, Madrid: Arco/Libros.

Mainou Pla, Roberto (1956) *La interpretación cinematográfica: Ensayo sobre su fundamento y su técnica*, Roberto Ortegas (pseud.), Barcelona: Sala, Mariano Galve.

Mamet, D. (1997) *True and False. Heresy and Common Sense for the Actor*, New York: Vintage Books.

Mamet, D. (1999) *Verdadero y falso: Herejía y sentido común para el actor*, trans. Josep Costa, Barcelona: Ediciones del Bronce.

Meeuf, Russell and Raphael Raphael (2013) *Transnational Stardom: International Celebrity in Film and Popular Culture*, London: Palgrave Macmillan.

Naremore, James (1998) *Acting in the Cinema*, Berkeley: University of California.

Naughten, Rebecca (2014) 'Subtle Gestures and Tonsorial Distractions: Javier Bardem as a Travelling Performer', *Cine-Files*, 6, Spring.

O'Rawe, Catherine (2014) *Stars and Masculinities in Contemporary Italian Cinema*, London: Palgrave Macmillan.

Peberdy, Donna (2011) *Masculinity and Film Performance: Male Angst in Contemporary American Cinema*, Houndmills, Basingstoke: Palgrave Macmillan.

Perriam, Chris (2003) *Stars and Masculinities in Spanish Cinema. From Banderas to Bardem*, Oxford: Oxford University Press.

Perriam, Chris (2013) '*Vicky Cristina Barcelona*: Penélope Cruz and Javier Bardem Acting Strangely', in Maria M. Delgado and Robin Fiddian (eds), *Spanish Cinema 1973–2010: Auteurism, Politics, Landscape and Memory*, Manchester: Manchester University Press.

Santaolalla, Isabel (2012) *The Cinema of Iciar Bollaín*, Manchester: Manchester University Press.

Serna, Assumpta (1999) *El trabajo del actor de cine*, Madrid: Cátedra.

Shingler, Martin (2012) *Star Studies: A Critical Guide*, London: Palgrave Macmillan

Taylor, Aaron (2012) *Theorizing Film Acting*, New York: Routledge.

Vincendeau, Ginette (2000) *Stars and Stardom in French Cinema*. London: Continuum.

Wheeler, Duncan (2014) 'Acting and Directing in Spain: Historicising Stardom and the Author-Function', in Duncan Wheeler and Fernando Canet (eds), *(Re)viewing Creative, Critical and Commercial Practices in Contemporary Spanish Cinema*, Bristol: Intellect, pp. 273–90.

Wojcik, Pamela Robertson (2004) *Movie Acting, the Film Reader*, New York: Routledge.

1

Acting for the camera in Spanish film magazines of the 1920s and 1930s

Eva Woods Peiró

Strolling through the pages of Spanish cinema magazines of the 1920s and 1930s, the reader tours endless photographic galleries of actors, stars and objects. Poised for consumption, these choreographed images kaleidoscopically transmit what seems to be the entirety of the cinematic apparatus (industry, image, content, stars, spectators). Portable and spreadable, film magazines succinctly rendered the act of wandering through the visual panorama of city streets lined by shop windows and signs, a practice Walter Benjamin defined as *flânerie* (2007: 36–7). Benjamin's attempt to understand a new phenomenology of vision enabled by mass reproduction was premediated in the textual medium of film magazines, in particular those published after 1910 and the inception of full-length narrative film. Yet several years before Benjamin's 1936 essay on mechanical reproduction, in magazines such as *Cine Popular*, *Cinegramas*, *Fotogramas* and *La Pantalla*, to name only a few, we find a running commentary on the same technological shifts that concerned Benjamin: the advancements of camera technology, the commodification of acting, the significance of the shift from stage to screen, the shift from recorded motion pictures as pure display to film narrative, and that from silent film technology to sound.

A survey of the content and full runs of forty film-fan magazines from 1917 to 1936 makes it evident that historicising or theorising film acting and performance by studying the film alone provides a wholly inadequate picture of the richness and diversity of the discourse that surrounded film acting. One aim of this chapter is thus to demonstrate that film magazines are essential for understanding film acting in the context of Spanish cinema. Cinema magazines provided a forum for conversation between critics, spectators and professionals about film acting. They also shaped the direction and development of acting as both industry professionals and actors themselves read these magazines and incorporated the ideas received from magazines into their works and performances. Despite their mass-culture sheen, this form of media housed some of the most avant-garde ideas about cinema. A second goal is to demonstrate, through citation of magazine text and image, how camera technology and the specific written or visual mention of the camera in discussions of acting – through photographs, advertisements and drawings – influenced how acting was discussed. Analysing discourse on acting in instances when the camera was explicitly invoked shows how subjectivity was increasingly determined by the object of the camera.

The application of systematic study of these publications reveals the extent to which awareness of the camera had already deeply penetrated how filmgoers thought and talked about acting, what they expected from it and what they projected onto it. As 'El arte fotográfico en el cine' notes, the camera was no longer an observer, 'sino un intérprete más' [but another actor] (Anon. 1934c: 25).[1] Camera technology persistently appeared in advertisements, while Spanish film critics regularly mused about the secret of photogeneity, the need for actors to physically and psychologically adjust their performances to the requirements of the camera medium, or the difficulties faced by actors due to the material exigencies of the cinema studio and the rhythm of film production.

Two intercombined logics that aided in this entertaining, educative mission were the 'magic' of the science of the camera and the concept of *fotogenia* [*photogénie*, or the photogenic]. Magazines carried the reader beyond the immediate experience of watching a film to help spectators develop a consciousness about cinemagoing so as to mould her or him into a more discerning and active cinemagoer, one that might consider becoming a director, or even a star. Yet, as I discuss presently, many writers tried to caution star-struck fans from racing to Madrid or Barcelona's studios. The intention of this rhetoric was to delimit the gender and racial boundaries of spectatorship. By instructing the reader how to think about acting and actors, magazine content surveilled the borders of star culture by defining who was either a floozy, an effeminate dandy, or a subject too racialised or downtrodden to be a star.

The panorama of cinema magazines

Cinema magazines manifested the power of recording technology, photographic montage and motion picture editing, which, like the cinema, captured reality and reorganised it onto a two-dimensional rectangular surface. They were an everyday visual encounter at the Spanish kiosk's expandable display boards. Their affordability guaranteed their abundance: by 1936, fifty-eight different cinema magazines were in circulation in Spain, and several magazines offered subscriptions.[2] Magazines cost between 20 to 50 *centavos* [cents] during the 1920s and usually

10 cents more in the 1930s, while a subscription for *Arte y cinematografía*, for instance, cost 10 pesetas for a year. Spectators were familiar with magazine covers' visual messages even if they couldn't buy
or read them. Magazine images occupied the peripheral vision of the
citizen spectator who subliminally stored them, and inadvertently or
consciously recalled these images while watching films or doing other
cinema-related activities.

Cinema magazines both educated and entertained the reader-spectator.
Magazines seduced readers through their sheer variety of content on
every facet of the cinema industry and its dream-machine: overviews of
national cinemas, genres, biographies, interviews and confessions of not
only stars but also directors, cameramen, costume or make-up design-
ers; opinion columns; fashion and make-up columns, debates about
the direction of the Spanish cinema industry or the transition to sound;
interactive content such as contests; and, of course, plenty of ads. Skilled
male and female writers directly and affectionately addressed a male and
female readership, pulling them into this dual-focused goal of leisure and
learning, while serialisation lured readers into buying the next issue, and
seduced them with promises of upcoming features and 'to-be-continued'
cliffhangers.

Conveying such teeming diversity here is impossible given the limits
of space, but even a sampling of the variety that foregrounds the camera reveals the importance of this technology to discourse on acting.
For example, at some point during their run, several magazines featured
a history of early cinema and moving camera technology spread out
over several issues. *Fotogramas* offered the multi-page spread 'Treinta
años de cinematógrafo: Conmemoración de la primera representación
pública'/'Thirty Years of Film: Anniversary of the First Public Screening',
which discussed technologies such as the praxinoscope and the muto-
scope accompanied by several photographs (Anon. 1926: 47–8).[3] Many
offered news about developments in camera technology such as an
article in *Cinegramas* on the *cámara tomavistas* [cine camera], 'El arte
fotográfico en el cine: La Naturaleza, como escenario auxiliar incomparable de la cámara tomavistas'/'Photographic Art in the Cinema: Nature
as the Unparalleled Setting for the Cine Camera' (Anon. 1934e: 5). Even
the idea of 'news' was merged with that of the camera. A regular news
column in *Cinegramas*, 'Instantáneas'/'Snapshot', played on the instant
snapshot and news 'flashes', but also included news pieces about anything remotely associated with photography. For instance, we learn from
a 1934 issue that Claudette Colbert 'jamás tuvo la intención de ser actriz
… Como pasatiempo le gusta tomar instantáneas de gente desconocida,
y a veces ella misma desarrolla los negativos' [never had any intention of

becoming an actress ... [and that] for a hobby she likes to take instant snapshots of people she doesn't know, and sometimes she develops the films herself] (Anon. 1934h: 40).

Through the camera, advertising occupied a fine line between educating and entertaining, or attracting product consumption. As a central feature of the magazine's visual education, camera ads were not relegated to trade magazines but rather populated fan magazines as much as other products. Also frequently featured was equipment related to the camera: Erneman projectors, Ray studio lighting, Brifco film stock, film labs like Castelló y Donoso, and movie studios such as Estudios Ballesteros, CEA, Roptence or Silver Star Films, to name only a few. Doubling as ads and entertainment, sometimes articles featured 'tours' of Spanish movie studios.[4] One possible explanation for this practice lies in what we could oftentimes call a dual-gender focus on advertising in Spanish cinema magazines. Differently from the US film magazines of the period, the magazines studied here interpellated both genders by including male and female cosmetic products (creams, girdles, hair removal products, soap), comestibles (biscuits, alcohol) and appliances (Edison and Philips radios, Citroen cars, tyres, sewing machines and refrigerators).[5]

Stars and cameras: becoming and policing

The promotion of stars was enmeshed with visual and textual citations of the camera. The reliance on stars for attracting and sustaining spectatorship was clear: virtually all cinema magazines I surveyed featured a star or a popular actor on their cover.[6] This dominance of star photography on the most prominent page reinforced the fusion of the star-actor with the camera object. Like Claudette Colbert in 'Instantáneas', stars were imagined in their interactions with cameras even when an article was not explicitly about stars. In the exposé 'En el estudio de Clarence Sinclair: El fotógrafo artista de las "star" yanquis'/'At Clarence Sinclair's Studio: The Photographer of the American Stars', we see a montage of six photos, most likely by Clarence Sinclair (Figure 1). Leaning against photo developing equipment, Sinclair stands over a pretty blonde model, as if giving her feedback before or after a pose. The remaining five photos show this same model-actress performing the steps involved in photochemical processing. In the last photo she holds up a photo of herself, in the pose she had just performed. The reader's delight comes from the neatly portrayed ideas that the camera produces stars, but a star also gives rise to the machine, and that the innards of the industry might be run by workers who look as lovely as this gal. As photography had proved the presence of a real object, the beautiful woman was a fact, but the cleverness of it all was still magical. The technical process could therefore be exposed while piquing desire for the wondrous (Anon. 1934f: 42).

Although a reader had never been in a film studio or seen a movie camera up close, an ad or an article and its photos could help her

Figure 1 'En el estudio de Clarence Sinclair: El fotógrafo artista de las "star" yanquis'. *Cinegramas*, 4, 30 September 1942, p. 42.

or him imagine these spaces and objects. Photographs of rehearsals and shoots were the essence of the 'behind-the-scenes' view. These shots were so popular in magazines that they became self-referential, a genre in their own right: 'fotos de héroes' [hero photos] (Figure 2). According to a photo caption of a montage of five such photos in *La Pantalla*,

Figure 2 'Fotos de héroes', *La Pantalla*, 55, 1929, p. 924.

Se denominan 'fotos de heroes,' en el argot professional, aquéllas tomadas desde puntos distintos en que está situada la máquina tomavistas y en las cuales aparecen, no solo los intérpretes de la farsa que luego veremos en el lienzo, sino también el director, ayudantes, fotógrafos y cuantas personas intervienen en la realización de la complicada tramoya'. [Hero photos, denominated as such in professional argot, are those shots taken from different points in which the cine camera is situated and in which there not only appear the actors of the farce that we will later see on the screen, but also the director, the assistants, cameramen and all those who intervene in the realisation of the complicated stage machinery.](Anon. 1928: 924)

Fotos de héroes summarised in one image the inside scoop. At the same time that they 'scientifically' dissected cinema, they indulged readers' imagination in the magical feats of the camera. As Alice Maurice argues, in the context of many US silent films, the scientific prowess of 'the new medium was always the underlying subject' and revealed 'film's doubly dexterous display by denoting two simultaneous spectacles: in essence, these films say, "Look at what these bodies can do and look at what the camera can do"' (2013: 3).

Acting: magic versus science

The presence of the camera transformed discourse around acting in two distinct ways. On the one hand, it contributed to the magic of the cinema; and on the other, it increased the scientific knowhow of acting. Both logics were steeped in racial and gendered assumptions and their assumptions had profound implications for the policing of these subjects. Demystifying the cinema apparatus, magazines may well have fostered sophisticated viewers but they also satisfied the insatiable spectator and her or his demand for more magic, more mystery and yet more knowledge. Edgar Morin's fascinating psycho-cultural study of identification with stars, although written in 1972, uses the silent film star Greta Garbo to illustrate how stars were divine idols, and gods of a modern religion (2005: 6–10). That some stars were like magicians, capable of transforming themselves and their spectators, was a common trope in Spanish film magazines. In 'El mago de la caracterización'/'The character magician', an homage to a longtime cinema actor, whose name the reader is forced to guess, and who can magically mould himself into any role, body shape or age, like clay in the hands of a sculptor:

Dijérase que su rostro era como un bastidor dispuesto para recoger la pintura, y su cuerpo, como el barro preparado por el escultor ... A pesar de haber trabajado durante muchos años ante la cámara, el mago de la caracterización no se había agotado, como tantos otros actores, y gozaba de la admiración del público. [One could say that his face was like a canvas waiting to receive paint, and his body like clay prepared by the sculptor … In spite of having worked in front of the camera for many years, the character magician had not been worn out, like so many other actors, and he enjoyed public admiration.] (Anon. 1934e: 42)

Audiences delighted in an actor's ability to present the most surprising appearance. But, as the article insinuates, the gruelling nature of camera acting (a nod to the science of acting) did not cause this actor's magic to wear out, thus testifying to that quality of genius inherent in a 'good' camera actor.

Magazines prolonged screen magic by endeavouring to 'scientifically' understand magic. They postponed the end point of desire by continually and serially publishing that which sustained desire: article after article on the 'science' of beauty, make-up, the kiss or the 'science' of acting. Because creating magic required exposing the artifice of cinema, an interdependent tension between science and magic was generated, becoming a powerful magnet for young Spaniards who fled homes in search of acting jobs, a trend that alarmed educational and religious authorities keen on safeguarding traditional gender roles. This concern has been amply documented in studies that have tracked laws that censored or surveilled minority populations (children especially and, by extension, women), cinema locales and cinema content (García Fernández 2002: 28, 55–8, 191–202; Scanlon 1986: 115). Cinema magazines logically referred to this 'problem'. As early as 1921, a series of articles published in ten instalments of *Cine Popular* introduces 'Para ser actor cinematográfico'/'How to Become a Movie Actor', with the justification that the magazine has received a large number of letters from readers 'motivados por el deseo de dedicarse al tentador arte cinematográfico, [quienes] nos preguntan acerca de las condiciones que se requieren para triunfar en la escena muda' [motivated by the desire to dedicate themselves to the tempting art of cinema, who ask us about the conditions required to triumph on the silent stage] (Ferry 1921b: 2).[7] According to the author, an expert in the business, these young people who dream of being the next Wallace Reid or Mary Pickford are 'legion'.

Cinema magazines sparked ideas about the new modern woman and social mobility through the conceptual framework of the science of magic, or the magic of science. In *La Pantalla*'s contest 'Extraordinario concurso de belleza: La Eva moderna'/'Extraordinary Beauty Contest: Modern Eve', which functioned as a feeder for casting companies, the new modern woman is 'La Eva moderna':

As a role model, she is the type of woman, let it be understood, whose style easily and admirably lends itself to feminine beauty. Today's young woman, with her concern for sportiness, refined manners, her readings, her

household chores – done with the help of electricity, which aids in everything – her work in the shop and the office, her taste for jazz, dance, and
new art and hygiene, and mainly because of her moral and spiritual uplift,
is the topic we have chosen as it encompasses everything in our Beauty
Contest program. (*La Pantalla* 35: 547)[8]

Science had allowed women to further enhance their magical attributes – their ability to excel in practically everything – while still carrying
out their traditional mandate as a pillar of morality.

Given the interest in stars and stardom, acting was a constant topic in
Spanish cinema magazines. Rebecca Swender, in her analysis of German
silent film, implies that acting style was internationally described in terms
of 'two distinct codes of silent-film acting: the histrionic and the verisimilar', or the shift from pantomime to more realistic styles (2006: 7–8).
Spanish film magazines referred frequently to these paradigms. In 'El
cine de mañana: Artistas esencialmente cinematográficos'/'The Cinema
of Tomorrow: Purely Cinematic Artists', actors are grouped according to
two styles: mimes like Chaplin, and rhythmic actors like Emil Jannings
(Ginestral 1929: 2–3). Up to that point, the author argues, pantomine,
considered banal and theatrical, was in decline. Chaplin's mimicry had
proved an exception, as it had been inspired by camera technology: 'El
arte de Charlot es puramente cinematográfico … Y es que Charlot posee
el secreto del cine actual: la mímica, exclusivamente cinematográfica'
[The art of Chaplin is purely cinematic … For Chaplin possesses the
secret of modern-day cinema: the exclusively cinematic art of mimicry]
(Ginestral 1929: 2–3). Cinema's increased autonomy from theatre, the
author further argues, has given rise to actors such as Jannings, who had
mastered rhythm, the key ingredient for believable acting: '[Jannings]
adopta un ritmo adecuado a la situación en que se halla; sus pasos len-
tos, cuando se dirige a la habitación para lavarse las manos tintas en
sangre de su víctima; sus movimientos rítmicos (de espaldas al público
y por lo tanto sin que se vea su gesto) relata al jefe de la cárcel el cri-
men que cometió' [Jannings is adopting a rhythm that is adequate to his
situation; his slow gait, as he goes toward the room to wash his hands,
stained with his victim's blood; his rhythmic movements (with his back
to the audience so that we can't see his gesturing) convey to the prison
warden the crime he committed] (Ginestral 1929: 2–3).

However, comments about acting style in magazines took on different
tones depending on the gender of the actor. Male actors tended to be
described in neutral or historical ways, while comments about actresses
adopted a critical, if not a depreciative, tone. In 'Consejos a las estrellas
españolas: Al oído de una de ellas, para que todas se enteren'/'Advice
for Spanish Stars: Whispering to One of Them, So that They All Know',

advice to Spanish stars centres on being natural, spontaneous and sincere, rather than automatic. When addressing actresses, the key ingredient to good acting was 'simpatía' [charm, likeability], the vague notion that the camera must 'like' the actress. Note that the advice also doubles as a conduct manual:

> Make sure you remain lifelike in front of the camera, not a puppet manipulated from the director's chair. Don't be a robot that mimics a person ... Act sincerely, spontaneously, and without artifice. Don't ever think of this or that star, or such and such a film. That memory will weigh you down, muddy your movements and you'll no longer be yourself ... Don't look for or ask the director for the most appropriate pose so as to double the value of your charm because a woman is never as pretty as when she is simply natural. This is the secret of *likeability* that you should produce and command from the screen. (Anon 1934b: 21, emphasis mine)[9]

Warnings were thus couched in contradictory advice about how to be likeable or charming, not just for the audience but for the overly scrutinous camera as well. Although the camera manifested capitalist thinking through its breakdown and reproduction of the body, economic thinking should be the furthest thing from a girl's mind when acting.

In 'Es fácil llegar a ser estrella cinematográfica?'/'Is Becoming a Movie Star Easy?', advice to *ingénues* comes in the form of a warning about the camera personified as an overbearing mother or mother-in-law:

> The moving camera is an arbitrary, capricious and temperamental creature. It is so crude, frank and brutally honest, that there are few people who can resist her gaze. Generally he who exposes himself to a 'judgment' of this 'lady' must disguise himself first with the intention of deceiving her, even though he might rarely achieve this. (Torrence 1927: 11)[10]

Indeed, the camera was a 'cruel' dame. Its vision surpassed that of human vision, and it was capable of reproducing detail so perfectly that bodily 'imperfections' like dimples, moles and scars were also reproduced, showing up as dark spots on the film. Unlike photography, experts lamented that film could not be retouched in the same way, as D. W. Griffith had already pointed out in 1917 in a seminal essay, 'What I Demand of Movie Stars',[11] which was liberally plagiarised and expanded upon in Spanish (and other national) cinema magazines throughout the 1920s and 1930s.[12] As Griffith writes, 'he or she knows there is no audience in front, but a grim, cold-blooded, truth-in-detail-telling camera lens which will register every quiver of the facial muscles, every gleam of the eye, every expression of the face, every gesture, just as it is given' (1917: 40).

Acting was thus a response to the demands of the camera as a device and a witness that could reproduce reality in minute detail, but the camera could also focus on just a part of this reality as opposed to an entire body. Cinema offered a new way of seeing the actor's body, permitting the spectator to see through the lens of industrial capitalism, which, as Benjamin later noted, dissected and fragmented the body into smaller, consumable bits through the breakdown of shots. Although an explicit critique of capitalism in Spanish film magazines would not arrive until publications like *Nuestro Cinema* (1932–), the ingredients for this analysis were already present in cinema magazines of the 1920s and 1930s, albeit in a mixed consciousness format.

The article 'Los imitadores'/'The Impersonators' illustrates how mechanical reproduction influenced how acting was conceived. By playing with the words 'myth-makers' and 'imitadores' it designated the gestures-cum-brands that film stars developed because of the camera's presence (Marlene's legs; Chaplin's cane and walk) (Anon. 1934i: 8). In a review of *Los hijos del trabajo/The Children of Work* in *Popular Film*, author Mateo Santos's focus on specific gestures demonstrates the influence of the camera on descriptions and expectations of acting: 'Manolo González, a former theatre actor, demonstrates gestures and expressions differently on stage than on screen. And Pepe Nieto is competitive with American actors because his facial muscles can just as easily register somber despair as they can a generous laugh' (1927: 12).[13]

The passage is significant for several reasons. First it joins many other articles that regularly documented the shift from theatre to cinema such as 'Los actores de teatro en el cinematógrafo'/'Theatre Actors in the Cinema' (Aldecoa 1927: 100) or 'Martha Eggerth habla de sus recuerdos y de sus proyectos: Cómo saltó de la escena a la pantalla la gran "star"'/'Martha Eggerth Speaks About Her Memories and Projects: How the Big Star Went from the Theatre to the Big Screen' (Anon. 1934j: 22–3). Second, the quote shows us how the transition from theatre to film became a trigger for a contradictory and discriminatory discourse about camera acting. As Carrasco notes, Manolo González and Pepe Nieto have endured the rapid changes involving this shift, and this made them better camera actors. A value judgment has thus been implied, valorising camera acting over stage acting and those actors who had survived the transition. Camera actors evolved, and are better.

Like most filmgoers of the late 1920s, Santos was conditioned to see what the camera saw. Thanks to the technology of the closeup, he focuses on the face, the smile, the eyes and the shape of the mouth, giving no further thought to acting with the whole body but only the magnified visual morsels that the camera allows us to see. He thus describes Celia Escudero as 'posee además una depurada sensibilidad artística, que le permite expresar fielmente con el gesto y la actitud los más diversos elementos psicológicos del personaje que interpreta ante la cámara fotográfica' [possesses a refined artistic sensibility that allows her to express the most diverse psychological elements of the character she is playing for the camera] (Santos 1927: 12). 'Sus ojos, de pupilas fulgurantes, saben dar picardía a su cara, cuando conviene; pero saben, también, dramatizarla, rimando con el frunce del ceño, levísimo surco abierto entre las finas cejas, y con el pliegue de la boca sensual en la que la barra de carmín finge un rojo corazón de baraja francesa' [Her eyes – with shining pupils, when it suits her; knowingly lend naughtiness to her face; but she also knows how to make them dramatic, rhyming with a frown, opening the lightest little furrow between her slim brows, folding her sensual mouth into a red French heart of cards drawn with scarlet lipstick] (Santos 1927: 12). Awareness about the wonderful yet problematic effects of the camera on bodies translated into greater efforts to understand the science behind the camera. But science could only be understood by assigning it criteria based on gendered and racial assumptions.

Fotogenia

Comments by magazine writers on the drawbacks to dependence on the camera, later reiterated by Benjamin – such as the fragmentation, monotonisation, repetition and alienation – were also couched in a discourse of morality.[14] The aim was to temper the cinephilia of young male and female fans and admonish against the dangers of cinemagoing. At the same time, authors reveled in intimidating tales about stars who had suffered from exploitation, the connotation being that this injustice was partly due to the actor's race and gender (Ramón Novarro being exemplary). Consequently they cautioned aspiring actors to perform to a prescribed whiteness.

The solution was to search for a good 'mate' for the camera, i.e., actors who were already, before they were shot by the camera, as close to perfection as possible. The possibilities had to be narrowed down. Not everyone could be a star. In this sense, other vague qualities were added to the list of photogenic criteria such as intelligence, or education – qualities that could narrow the pool in terms of not just race or gender, but also social class.

Again we return to Griffith, who set the tone for this discourse by supposedly locating the secret of photogeneity within an abstract and ineffable quality that could be applied as needed: 'Granted that the person has a moving-camera face – that is, a person who photographs well – the first thing needed is "soul"' (1917: 40). Originally coined by

Louis Delluc in 1920 but only vaguely described, Jean Epstein and other avant-garde French filmmakers employed 'photogeneity' widely in an attempt to explain 'the vitality of the moving image from the deadness (*nature morte*) of still photography' (Okada 2008: 370). Indefinable notions about what constitutes the mix of moving picture photography and 'genio' or genius/magic equally emerge in countless Spanish articles over the next decade in the form of 'character', 'intensified realism' or 'simpatía'. As Jun Okada rightly argues in the context of French cinema of the same period (that looked to US cinema as its point of reference), of the same period, favouring a term so apolitical, intuitive and rife with subjective aesthetics led to the elision of racial politics: photogeneity becomes a translation of racial anxieties as aesthetic effect (2008: 370).

By 1921, the word '*fotogenia*' was already at the centre of cinema discussions in Spain. In the first instalment of a series of articles dedicated to 'Para ser actor cinematográfico'/'In Order to Be a Cinematographic Actor', published in *Cine Popular* in 1921, the article 'La fotogenia' asserts that 'para ser actor cinematográfico es condición indispensable ser *fotogénico*' [an indispensable condition for being a cinema actor is to be *photogenic*] (Ferry 1921b: 4). It continues: 'en cinematografía es "fotogénico" todo lo susceptible de dar una hermosa imagen en la proyección y el conjunto de cualidades requeridas para contribuir a la plasticidad y a la armonía de un cuadro animado' [in cinema, the photogenic is anything that can project a beautiful image and the set of required qualities that contribute to the plasticity and harmony of a moving image] (Ferry 1921b: 4). Photogeneity's undefinability, its 'je ne sais quois', could mask discriminatory assumptions about race and gender by valuing certain kinds of whiteness or gendered traits over others.

The search for the secret of *fotogenia* overlapped with the need to respond to fan enquiries asking how to become a star. Magazines answered this call for help by attempting to define *fotogenia*. In a 1929 article in *El norte cinematográfico*, 'La fotogenia y el maquillaje en la cinematografía'/'Photogeneity and Make-up in Cinematography', we see an overt acknowledgement of the frustration (yet delight) with this abstract term:

> In the language of the movie studio, to be photogenic is to be liked by the camera's lens. Photogeneity is the quality of possessing a face that pleases the camera's eye. Oh the whims of the camera's eye! The lens deforms, augments, highlights, animates, and obtains unsuspected effects and surprises us with portentous revelations. But what mysterious quality is that which pleases the camera lens? We will say it once and for all: the facial expression of intelligence that expresses ideas without words. (Martínez de la Riva 1929: n.p.)

Here intelligence is no more specific than being likeable, but it functioned as an important criterion for what constituted beauty and often, by nature, racial and sexual norms. Gentlemanliness and, by extension, an education in class distinction also served as the gateway to *fotogenia*. However, 'la educación no se improvisa, y el que ha sido patán o ha vivido en medios modestos, sin salir de ellos, no podrá representar jamás al perfecto "gentleman"' [education can't be improvised, and he who has been a lout or lived with modest means without ever leaving that condition, could never represent the perfect 'gentleman'] (Ferry 1921a: 7–8).

Scientifically speaking, there was a factual base to some of the claims of photogeneity. Shooting black eyes as opposed to blue eyes yielded different results and the colour of skin or hair was affected by the filter, lighting and film stock used. Griffith had also spoken to this problem in 1917: 'People with very light hair and light blue eyes are seldom successful before the movie camera, because the eyes look white and wild or startled' (1917: 41). But what concerns us here is not the technical issue but rather the effect of this discourse on readers: how did readers absorb the conclusions about certain physical characteristics being more photogeneic than others, and how did these ideas reinforce normative identity? In any case, this issue consistently re-emerged throughout the period in contradictory fashion.

'Para ser actor cinematográfico' states that 'los ojos azules son fotogénicamente muy mediocres, porque en la proyección resultan en exceso pálidos. Los ojos azul oscuro y negros son, en general, sombríos en la proyección. Son preferibles los ojos verdes, los amarillos y los morenos' [blue eyes are photogenically speaking very mediocre because, when projected, they result in an excessive paleness. Dark blue eyes and black are generally sombre when projected] (Ferry 1921b: 4). Yet in the same article, 'la piel muy morena no es una buena condición' [brown skin is not a good condition [for photogeneity] (Ferry 1921b: 4). And in 1928 in the *ARS Programa de los espectáculos del Palacio de la Música, Madrid*, we learn that

> Cecil Holland, a make-up expert, says that black eyes don't photograph as well as blue because blue lend themselves to a variety of expressions that are impossible in the case of black eyes. The eyes of actors such as Ramón Novarro, John Gilbert and Ricardo Cortez only lend themselves to romantic roles as poets or fiery lovers … and the woman with dark eyes must resign herself to roles as mermaids, vampires, etc. (Anon. 1928: 10)[15]

Descriptions of *fotogenia* become increasingly racialised as we move through this time period. As Alice Maurice has argued in the context of early US cinema, 'in moments of transition or technological vulnerability is when we see most clearly racialised bodies and connection of race to cinema' (2013: 3). Maurice's overall point, that race becomes more visible in moments of technological change, and that the camera offered a site for working out social problems, is certainly true in the context of Spanish cinema and its surrounding discourse around it in the 1920s and 1930s (2013: 3). Perhaps for this reason, towards the end of the decade, race and photogeneity were being discussed in reflexive terms. In *¡A mí … películas!* in 1929, Francisco Ginestral writes about 'la fotogenia de las razas y la naturalidad en el "cine"' [the photogeny of race and naturalness in 'film'], recognising that 'generally certain types of individuals or races are said to be photogenic in that the light favours them more than others.' But 'any other race is more photogenic than ours … and leaves a better impression than we do on the photographic plate' (1929: 2–3).[16] The author continues, asking the reader to observe the Chinese, Indians or blacks in films, and in particular the 'esquimos' in *Perdidos en el Árctico/Lost in the Arctic* (H. A. Snow & Sydney Snow, 1928). Because of their distance from civilisation, their lack of prejudice, vanity, simplicity and their naturalness before the camera, these individuals are innately capable of charming the spectator. He concludes that screen actors should copy individuals of all the races of colour and the 'esquimos' so that 'no siga viendo el público vanidad en vez de arte y artificio en lugar de buen gusto' [audiences don't have to keep watching vanity instead of art, and artifice instead of good taste]' (Ginestral 1929: 2–3).[17] On the one hand, revealing the secret of photogeneity to aspiring actors amplified the possibilities for entering showbiz; on the other, this generosity was mitigated by a cautionary tone and an ensuing discussion of the inconveniences of this magical business.

Exploitation is horribly delightful

The tone of magazine writers is celebratory of actors and film in general, but some columns avidly discuss the downside of this magical business. These moments of criticism were exceptions in the larger scheme of adulatory discourse, unanticipated slippages, and by the end of an article they are mostly subsumed back into the anodyne glorification of showbiz. Admissions of the unpleasant aspects of the film world tend to closely follow mention of the actual word, '*cámara*'. Such iterations focus on the camera as cause of suffering, a relentless machine that ruthlessly extracts physical and emotional labour from the actor and whose causes and effects can be scientifically explained; and the interconnected wondrous magic produced by the camera without any apparent effort.

Indeed, these revelations about the hidden side of film did not deter the reader from consuming magazines, going to films, imitating stars through fashion, entering contests or even trying their hand at acting, but instead tantalised the reader by portraying prohibitive pleasures. Moreover, pointing out the dangers further obscured the hard reality of film acting and promoted the magazine as a secondary, but equally desirable kind of screen, which showed exploitation or addiction to cinema, only to dispel it through the sumptuous, dynamic graphics and content of its pages.

'La vida de Cinelandia'/'The Life of Movieland', a weekly column in *Popular Film*, educates the filmgoer about the pressures actors face before the camera, as opposed to stage acting. Unlike most articles, it is dedicated to listing the 'deceptions and tragedies' related to camera acting.

> Most audience-goers sincerely believe that the people of Cinelandia live a life regulated by pleasure, luxury, extravagances and continual merriment ... most never hear about the declarations of some actors who upon retiring from the screen express how intense, agitating and demanding their life has been relative to many other current professions. Rarely does the audience hear about statements made by actors upon retiring from the screen in which they refer to their intense, hectic lifestyle, more demanding, perhaps than many other current professions ... None too few actors have said that if they were made to choose between being a cinema actor or digging dirt, without doubting in the least, they would choose the latter. (Vargas de la Maza 1928: 4)[18]

Film actors, he instructs us, expend far more labour than stage actors because they must act out scenes that are out of sequential order, thus violating the integrity of a stage performance; they must act the same scene multiple times, submitting to any directorial whim; they should endeavour to ignore the film crew members; they must underact, which ironically took more work; they must endure the intense heat and light of the mercury lamps and potentially suffer eye diseases as a result; and, finally, they must face the often vicious publicity apparatus.[19] This unambiguous confirmation of the exploitation of actors ends with the pessimistic prediction that all this toil and humiliation will only land them roles as extras.[20] Yet the grippingly recounted shattered illusions are precisely what reproduce the magic of Cinelandia: a seemingly deeper connection to one's humanity, in reality, further alienates the viewer from the conditions that led to this victimisation.

In these dramas ancillary to the film, the reader is encouraged to empathise with the child actor, doubles or extras. By peering into the mechanisms of the set, we see how profit is made from invisible labour but also we are enticed to know more about the inner workings of the fetishised object without changing it in the least. In 'Héroes anónimos del estudio: Los dobles'/'Doubles: the anonymous heroes of the studio', the writer tells us that the life of doubles is 'monotonous and bothersome, exhausting, poorly paid and wholly unrecognised'. The lights 'braze' the skin, the shouts of the director and the hammering of carpenters 'stun and mortify' the ears; but the worst is that once everything has been fastidiously checked in all possible combinations, the double is supplanted by the star, who can't be bothered in the least.[21] The job most likely to be advertised and available to an average magazine reader was portrayed here as dead-end and humiliating, if not the vision of a shattered dream.[22]

These severe warnings could be especially terrifying for women. In '¡Quién fuera vedette!'/'Who Would be a Showgirl', author Ricardo Valls records 'las torturas más espantosas' [the most horrid tortures] which the 'bellas mujercitas' [beautiful little women], who covet the celebrity of Greta Garbo, should know about before subjecting themselves to the 'infierno de los proyectores' [the hell of the film projectors], the powerful spotlights that, like lead pouring down over the head, melt the most polished and preventative make-up job, and the ultraviolet rays, that, like arrows, are nailed into the eyes (Valls 1934: 17–18). He continues:

> Pretty photo, right? It certainly is. In order to shoot it, the cameraman would have to have submitted the star to the torture of posing who knows how many times in front of the camera's scrutinising pupil. While he studies the diverse light combinations that will allow for a perfect work. Will the actress have suffered unspeakably in front of the lights that ruin her sight and boil her skin? Bah! No matter! (Valls 1934: 17–18)[23]

'We do not intend to dishearten those whose seek fame', he says, 'we only want to express to our readers how far the life of the stars is from what they have imagined. If your resistance succumbs and one day you become one of those tyrannical, intransigent and despotic stars, won't there be an excuse for your tyranny?' (Valls 1934: 17–18). The message delivered is ambiguous on several registers: good girls should not want to expose themselves to such dangers; but attaining stardom, which requires passing through these tortures, will license one to abuse your worshipping crewmen and fans. Most confusing of all is that reading about these tortures is both horrible and titillating.

But what happens when the individuals in danger of succumbing to the cinema are non-normative subjects, second-class minorities, considered deviant, or racialised others? 'Niños sin infancia: El gesto de los pequeños actores'/'Children Without Childhood: The Performance of Child Actors' provides an ambivalent description of the acting styles of child actors, Baby Leroy and Jackie Cooper. From the beginning, the writer is on the fence about this practice: 'It could be that it's convenient for the respective parents, or protectors, of the little ones who monkey around on the screen, or maybe these precocious artists just *love* being under the burning beams of the sunlights' (Anon. 1934k: 21, emphasis original).[24] While the author sympathises with these 'delicious dimples', he is also 'won over by them'. Here we see the very process of exploitation justified in the name of entertainment, a mechanism similar in form to that of racism.

And in this spirit the author's interest turns toward the science of achieving photogeneity from child actors.[25] With Baby Leroy, he continues, 'no more is involved than tapping into that imitative instinct,' for 'Baby Leroy is a genius, but also, a mere copycat. With the biblical patience of Job, he must perform that whole series of gestures, attitudes, and guttural shouts that he can then repeat automatically after long hours of rehearsal' (Anon. 1934k: 21).[26] With Jackie Cooper, the procedure differs: 'The demanding director minutely explains how he has to perform the gesture to the point at which he moves and acts consciously and precisely, until the job is considered valid.' But until he does, how many metres and metres of useless celluloid!' (Anon. 1934k: 21).[27] The tone has shifted to impatience, slight disregard and even dismissal. The exploitation of children is no longer at stake, but rather the demands and 'needs' of the filmgoer.

In 'Confesiones de artistas: Ramón Novarro habla de su vida artística y de lo caros que resultan los divorcios'/'Confesions of an Actor: Ramón Novarro Talks about His Artistic Life and the Expense of Divorce' (Anon. 1934a: 16–17), we shift even further away from the worries about exploitation and conduct, and closer to the suspicion that this exotic actor might have deserved his torture. Ramón Novarro, born José Ramón Gil Samaniego, was a Mexican actor who became Rudolph Valentino's successor after the latter's death in 1926. 'Ravishing Ramón', as they called him, was limited to Latin lover roles but he did attain wealth and fame. His homosexuality was insinuated, but not explicitly publicised, until his sensationalised murder in 1968. His androgynous beauty challenged prevailing norms of masculinity in the 1920s and 1930s (Holliday 2002, n.p.). Yet, as the surplus of meanings in the *Cinegramas* article reveal, it also colored the estimation of his talent. The writer describes his ascent to stardom as a 'un dilatado calvario' [drawn-out calvary]. While Novarro was still unknown, Rex

Ingram chose him for *The Prisoner of Zenda* (1922) 'and the obscure novice found himself under the powerful lights of an immense studio with Ingram's eyes fixed on him; a *machine* before him inexorably registered all of his gestures and changes in facial expression, no matter how insignificant' (Anon. 1934a: 16–17).[28] During preparations for the film, Novarro says 'his life was subject to the strictest discipline for the sake of acting: 6.00 a.m. rowing workouts and intensive rehearsals in which scenes were retaken 20–30 times.' When it was time to film the galley scene, he recalls, 'my whole body felt like it had been burned to a crisp. I applied a pomade that when it dried made my skin look desiccated and rough … the sun burned, and the sufferings of the slaves chained to the oars was not always fiction' (Anon. 1934a: 16–17).[29] Life greatly improved for Ramón after this St Sebastian-like episode. But nevertheless, this revelatory fantasy reproduces, perhaps even more than a camera would, the objectifying gaze on the sexualised body.

In 'También los negritos hacen contratos de miles de dólares'/ 'Black Actors Also Get Contracts of Thousands of Dollars', the focus is on Allen Clayton Hoskins, aka 'Farina' from *The Little Rascals*, who acted in these serial films from their inception in 1922 through 1931. Hoskins spent several years trying to secure an acting career in Hollywood but 'aged out', and received no payments after he was let go, even though reruns were shown up through the 1970s. Written in 1923, this article applauds cinema for its cosmopolitanism and universality, which allow for 'la mano amarillo o negra' [the yellow or black hand] to pick up a pen and sign contracts worth 'un infinidad de miles de dólares' [an endless number of dollars] (Anon. 1923: 7). But, unlike Baby Leroy or Jackie Cooper, Little Farina has a tinge of rebellion in him. The caption of the bottom photo, in which Hoskins sits next to the director eating watermelon, provides the following pun: 'El famoso negrito discute con su director los derechos de hegemonía sobre una tajada dulce y refrescante' [The famous *negrito* debates with his director over the rights to a sweet and refreshing slice of melon/money]. For the targeted normative reader, the "fun" here is partly in questioning Farina's photogeneity. But it is mainly that the risqué subject of color dares to argue with the director when he should know his place (tragically he would).

In sum, two conclusions can be drawn from this chapter. First, the new ways in which the camera intercepted acting and awareness about cinemagoing contributed to the (self-)policing and racialisation of subjects, implicating both actors and readers of film magazines. Second, from its inception, discourse around cinemagoing in Spain grew from its relationship to other national cinemas, specifically Hollywood, and for this reason our analyses should not treat Spanish cinema as a discrete national phenomenon. Racial anxieties were transnationally present, whether in the US, France or indeed Spain. Yet the translation of racial difference from its visual format into textual discourse and subsequent interpretation, depended on the specific social and economic framework of Spanish film culture. Discussions about race, for instance, resonated differently in France or in Spain because of their particular colonial experiences, but the mechanism of racism was still present in both, and enhanced by the ubiquity of the camera.

Notes

1 All translations throughout are mine.
2 *La Pantalla* in 1927 cost 20 cents; *Films selectos* in 1930 cost 30 cents; *Metrópolis* in 1930 cost 50 cents; *Popular Film* cost 20 cents in 1927 and 30 in 1932. Throughout the 1920s, *Arte y cinematografía* (begun in 1910) cost 1 peseta, but it had over 50 pages.
3 Similar histories were also published in *La Pantalla* and *Nuestro Cinema*.
4 For example, 'Los nuevos estudios de Serafin Ballesteros, Tono Film', *Cine espanol*, November 1935, 5.
5 See Studlar (1996) for one of the few studies on film magazines of this period.
6 Magazines that featured stars on their cover as part of their brand: *Popular Film* (Barcelona, 1926–36); *Cinegramas* (Madrid, 1934–36), *La Pantalla*, *El mundo cinematográfico*, *Cine Popular*, *El teatre Catalá*, *Películas*, *Tras la Pantalla*. Exceptions were the leftist *Nuestro Cinema* (1932–35, Paris), regional publications such as *La Reclam* (Valencia), ones focused on photography such as *Art de la Llum* (1933–35, Barcelona), *Revista Kodak* or *24x26: Revista Fotográfica*, or trade magazines directed at unions or professional organisations.
7 This *Cine Popular* series by Ferry starts with 'Preámbulo' on 22 June 1921, and continues with titles such as 'El tipo'; 'Condiciones generales'; 'La belleza femenina'; 'El maquillaje'; 'La educación física'; 'El arte de saber vestir'; and 'El estudio de la actitud.'
8 'Es tipo que, bien entendido, se presta a la más fácil y admirable estilización de la belleza femenina. La *mujercita de hoy*, con sus inquietudes por los sanos deportes, sus gestos refinadísimos, sus lecturas, sus labores domésticas, realizadas al amparo de la electricidad, que ayuda *a todo*, sus trabajos en el taller y en la oficina, su afición al *jazz-band*, al baile, al arte nuevo y a la higienes, y principalmente por su elevación espiritual y moral, es el tema que hemos escogido para plasmar todo ello en el programa de nuestro Concurso de Belleza' (*La Pantalla*, 35, 547).

9 'Procura mantenerte ante la cámara como ser que vive, no como "marion-eta" manejada desde la silla del director. No seas el autómata que remeda a la persona ... Actúa sincera, espontánea, sin artificiosidades. No te acuerdes para nada de la estrella tal y de la escena cual. El peso de aquel recuerdo te embarrará los movimientos y ya no serás tú. ... No busques ni pidas al direc-tor la "pose" más afortunada para que tus encantos resalten duplicando su valor, porque nunca es más bella una mujer que en su sencilla naturalidad. Este es el secreto de la *simpatía* que tú debes producir y mandar desde la pantalla' (Anon 1934b: 21, emphasis mine).

10 'La cámara cinematográfica es una criatura arbitraria, caprichosa y temper-amental. Es tan cruda, franca y brutalmente fiel, que hay muy pocas perso-nas que resistan a su análisis. Generalmente el que se expone a un "juicio" de esta "señora" tiene que disfrazarse antes, con objeto de engañarla, aunque muchas veces no lo consigue' (Torrence 1927: 11).

11 As Griffith writes, 'Retouching is out of the question, because one could not retouch a mile or two of film with thousands upon thousands of pictures' (1917: 40).

12 'La cámara impresiona las cosas tal cual las ve su único ojo, y teniendo un solo ojo ve mucho más que nosotros con dos. Ocurre con ella que teniendo un solo punto de mira, ve las cosas planas y las impresiona sin darle propor-ción de amplitud. Si hay alguna curva o protuberancia, aparecerá en forma obscura. Y cuando más honda o sobresaliente sea, más obscura será la som-bra que imprima. De ahí a la necesidad de que los rostros que se impresionen puedan resistir esta crueldad de la cámara fotográfica' (Torrence 1927: 11).

13 'Manolo Gómez, que procede del teatro, ha demostrado saber que el gesto y el ademán en la pantalla, tienen un valor distinto que en el tabladillo de la farándula hablada. Pepe Nieto ... podrá competir con muchos del film americano cuando sus músculos faciales adquieran para el gesto sombrío, para la expresión dramática, la misma 'facilidad' que tienen para la sonrisa, que acaso prodiga con exceso' (Santos 1927: 12).

14 The term 'monotonisation' was used by theorists in the 1920s to mean 'that which makes life monotonous or uniform' (Zweig 1994: 397–400).

15 'Cecil Holland, experto en maquillaje, dice que los ojos negros no fotografían tan bien como los azules, porque éstos dan una gran variedad de expresiones que no pueden producir los negros. Los ojos de artistas como Ramón Novarro, John Gilbert y Ricardo Cortez, sólo se prestan para papeles románticos, de poetas o de fieros amantes ... y la mujer de ojos oscuros tiene que contentarse con papeles de sirena, vampiresa, etc.' (Anon. 1928: 10).

16 'Generalmente se dice que tal o cual individuo es fotogénico o ésta o aquella raza favorece mejor la luz que la otra. Respecto de los individuos esencial-mente blancos hablar de fotogenia es abusar de la palabra; cualquier otra raza es más fotogénica que la nuestra. Las de color, por muy tenue que sea éste, impresionan mejor una placa fotográfica que nosotros' (Ginestral 1929: 2–3).

17 The quote in its entirety: 'Observen ustedes a los chinos a los indios, a los
   negros que aparecen en las películas y se convencerán de lo que digo. En
   Perdidos en el Árctico los hombres curtidos, los que aun siendo blancos,
   no tienen ya la blancura de la tez y ni el tinte del individuo de la cuidad,
   resultan muy fotogénicos. Los esquimales, sus mujeres y sus hijos, extraños
   a la gran civilización, o las últimas baluartes de esta y carentes del prejuicio
   y de la vanidad, encantan al espectador por su sencillez y por las maneras
   tan naturales que adoptan ante el objetivo. Ni en un solo momento recur-
   ren a la afectación o a la "belle pose" para gustar. Y sin embargo, ni las
   más diestra cuadrilla de figurantes y actores representaría sus papeles como
   ellos. Especialmente los artistas de la pantalla deben copiar a los individuos de todas las razas de color y a los esquimales, si quieren que a través
   de sus gestos estudiados y de sus maneras ramplonas, no siga viendo el
   público vanidad en vez de arte y artificio en lugar de buen gusto' (Ginestral
   1929: 2–3).
18 'La generalidad del público que asiste a las exhibiciones de películas cree
   sinceramente que los actores de Cinelandia viven una vida regalada de placeres, de lujo, de extravagancias y de jolgorio continuo … Pocas veces llegan
   a oídos de este público las declaraciones que han hecho algunos actores en
   el momento de retirarse de la pantalla y en las que expresan su vida intensa
   y agitada, más exigente, quizás que muchas otras de la profesiones corrientes
   … No ha faltado actor que haya dicho que si se le pusiera a escoger entre ser
   actor cinematográfico o cavar la tierra, sin dudar un solo instante escogería
   lo último' (Vargas de la Maza 1928: 4).
19 The quote in its entirety: 'Ya en el taller los actores tienen que presentarse
   con una absoluta puntualidad, proceder a caracterizarse con sumo cuidado,
   de tal modo que su figura no cambie en lo absoluto de un día a otro; atender
   a todas las órdenes del director y pasar horas y horas frente a la cámara bajo
   los rayos de las lámparas mercuriales que tantos daños causan a la retina
   hasta el extremo de que en algunas ocasiones ha habido actores que han
   tenido que sufrir largas enfermedades en los ojos; … las compañías gastan
   millones de dólares [para al final] desdecir mucho de su honorabilidad. Los
   más insignificantes detalles son amplificados por los publicistas … algunos
   han visto desaparecer su fama como humo de paja y otros han sufrido per-
   juicios en su reputación' (Vargas de la Maza 1928: 4).
20 Benjamin described the effects of the alienation of doubles in the following
   terms: 'with a vague sense of discomfort, he feels inexplicable emptiness …
   estrangement' (2007: 230); the image of the actor has become 'separable,
   transportable …' (2007: 231) to the public, 'the consumers who constitute
   the market' (2007: 231).
21 The quote in its entirety: 'monótono y molesto, sin descanso, un salario
   reducido, una falta absoluta de reconocimiento … y la seguridad de un completo anónimo. Mientras se prueban los potentes foco que iluminan el set

y abrasan la piel; mientras aturden los gritos del director y sus ayudantes y mortifica el oído el constante martilleo de carpinteros y tramoyistas ... el "doble" está en el centro de la escena, sofocado, abrasado, mortificados sus ojos por la luz casi irresistible; pero apenas han terminado los preparativos, cuando se han probado todas las combinaciones posibles de luz y sombra, ya tomadas las medidas de los diferentes puntos de la escena a la cámara y al micrófono ... cuando todo lo que es molestia y fastidio ha cesado, ¡el doble abandona su puesto, para que lo ocupa la estrella, a la que no debe molestarse sino lo menos posible, y se retira a un rincón, olvidado, ignorado, hasta que empiecen a disponerse a preparar otra escena!' (Anon. 1934g: 6).

22 'Es la suya una vida de paciencia, de sacrificio, de constancia, de lealtad, sin recibir jamás una ligera felicitación, sin la probabilidad de un aplauso futuro. Son los "dobles" de las estrellas forma y sombra del artista que representan, que por razones técnicas tienen importancia capital frente a la cámara ... aunque nunca los vemos en la pantalla. Se visten y mueven como los principales actores o actrices; toman de momento su lugar; juegan a ser príncipes o princesas, ídolos adorados por las multitudes fanáticas ... y a veces suenan que lo son. Pero el sueño se desvanece pronto, no tardan en despertar para darse cuenta de que su vida no es más, es probable que nunca sea más, que una permanente farsa, un constante engaño, una simple sustitución de la persona que ha de recibir el aplauso del público, la alabanza de la crítica y el respeto de los productores' [Theirs is a life of patience, sacrifice, constancy, and loyalty, without ever a hope of a passing compliment/congratulations, and probably no future applause. Star doubles are the form and shadow of the actor whom they represent; for technical reasons, in front of the camera, they are of capital importance ... yet we never see them on the screen. They dress and move like the principal actors; they take the same positions; they play princes and princesses, adored idols by fanatical multitudes ... and sometimes they dream that they really are these people. But the dream fades fast, and soon they wake realising that theirs) will never be more than a permanent farce, a constant ruse, a simple substitution of the person who receives the applause, the praise, and the producer's respect] (Anon. 1934g: 6).

23 'Bella foto, ¿verdad? Lo es, ciertamente. Para obtenerla, el 'camaraman' Habrá sometido a la estrella a la tortura de posar quién sabe cuánto tiempo ante la pupila escrutadora de la cámara, mientras él estudia las diversas combinaciones lumínicas que permitirán lograr la obra perfecta. ¿Que para ello la artista ha padecido indeciblemente ante los focos que deslumbran la vista y hacen hervir el cerebro? ¡Bah! '¡Eso no cuenta!' (Valls 1934: 17–18).

24 'Puede que a sus respectivos papas o *protectores* les convenga que los pequenines hagan monadas en la pantalla, y que hasta esos precoces artistas se encuentren tan a gusto bajo los focos de luz ardiente de los *sunlights*' (Anon. 1934k: 21, emphasis original).

25 'Cómo se consigue que se infundan tanta expresión a sus interpretaciones y se sometan a la dura labor del set? … De qué modo actúan estos pequeños actores?' (Anon. 1934k: 21).

26 'No hay mas que desenvolver el instinto imitativo, tan desarrollado en la infancia. Con una paciencia del bíblico Job hay que ir haciéndole antes toda esa serie de gestos, actitudes y gritos guturales que luego va repitiendo de modo casi automático, después de largas horas de prueba' (Anon. 1934k: 21).

27 'Con Jackie Cooper el procedimiento varía. Se le explica con minuciosidad como ha de hacer el gesto, a tal punto que se mueva y obra ya de modo consciente. Tiene la preocupación de dar al gesto que le han ensenado la expresión adecuada … pero hasta que la cámara capta ese momento feliz, ¡cuantos y cuantos metros de celuloide inútil! … El director se muestra muy exigente en los ensayos y el gesto, el ademan, el movimiento, la escena entera, se repite una y otra vez, cien veces si es preciso, hasta que se da por valido el trabajo' (Anon. 1934k: 21).

28 '[Y] el obscure novicio se encontró bajo los potentes reflectors, en un inmenso Estudio, con los ojos de Ingram fijos en él, y frente a una máquina que registraba inexorablemente todos sus gestos, todos los cambios de expresioón de su rostro, por insignificantes que fueran' (Anon. 1934a: 16–17).

29 '[T]odo mi cuerpo daba la sensación de estar completamente achicharrado. Me ponía una *pomade* que al secarse daba a la piel la apariencia de estar reseca y desollada … El sol quemaba y los sufrimientos de los esclavos encadenados al remo no siempre eran de ficción' (Anon. 1934a: 16–17).

References

Anon. (1923) 'También los negritos hacen contratas de miles de dólares', *Cine Popular*, 10 October, 7.

Anon. (1926) 'Treinta años de cinematógrafo: Conmemoración de la primera representación pública', *Fotogramas*, June, 47–8.

Anon. (1928) 'Noticiario cinematográfico', *ARS Programa de los espectáculos del Palacio de la Música, Madrid*, 1 February, 10.

Anon. (1929) 'Fotos de héroes', *La Pantalla*, 55, 924.

Anon. (1934a) 'Confesiones de artistas: Ramón Novarro habla de su vida artística y de lo caros que resultan los divorcios' *Cinegramas*, 9, 11 November, 16–17.

Anon. (1934b) 'Consejos a las estrellas españolas: Al oído de una de ellas, para que todas se enteren', *Cinegramas*, 3, 23 September, 21.

Anon. (1934c) 'El arte fotográfico en el cine', *Cinegramas* 6, 21 October, 25.

Anon. (1934d) 'El arte fotográfico en el cine: La Naturaleza, como escenario auxiliar incomparable de la cámara tomavistas', *Cinegramas* 9, 11 November, 5.

Anon. (1934e) 'El mago de la caracterización', *Cinegramas*, 5, 14 October, 42.

Anon. (1934f) 'En el estudio de Clarence Sinclair: El fotógrafo artista de las "star" yanquis', *Cinegramas*, 4, 30 September, 42.

Anon. (1934g) 'Héroes anónimos del estudio: Los dobles', *Cinegramas*, 9, 11 November, 6.

Anon. (1934h) 'Instantáneas', *Cinegramas* 7, 28 October, 40.

Anon. (1934i) 'Los imitadores', *Cinegramas*, 8, 4 November, 8.

Anon. (1934j) 'Martha Eggerth habla de sus recuerdos y de sus proyectos: cómo saltó de la escena a la pantalla la gran "star"',*Cinegramas*, 9, 11 November, 22–3.

Anon. (1934k) 'Niños sin infancia: El gesto de los pequeños actores', *Cinegramas* 1, 1 September, 21.

Benjamin, Walter (2007) *Illuminations*, ed. Hannah Arendt, New York: Schocken.

De Aldecoa, Luis E. (1927) 'Los actores de teatro en el cinematógrafo', *La Pantalla*, 7, 100.

Delluc, Louis (1920) *Photogènie*, Paris: M. De Brunoff.

Ferry, L. (1921a) 'Condiciones generales', *Cine Popular*, 10, 6 June, 7–8.

Ferry, L. (1921b) 'La fotogenia', *Cine Popular*, 17, 22 June, 2–4.

García Fernández, Emilio C (2002) *El cine español entre 1896 y 1939: Historia, industria, filmografía y documentos*, Barcelona: Ariel.

Ginestral, Francisco (1929) 'El cine de mañana: Artistas esencialmente cinematográficos', *A mí … películas!*, 17 February, 2–3.

Griffith, D.W. (1917) 'What I Demand of Movie Stars', *Moving Picture Classic*, 3, 40–1, 68.

Holliday, Peter J. (2002) 'Navarro, Ramon (1899–1968)', *glbtq: An Encyclopedia of Gay, Lesbian, Bisexual, Transgender and Queer Culture*, www.glbtq.com/arts/novarro_r.html, accessed 1 January 2015.

Martínez de la Riva, R. (1929) 'La fotogenia y el maquillaje en la cinematografía', *El norte cinematográfico*, 2, 10 March, n.p.

Maurice, Alice (2013) *Cinema and Its Shadow: Race and Technology in Early Cinema*, Minneapolis: University of Minnesota Press.

Morin, Edgar (2005) *The Stars*, trans. Richard Howard, Minneapolis: University of Minnesota Press.

Okada, Jun (2008) 'Fortaiture: Photogenie, Race, and Homoerotic Homage in the French Remake of DeMille's *The Cheat*', *Quarterly Review of Film and Video*, 25, 5, 368–81.

Santos, Mateo (1927) 'Review of *Los hijos del trabajo*' *Popular Film*, 23 June, 12.

Scanlon, Geraldine M. (1986) *La polémica feminista en la España contemporánea 1868–1974*, trans. Rafael Mazarrasa, Madrid: Akal.

Studlar, Gaylyn (1996) 'The Perils of Pleasure? Magazine Discourse as Women's Commodified Culture in the 1920s', in Richard Abel (ed.), *Silent Film*, New Brunswick, NJ: Rutgers University Press.

Swender, Rebecca (2006) 'The Problem of the Divo: New Models for Analyzing Silent Film Performance', *Journal of Film and Video*, 58, 1–2, 7–20.

Torrence, Ernest (1927) 'Es fácil llegar a ser estrella cinematográfica?', *ARS Programa de los espectáculos del Palacio de la Música, Madrid*, 24 January, 11.

Valls, Ricardo (1934) '¡Quién fuera vedette!', *Cinegramas*, 10, 18 November, 17–18.

Vargas de la Maza, Armando (1928) 'La vida de Cinelandia', *Popular Film*, 19 April, 4.

Zweig, Stefan (1994) 'The Monotonization of the World', in Anton Kaes, Martin Jay and Edward Dimendberg (eds.) *The Weimar Republic Sourcebook*, Berkeley: University of California Press, pp. 397–400.

2

Performance and gesture as crisis in *La aldea maldita/The Cursed Village* (Florián Rey, 1930)

Sarah Wright[1]

Film acting has come to be understood as the production of 'communicative signs that conceal their own ostensiveness under the guise of quotidian behaviour' (Swender 2006: 7). As David Mayer similarly notes, 'we expect that a cinema actor, with facial nuances, small suggestive gestures, and vocal modulations such as those we might use in our daily lives, will try to confirm the corporeality and actuality of the environment he or she inhabits' (1999: 10). Yet, as Mayer also notes, problems arise when we apply the same descriptive criteria from our twenty-first-century perspective to silent film performances. Analysing silent film acting through the lens of present-day practice, then, tends to result in what Swender terms a 'vague and often pejorative teleology' (Swender 2006: 8). As early as 1930 in Spain, Guillermo Díaz Plaja also noted the marked ostensiveness of silent film from an earlier era: 'hoy esa expresión exagerada nos parece grotesca. En el porvenir parecerán violentísimos algunos gestos que ahora estimamos normales' [today that exaggerated expression seems grotesque to us. In the future some gestures that now seem normal to us will seem awkward] (1930: 97). 1930 was also the year that Florián Rey's *La aldea maldita* was first screened, dubbed 'Spain's last silent film'. But, in the case of this film, the performance styles contribute not towards a jarring 'disjuncture' (Mayer 1999: 11) even when viewed today, but rather towards what is described in terms of the eloquent silent beauty of the film.

In 1942, Florián Rey remade *La aldea maldita*.[2] Where the 1930 version had been filmed on a shoestring, a labour of love funded by Rey and his star Pedro Larrañaga for just 22,000 pesetas, the remake was a big-budget epic. The original was released against the demise of the Primo de Rivera regime and the 1942 version under the tenets of National Catholicism.[3] Both are regarded as biblical parables expressive of conservative visions of gender and Spanishness. If gesture can be understood as an 'always historical conditioning of the body and the world around it' (Levitt 2002: 24), then each might be read as an articulation of gestural practice in cinema and there are marked differences in terms of the performance styles of these two works. Thus, while in the earlier work the performances add to its stark beauty, the remake moves from an overly theatrical, wordy style to static performances which seem to crystallise into tableaux with religious themes. Furthermore, where the first version is considered a masterpiece of silent cinema, the remake is 'cartón-piedra' [cardboard cinema] and 'demodé' [outmoded] (Zumalde Arregui 1999: 459). Thus, both versions appear anachronistic to us now. But in the earlier version the out-of-timeness is central to the film's poignancy and its critical work, while in the remake this has to do rather with our perception of the effects of the crushing biopolitical project at the heart of National Catholicism.

In this chapter, I focus on performance in the early version in order to explore the ways that this film has come to be regarded as Spain's most important silent film, and to unpack some of the elements which contribute to its poignancy. At the same time, I will explore the film's stark gender politics and the way that its performance style may contribute to a meditative critique of the passing of outmoded tradition in the face of encroaching modernity. Above all, performance is seen to stage a gestural crisis which is overcome as the film performs a therapeutic transition to modernity.

Silent gesture in *La aldea maldita* (1930)

The plot of the 1930 version is as follows: Juan (Pedro Larrañaga) and his wife Acacia (Carmen Viance) live with their baby son and Martín, Juan's blind father (Víctor Pastor) in a village that has been the victim of three successive bad winters that have destroyed all of the crops. When Juan sees how the local moneylender has benefited from the misery of the village, he almost throttles him and is thrown into jail. Meanwhile, the villagers leave in droves to seek their fortunes in the city. Magdalena (Amelia Muñoz) persuades Acacia to accompany her to the city. Martín takes the baby to a hideout and Acacia leaves without her child. Three years later, Juan, who has been released from jail and has now reached a comfortable position as head of a group of labourers, goes to a tavern/brothel in the city. There he meets Madgalena, who is now a prostitute, who pulls aside a curtain in a backroom to reveal Acacia, who is with a man. Juan drags his wife home and tells her that she may stay only until his father dies, so that his father may never know of her dishonour. She may not, however, speak to or look at the child. On Martín's death, Acacia leaves home and becomes mad – she is obsessed with the village children, but they throw stones at her. Lucas, the moneylender, summons

Juan to the village and in his old home he finds Acacia rocking an empty cradle. Finally, he pushes his son towards her, saying: 'Dale un beso a tu madre, hijo' [Give your mother a kiss, son]. Acacia is roused from her madness but hides her face in shame: 'haces bien en perdonar, Juan' [you are right to forgive], offers Lucas at the end of the film.

La aldea maldita appears on the cusp of what Román Gubern has termed 'la traumática transición al sonoro' [the traumatic transition to sound] (1993). In fact, there were two versions of the first film: a silent one which was shown privately in Madrid in March 1930 and the second, a post-synchronised sound version, created at the Joinville dubbing studios outside Paris (with the same cast), which was first shown in Paris in August 1930 and then later travelled to Madrid. Nevertheless, it appears that Rey, who had had a disastrous experience with post-synchronised sound on his 1929 film *Fútbol, amor y toros*/*Football, Love and Bullfighting*, planned *La aldea maldita* as a silent film.[4] The advent of sound brought casualties of the 'talkies', as Gene Kelly and Stanley Donen's *Singin' in the Rain* would parody so mercilessly in 1952. Thus, although one director of Paramount maintained that 'anyone who can speak on the telephone can work in sound films as long as they have the aptitude for acting' (Anon. 1930b: 7), actors and actresses who had made their names in silent cinema nevertheless suddenly found that their voices simply did not fit the new aural medium. This was similarly the situation in Spanish cinema, and in fact this appears to have been the case for Carmen Viance, whose career, in spite of her assurances in one interview that 'mi voz no "da" muy mal. Canto una nana, pero sin música' [my voice isn't bad. I sing a lullaby, but without musical accompaniment] (Torres 1930: 9), waned quickly after the introduction of sound.[5] An article from the Spanish film journal *Popular Film* from 1930 announced dramatically that sound engineers threatened to displace the authority of the director on a film set (Anon 1930a: 11), while another in the same journal that same year proclaimed that Lon Chaney, the American actor, 'siente repulsion por las palabras' [feels repulsion for words]. Chaney's family members, we are told, were born mute and 'él debe considerar que es una traición a los suyos usar con prodigalidad de un don que la Naturaleza no concedió a sus familiares' [he must feel that it is a betrayal to his family to have the prodigious use of a talent that Nature didn't give to his family members]. It was this family situation that led Chaney to act as well as he does in silent cinema, giving his face 'extraordinary mobility': 'se le llama el hombre de la cara de goma' [he's called the man with the rubber face], but now he will have to star in sound films ('films hablados') or else his career will come to an end ('terminará') (de España 1930: 11).

Paradoxically, Adorno and Eisler maintained that audiences of silent cinema felt fear at 'being threatened by muteness'. Music existed 'to spare the spectators the unpleasantness involved in seeing effigies of living, acting and even speaking persons, who were at the same time silent' (Adorno and Eisler 1994: 75). Grover-Friedlander takes this further: all films, both silent and with sound, are involved in such a matrix of loss for 'picture and speech are intrinsically contradictory: those who seem to speak on the screen are really mute. Sound pictures do not overcome this, for film, like ballet and pantomime, is fundamentally gestural' (2005: 22). In at least one scene of *La aldea maldita*, the voice is presented as a lost object: when Acacia leaves the village for the city, Juan watches her from behind bars. He shouts to her (we see how his lips form the words) but the inter-titles inform us that 'la voz del prisionero se perdió en el ruido de las carretas' [the voice of the prisoner was lost in the noise of the wagons], leaving just the image of Juan's agitated face and the picture of cart-wheels accompanied by the non-diegetic musical accompaniment. If that scene suggests that Juan has been robbed of his voice, another later scene presents Acacia as gagged by her situation, when she hears her son fall down the stairs and she cries out, but her husband prevents her from comforting him.

Filmed as silent cinema, *La aldea maldita* might seem to fall somewhere closer to Roberta Pearson's classifications of early film 'verisimilar' naturalism and away from the earlier 'histrionic poses' between 1910 and 1920 (1992). Janet Staiger explains further that facial expression, and in particular the eyes, was the new way for actors to express emotion (1985: 19). José Nieto, responsible for composing a score for the film in 1986, noted that at a time when 'directors and actors tried to supplement the lack of voice with an acting style full of large gestures, almost always emphatic and external, Florián Rey had achieved a sober acting style, contained and rich, very close to what would later be the most modern techniques of cinematographic acting' (Alvares 1996: 105).[6] But, unlike much later sound film, the performances of *La aldea maldita*, often feature little speech, and instead seem to use a gestural style more in keeping with the silent soliloquies of mime.[7]

It is worth remembering, perhaps, that silent film only came to be known as silent or mute after the introduction of sound. It is not just that, as Abel and Altman remind us, silent film was rarely silent, being supplemented by a variety of external accompaniments (2001: xii). But, as Jane Gaines notes in her critique of Molly Haskell's designation of women in silent film (in her 1974 book *From Reverence to Rape*) as 'condemned to speechlessness', 'it isn't that the silent screen took articulate speech from female characters, leaving them expressionless'

(2013: 290), it is merely that this world filled with sound is unheard by us.[8] Moreover, as Gaines notes, 'the silent cinema had many more kinds of expressive systems at its disposal, from color to camera movement, to the full gestural continuum' (2013: 290). She goes on: 'even if we start to think about the silent cinema *mise-en-scène* as comprised of sound substitutes we start to go down the wrong track and begin to think of the so-called "non-verbal" as second order signs' (2013: 290). Rather, she suggests that we pay attention to bodily expression, and not to forget the 'rich traditions of theatrical pantomime and stage melodrama' at work in silent film.[9] As Mary Ann Doane noted: 'The absent voice re-emerges in gestures and the contortions of the face – it is spread over the body of the actor' (1980: 33).

In *La aldea maldita* the actors' gestures are minimalist, with small movements of the mouth as they silently speak. At the same time, the silent speeches are few and far between (an aspect of silent film noted by Luis González Alonso in his *Manual de cinematografía* of 1929, which covers aspects of cinema from the industrial to the commercial and artistic, including advice to actors and the sorts of material for clothing which shows up best on camera). González Alonso notes with irony silent cinema's difference with theatre: '¡y aún hay quien afirma que el cinema es el teatro mudo!' [and there are still some people who say that cinema is silent theatre!] (1929: 20), he exclaims. But at times we have to lip-read in order to 'hear' an answer which is not given an inter-title. Following Raynauld (2001), we might suggest that a spectator conjures up the voice in her or his mind – perhaps we could add that at times this voice is also delayed through the inter-titles. Naremore notes that actors in silent film had to give 'slightly exaggerated ostensiveness to expressive movements of eyes, face and hands' (1992: 48). Through the close-up, we focus on the micro-movements of the face, and on the expressivity of gesture in performance. Meaning is made through gesture which, here, although not 'histrionic', may tend towards ostensiveness, and at times towards mime. Furthermore, gestures often seem orchestrated around moments of pose, an absorbing stillness which signals that an inter-title is about to be inserted.[10]

Gesture and crisis

The silence (or even the lack of it) of *La aldea maldita* is not therefore traumatic. Nevertheless, a sense of crisis is conferred on the film by the perceived threat of encroaching modernity. Thus, amidst the slow-moving rhythms of village life and the mass exodus of the villagers following a crop destroyed by hailstones, Magdalena and Acacia speak in confidence together against a stone bridge, their heads bent low towards each other. The inter-titles tell us that Magdalena is speaking to Acacia of the city and, as she does so, a series of dissolves of city life fills the screen. The sequence has the effect of what Georg Simmel termed 'the rapid crowding of changing images … and the unexpectedness of onrushing impressions' (1950: 410), as buses, cars and trams crisscross the screen, suggesting the acceleration and speed of city life. The unexpectedness of these urban images, which emerge against the rural backdrop of the film, suggests the sudden assault of modernity, rendered formally through dissolves which create chaos. Magdalena, with her seductive fineries brought from the city, her heavily made-up eyes and sly, darting, sideways glances, is the incarnation of the cinematic vamp – she is predatory both culturally and sexually (Figure 3). Both filmically and thematically she represents modernity and its ills.

When Magdalena tells Acacia to consider leaving her child at home while she goes to find work, her status is confirmed as the non-maternal, non-procreative dangerous female. Femininity is here associated with change and infidelity. As Marsha Kinder notes of this film, 'clouds and wind moving across a dark sky, vehicles and crowds moving dynamically across the frame' are the domain of the feminine (1992: 45). The bewildering uncontrollability of the natural elements which have destroyed the crops is aligned with femininity which likewise threatens to disrupt the patriarchal order, unless controlled, regulated and managed. Acacia looks out

Figure 3 Amelia Muñoz as Magdalena in *La aldea maldita* (Florián Rey, 1930). Florián Rey-Pedro Larrañaga Productores.

thoughtfully to the middle distance and, when she rises, she walks towards the screen, blocking it completely, and the next shot from her back as she walks away shows that an ellipsis has taken place.[11] In a series of articles, Jodi Brooks has explored the ramifications of this move towards the spectator along the Z-axis in such a way as to hail the spectator 'through a missed beat' (2012). In our case, the 'missed beat', or temporal disjunction, is rendered as an ellipsis or a jump-cut which is seen to be part of Acacia's technological body. The sequence appears to jolt in reminiscence of the bursts and fits characteristic of much earlier cinema. In 'Notes on Gesture', Giorgio Agamben finds a correlation between the 'proliferation of tics, involuntary spasms and mannerisms that can be defined only as a generalized catastrophe of the gestural sphere' (and, moreover, the measuring of these dislocated fragments of gesture), which are involuntarily repeated and interrupted to be found in conditions such as Tourette's syndrome, and the corporeal movements of early cinema (2000: 54). These are the jerky rhythms of a convulsive, hysterical cinematic body, reminiscent of what Väliaho calls the 'deep crisis' of the body 'at the limits of technological automatism' characteristic of early cinema: the scene constitutes a surprising assault on the spectator. Haunting the borders of the alternative logic of vision established by this move into the 'blind field' (Brooks 2013) is the technologised body of cinema, and the attendant fears about modernity. When Acacia walks towards the screen, she has swallowed the technology whole – the incarnation of modernity's shocks.

When we next meet Magdalena, in a brothel/tavern in the city, she now resembles other vamps of the era such as Theda Bara, and the tone of the sequence is markedly out of tune with the rural settings of the rest of the film.[12] Juan, who marks the calendar time of the worker (represented by the camera's obsessive dwelling on the date of the calendar on the wall), goes to a tavern/brothel in the city to celebrate his saint's day. As he laughs and drinks, we see how a hand rests on his shoulder – in dramatic effect, it takes time for Juan, and us, to realise that this hand belongs to Magdalena. He throws her to the floor, and she responds, '¡Cobarde!' [coward!], hair dishevelled, eyes narrowed, eyes darting sideways. Magdalena responds by drawing back a curtain to reveal Acacia with a man. Magdalena and Acacia are technologised by modernity's shocks, producing a sense of crisis. Acacia appears, arm across her face, as a shadow – in an image borrowed straight from Murnau's *Nosferatu* – advances over her. Juan drags Acacia home, throwing modest clothes at her and telling her that she will live with them for the sake of his father, but that she must not speak to nor look at his son.

By contrast, village life is rendered through the faces of the villagers, ravaged by time and hunger, with an air of the microscopic gaze of Buñuel's *Las hurdes, tierra sin pan/Land without Bread* (1933). It is interesting that Juan Piqueras, contemporary film scholar and devotee of the film, should note that, for audiences of the film, 'era la primera vez que no se veían tópicos regionales: que no aparecían toros, ni toreros, ni flamenquismos andaluces' [it was the first time that regional clichés were not in evidence: there were no bulls, nor bullfighters, nor Andalusian flamenco flourishes] (Sánchez Vidal 1991: 136). Marta García Carrión (2007) has noted that *La aldea maldita* appears against anxieties that the number of films being produced in Spain was on the decline and had almost stalled towards the end of the century. In addition, there were numerous debates regarding a degeneration of the portrayal of folklore on screen in the form of the *españolada*. Against this background, technological advances in sound were trailing behind those of other countries, contributing to a fear that Spanish cinema may be overtaken by Hollywood.[13] Nevertheless, Piqueras also declares that Spanish films will have to be 'más españolas de lo que hasta aquí lo fueron [more Spanish than they have been in the past] in the face of the loss of the 'universalidad que le prestaba el silencio' [universality afforded by the silent film] (Piqueras 1930b: 12). Notably, critics of the sound version of *La aldea maldita* in Paris would laud it as 'el primer film sonoro racialmente español' [the first Spanish sound film] (García Carrión 2007: 147), but in spite of this the film articulates a sense of the fears of the passing of the authentic in the face of the fracturing of Spanish filmic identity on the global stage.[14] In *La aldea maldita*, as the camera focuses on the villagers as they prepare to leave the village, they are dressed in local folkloric dress, which adds a self-consciousness to the *vérité* scenes reframed as performance. The sequences tend towards stasis, breaking down the motion picture into stills which recall the paintings of Ignacio Zuloaga or the photographs of José Ortiz Echague.[15] The effect is of a pinning down of tradition in the face of the relentless march of time, in both thematic and formal terms. As Rey noted in 1943, he wished to shun the dynamic camera, which was then associated with Hollywood, and instead create a series of tableaux (quoted in Sánchez Vidal 2005: 15).[16] Martín, the blind grandfather, has a face which is as craggy as the ruins he hides in. There is a sense of crisis here too, as if the technology itself were responsible for the creation of stillness out of motion.

The gestural revolution that took place in the spheres of early silent cinema can be seen as a recuperative process in the broader historical context of the *fin-de-siècle* crisis of the body theorised by Béla Balázs, who maintains that the expressive capacity of the body had deteriorated between 1850 and 1900, and that the physical arts (in particular, theatre) had floundered with the proliferation of the printed word (2010: 41). For

Balázs, silent film is a drama of faces. What Balázs calls the 'submerged', 'unexpressed' realm of the inner was becoming visible again for the first time since the invention of the printing press: 'The whole of mankind is now busy relearning the long forgotten language of gestures and facial expressions' with the result that 'Man has again become visible' (Balázs 2010: 41). With the arrival of synchronised sound, however, all of this would change, according to Balázs. Actors would revert to spoken language to express the interior, and the new education being offered by cinema in the silent era would be cut short. With its stark aesthetics and gestural performance styles, *La aldea maldita* might be described as an eloquent elegy to silent film, poised at the entrance to sound.

Erin Brannigan has identified a 'transitional period' in silent cinema, a period after the exaggerated grotesque gestures of the early cinema outlined by Balázs, but nevertheless characterised by a 'gestural mediality' which 'is fascinated by the unassimilable, expressive potential of the performing body' (2011: 65). In the final sequence of the *La aldea maldita*, Lucas, the usurer, tells Juan to return to his home in the village. Acacia, who has now become mad, is living there. Acacia at first does not notice the presence of the onlookers and crooks her head towards an imaginary baby. Then, when she sees that the visitors have arrived, she motions to the onlookers to be quiet, drawing her fingers to her lips to signal the sound 'ssshhhhh' (Figure 4). She sings to the baby. As her head turns

Figure 4 'Sssshhhh': Carmen Viance as Acacia in Florián Rey's *La aldea maldita* (1930). Florián Rey-Pedro Larrañaga Productores.

sideways to comfort the imaginary baby, she looks animated and happy. If earlier scenes have betrayed an anxiety regarding the technologisation of the corporeal, here the ostensiveness of the scene (the ghosting of mime, reminiscent of an earlier stage of cinema) stages the crisis of the technologised body, while at the same time celebrating the recuperative power of cinema to bring body and technologised movement beautifully into relation through the cinematic gesture. Thus the film records cinema's decomposition of the human body at the same time that it shows how cinema itself may restore the body's expression.

With its focus on gesture and facial expression, *La aldea maldita* seems to share the nostalgia for the silent film expressed by Balázs (and later by Spanish theorists such as Guillermo Díaz Plaja and Fernando Vela who drew on Balázs in their writing).[17] Balázs wrote that what film contributes to the world is the ability to read faces. The micro-movements of the face could change the meaning of a given film sequence. In Balázs's terms, the close-up of the face allows us to understand that 'we can see that there is something that we cannot see' (2010: 37). He goes on:

> In a truly artistic film the dramatic climax between two people will always be shown as a dialogue of facial expression in close-up … Since film permits of no psychological explanations, the possibility of a change in personality must be plainly written in an actor's face from the outset. What is exciting is to discover a hidden quality, in the corner of the mouth, for example, and to see how from this germ the new human being grows and spreads over his entire face. (2010: 36)

Doane reminds us that for Balázs, the face is at once legible and phenomenological. It is sheer presence. 'The closeup transforms whatever it films into a quasi-tangible thing, producing an intense phenomenological experience of presence, and yet, simultaneously, that experienced entity becomes an sign, a test that demands to be read' (Doane 2003: 94). The gigantic face projected on the screen can threaten to overwhelm the subject – what saves it and us is the fascination we feel for the face of another, given an 'aura' in Benjamin's terms. If the film has had to do with the crafting of the control of the feminine (Acacia moves from vamp to *mater dolorosa*) and performance styles similarly exercise restraint and control, the final scene sees the abandonment of control. In this final scene of the film, while Lucas looks on in astonishment, Juan's face plays out his emotions. Juan's eyes well up in tears, giving full rein to the emotions in a way which exceeds the dominant narrative provided by the inter-titles ('Haces bien en perdonar, Juan' [You are right to forgive her, Juan], remarks Lucas). But Juan's face speaks of love, shame and recognition of his ill-treatment of Acacia (the tragedy of the moment is underlined by the poignancy of the lost years away from a child who has now grown up), the product of an outmoded Calderonian honour code. The final scene, then, acknowledges change.[18] Crisis is present in Acacia's madness, but Juan's admission appears as a critique and is therefore recuperative.[19]

The final sequences of the film, in which Acacia silently mimes her actions, recall the heard/unheard dialectic hailed by a silent film poised at the entrance to sound. Even for those audiences who experienced the sound version after post-synchronisation, the final performances of *La aldea maldita*, draw on the silent beauty of mime. Deborah Levitt has written that 'art in the age of mechanical reproduction prepares itself for bodies, whose configuration both determines and reproduces a cultural and corporeal logic proper to its historical moments' (2002: 24). Brooks explains that film can enable a 'rehearsing of shock experience and a release of what we could call its side effects' (1999: 81). At the same time, we may be reminded that, for early film theorist Ricciotto Canudo, it was mime that could 'establish for the cinema the degree of poetics necessary to exorcise it of the phantoms that were the result of its supreme reliance on mechanical and technological processes. (The screen was at once a product of and a vehicle for these realities)' (Piccardi 2013: 4).[20] If *La aldea maldita* charts the way that early cinema decomposes the human body, it also shows us the way that cinema itself may restore the body's expressions. The slowness introduced by the mime-like performance in some respects acts as a foil to earlier anxieties expressed in the film at the jerky rhythms of modernity, the passing of calendar time and the chaos of the seasonal destruction of the harvest by the elements. The final sequence, which depicts Acacia unaware of Juan observing her, reads like a meta-cinematic staging of Stanley Cavell's maxim that the cinema allows us to view the world unseen (1980: 40). Poignancy is achieved through this matrix of silence, loss and recognition. Finally, then, *La aldea maldita* performs a therapeutic transition to modernity by restoring beauty and silence to the technologised body, even after the transition to sound.

Notes

1 I am very grateful to the editors and to Jodi Brooks and Julie Brown for their very helpful comments on this chapter. I am also grateful to Laura Gómez Vaquero for the location of materials and to Natalja Poljakowa for locating the Soviet film *Baby Ryanzanskie*, and for other information about the the that film.

2 With Julio Rey de Heras and Florencia Bécquer in the starring roles.

3 Sánchez Vidal notes that filming began in January 1930 with a silent version shown privately in Madrid in March. Sound was added in Paris in August and this version was shown in Paris in October and in Madrid in December of the same year (Sánchez Vidal 1997: 84).

4 Sally Faulkner notes the irony that 'Rey's much-celebrated mastery of the silent film was in 1930 sabotaged for the majority of audiences who could only experience a sonorized version'. She observes that we are now 'working with a text that differs from the one known at the time' (2013: 31).

5 Amelia Muñoz (Magdalena), meanwhile, primed for stardom and playing opposite Carlos Gardel (Waldman 1998: 136), would tragically suffer a cardiac arrest while dubbing at the Paris Joinville studios. For the background to the introduction of sound in Spanish cinema, see Vernon and Gubern (2012).

6 'Realizadores y artistas trataban de suplir la falta de la voz con una interpretación de gran gesto, casi siempre enfática y por tanto externa, Florián Rey había conseguido un trabajo actoral sobrio, contenido y rico, muy cercano a lo que más tarde iban a ser las técnicas más modernas de la interpretación cinematográfica' [Filmmakers and artists tried to compensate for the absent voice with a gestural acting style which was almost always emphatic and therefore external, Florián Rey had achieved a sober, contained and nuanced acting style, very close to what would later be the most modern acting techniques for the cinema] (Alvares 1996: 105).

7 A note on the DVD extras to the Divisa Red edition of the film notes that Carmen Viance insisted on having children throw stones at her for real in the scenes where she is ostracised from the village.

8 Haskell writes: 'by definition, silent cinema is a medium in which women can be seen, but not heard' (1974: 175).

9 Carlo Piccardi has explored the connections between early cinema and pantomime (a rich theatrical tradition featuring the Pierrot character amongst others and derived in part from the *commedia dell'arte*): both had both grown out of theatrical shows at fairs (Piccardi 2008: 37). See also Piccardi (2009, 2013).

10 Films had to be run at the correct speed so as to avoid movements looking jerky or unnatural. González Alonso provides a guide to actors, noting: 'como que la velocidad de proyección debe estar sincronizada con la de impresión para que el ritmo mímico no se destruya, éste ha de ser – en general – algo más lento que la acción normal, a fin de que los gestos y las actitudes provoquen todo su efecto expresivo' [as the projection speed should be synchronised with that of the imprint so that the rhythm of the performance is not destroyed this must be, in general, slightly slower than normal action so that the gestures and attitudes are adequately expressive] (1929: 113).

11 Juan also appears to walk into the camera in the same way at times.

12 Sánchez Biosca relates these scenes to Murnau's *Sunrise* (2012: 349).

13 Cf. Juan Piqueras's (1930b) defiant article in *Popular Film*, which declares that Spanish and English talkies will lead the way in the new era of sound.

14 Rey would famously later become involved in the dual-language version through films with Imperio Argentina made in Germany under the Nazis. See, for example, Yraola (1999) and, for the wider picture, Vincendeau (1999).

15 See Alcaide (2004).

16 Rey's explorations of the static tableaux would reach their apogee in the 1942 version, where Acacia's languid slowness breaks down the sequences into gestures. In a memorable contemporary review, Ernesto Giménez Caballero encoded the film's wayward femininity as a means to purge the land from the 'red threat'. Acacia (here played by Florencia Becquer) appears almost to collapse under the weight of the biopolitical project. In the film's final scene, the image crystallises into a static tableau with a religious theme. Gesture in cinema from during the 1940s and 1950s in Spain was seen as something that, if imitated, might lead to corrosive ideological effects (i.e. behaviour which was not in keeping with National Catholic ideology). See Marañón's article on gesture (1947) and my earlier article on the writings of Catholic ideologues in the 1950s (Wright 2005).

17 See Lorenzo Benavente (1995) and Díaz Plaja (1930).

18 Sánchez Vidal also notes a sort of nuance in the film with respect to the outmoded honour code, Juan's forgiveness, and the child who plays with the aeroplane, seen as symbolic of an acceptance of modernity (1997: 85). See also Faulkner (2013: 34) and Sánchez Vidal (2005).

19 Despite the more recent classification of this film as wholly conservative, contemporary reviews reflected diverse opinions. Thus, whilst a review from *La Gaceta Literaria* celebrated the depiction of honour, religious iconography and Acacia's punishment, a review from 1930 from Juan Piqueras nevertheless observed the following: 'el honor castellano, todavía arraigado y aformado sobre viejas apreciaciones, sobre ideas antiguas, en hidalgas creencias, basado en experiencias demasiado rancias, provistas de una humildad y de una lógica inaceptable en la hora presente. En el film, la vuelta de la esposa – tratada por el marido con una dureza ejemplarizante, se resuelve de forma calderoniana. Se prosigue la linea de la vieja dramatica espanola. Pero al final se le da un sentido más moderno y humano. Más lógico y admisible' [Castillian honour, still deeply entrenched and formed through old values, ancient ideas, bygone beliefs based on rancid experiences derived from a humility and logic that is unacceptable in the present day. In the film, the return of the wife – treated by the husband harshly as an example, is resolved in a Calderonian manner by following the line proscribed by classical Spanish drama. But the ending is more modern and more human. More logical and acceptable] (Piqueras 1930a: 89). Comparisons with the Soviet film 'The Women of Ryazan' (1927) by Olga Preobrazhenskaya, with which *La aldea maldita* has been compared (the film was released in Spain as *El pueblo del pecado*), are also interesting. Sánchez Vidal (1991: 130) refutes the possible influence (citing lack of opportunity for Rey to see the film and Rey's own statements), but Rey Reguillo notes that Pedro Larrañaga stated

that he was influenced by Soviet cinema (Rey Reguillo 1992: 8). The Soviet film features a plot in which a woman is raped by her father-in-law and then commits suicide when she and her child are rejected by her husband. It appears to us now like a proto-feminist film made by a female film director, in which dizzying camera angles are employed to show the female point of view.

20 Canudo was one of the earliest film theoreticians, and coined the phrase 'the Seventh Art'. In 1908 he wrote about the structural affinities between cinema and the (panto)mime. See Piccardi (2009: 7).

References

Abel, Richard and Rick Altman (2001) 'Introduction', in Richard Abel and Rick Altman (eds), *The Sounds of Early Cinema*, Bloomington: Indiana University Press.

Adorno, Theodor and Hanns Eisler (1994) *Composing for the Films*, London: Athlone Press.

Agamben, Giorgio (2000) *Means Without End: Notes on Politics*, trans. Vicenzo Binetti and Cesare Casarino, Minneapolis: University of Minnesota Press.

Alcaide, José Luis (2004) '*La aldea maldita* y la cultura fin de siglo', *Ars Longa*, 13, 121–45.

Alvarcs, Rosa (1996) *La armonía que rompe el silencio: Conversaciones con José Nieto*, Valladolid: SGAE.

Anon. (1930a) 'Va desapareciendo el antiguo tipo de director de películas', *Popular Film*, 195.5, 11.

Anon. (1930b) 'El teléfono y la voz de los actores de cine', *Popular Film*, 183.5, 7.

Balázs, Béla (2010) *Early Film Theory: Visible Man and The Spirit of Film*, ed. Erica Carter, trans. Rodney Livingston, Oxford: Berghahn Books.

Brannigan, Erin (2011) *DanceFilm: Choreography and the Moving Image*, New York: Oxford University Press.

Brooks, Jodi (1999) 'Crisis and the Everyday: Some Thoughts on Gesture and Crisis in Cassavetes and Benjamin', in Lesley Stern and George Kouvaros (eds), *Falling for You: Essays on Cinema and Performance*, Sydney: Power Publications, pp. 73–104.

Brooks, Jodi (2012) 'Missed Beats: Unseen Cinema and a Cinema of the Unseen (or *Stella Dallas* again)', *Screening the Past*, 34. www.screeningthepast.com/2012/08/missed-beats-unseen-cinema-and-a-cinema-of-the-unseen-or-stella-dallas-again/, accessed 25 April 2015.

Brooks, Jodi (2013) 'Invisibility's Beat: Ralph Ellison, Rhythm, and Cinema's Blind Field', in Jan Hein Hoogstad and Birgitte Stougaard (eds), *Off Beat: Pluralizing Rhythm*, Amsterdam/New York: Thamyris/Rodopi, pp. 149–68.

Cavell, Stanley (1980) *The World Viewed: Reflections on the Ontology of Film*, Cambridge, MA: Harvard University Press.

de España, Juan (1930) 'El hombre que siente repulsión por las palabras', *Popular Film*, 184.5, 11.

Díaz Plaja, Guillermo (1930) 'Estética del cine mudo', in *El engaño a los ojos*, Barcelona: Destino, pp. 81–120.

Doane, Mary Ann (1980) 'The Voice in Cinema: The Articulation of Body and Space', *Yale French Studies*, 60, 33–50.

Doane, Mary Ann (2003) 'The Close Up: Scale and Detail in the Cinema', *differences: A Journal of Feminist Cultural Studies*, 14.3, 89–111.

Faulkner, Sally (2013) *A History of Spanish Film: Cinema and Society 1910–2010*, London: Bloomsbury.

Gaines, Jane (2013) 'Wordlessness, to be Continued ...', in Monica Dall'Asta and Victoria Duckett (eds), *Women in Silent Cinema: New Findings and Perspectives*, Bologna: Dipartimento delle Arte, pp. 288–302.

García Carrión, Marta (2007) *Sin cinematografía no hay nación: Drama e identidad nacional española en la obra de Florián Rey*, Zaragoza: Diputación de Zaragoza.

Giménez Caballero, Ernesto (1943) 'Significación nacional de *La aldea maldita*', *Primer Plano*, 18 April, n.p.

González Alonso, Luis (1929) *Manual de Cinematografía*, Madrid: CEC.

Grover-Friedlander, Michal (2005) *Vocal Apparitions: The Attraction of Cinema to Opera*, Princeton, NJ: Princeton University Press.

Gubern, Ramón (1993) 'La traumatic transición del cine español del mudo al sonoro', in *El paso del mudo al sonoro en el cine español: Actas del IV Congreso de la AEHC [Asociación Española de Historiadores del Cine]*, Madrid: Complutense, pp. 3–24.

Haskell, Molly (1974) *From Reverence to Rape: The Treatment of Women in the Movies*, New York: Holt, Rinehart and Winston.

Kinder, Marsha (1992) *Blood Cinema: The Reconstruction of National Identity*, Berkeley: University of California Press.

Levitt, Deborah (2002) 'Image as Gesture: The Saint in Chrome Dioxide', *Spectator*, 21.2, Fall, 23–39.

Lorenzo Benavente, Juan Bonifacio (1995) 'Fernando Vela, frente a la pantalla cinematográfica', *Actas del V Congreso de la AEHC.*, A Coruña, CGAI, pp. 281–90.

Marañón, Gregorio (1947) 'Psicología del gesto', *Ensayos liberales*, Madrid: Espasa Calpe, 13–70.

Mayer, David (1999) 'Acting in Silent Film: Which Legacy of the Theatre', in Alan Lovell and Peter Krämer (eds), *Screen Acting*, London: Routledge, pp. 10–30.

Naremore, James (1992) *Acting in the Cinema*, Berkeley: University of California Press.

Pearson, Roberta (1992) *Eloquent Gestures: The Transformation of Performance Style in the Griffith Biograph Films*, Berkeley: University of California Press.

Piccardi, Carlo (2008) 'Pierrot at the Cinema: The Musical Common Denominator From Pantomime to Film. Part I', trans. Gilliam B. Anderson, *Music and the Moving Image*, 2.2, Summer, 37–52.

Piccardi, Carlo (2009) 'Pierrot at the Cinema: The Musical Common Denominator from Pantomime to Film. Part II', trans. Gilliam B. Anderson, *Music and the Moving Image*, 2.2, Summer, 7–23.

Piccardi, Carlo (2013) 'Pierrot at the Cinema: The Musical Common Denominator from Pantomime to Film. Part III', trans. Gilliam B. Anderson, *Music and the Moving Image*, 6.1, Spring, 4–54.

Piqueras, Juan (1930a), 'Sentido social de *La aldea maldita*', *La Gaceta Literaria*, September, 7.

Piqueras, Juan (1930b) 'Florián Rey en París', *Popular Film*, 212, 12–13.

Raynauld, Isabelle (2001), 'Dialogues in Early Silent Sound Screenplays: What Actors Really Said', in Richard Abel and Rick Altman (eds), *The Sounds of Early Cinema*, Bloomington: Indiana University Press, pp. 70–78.

Rey Reguillo, Antonia (1992) 'La influencia del cine soviético de los años veinte en *La aldea maldita* (Florián Rey, 1930)', *I Jornadas Andaluzas de Eslavística*, Universidad de Granada, http://roderic.uv.es/bitstream/handle/10550/32847/Cine_soviético_años%20veinte_y_La_aldea_maldita_RODERIC.pdf?sequence=1, accessed 25 May 2015.

Sánchez Biosca, Vicente (2012) 'Photography, Production Design and Editing: An Anomalous Cinema?', in Jo Labanyi and Tatjana Pavlovic (eds), *A Companion to Spanish Cinema*, Oxford: Wiley-Blackwell, pp. 346–70.

Sánchez Vidal, Agustín (1991) *El cine de Florián Rey*, Aragón: Caja de Ahorros de la Inmaculada.

Sánchez Vidal, Agustín (1997) '*La aldea maldita* 1930', in Julio Pérez Perucha (ed.), *Antología crítica del cine español 1906–1995*, Madrid: Cátedra, 83–5.

Sánchez Vidal, Agustín (2005) '*La aldea maldita/The Cursed Village*', in Alberto Mira (ed.), *The Cinema of Spain and Portugal*, London: Wallflower Press, pp. 12–21.

Simmel, Georg (1950) 'The Metropolis and Mental Life (1903)', in Kurt H Wolff (ed.), *The Sociology of Georg Simmel*, New York: The Free Press, pp. 409–24.

Staiger, Janet (1985) '"The Eyes Really Are the Focus": Photoplay Acting and Film Form and Style', *Wide Angle*, 6.4, 14–23.

Swender, Rebeccca (2006) 'The Problem of the Divo: New Models for Analyzing Silent Film Performance', *Journal of Film and Video*, 58.1–2, 7–20.

Torres, Mauricio (1930) *Heraldo de Madrid*, 10 December, 9.

Vernon, Kathleen and Ramón Gubern (2012) 'Soundtrack', in Jo Labanyi and Tatjana Pavlovic (eds), *A Companion to Spanish Cinema*, Oxford: Wiley-Blackwell, pp. 370–90.

Vincendeau, Ginette (1999) 'Hollywood Babel. The Coming of Sound and the Multiple-Language Version', in Andrew Higson and Richard Maltby (eds), *'Film Europe' and 'Film America': Cinema, Commerce and Cultural Exchange, 1920–39*, Exeter: University of Exeter Press, pp. 207–24.

Waldman, Harry (1998) *Paramount in Paris: 300 Films Produced at the Joinville Studios, 1930–1933, with Credits and Biographies*, Lanham, MD: Scarecrow Press.

Wright, Sarah (2005) 'Dropping the Mask: Theatricality and Absorption in Sáenz de Heredia's Don Juan (1950)', *Screen*, 46.4, 415–31.

Yraola, A. (1999) 'Misión españolista: Los camaradas Florián e Imperio con Hitler y el doctor Goebbels', *Film Historia*, 9.3, 131–48.

Zumalde Arregui, I (1999) 'Los sonidos de la reconciliación: Estudio comparativo de dos versions de *la aldea maldita* de Florian Rey', in *Los límites de la frontera: la coproducción en el cine español. Actas VII Congreso de la AEHC*, Madrid: AACCE, 455–66.

3

Exaggeration and nation: the politics of performance in the Spanish sophisticated comedy of the 1940s

Stuart Green

Introduction

It is perhaps not surprising that the ideologically charged atmosphere of the decade immediately following the Spanish Civil War is reflected in academic studies of the cinema of this period. On the one hand, there is a wealth of scholarly analyses of the military and historical epics subsidised by state institutions.[1] This is accompanied by approaches to the *españolada* (folkloric film) rooted in popular theatrical forms, sometimes employing a theoretical framework that draws on the writings of Antonio Gramsci – in particular the terms 'consent', 'hegemony' and the 'national-popular' – to nuance our understanding of the cultural politics of 1940s Spain. Yet these two rich seams of research in Spanish cinema studies have meant that the genre which comprised the majority of productions at the time – the sophisticated comedy – has been largely neglected.[2] Despite their popularity, these films – many directed by heavyweights of Spanish cinema during the Franco dictatorship such as José Luis Sáenz de Heredia, Rafael Gil and Juan de Orduña[3] – are often ignored because they neither glorify the military and moral values of the new regime,[4] nor exploit Andalusian popular culture (and therefore enter into Gramscian negotiations with the ruling elite) as did the folkloric genre.[5] At best, the political ambivalence of these high-society comedies' settings, storylines and characters has led to confusion. Thus when Núria Triana-Toribio wonders why there were 'never worthy Castilian peasants in these comedies if it is them and not this "smug bourgeoisie" who embody *Hispanidad*' (2003: 41) in her analysis of national cinema,[6] she falls back on explanations of escapism and the mismatch between the comedy genre and the noble poverty of the peasant – answers she implicitly grants are insufficient – before moving on to focus on other genres whose links with questions of nation and national identity are more easily perceived (the *españolada* and the military film).

In this chapter, I show that scholarly engagement with the issue of screen performance – encumbered in film studies as a whole by the predominance of ideological approaches to cinema (Krämer and Lovell 1999: 3–4) – actually enables us to answer Triana-Toribio's question. By exploring ways in which sophisticated comedies and discourses of nation in the post-war decade intertwine vis-à-vis the performance of their stars and supporting actors,[7] and in the media discourse surrounding screen acting, I shed new light on the politics of Spanish cinema during the post-war decade. To this end, I problematise and elaborate upon those references to comic performance hidden away in the handful of academic analyses of this genre. My study focuses particularly on the supporting actor Guadalupe Muñoz Sampedro and romantic lead Rafael Durán.

In his book on Spanish film of the 1940s, José Luis Castro de Paz draws on Santos Zunzunegui's identification of a general 'desvío de la técnica meramente reproductiva del realismo' [deviation from the merely reproductive technique of realism] (Zunzunegui 2002: 493), supposedly characteristic of Spanish cinema and national culture more broadly, writing that the sophisticated comedy 'triunfa ... porque juega la baza de la tradición de la comedia americana insuflándole un *cierto tipismo castizo de los registros interpretativos* u otras formas de espectáculo popular de honda raigambre hispana' [triumphs by cleverly suffusing American comedy convention with the *authentic local colour provided by performance models* or other mannerisms of popular theatre of profoundly Spanish roots] (Castro de Paz 2002: 86; original emphasis). Subsequently, Castro de Paz attributes the lengthy run of *Ella, él y sus millones/She, He and Their Millions* (Juan de Orduña, 1944) to

> los registros interpretativos y la velocidad del recitado de los diálogos que, proveniente del Howard Hawks de *La fiera de mi niña* (Bringing Up Baby, 1938) o *Luna nueva* (His Girl Friday, 1940), toma [sic] cuerpo en unos excelentes actores que – con José Isbert a la cabeza – sitúan al filme en la línea de lo grotesco, lo desmesurado y lo esperpéntico [the performance ranges and the dialogue delivery speed which, their origins in the Howard Hawks of *Bringing Up Baby* or *His Girl Friday*, are executed by various superb actors who – José Isbert at their head – locate the film in the domain of the grotesque, the over-the-top]. (2002: 89)

In a more recent publication, Zunzunegui describes this mode of performance as one centred on 'the subtle exaggeration of a tiny detail, the calculated exaggeration of a gesture' (2013: 207) and dominated by supporting actors. Examples of those who perform in this stylised way, according to Zunzunegui, which he sees as a defining trait of Spanish cinema, include José Isbert and Guadalupe Muñoz Sampedro (from the decade that concerns us here), as well as Javier Gurruchaga and Chus Lampreave (2013: 209). Disappointingly, this and other academic writings on this subject rarely support their claims with detailed analysis of screen performances, a failing the present chapter aims to correct.

While such figures often crop up in Spanish comedies, I dispute Zunzunegui's contention that their performance style can be traced back to an incipient nationalism in the sixteenth and seventeenth centuries and which is thus unique to Spain (2002: 493). As Steven Marsh points out in his brief survey of these secondary actors, they embody a paradox: 'they are typecast as Spaniards yet they are universally recognizable as comics who span spatial and temporal boundaries: Julia Lajos is Hattie Jacques, Manolo Morán is Lenny Bruce, Eric Morecambe or Leo Bassi' (2006: 26).[8] As opposed to some Spanish essence passed down the generations, these performances are informed by the actors' theatrical backgrounds. Curiously, both Zunzunegui and Castro de Paz acknowledge this influence, yet they do not perceive the contradiction in the claim there exists a '"typically Spanish school" of acting' (Zunzunegui 2013: 207) prolonged by the absence of innovation on the stage in the first half of the twentieth century. While I do not deny the influence of theatre on cinema at this time – and not just in the case of these supporting actors – greater care is required in any attempt to discuss the notion of what might be termed a national imaginary of performance in its light.

Exaggerated performance styles: supporting actors and romantic leads

Most importantly, we need to recognise that the performance style of actors such as Isbert and Muñoz Sampedro was to a great extent determined by industrial factors operative in the theatre throughout the first half of the twentieth century. On the one hand, they were comic actors working at a time when comedy was by far the most popular genre on the stage,[9] and within a specific, nearly universal, company structure that demanded that dramatists create stock characters rather than psychologically complex individuals.[10] Coupled with the lack of rigour in rehearsals, therefore, it is perhaps no surprise that the actor 'entraba y salía de situación contínuamente, y para mantener el recorrido del personaje acudía a codificaciones gestuales más bien externas, buscando sólo el efecto sobre el público' [jumped in and out of character constantly, and to maintain the notion of a coherent character, fell back on mostly external gestural codes, seeking no more than to impress the audience] (Joya 1999: 222). Furthermore, theatres during this period were proscenium stages and possessed several balconies. Consequently, in the absence of professional training which might enable an actor to project his or her voice appropriately, 'se grita para la galería' [actors shout in the direction of the circle] (López Rubio, in Abizanda 1943: 39). This corporeal and vocal excess was perpetuated by the system of *meritoriaje* [apprenticeship] which required novices to observe and repeat, skills facilitated by the predominance of types among the roles they might hope to play. When stage actors were recruited for the screen, then, 'en ningún momento se planteó la necesidad de que modificaran sus técnicas para adecuarlas al medio cinematográfico' [at no point was it thought their techniques needed to be modified for the medium of film] (Ríos Carratalá 2002: 124). This performance style rooted in the theatre was able to continue on screen, as many films of this time were adaptations of stage plays.[11] More generally, it was facilitated by the marked preference in these comedies for medium and medium-long shots framing the interaction of two characters. Scant use is made of close-ups. In addition, the shot/reverse shots and alternating eyeline-matched medium shots which David Bordwell (Bordwell, Staiger and Thompson 1985: 66) identifies as the building blocks of the typical classical Hollywood sequence are virtually absent. These sequences thus facilitate the kind of interaction between actors to which they (and spectators) had been accustomed by the stage. The theatrical feel of these shots is strengthened further still by their consistently long duration.

This state of affairs is exemplified by the case of Guadalupe Muñoz Sampedro. Born into a theatrical family in 1896, Muñoz Sampedro was a well-established comic actress by the time she appeared in her first film, *La Dolores/Mrs Dolores* (Florián Rey, 1940). Her screen performances are memorable for her wide-eyed expressions of surprise and fear, gesticulations and high-pitched voice. As Clotilde in *Eloísa está debajo de un almendro/Eloísa Under an Almond Tree* (Rafael Gil, 1943), her reaction on reading what she suspects is Ezequiel's murder diary – a screech, raised eyebrows, open mouth and hand on cheek – no doubt draws on her stage performance in this role when Enrique Jardiel Poncela's original play premiered in May 1940. In *Ella, él y sus millones*, her singsong voice, lively face and constantly busy hands help define the eccentricity of the family to which she belongs.

The impact of industrial and individual factors on the screen performance of Muñoz Sampedro is epitomised in *Tuvo la culpa Adán/Adam's Fault* (Juan de Orduña, 1943), when her character Sandalia reunites with Nazario (Juan Espantaleón) – the man she left at the altar some two decades previously – at the wedding of her nephew. This sequence lasts slightly under four minutes and consists of just eight shots: an average of 28 seconds each, the shortest two lasting 10–11 seconds, the two longest being 47 and 78 seconds in duration.[12] The sequence actually commences in the middle of a take in which Nazario is ushered into the ballroom by the father of the bride. Feeling ill at ease upon being left alone to watch the dancing, Nazario is followed by the camera in medium-long shot as he disappears up the stairs. The camera then cuts to another medium-long shot from the first floor as Nazario walks to his bedroom door, where he bumps into Sandalia. Exaggerated facial expressions on the part of both actors – and marked hand gestures in the case of Muñoz Sampedro – thus ensue: in a medium shot when the two former lovers exchange their first awkward words; in a medium-long shot when Sandalia apologises to Nazario for her behaviour; in two medium close-ups – halfway between a two shot and an over-the-shoulder shot – when Nazario expresses his anger and when Sandalia explains her decision (Figure 5); and in one final medium-long shot as they settle their

Figure 5 Sandalia (Guadalupe Muñoz Sampedro) explains to Nazario (Juan Espantaleón) why she left him at the altar. *Tuvo la culpa Adán* (Juan de Orduña, 1943), CIFESA (image reproduced by kind permission of Video Mercury Films).

differences and head downstairs. A dissolve to a medium shot of the couple dancing brings the sequence to an end, and segues uninterrupted into a conversation between her nephew Germán and Nora. These gestures and expressions, coupled with lengthy takes (in which movement of the camera is preferred to editing), lend the sequence a bold theatrical feel. This impression is strengthened further still by the large rises and falls in intonation of dialogue, often accompanied by exaggerated movement of the head, especially in Muñoz Sampedro's performance.

Similarly animated facial expressions, nods, gesticulations and vocal inflections characterise the performances of a host of other supporting actors in these comedies: the gruff voice and lack of (physical) grace of José Isbert as a wealthy grandfather in *La vida empieza a medianoche/ Life Starts at Midnight* (Juan de Orduña, 1944) and as an aristocrat-cum-academic in *Ella, él y sus millones*;[13] the stiff movements and painstaking enunciation of Fernando Freyre de Andrade as butlers in *Deliciosamente tontos/Delightfully Foolish* (Juan de Orduña, 1943) and *Ella, él y sus millones*, as gambler-turned-valet in *El hombre que las enamora/The Heartbreaker* (José María Castellví, 1944), and as a double-dealing diplomat in *Huella de luz/A Sight of Light* (Rafael Gil, 1943); the jerky upper body and raised brow of Alberto Romea as a serially jilted groom in *El hombre que las enamora*, as a hapless father in *Deliciosamente tontos*, and as a man haunted by his son's death in horror-comedy *Viaje sin destino/Journey to Nowhere* (Rafael Gil, 1942); and the oleaginous deference oozed by Antonio Riquelme as a telegraphist with a poetic streak in *Deliciosamente tontos* and as an accountant in *Ella, él y sus millones*. While such actors never enjoy the same screen time as the stars of these films, then, their gestural traits, coupled with their unconventional physical appearance, make them just as recognisable. It might therefore be argued that this enabled producers to benefit from the 'capital value' that Susan Hayward identifies as one of the functions of stars (2013: 353).

As noted above, Muñoz Sampedro, Espantaleón *et al.* were never romantic leads in the theatre. Instead, they mostly provided comic relief.[14] Analysis of the performance styles of romantic leads in film comedies of the 1940s reveals a more restrained performance style, albeit one that still bears the hallmark of a background in the theatre and shaped by the dominant approach to filmmaking in Spain at this time.

As he recounts in his contribution to a series of brief autobiographies of homegrown stars published in 1943–44, Rafael Durán began his stage career in the early 1930s as a novice (1944: 5). Having plied his trade sufficiently well to occupy a modest position in various companies by the middle of the decade, he spent the next few years dubbing male leads in Hollywood films. Durán rose to prominence as a screen *galán* in the hugely successful *La tonta del bote/The Foolish Girl* (Gonzalo Delgrás, 1939).[15] On account of the greater screen time he enjoys, Durán displays a wider range of performance styles in his films of the 1940s than the aforementioned supporting actors. In *Un marido a precio fijo/The Hired Husband* (Gonzalo Delgrás, 1942) and *Tuvo la culpa Adán*, he plays the self-assured, witty Miguel and Gerardo with a loud, nasal voice whose cadence (his intonation often falls at the end) gives the impression he is gently mocking the listener, an impression Durán sometimes reinforces with a cock of the head or by arching an eyebrow.[16] In other films, Durán plays more serious roles – for instance, the wistful Fernando Ojeda in *Eloísa está debajo de un almendro*, the tragic Javier Zarco in *El clavo/ The Nail* (Rafael Gil, 1943) – for which he adopts a gruffer voice and more measured mannerisms. At times, Durán switches between these two styles in the same film, such as in *El 13.000/Number 13000* (Ramón Quadreny, 1941), where he begins rather stiffly as a captain in the air force during the melodramatic first half, and adopts his more laid-back, jovial style when the film becomes more of a romantic comedy. In none of these films does Durán strike the larger-than-life facial expressions of his fellow supporting actors. Yet traces of his theatrical background are evident in the slight head movements he often makes when speaking (a tic assisted by the aforementioned predominance of medium and medium-long shots, and which would have had to be suppressed had the close-up been employed more habitually), and in his occasional gesticulations. These features can be seen in *Tuvo la culpa Adán*, for instance, when he explains over the telephone to Marisa (Luchy Soto) why he failed to make their wedding (Figure 6). A similar physicality is displayed by other male romantic leads of the time at certain moments of their films, such as Alfredo Mayo when unjustly imprisoned in *Deliciosamente tontos* and Armando Calvo on his return from a year abroad in *El hombre que las enamora*.[17]

Conversely, the performances of female stars are more measured than their male peers. Despite scenes such as Lina Yegros's tantrum upon being left waiting at the altar in *Tuvo la culpa Adán*, the characters created for female stars tend to be more diffident than their (more proactive) male counterparts. The relative lack of protagonism to which they are relegated as love interest is exemplified in the fact that, in many of these comedies, the female stars are virtually absent for the opening 15–20 minutes. A performance that features less exaggerated facial expressions is also required in part by the fact that these female romantic leads are more often shot in close-up and soft focus as figures of desire.

Arguably the clearest example of the notable influence of theatre on screen performance in 1940s comedy is the use by both supporting

Figure 6 Germán (Rafael Durán) argues on the telephone with Marisa about why he did not turn up to their wedding. *Tuvo la culpa Adán* (Juan de Orduña, 1943), CIFESA (image reproduced by kind permission of Video Mercury Films).

actors and leads of the aside; that is, a comment or exclamation made to oneself on screen, in lieu of a physically present audience as when on stage. In *Ella, él y sus millones*, for example, Diana (Josita Hernán) – recalling her husband's statement that their marriage is merely an economic transaction while she brushes her hair alone on their wedding night – muses that 'Ya lo veremos ...' [We'll see ...].[18] *El hombre que se quiso matar/The Man Who Wanted to Kill Himself* (Rafael Gill, 1942) features several such indications of internal thought processes, such as when Federico (Antonio Casal) laments '¡La vida! No vale la pena vivir así' [Life! There's no point in living like this]. The most obvious instance of the theatrical origins of these asides occurs when Dimas (Antonio Riquelme) cries out '¡Atiza!' [Crikey!] on overhearing news that his master's wedding has again been called off in *El hombre que las enamora*.

It is, I would argue, for reasons related to the performance traits of both stars and supporting cast that Antonio Casal proved such a popular lead in his romantic comedies of the early 1940s. In addition to his good looks, Casal exhibits – as Castro de Paz proffers regarding his performances as Federico Solá in *El hombre que se quiso matar* and as Octavio Saldaña in *Huella de luz* – 'un cuerpo, un gesto y una voz directamente vinculados con bien arraigadas formas del espectáculo popular español' [a body, a motion and a voice linked directly to firmly rooted Spanish popular theatre models] (2002: 95–6). What is more, as noted above, these roles include the asides familiar to spectators from the theatre.[19] It is significant in this respect that Casal began his career in the theatre as a *galán cómico*, that is, as a supporting actor who had to combine charm and wit in equal measure. The only other actor to make a similar leap from *galán cómico* on stage to successful screen *galán* was Fernando Fernán Gómez, who continues to employ the nervous tics seen in *Cristina Guzmán* (Gonzalo Delgrás, 1943) in later films such as *El destino se disculpa/With Apologies from Fate* (José Luis Sáenz de Heredia, 1945).

The aforementioned elements of these performance styles, marked to a greater or lesser extent by the theatrical background of the actors, are also to be found in the *españolada* of the Second Republic and the early Franco dictatorship. Since they are more prominent in the performances of comic actors rather than the romantic leads, Ángel Comas (2004: 84) groups all these actors together under the label of *gracioso* [comedian]. Yet these elements are far more manifest – both quantitatively and qualitatively – in the comedians of the folkloric film. In *Suspiros de España/Sighs of Spain* (Benito Perojo, 1938), Concha Catalá's performance as Dolores is characterised by saucer-like eyes, huge gesticulations and a clamorous voice. In the same film, Miguel Ligero as Relámpago also employs over-the-top bodily movements, most notably when walking (raised arms bent at the elbow) and when speaking (finger pointing, open hand, swaying head, shrugs). Ligero's unique screen persona is also to the fore in *Rumbo al Cairo/Bound for Cairo* (Benito Perojo, 1940) and *Pepe Conde* (José Luis Rubio, 1941). The centrality of Ligero's performance to the success of the film is evidenced by the fact he is often captured in close-up, unlike the supporting actors in the sophisticated comedy of the period concerned. Likewise, the fireman's cry of '¡Atiza!' [Crikey!] in *Rumbo al Cairo* is addressed directly to the camera rather than to oneself, as in the above case of Antonio Riquelme. The greatest exaggeration characteristic of the *españolada* can be seen in Antonio Casal's performance in *Pepe Conde* as Conde Juan José, whose use of hands, arms and shoulders (especially in the sequence when he reads a telegram) is far more affected than in Casal's sophisticated comedies.

Media criticisms

Viewed in the light of the *españolada*'s more explicit literary, thematic and geographical connections with national popular culture, (exaggerated) screen performance can be related to the question of nation and the national imaginary. Indeed, this appears to be the case in comments regarding actors made by film critics of the early post-war period. As Triana-Toribio notes, the first film magazine of the Franco dictatorship, *Primer Plano*, was conceived in 1940 as a mouthpiece for Falangist sympathisers wishing to exploit cinema to their political ends. This involved 'paradoxically demanding the undoing of already existent 'nation-building' narratives and strategies' (2003: 40) associated with the Second Republic. Those demands she mentions are 'that Spanish cinema should not represent poverty and only celebrate the 'right' masses' (2003: 40) and thus 'the banishment of the *españolada* from the national screens (2003: 43), 'adaptations of classic Spanish plays and novels' (2003: 44), as well as celebrations of 'the *crusade* (the Civil War), its participants, and the resultant militarist state' (2003: 44). An analysis of reviews of Spanish films in *Primer Plano* throughout 1943 also reveals that this nation-building exercise extended to screen performance.

In 1943, responsibility for the film review page published in each weekly edition of *Primer Plano* passed through the hands of three men: Antonio Mas-Guindal, Ubaldo Pazos and José Luis Gómez Tellos. The first and third of these clearly sympathised with the ideology of the Movimiento at this time. Mas-Guindal, better known as a scriptwriter, had recently published a review of the controversial *Rojo y negro/Red and Black* (Carlos Arévalo, 1942) which disapproved of the compassion the film showed for its Communist protagonist (see Castro de Paz 2010: 73, n.25). Gómez Tello had fought in the División Azul, an experience about which he later wrote 'La simiente que José Antonio dejó, nosotros somos' [We are the seed that José Antonio [Primo de Rivera] left behind] (cited in Rodríguez-Puértolas 2008: 715) in his 1945 memoir *Canción de invierno en el Este/Winter Song in the East.*[20]

The reviews of Spanish films written by Mas-Guindal from January until late February are short texts in comparison to his longer reviews of Hollywood and other foreign films. For the most part, his reviews focus on storyline, themes and stylistic issues; details concerning performance are limited to one or two sentences. While the insipidness of many of his comments testifies to a general lack of critical interest in this aspect of cinema at the time – the cast in *¡¡Campeones!!/*

Champions!! (Ramón Torrado, 1943) deliver an 'adecuada inter-pretación' [adequate performance] (Mas-Guindal [1943d]) – a few remarks imply a rather dismissive opinion of the exaggerated performance styles outlined above. In reference to *Su excelencia, el mayordomo/His Excellency, the Butler* (Miguel Iglesias, 1942), he writes that Luis Prendes' performance is 'desenvuelta y a tono con el matiz de vodevil que marca la cinta' [relaxed and in keeping with the spirit of farce that defines the film] (Mas-Gunidal [1943a]). This attitude is much more patent in the subsequent reviews by Pazos, the majority of which devote greater space to Spanish films and are divided into sections regarding storyline, dialogue, sound, editing, music, cinematography, *mise-en-scène*, acting and direction. In the first such review, Armando Calvo is reproached for his 'exagerada afectación ante la cámara' [exaggerated affectation before the camera] (Pazos [1943a]) in *Correo de Indias/Courier of the Indies* (Edgar Neville, 1942). Likewise, Josita Hernán is lambasted for her 'gritos extemporáneos, gestos fuera de lugar, afectados, ademanes exagerados' [incongruous screams, inappropriate gesticulations, exaggerated mannerisms] (Pazos [1943d]) in *La niña está loca/The Kid Is Crazy* (Alejandro Ulloa, 1943). Affectedness and a propensity to gesticulate are repeatedly flagged by Pazos throughout his six-month spell as film critic. These flaws Pazos attributes to the theatre. Guadalupe Muñoz Sampedro in *Mi vida en tus manos/My Life in Your Hands* (Antonio de Obregón, 1943), for instance, 'tiene a su cargo un papel que siempre es el mismo en las últimas películas y que ella desempeña con la misma gracia y algo de exageración y amaneramiento teatral' [is given a role the same as all those in her recent films and which she performs with the same wit and somewhat theatrical exaggeration and affectedness] (Pazos [1943f]). Those qualities praised or demanded by Pazos are, conversely, 'naturalidad' [unaffectedness] and 'sencillez' [simplicity]. A lack of the former, for instance, defines Rafael Durán's performance in *Mosquita en palacio/Mosquita at the Palace* (Pazos [1943c]). These qualities are said by Pazos to be inherently cinematic in his comments as regards Julio Peña in *Intriga/Intrigue* (Antonio Román, 1942): 'Es el perfecto galán, ajustado y preciso, que, con el debido desenfado, hace una maravillosa creación de su papel, teniendo los dos matices para mostrarnos con amplitud y profundidad lo que es teatro y lo que es cine' [He is the perfect romantic lead, meticulous and precise, which, coupled with the right degree of effortlessness, renders a magnificent creation of his role, displaying both qualities in order to show us clearly and truly what is theatre and what is cinema] (Pazos [1943e]). While Gómez Tello reverts to the earlier format of relatively brief reviews not divided into sections, he displays the same concern as Pazos about exaggerated mannerisms on screen. In reviews of *Todo por ellas/Everything for the Ladies* (Adolfo Aznar, 1942), *Se vende un palacio/A Palace for Sale* (Ladislao Vajda, 1943) and *La boda de Quinita Flores/Quinita Flores' Wedding* (Gonzalo Delgrás, 1943) ([1943a]), *Rosas de otoño/Autumn Roses* (Juan de Orduña, 1943) ([1943b]), *El abanderado/The Flag Bearer* (Eusebio Fernández Ardavín, 1943) ([1943c]) and *La chica del gato/The Girl with the Cat* (Ramón Quadreny, 1943) ([1943d]), Gómez Tello consistently associates these traits with the theatre.

These calls for a less affected, supposedly more cinematic performance style in *Primer Plano* can tentatively be interpreted as another means by which Spanish film of the post-war period was to be cleansed of the 'wrong' kind of Spanishness. The 'right' alternative advanced appears to have been more than just a style free of affectation. What is more, this (ostensibly utopian) goal was not politically neutral. On a number of occasions in these reviews, the critics praise the qualities of *sobriedad* [solemnity] and *vigor* [force]. For example, according to Pazos, Rafael Durán fails to strike the correct level of the former ([1943c]), while Isabel de Pomés lacks the latter ([1943b]). Significantly, the actor most frequently associated with these qualities is the darling of official post-war cinema and the embodiment of the values of the recently established military dictatorship: Alfredo Mayo (Mas-Guindal [1943b] and [1943c]).

Nevertheless, such calls went unheeded during this period. Neither official cultural organisations nor producers showed any interest in formalising actor training during the first half of the 1940s as Hollywood had since the mid-1930s (Baron, 1999). The screen acting school in which A. Abad Ojuel sought to instruct actors how to 'andar, llevar las manos en su sitio, moverse, sonreír, parpadear, dirigir la mirada sin incurrir en empaques grotescos o en actitudes falsas' [walk, hold one's hands in place, move, smile, blink, look without resorting to grotesque incarnations or false poses] (1943) was not to materialise until the founding of the Instituto de Investigaciones y Experiencias Cinematográficas (National Film School) in 1947, by which time the sophisticated comedy had disappeared (Monterde 1995: 231). The subgenre's fall from grace in the second half of the 1940s, I would argue, is less on account of a rejection of such affected performance styles – actors such as Pepe Isbert and Alberto Romea continued to enjoy an outlet for their skills, often (ironically) in the films of IIEC graduate Luis García Berlanga – than because audiences had tired of the Hollywood *mise-en-scène* of the films' sophisticated settings.

Conclusion

This chapter deems that the exaggerated performance style of support-ing actors as well as romantic leads, rooted in the theatre, made possi-ble the commercial success of the sophisticated comedy at a time when demand was high for something to help forget – even if only for an hour or so – the dreary reality of the immediate post-war period. Yet this is not because certain 'gestural codes', as Susan Hayward contends, 'are deeply rooted in a nation's culture' (2013: 200). While such exaggeration was clearly crucial in articulations of what might be called a national imaginary of performance in Spain, I would also draw attention to the affected performances in Hollywood comedy at this time of romantic leads such as Cary Grant and Katharine Hepburn, or supporting actors like Roscoe Karns and Franklin Pangborn.[21] Considerable similarities exist across national borders, as Steven Marsh notes as regards comic types (see above). It is therefore more appropriate to talk about general performance paradigms which then feed back discursively into percep-tions of nation rather than actual national models. If exaggerated perfor-mances are more prominent in Spanish film of the time, this is the result of the persistence of a paradigm better suited to the large theatre than the big screen and not the manifestation of national character.

Notes

1 See, for example, José María Caparrós Lera's analysis of *Raza* (2000: 15–31) and Alberto Mira's of *Alba de América* (1999).

2 For statistics, see Monterde 1995: 230. As Steven Marsh notes in what remains the most systematic analysis of examples of screen comedy during this era, propaganda films numbered barely twenty in a total of over five hundred productions (2006: 1–2); of the folkloric musical, Aurea Ortiz writes, 'hay muy pocos trajes de faralaes, muy pocos bandoleros, poca canción española y ningún niño prodigio' [there are very few frilly dresses, very few bandits, barely any traditional Spanish song and no child prodigies] (2001: 116). This and all subsequent translations in this chapter are my own.

3 Sáenz de Heredia is best known for his 1941 film *Raza*, based on Francisco Franco's script. Rafael Gil's *El clavo/The Nail* (1944) is often held up as a commercial classic of this decade. Juan de Orduña's *Alba de América/Dawn of America* (1951) was conceived as a response to *Christopher Columbus* (David McDonald, 1948) and consequently showered with official financial rewards, forcing the dismissal of José María García Escudero as Director General of Cinema and Theatre.

4 Indeed, as Ortiz points out (2001: 120–1), many of these films can be seen as critiques of the Catholic-bourgeois marriage advocated in films such as *Raza* (José Luiz Sáenz de Heredia, 1941).

5 While this chapter argues that a significant factor in the Spanish sophisticated comedy's success at this time is the theatrical performance style displayed by its romantic leads and supporting cast, its social causes are more difficult to determine: details of the consumption and reception of Spanish film at this time of vainglory for the victors, and of crippling food shortages and bloody reprisals for the vanquished, are frustratingly scant.

6 In its original context of the quasi-manifesto of Falangist film published in *Primer Plano* in 1940 (translated by Triana-Toribio 2003: 39), the phrase 'smug bourgeoisie' refers to spectators of these sophisticated comedies rather than their protagonists. Triana-Toribio's citation of her own translation widens its semantic field to include the latter.

7 The sophisticated comedy is of particular value for the study of screen performance, for it was here 'donde labraron su popularidad las principales estrellas de la época y donde se refugiaron con éxito los consagrados en los films histórico-político-militares' [where the biggest stars of the age fabricated their popularity and to where those acclaimed for their historico-politico-military films retreated with great success] (Comas 2004: 66)).

8 Prior to this, Marsh states that 'There is … absolutely nothing to sustain the nationalism implicit (and often explicit) in claims of intrinsic Spanishness attributed to these actors' (2006: 25).

9 In his study of theatre in Madrid during the Second Republic, Luis M. González (1996: 34) notes that, of some 600 productions staged during this nine-year period (excluding *zarzuelas* and similar musical genres), nearly 450 were *comedias*. While not necessarily comedies strictly speaking, these plays inevitably included a significant comic element.

10 With very few exceptions, theatre companies in the first half of the twentieth century in Spain comprised a leading lady supported by two men – one older and one younger (the *primer actor* and *galán*) at their centre, around which moved the indispensable comic actors (male and female) alongside a selection of other more modest roles such as older or younger women (*damas*), roles for actors specialising in servants (*actrices* and *actores de carácter*) as well as walk-on parts for novices. Víctor García Ruiz (1999: 23) provides a list of these roles as indicated in the first official attempt to regulate the theatre industry under the Franco dictatorship in 1949.

11 In the mid-1930s, as Román Gubern notes (1995: 155), more than half of national film productions were adaptations of stage plays.

12 According to Bordwell, the average shot length of Hollywood films of this time is 10–11 seconds (in Bordwell, Staiger and Thompson 1985: 61), while sequences were generally 2–5 minutes in length and consisted of 12–30 shots (1985: 62).

13 Isbert played this latter character in the 1928 premiere of the play on which this film was based, Honorio Maura's *Cuento de hadas/Fairy Tale*.

14 That is not to say they were always consigned to a supporting role: by the mid-1930s, Isbert was sufficiently popular with audiences to create a company of his own in partnership with Milagros Leal. Leaving the Compañía María Isabel, where he had been *actor de carácter*, at the turn of 1935, he played the lead in Luis Manzano's *Tú y yo solos/On Our Own*, which opened at the Teatro Benavente on 8 February. This was not a romantic role, as convention regularly dictated, but a bossy father, Paciano (Manzano 1935).

15 Regrettably no copy of this film survives today.

16 This performance style was clearly the reason why Edgar Neville chose Durán to play Miguel in *La vida en un hilo/Life on a String* (Edgar Neville, 1945), the bohemian artist who trivialises bourgeois values, much to the delight of protagonist Mercedes (Conchita Montes).

17 Curiously, on many occasions in the films watched for this chapter, the actors hold an object or have their hands in their pockets, perhaps in order to curtail such hand movements.

18 The spectator is reminded of this statement by the repetition at this moment of the film – in the form of an internal monologue 'heard' by Diana – of the earlier remark by Salazar (Rafael Durán) that 'La vida sentimental no me interesa' [I'm not interested in having a love life]. This is a device far less suited to the stage, but Hernán's response to this comment is an aside all the same.

19 These asides, I would argue, belie Castro de Paz's claims of Casal's 'pasmosa naturalidad' [stunning lack of affectation] (1997: 20).

20 I have been unable to locate literature concerning the political beliefs of Pazos.

21 Indeed, one of the actors who dubbed Cary Grant into Spanish most frequently during the late 1930s was Rafael Durán.

References

Abad Ojuel, A. [as A. Abad Ojual] (1943) 'Una escuela española de actores', *Primer Plano*, 22 August, n.p.

Abizanda, M. (1943) 'López Rubio cuenta sus aventuras', *Cámara*, December, 38–9.

Baron, Cynthia (1999) 'Crafting Film Performances: Acting in the Hollywood Studio Era', in Alan Lovell and Peter Krämer (eds), *Screen Acting*, London: Routledge, pp. 31–45.

Bordwell, David, Janet Staiger and Kristin Thompson (1985), *The Classical Hollywood Cinema: Film Style and Mode of Production to 1960*, London: Routledge and Kegan Paul.

Caparrós Lera, José María (2000) *Estudios sobre el cine español del franquismo (1941–1964)*, Valladolid: Fancy Ediciones.

Castro de Paz, José Luis (1997) 'Antonio Casal, comicidad y melancolía', in José Luis Castro de Paz (ed.), *Antonio Casal, comicidad y melancolía*, Ourense: Concello de Ourense, pp. 17–24.

Castro de Paz, José Luis (2002) *Un cinema herido: Los turbios años cuarenta en el cine español (1939–1950)*, Barcelona: Paidós Ibérica.

Castro de Paz, José Luis (2010) 'Propaganda, metáfora, memoria: La Guerra Civil en el cine español (1939–1965)', in Juan Carlos Ibáñez and Francesca Anania (eds), *Memoria histórica e identitdad en cine y televisión*, Zamora: Comunicación Social Ediciones y Publicaciones, pp. 59–82.

Comas, Ángel (2004) *El star system del cine español de posguerra (1939–1945)*, Madrid: T&B Editores.

Durán, Rafael (1944) *Mi vida*, Madrid: Ediciones Astros.

García Ruiz, Víctor (1999) *Continuidad y ruptura en el teatro español de la posguerra*, Pamplona: Eunsa.

Gómez Tello, José Luis (1943a) 'Crítica de los estrenos', *Primer Plano*, 5 September, n.p.

Gómez Tello, José Luis (1943b) 'Crítica de los estrenos', *Primer Plano*, 10 October, n.p.

Gómez Tello, José Luis (1943c) 'Crítica de los estrenos', *Primer Plano*, 24 October, n.p.

Gómez Tello, José Luis (1943d) 'Crítica de los estrenos', *Primer Plano*, 26 December, n.p.

González, Luis M. (1996) 'La escena madrileña durante la II República', *Teatro*, 9–10, 7–73.

Gubern, Román (1995) 'El cine sonoro (1930–1939)', in Román Gubern et al., *Historia del cine español*, Madrid: Cátedra, pp. 123–79.

Hayward, Susan (2013) *Cinema Studies: The Key Concepts*, 4th ed., London: Routledge.

Joya, Juan Manuel (1999) 'El actor en la primera mitad del siglo XX', *ADE Teatro*, 77, 220–33.

Krämer, Peter and Alan Lovell (1999) 'Introduction', in Alan Lovell and Peter Krämer (eds), *Screen Acting*, London: Routledge, pp. 1–9.

Manzano, Luis (1935) *Tú y yo solos*, Madrid: La Farsa.

Marsh, Steven (2006) *Popular Spanish Film Under Franco: Comedy and the Weakening of the State*, London: Palgrave.

Mas-Guindal, Antonio (1943a) 'Crítica', *Primer Plano*, 3 January, n.p.

Mas-Guindal, Antonio (1943b) 'Crítica', *Primer Plano*, 14 February, n.p.

Mas-Guindal, Antonio (1943c) 'Página de crítica', *Primer Plano*, 10 January, n.p.

Mas-Guindal, Antonio (1943d) 'Página de crítica', *Primer Plano*, 7 February, n.p.

Mira Nouselles, Alberto (1999) 'Al cine por razón de estado: estética y política en *Alba de América*', *Bulletin of Spanish Studies*, 76.1, 123–38.

Monterde, José Enrique (1995) 'El cine de la autarquía (1939–1950)', in Román Gubern *et al.*, *Historia del cine español*, Madrid: Cátedra, pp. 181–238.

Ortiz, Aurea (2001) 'La comedia española de los años cuarenta', *Cuadernos de la Academia*, 9, 115–25.

Pazos, Ubaldo (1943a) 'Crítica de los estrenos', *Primer Plano*, 7 March, n.p.
Pazos, Ubaldo (1943b) 'Crítica de los estrenos', *Primer Plano*, 28 March, n.p.
Pazos, Ubaldo (1943c) 'Crítica de los estrenos', *Primer Plano*, 18 April, n.p.
Pazos, Ubaldo (1943d) 'Crítica de los estrenos', *Primer Plano*, 2 May, n.p.
Pazos, Ubaldo (1943e) 'Crítica de los estrenos', *Primer Plano*, 23 May, n.p.
Pazos, Ubaldo (1943f) 'Crítica de los estrenos', *Primer Plano*, 20 June, n.p.
Ríos Carratalá, Juan A. (2002) 'Relaciones entre el teatro y el cine en la España del Franquismo: la perspectiva del actor', *Anales de la Literatura Española Contemporánea*, 27.1, 121–36.
Rodríguez Puértolas, Julio (2008) *Historia de la literatura fascista española II*, Madrid: Ediciones Akal.
Triana-Toribio, Núria (2003) *Spanish National Cinema*, London: Routledge.
Zunzunegui, Santos (2002) 'La línea general o las vetas creativas del cine español', in José Luis Castro de Paz, Julio Pérez Perucha and Santos Zunzunegui (eds), *La nueva memoria. Historia(s) del cine español*, A Coruña: Vía Láctea, pp. 489–504.
Zunzunegui, Santos (2013) '*Queridos cómicos*: Actors and Entertainment', in Jo Labanyi and Tatjana Pavlovič (eds), *A Companion to Spanish Cinema*, Malden MA: Blackwell Publishing, pp. 203–9.

4

The voice of comedy: Gracita Morales

Kathleen M. Vernon

Recent scholarship on mid-twentieth-century Spanish cinema has witnessed a re-evaluation of the comic performances and persona of a number of well-known actors, including José Isbert, Manolo Morán, José Luis López Vázquez, Alfredo Landa and Tony Leblanc.[1] Writing in *The Companion to Spanish Cinema* on the 'politics of stardom', Chris Perriam and Nuria Triana-Toribio have noted the mechanisms and effects of this critical rehabilitation whereby the reputations of certain performers were purged of associations with popular genres perceived as crudely commercial and reactionary (2013: 330–3). In contrast, Gracita Morales, one of the most recognisable comediennes and comic voices of the period, although frequently paired with López Vázquez (see Whittaker, chapter 5 this volume) as well as Landa, never benefited from such a second look at her career and influence. In proposing both to understand and remedy this neglect, I will situate Morales' career and performances with respect to the body of critical work on women and comedy in various film traditions and within the context of a specifically Spanish history of film types and performance norms. In particular, I will consider the role of Morales' distinctive vocal style as a source of success but also as a limitation that kept her confined to a pattern of stereotypical roles.

Women and comedy

From its origins across the globe in popular theatrical forms such as vaudeville, music hall and the *sainete* [popular farce], film comedy has been seen as a masculine genre. In a study of comedy and femininity in early twentieth-century film, Kristin Anderson Wagner points to the 'pervasive belief that comedy was inappropriate for women' (2011: 35). Both verbal comedy, with its reliance on intellect, wit and critical distance, and the more physical varieties like slapstick, with a base in bodily spectacle and ridicule, were thought to be antithetical to the quintessential feminine qualities of emotion and empathy, beauty and grace (2011: 35–8). In many respects little has changed over the last century. Analysing Anglo-American female comedy of the 1990s, Yvonne Tasker writes that women are not expected to be funny; 'they are expected to be beautiful' (1998: 165). Even while arguing for the anti-authoritarian and potentially subversive function of comedy as a genre that erases social and cultural distinctions, displacing the hero of tragedy in favour of the everyman, scholars such as Frank Krutnik emphasise its male-centred character. In that view, the male comic performer is defined by his rejection of a conformity that is 'projected onto women and thence disowned and devalued' (cited in Tasker 1998: 163).

For many feminist critics, it is precisely the supposed inappropriate and unfeminine nature of comedy that makes it a potent vehicle for woman performers who would dare to challenge the established social order and gender roles. In her key study of the disruptive power of women comics, *The Unruly Woman*, Kathleen Rowe highlights comedy's attack on patriarchal power, its capacity to level, disrupt and destroy hierarchies. 'Comedy breaks taboos,' she affirms, and 'expresses those impulses that are already outside the social' (1995: 101). Wagner echoes this claim in her analysis of the boundary-levelling effects of physical, slapstick comedy wielded by women that 'moves toward an obliteration of traditional gender roles', in the 'chaos and anarchy' of 'pervasive and persistent gender confusion' (2011: 36).

Breaking with standards of female decorum, the woman comic embraces excess; she makes a spectacle of herself, she laughs and invites laughter at her own expense. As Tasker notes, comedy 'emphasizes performance: facial expressions, intonation, delivery and body language' (1998: 165). In this respect the practice of female film comedy also challenges the gender binaries of canonical feminist film theory. Wagner argues that '[u]nlike the passive and sexually objectified, "to-be looked at" mode of display that Laura Mulvey describes as the inescapable position for women in classic Hollywood cinema, comic display is aggressive and assertive' (2011: 42). For her part Rowe affirms the need for women to claim a sense of spectacle for themselves, noting that 'visual power flows in multiple directions and the position of spectacle is not necessarily one of weakness. Because public power is predicated largely on visibility, men have long understood the need to secure their power not only by looking, but by being seen.' She asks: 'How might women use spectacle to disrupt that power and lay claim to their own?' (1995: 11).

The film comedienne's deployment of spectacle is, of course, not limited to the strictly visual performance of movement and gesture but, as noted by Tasker, also relies on the use of voice and speech. Both types run counter to conventional feminine ideals, in which stillness and silence are considered a virtue 'that enhances a notion of female beauty dependent on passivity and mystery' (Rowe 1995: 126). Likewise, Mulvey's notion of the woman in patriarchal culture as the passive object of male projections rests on a conception of the '*silent image of the woman* still tied to her place, as bearer, not maker, of meaning' (2000: 35, emphasis mine). Rowe points instead to the demystifying role of sound: 'When a woman's image is accompanied by the sound of her voice, that image is less readily reduced to a screen for the projection of male fantasy' (1995: 125–6).

Funny women, funny voices

The various expressions of vocal excess were a key component of the performance repertoire of many of the most successful and disruptive film comediennes of the past century. Writing about early Hollywood sound cinema, Henry Jenkins describes the effects of the 'ear-piercing voice' and vulgar use of language of 'wild woman' actress Charlotte Greenwood (1992: 245–7). Rowe offers a qualifier to such characterisations, observing that 'voices in any culture that are not meant to be heard are perceived as loud when they do speak, regardless of their decibel level' (1995: 63). Nevertheless, funny voices, prolix and non-standard speech were central to the careers of well-known figures like US vaudeville, radio, film and television comedienne Gracie Allen, theatre and film actress Judy Holliday and Argentine radio and film performer Niní Marshall. In contrast to the case of Gracita Morales, the work of these female comedic forebears has been the subject of a number of academic studies.

While attentive to specific cultural, socio-economic and technological contexts of these artists' careers, scholars identify a cluster of common features pertaining to their distinctive vocal performance and evident in their most celebrated roles. With voices described as (Allen) 'feminine and high-pitched' (Lowe 2003: 243), (Holliday) 'slightly squeaky' and akin to a 'toy whistle' (Wojcik 2010 : 215) and (Marshall) 'squeaky and high-pitched' (Karush 2012: 127), these actresses employed vocal typing and a 'peculiar use of language' as key elements in a performance arsenal used to construct their characters and feminine image (Lowe 2003: 241). In the cases of Holliday and Marshall, speech is also inflected by ethnicity and class. Marshall had created two comic personas for radio that she later transferred to film: the Spanish maid Cándida, a stock character familiar from the *porteño* [from Buenos Aires] stage who was 'ridiculed for her uneducated forms of speech, smelly food and stupidity' (Karush

2012: 123); and the wise-cracking Italian immigrant Catita, who 'steals every scene she is in, deploying all of the comic devices she developed for radio: rapid-fire speech, a squeaky, high-pitched voice, a tendency to run words together, and a grab bag of uncultured catch phrases' (Karush 2012). As for Holliday, as Billie Dawn in *Born Yesterday* (George Cukor, 1950), a role she originated on Broadway and reprised in the 1950 film version, she is said to exaggerate Billie Dawn's unruliness 'through the character's body language, her voice [and working class, Brooklyn accent] and her blond "dumbness"' (Rowe 1995: 175).

Although most highly developed in Allen's dizzying verbal exchanges with her straight man and off-screen husband George Burns, all three performers also engage in the kind of wordplay – including the use of malapropisms, *non sequiturs* and shifts in register – that Susan Douglas has dubbed 'linguistic slapstick' (cited in Lowe 2003: 242).[2] In taking on the most derided qualities of female (and ethnic) speech and behaviour and turning them on their comic heads, these comediennes delivered a blow against cultural hierarchies and social norms. Patricia Mellencamp is speaking of Allen's performance in her 1950s television show when she explains that, '[d]espite being burdened by all the clichés applied to women – illogical, crazy, nonsensical, possessing their own peculiar bio-logic and patronized accordingly – in certain ways she [the TV Gracie] seemed beyond men's control' (1986: 83). In this she might also be describing the topsy-turvy verbal logic wielded in Marshall's and Holliday's on-screen roles.

Gracita Morales and Spanish comic traditions

Similar to her predecessors Allen, Marshall and Holliday, Gracita Morales, born María Gracia Morales Carvahal in Madrid in 1928, honed her performance style and comedic persona in popular theatrical productions, in her case as a member of the repertory companies of well-known figures from the Spanish stage, including Rosita Hernán, Luis Peña, Catalina Bárcena, Ernesto Vilches and Tina Gascó ('Los plazos de la vida' 1995: 104). Following her début in 1949, Morales took on a wide variety of roles, but achieved her greatest impact with comic performances and by the mid-1950s authors were writing parts with her in mind. Over the years she would earn great success in works by well-known playwrights such as Alfonso Paso, Miguel Mihura and José Alonso Millán, and even after she began to make films she continued to perform on stage in a kind of 'double shift'.[3] By the early 1960s she was working regularly in films, initially in supporting roles, joining a group of largely male contemporaries who also came from the comic theatre tradition.

In recent years, historians of Spanish cinema have made much of the autochthonous roots of Franco-era popular film comedy in the theatrical traditions of the *sainete*.[4] In his book *Lo sainetesco en el cine español*, Juan A. Ríos Carratalá offers particular insight into the performance styles derived from the form. A genre built upon the use of recurring character types and a loosely-woven, episodic plot structure in its representation of the quotidian details of (generally) urban life, its appeal rested on the capacity of a group of virtuosic comic actors to convey the material as economically as possible (1997: 20–1). Key to the performer's success was the ability to develop a distinctive voice and vocal type:

> Much has been said about the extraordinary importance of character actors in Spanish cinema, of those who were able to communicate the nature of a role or type on the basis of a brief appearance on screen. To achieve this feat they work with their image but also with a deliberate and intelligent use of their voices. In contrast with the hyper-correct uniformity of dubbed voices that seems to have become generalised among contemporary actors, many of the performers who played important roles in films with roots in the *sainete* came from a theatre tradition in which such uniformity was to be avoided, especially in the case of comic works and those that focused on local customs. Each of those actors created her or his particular and unmistakable voice, capable on its own of delivering an important dose of characterization to the types they played. (Carratalá 1997: 53)[5]

Not surprisingly, the majority of the most distinctive film voices of mid-twentieth-century Spanish cinema – one thinks of José Isbert, Alberto Romea, Rafaela Aparicio, Lola Gaos and, of course Morales – emerged from the ranks of performers who cut their teeth in the *sainete*. But the history of dubbing evoked by Ríos Carratalá had its effects on the kinds of films and roles in which those actors and actresses appeared. Beyond the ideological effects of the obligatory dubbing of all foreign language films, the practice resulted in a demonstrable standardisation and typification of voices in Spanish original productions. Film historian Alejandro Avila's book *El doblaje* provides a perhaps inadvertent illustration of this phenomenon in a table enumerating a series of character types (male lead, male villain, female lead, female villainess, child, etc.) and their vocal equivalents (1997: 67). This prescriptive codification in which the male lead is characterised by a *grave* [deep] voice and the female lead by her *dulce y femenina* [soft and feminine] one alludes to a series of unwritten rules and expectations that continue to shape and restrict the kinds of voices Spanish audiences hear on screen. While non-standard voices were permitted and even cultivated for comic and character actor parts, lead roles would continue to require the 'phonogenic' expression of the unproblematically feminine *dama buena* [virtuous heroine] and appropriately masculine *galán bueno* [virtuous hero].[6]

Articles and interviews in the general press on Morales over the years repeatedly mention her unmistakable voice, employing a catalogue of less than positive terms. Several address its qualities of pitch and tone: 'atiplada' [high-pitched], 'voz de pito' [shrill], 'voz aniñada' [childlike], 'aguda vocecilla' [sharp little voice]; others, its volume and duration: 'peculiarísima y chillona' [highly particular and piercing], 'chirriante' –[screeching], 'el gritito que no cesa' [unceasing little cry].[7] This total identification between performer and voice proved a double-edged sword for Morales' career. Asked in an 1985 interview how much of her success could be attributed to her voice, she answered: 'all of it', or 'al menos un noventa por ciento porque como tengo una voz un poco peculiar, que hace gracia, pues me ha ayudado mucho' [at least 90 per cent, because I have a voice that is a little bit particular and it makes people laugh so it has helped me a lot]. When pushed to consider whether it might have hurt her a little as well, she answers 'no' ('Gracita Morales, gente honrada' 1985, n.p.). There is no question that Morales' voice played a central role in shaping a comic persona that followed her from film to film. Physically unprepossessing, Morales might easily have disappeared into the background of a scene, were it not for the notable mismatch between sound and image, her high-pitched, childlike voice issuing from a grown woman's body. Her most recognisable film performances exploit this dissonance, initially with a series of characters whose innocent demeanour and candid chatter cast them as comic embodiments of the clash between traditional values and urban modernity. Other films would insist further on the incongruity between the stereotypical conventions of feminine glamour on screen and Morales' established comedic image. In what follows we will focus on examples of these two tendencies, looking at the specific details of individual performances, and the broader social context in which they were created and consumed.

'La chacha del cine español'

Reporting on the death of Gracita Morales in April 1995, Spanish newspapers invariably identified the actress with reference to her role as a *chacha* [a maid, in familiar Spanish slang] in several of the most popular comedies of the 1960s, although many of the articles lamented the typecasting that confined her to such parts.[8] There is of course a long history across various performance traditions of servant roles functioning as comic relief, with stories and characters that provide a farcical counterpart and satirical commentary on the primary plot and main leads. Such is the case, as we saw, of Marshall's Cándida. For some, these minor roles offered a way to break into the profession on the way to better things, but there were also many actors of both genders who specialised in such characters. For performers whose faces and bodies placed them on the wrong side of the beauty standards of their era, the role of maid, butler or manservant offered a recurring option in constructing a extended career as a supporting player. Morales was not the only Spanish actress of her generation pigeon-holed as a *cha-cha*; in this she joined performers such as Florinda Chico and Rafaela Aparicio, whose matronly looks (and, in the case of Aparicio, equally distinctive vocal styling) confined them to secondary status. In addition, during a lengthy stretch of Western entertainment history, dark skin and other markers of racial and ethnic otherness posed an insurmountable obstacle to leading roles in mainstream productions, hence the familiar roster of African American female performers in 'mammy' roles, from Hattie McDaniel and Butterfly McQueen in *Gone with the Wind* (Victor Fleming, 1939) to Ethel Waters, McDaniel and Louise Beavers as the maid Beulah on radio and TV.

Like those of her 'sister' performers in other times and places, Morales' maid characters offered an oblique reflection on the conventions and canons of the entertainment industry at the same time as the broader socio-economic context of 'development'-era Spain. In a 1983 interview Morales offers a comment on the former, speaking of her scepticism when film directors who knew her work in theatre began to approach her with offers to perform on screen: 'Recuerdo que les decía: Vosotros sólo escogéis a las guapas' [I remember I used to tell them: You people only choose the pretty ones] (Ordóñez 1983: n.p.). Female performers in particular learned to internalise and abide by the disjunction noted by Tasker between beauty and comic talent. In 1960s Spain, the image of a woman working in the *servicio doméstico* [domestic service] evoked other meanings as well, in a society in which paid work for women was viewed as morally suspect. During the first two decades following the Civil War and under Francoist legislation designed to keep women out of the labour force, female employment stood at low levels, reaching 15 per cent in 1950 and only 28 per cent in 1975, with half of those employed in domestic service (Tusell 2012: 466). Among traditional female occupations, domestic service figured at the bottom of the scale, 'el último peldaño de la marginalidad en términos de cualificaciones, estatus y salario' [the bottom step of marginality in terms of qualifications, status and salary] (Borderías 1991: 107). As such, domestic service 'se convertía en la ocupación principal de muchas mujeres de clase humilde, buena parte

de las cuales procedía del medio rural en la época franquista' [became
the primary occupation for many lower class women, a good number of
whom during the Franco era were migrants from rural areas to the cities]
(Marías Cadenas 2010: 297–8). Then as now, work in the domestic sec-
tor offered one of the few entry points to the labour market for female
immigrants. Far from home and often without the support of family and
friends these women found themselves 'desprotegida[s]' [unprotected] in
terms of labour regulations (Marías Cadenas 2010: 297) but also more
generally. Domestic work, with its 'traditional and family-based character', existed in an in-between space and status, especially in the case of
live-in maids, under regulations and social attitudes that regarded such
employees as 'integral parts of the home' (Marías Cadenas 2010: 299).

Although played for laughs in Morales' maid roles, this socio-
economic referent filters through the broad comedy and outlandish situations of her films. In two of her more representative films, *Chica para
todo/A Girl for Everything* (Mariano Ozores, 1963) and *La ciudad no
es para mí/City Life is Not for Me* (Pedro Lazaga, 1966), Morales plays
a recent immigrant to the Spanish capital depicted in her life as a maid
working in middle- or upper-middle-class households. *La ciudad no es
para mí* is by far the better-known film, as the top grossing Spanish
production of the decade, featuring the quintessential country bumpkin,
the 'hombre de la boina' [man in a beret], actor Paco Martínez Soria
(García de León 1993: 329). Nathan Richardson identifies *La ciudad
no es para mí* as the first and most popular of the *cine de paletos* [the
country bumpkin or hick film] subgenre and as a film that inspired a
host of imitations (2002: 72). Nevertheless, *Chica para todo*, which
appeared three years earlier, presents the same themes and set pieces in
its portrayal of the rural immigrant's disorienting encounter with the
modern city, but from the perspective of its female protagonist, played
by Gracita Morales. Both films feature obligatory scenes showing the
rural immigrants' departure from the *pueblo* [village] and arrival by bus
(*Chica para todo*) or train (*La ciudad no es para mí*) in Madrid. Both
characters' appearance broadcasts their rural origins, most obviously in
the unwieldy collection of luggage they struggle with, in a bit of comic
business: suitcases, boxes and baskets, capped by a live chicken (two in
the case of Martínez Soria's Agustín). However, soon after laying out
their initial gambit, the films part ways. *La ciudad no es para mí*, to
which we will return, moves quickly in the direction of the comic family
melodrama and morality tale. *Chica para todo* proposes instead a kind
of female picaresque, as Morales' character, Petra or Petrita López, pursues her goal of becoming a *señorita* [proper lady], a status seemingly
only attainable in the big city, or so she believes.

The film opens with Petra's departure from the sleepy *pueblo*, as a handful of older women dressed in black bid a tearful farewell and a donkey-drawn cart crosses in the background. Once on the bus she introduces herself, unbidden, to her fellow passengers, 'Me llamo Petra y voy a la capital a servir' [My name is Petra and I'm going to the capital to serve (that is, work as a maid)]. In her distinctive, piping, high-pitched voice she keeps up a running commentary, her monologue a compendium of contradictory statements of popular wisdom and opinions: that staying in the *pueblo*, 'no se puede llegar a nada' [you can't get anywhere], but in the city you have to be careful, you can't trust anyone; that everyone was scandalised and said so when her friend Adela left for the city, but when she came back with 'medias de nilón' [nylon stockings] and a permanent in her hair, their tune changed; and now Adela has got Petra a job in the house where she has been working because she has another one, with some Americans. As the bus rolls on, Petra continues talking, until her seat companion, a young man home from military service (and her eventual love interest), passes her a piece of chewing gum to shut her up. Like the veteran Spanish comedienne she is, Morales uses her voice to convey the recognisable character type of the rural innocent, her optimism, good humour and determined independence but also her vulnerability. And Petra will be taken advantage of, starting after the bus's arrival in the Plaza Mayor with a pair of conmen who connive to sell her an entry ticket to Madrid. Although the plot of the *paleto* film depends on the contrast between city and *campo* [countryside], in contrast to *La ciudad no es para mí*, *Chica para todo* makes short work of the village, which is never seen after the opening sequence. The film is more concerned to follow Petra's dogged if unsuccessful efforts to 'pass' as a modern city dweller and leave behind her identity as a *pueblerina* [yokel] – a term thrown at Petra as an epithet by one of her employers.

Petra's passage through the city will consist of a series of apprenticeships, as she learns (or does not) the skills involved in various types of work available to newly arrived young women, and in the less defined role of *señorita*. The episodic structure of the picaresque plot, with Petrita going from employer to employer and job to job, also gives ample opportunity for Morales to demonstrate her comic gifts in a series of set pieces. In a scene that illustrates the cultural divide between the *pueblerina* Petra and her urban employers in their mid-century modern high rise apartment, the family is gathered at the dining table and the husband rings a bell to signal the new maid to bring out the first course. After various rings, and no sign of Petra, the wife goes to see what has happened, only to find the maid kneeling in the adjacent hall, eyes lowered and a soup tureen in her hands (Figure 7).

Figure 7 Culture clash: the '*chacha*' Petra (Gracita Morales) kneels at the sound of the dinner bell in *Chica para todo* (1963). Mariano Ozores Productores y Distribuidores Asociados S.L.

When asked what she is doing, Petra explains that she is on her knees as one is required to be when the '*santísimo*' [Jesus Christ] is passing by, a reference to the consecrated host raised at the climax of the Catholic Mass and signalled by the ringing of bells. Other scenes deal more directly with the details of domestic labour, as in a sped-up montage of a day in the life of a *chacha* as Petra dusts the furniture and lamps, scrubs the floor, does the laundry and ironing, and washes the dishes, dropping one plate and then another out of pique, only to end up sleeping in the bath. The particular vulnerabilities posed by the domestic servant's in-between position come into view in her dealings with both a randy *abuelo* [grandfather] and the coddled and overly familiar twenty-year-old son of the same well-to-do family, Carlitos, who demands entry to her bedroom at night with the apparent goal of borrowing small amounts of cash.

But Petra's biggest challenges come in her attempts to acquire the traits and behaviours of a *señorita*. Taking the more elegant and worldly Adela (Vicky Lagos) as her model, she paints her toenails and tries to walk in high-heeled shoes. When Adela tells her that if she wishes to move up to a job working in a cafeteria, like her, then she needs to learn a foreign language, Petra is shown listening to English lessons on records. Straining to match the sounds of words and phrases she does not understand, she produces a string of garbled nonsense syllables. Later, while waiting to meet Adela at an outdoor café, Petra studies the other women seated there, imitating their gestures as she stretches out her legs languorously in the sun or pretends that the straw in her *horchata* [almond milk drink] is a cigarette. She even mimes a conversation with an imaginary interlocutor, echoing the intonation and speech patterns of the women she aspires to be.

The film's concluding scenes portray the diverging fates of Petra and Adela. The former takes up job as a bar hostess at the night-club where Adela had been working, as scenes of a heavily made-up Morales in a cocktail dress are cross-cut with Adela's visit to the parents of her reluctant suitor. Following a night of drinking and dancing the cha-cha-cha, twist and conga with a man claiming to be a wealthy owner of coal-mines, Petra ends up at the police station, saved from a morally dubious fate by a veteran bar hostess who defends her as a confused *pueblerina*. Chastened by her failure to find the path to *señorita*-hood, Petra arrives at the Plaza Mayor the next morning to join her male counterpart, his military service concluded, who is returning to the *pueblo* for good. While the protagonist's departure would seem to provide the required reassuring ending to the *paleto* film, with its confirmation of the (moral) superiority of the country over the sinful city, Adela's story offers an ironic twist to both the immigrant's tale and the romance plot, although its socio-economic message is, if anything, more reactionary. Come to inform her fiancé's wealthy parents about their relationship, Adela is taken for an applicant for the domestic position advertised by his mother. Upon hearing the conditions, Adela decides to take the job of *doncella* [maid], with its promise of monthly salary of 3,000 pesetas, new uniforms, two days off a week and a private room, over the much more uncertain prospects of marriage to the woman's cowardly son.

In *La ciudad no es para mí*, Morales once again plays the role of maid, although this case in a secondary role. Her character, Filo, appears throughout dressed in the beribboned uniform and crown-like cap of the *doncella*, an indication of her function as a status symbol for the film's upwardly mobile family, comprised of a doctor, Agustín, his wife, Luchy, and their teenage daughter, Sara, themselves immigrants to Madrid from the *pueblo*. During the first half of the film, Filo is the source of irreverent commentary designed to skewer the social affectations of Luchy, with Morales' singsong delivery serving to accentuate her mocking attitude. Following the inopportune arrival of Agustín Sr (Martínez Soria) from the *pueblo*, he and Filo will make common cause as proponents of the traditional values of the *campo* against the modern behaviours and cultural chaos of the city. In Filo's telling, family unity has become a casualty of their modern lifestyles as the various members go their separate ways, with Agustín Jr at his clinic, Luchy out shopping with friends and daughter Sara left to come and go as she pleases. When the scandalised Agustín Sr inquires about mealtimes, Filo reports that they almost never eat together but subsist on a diet of canned and frozen food. Displaced to the sidelines, Morales' character is reduced from garnering her own laughs to providing an appreciative audience for the folksy observations of Martínez Soria's Agustín. She joins him in expressing nostalgia for the village, her own, where people enjoy simple pleasures singing and wading in the river. Ultimately, the disruptive potential of Filo (and Morales) is channelled into a supporting and supportive role in Agustín's restoration of family hierarchies and gender roles. When a teary Filo confesses she is pregnant, Agustín takes a patriarchal interest, muscling her seducer, an amateur actor who specialises in playing Don Juan Tenorio, the *huevero* [egg seller] Genaro, into marriage, after which she settles happily into the part of a dutiful wife.

Performing femininity

While the formulaic happy ends to the idiosyncratically Spanish genres of *paleto/chacha* films leave Morales' characters safely married off at the picture's conclusion, another series of successful comedies, inspired by the international genre conventions of the heist film and spy thriller, actively exploit the strain involved in emplotting the 'unruly woman' in a traditional narrative (Rowe 1995: 124). Films such as *Atraco a las tres/Robbery at 3 O'Clock* (José María Forqué, 1962), *Operación cabaretera/Operation Cabaret Dancer* (Mariano Ozores, 1967) and *Operación Mata Hari/Operation Mata Hari* (Mariano Ozores, 1968), give full scope to the actress's talent for mimicry and parody of conventional forms of femininity as well as self-mockery.[9]

Atraco a las tres, like its Hollywood antecedent, *Ocean's Eleven* (Lewis Milestone, 1960) (released in Spain as *La cuadrilla de los once* some two years earlier), relies for its effectiveness on the well-choreographed machinery of its 'star' cast of would-be crooks, in this case employed to comic ends. A group of bank employees led by José Luis López Vázquez and including Cassen, Manuel Alexandre, Agustín González and Alfredo Landa in addition to Morales, develop a plan to rob the bank after the dismissal of their longtime boss in favour of his conniving assistant. Morales works as a secretary and participates as one more member of the team (in contrast to the primarily decorative role of Angie Dickinson in *Ocean's Eleven*). As the bumbling group of would-be thieves rehearse their roles in the plan designed by mastermind López Vázquez, the mousy

Morales surprises her colleagues with a glamorous makeover. A muted bluesy trumpet and syncopated piano on the soundtrack accompany her as she languidly descends a long fire escape stairway. Decked out in a fuzzy 'fur' coat and sporting a swinging blonde ponytail and with a cigarette holder hanging from the side of her mouth, she slips the coat from her shoulders to reveal a slinky sheath dress underneath. One of her collaborators enquires about her 'disguise'. Responding as if to a backward child, she states that she's an *'atracadora'* [robber], and that 'clearly they don't get out to the movies much'. Equally immune to her enticements, López Vázquez warns her to cover up or she'll catch cold, whereupon she huffs that a person is not allowed to 'lucir sus encantos' [show off her charms].

This type of parodic performance of hypersexual femininity would become one of Morales' signature acts, carried to comic extremes in the two spy spoofs, *Operación Mata Hari* and *Operación cabaretera*. In *Mata Hari*, set during a farcical, stage set World War I, Morales first appears as Guillermina, the adventure-seeking maid to the real exotic dancer and international spy, Mata Hari. When the latter decides to retire from the spy game for the comforts of marriage to an accountant, Guillermina takes over her identity and her wardrobe. Recruited by the German spy Colonel Von Haber, played by López Vázquez, to help steal the plans for a new and potent Allied weapon, the pair adopts a series of disguises in their attempts to outsmart their equally hapless French and British competitors and the comely double agent, Paula (Pilar Vázquez). In the course of her transformation from the 'servicio doméstico al servico secreto' [domestic service to the secret service], Morales' character has occasion to engage in a series of impromptu comic numbers, each more spectacular than the last: a dance of the seven veils in a Berlin cabaret; a performance of the World War I patriotic French song 'La Madelon', famously revived in a 1939 appearance in Paris by Marlene Dietrich and by Sara Montiel in *El último cuplé/The Last Torch Song* (Juan de Orduña, 1957), in the home of an aristocrat; and an energetic can-can in a French theatre where the pair have taken refuge. In their roles as border-crossing spies, both Morales and López Vázquez also traverse gender boundaries, with Guillermina/Mata Hari dressing as a French soldier while Von Haber dons the costume of a can-can dancer. The joke, endlessly repeated across various films and performances, depends, as we have noted, on the underlying disparity between the sexually alluring roles the character is called on to assume and Morales' anti-glamorous image, a disjunction that goes to the heart of the funny woman paradox. Morales' singing bears this out. Her rendition of the French song lacks the grating shrillness of her speaking voice, but reinforced by broadly comic gestures and exaggerated costumes it marks her attempts at seduction as more clownish than convincing. Sara Montiel wasn't much of a singer either in *El último cuplé*, but her low and husky voice, in contrast to Morales' cartoonish tones, carried the promise (and threat) of a potent female sexuality.

Also featuring Morales and López Vázquez, *Operación cabaretera* takes place in the contemporary setting of the tourist 'paradise' of the Costa del Sol. Morales plays Hipólita, a woman employed in a resort complex as a less than successful bar hostess who is given a chance to perform as a singer (Figure 8). Emerging into the spotlight of a sparsely populated club, wearing a bejewelled headdress and long black dress, Lita swans about the dance floor to a tango rhythm, 'Para llegar a vampiresa' [How to Become a Femme Fatale], a song whose lyrics spell out an aspirational message reminiscent of Morales' character's pursuit of *señorita* status in *Chica para todo*:

> Para llegar a vampiresa
> Es necesario vocación
> Muchas fracasan en la empresa
> Por no tener preparación ...
> Saber fingir y suspirar
> aprender a adorar y sonreír
> Saber mentir y engatusar
> Y, más, a pervertir
> [To become a femme fatale
> One needs a vocation
> Many fail in the intent
> For lack of preparation ...
> Know how to pretend and to sigh
> Learn how to adore and to smile
> Know how to lie and entice
> And what is more, to pervert]

Of course nothing could be less enticing than this demystifying list of instructions for the would-be seductress. Lita would seem to approach the task as a job like any other while Morales' performance highlights the impossible distance between the everywoman Hipólita and the *vampiresa*, between reality and the figure of the femme fatale. As if her unsexy demeanour and marginal singing were not enough, Lita's performance is nearly upended by the antics of a travelling salesman peddling joke items, Daniel Antúnez (López Vázquez), who tries to cut short her number by tossing sneezing powder on the spotlight operator in order to pursue an assignation with an attractive fellow hostess, Angélica (Mara Cruz).

Figure 8 To become a femme fatale: Gracita Morales performs a parody of hypersexual femininity in *Operación cabaretera* (1967). Mariano Ozores Izaro Films, S.A.

Later her co-workers offer half-hearted compliments on her début, but one suggests that neither singing nor hostess work (characterised as a 'profesión perra' [miserable profession]) suits her. Once again, there are obligatory references to Morales' history of maid roles, in another's comment that, since Lita doesn't know how to type, her only option may be the *servicio doméstico*. Another convoluted plot, here involving Chinese spies selling nuclear secrets, ultimately finds Morales, López Vázquez and Angélica caught between two groups of gunmen in pursuit of the microfilm containing the nuclear plans hidden in a tube of toothpaste that ends up in Lita's handbag. With Antúnez obsessed with the pursuit of bikini-clad women on the beach of Marbella, Lita ends up taking charge of the situation. While one set of rivals is busy squeezing out toothpaste from the ninety-two tubes purchased by Lita to disguise the one that holds the microfilm, she presents herself in the guise of an entertainer hired for a fiesta at the oceanfront chalet of the second group where López Vazquez is being held. Taking off her mod-print coat and lampshade hat to reveal a dark suit and tie and slicked-back hair, Lita launches into a impassioned rendition of 'Tu eres aquel' [You are the one], a spot-on pastiche of Spanish singer Raphael's 'signature' ballad 'Yo soy, aquel', and Spain's entry for the 1966 Eurovision Song Contest. Both the words and the singer's emphatic gestures closely mimic the original, but in this case

Lita/Morales offers it as a declaration of love to her former nemesis, López Vázquez, who accompanies her on guitar.

In addition to their obvious comic effects, Morales' exercises in gender/genre-bending and -breaking serve to highlight the instability of the concept and category of the feminine. Rowe signals this dimension when she identifies the role played by the 'parodic excesses of the unruly woman and the comedy conventions surrounding her [to] provide a space to "act out" the "dilemmas of femininity" [and] to make not only "fantastic" and "incredible" but also laughable those tropes of femininity valorised by melodrama' (1995: 11). However, in Spanish comedies of the period such questioning and mockery was not limited to the dilemmas of femininity. Both López Vázquez and Antonio Ozores, playing a hotel employee and former boyfriend of Angélica, are portrayed as embodiments of the stereotypical *macho ibérico* [Iberian male], the sexually repressed male whose compulsive pursuit of scantily dressed, preferably blonde and foreign, women gave the name *landismo* to a host of similar films, many of which actually starred Alfredo Landa. The focus on the physical imperfections and social inadequacy of short Spanish males (see also Whittaker and Epps, chapters 5 and 7 this volume) finds a close parallel in the roles and 'look' assigned to Morales, who was also short and somewhat lumpy around the middle, even, or especially, when wearing a mini-skirt, as in much of *Operación cabaretera*. But, in contrast to her male co-stars, Morales' lack of sex appeal – in one conversation in the latter film she confuses the English phrase with '*pil-pil*' [garlic and pepper sauce], as in the dish *bacalao al pil-pil* [cod in pil-pil sauce] – is not presented as national trait or defect. In her films, as we have seen, she nearly always shares the screen with a conventionally attractive female companion or rival. The spotlight is always on Morales, although she may struggle to keep it there, and she gets the laughs, but there is also a sense that spectators were required to be reminded what 'real' femininity and female beauty should look, and sound, like.

Gracita Morales garnered enormous popularity as a film performer, appearing in a hundred or so features, with a salary, according to a 1980 article in the magazine *Interviú*, that topped a million pesetas per film – 'lo que nadie cobraba entonces' [what no one else was earning at that time] (Calabuig 1980: 91). Certainly no Spanish comedienne came even close. But by the early 1970s her career was in steep decline. Spanish audiences' tastes were changing and no Carlos Saura or Mario Camus would come calling, as they did in the cases of López Vázquez and Landa, to recast her image in the service of a new auteurist paradigm.[10] Morales' eclipse had many causes. Press reports mention bouts of depression and the actress herself speaks of her unsuitability for the *destape* [nudity] films that became prevalent at the time (Carvajal 1982; Ordóñez 1983). Unlike her fellow *chachas* Chico and Aparicio, who made appearances in films by Saura and other art cinema directors, Morales proved resistant to reappropriation, her career and roles too closely aligned with the embarrassing excesses and limitations of a not-yet-modern nation. Beneath the ridicule and laughter they generated, the maids and unsexy bar hostesses she gave voice to, far from vehicles of feminine conformity, emphasised the limited economic and social options available for women and members of the less-than-privileged classes. Although the films she starred in might seem to glory in a comic complacency that left the old hierarchies intact, Morales' performances revealed the precariousness and unsustainability of an economic, social and gender order already under siege.

Notes

1 See, for example, Marsh (2005) on popular film from the Franco era, as well as monographs on Isbert (Pérez Perucha 1984), Landa (Delgado 1991), Leblanc (Ordoñez 1999) and López Vázquez (Rodríguez 1989). See also Whittaker's analysis of López Vázquez's career in chapter 5 of this volume.
2 For more on the function of Allen and Burns' comic 'cross-talk,' see Wolfe (2011). For a sociolinguistic analysis of the comedic effects of 'funny voices,' see Georgakopoulou (2000).
3 A 1982 interview offers detailed insight into the overlap between film and theatre work and the 'double shift' many actors and actresses endured. Morales reports that, while she was making *Atraco a las tres*, 'trabajaba en *Las que tienen que servir* de Alfonso Paso, y no dormíamos nada, ni Agustín González, ni López Vázquez ni yo. Porque ¡hay que ver!: dos funciones al día y luego irte a rodar, Es muy difícil, estar cansada por el trabajo teatral y tener encima que hacer gracia. Hacía falta tener, y nosotros la teníamos, fuerza de voluntad y mucha ilusión' (Ortiz 1982).
4 See the studies by Zunzunegui (1999), Castro de Paz (2002) and Marsh (2005).
5 'Mucho se ha hablado de la extraordinaria importancia de los secundarios del cine español, de aquellos que deben dar cuenta de un tipo con tan sólo una breve aparición. Juegan para ello con su imagen pero también con … una deliberada e inteligente utilización de su voz. Frente a la correcta uniformidad del doblaje que parecer haberse extendido a bastantes de los actores actuales, muchos de los cómicos que protagonizaron las películas con presencia de lo sainetesco procedían de un teatro donde se evitaba dicha uniformidad, sobre todo cuando se trataba de obras cómicas y costumbristas. Cada uno de ellos creaba así su peculiar e inconfundible voz, capaz por si sola de

    aportar una importante dosis de caracterización a los tipos' (Ríos Carratalá, 1997: 53).

 6 Especially striking is the case of the actress Emma Penella. As Nancy Berthier notes in a study of Luis García Berlanga's *El verdugo*, Penella's voice was considered 'unusual' and her performances were frequently dubbed until Juan Antonio Bardem insisted on using her original voice in his 1953 film *Cómicos* (1998: 86). Unlike the character voices of Morales or Gaos, Penella's was deemed excessively sensual (de la Serna 1958). For a more detailed discussion of the history and consequences of dubbing on the vocal conventions and practices of the Spanish film industry, see Gubern and Vernon (2013: 376–82).

 7 These descriptions are drawn from the following: Otero (1992); Ordoñez (1983); Díez (1974); Villán (1995); 'La sinceridad de una actriz olvidada' (1977).

 8 See, for example, 'Muere Gracita Morales, "chacha" del cine' (1995); Ruíz de Villalobos (1995); Villán (1995).

 9 Whittaker offers a discussion of López Vázquez's performance style in the films of Ozores in chapter 5 of this volume.

10 López Vázquez would appear in three Saura films: *Peppermint frappe* (1967), *El jardín de las delicias* (1970) and *La prima Angélica* (1974) (See also Whittaker, chapter 5 this volume) Landa would share the best actor award at the Cannes Film Festival with Francisco Rabal for their performances in Camus' *Los santos inocentes* (1984).

References

Ávila, A. (1997) *El doblaje*. Madrid: Cátedra.

Berthier, N. (1998) 'Prénom Carmen (Images de la femme dans *El verdugo*)', in E. Larraz (ed.), *El verdugo*, Dijon: Hispanística 20, 83–105.

Borderías, C. (1991) 'Las mujeres, autoras de sus trayectoria personales y familiares: A través del servicio doméstico', *Historia y Fuente Oral*, 6, Otras Miradas, 105–21.

Calabuig, J. (1980) 'Gracita Morales, una chacha en paro' *Interviú* (20–6 March), 91–2.

Carvajal, M. (1982) 'Gracita Morales. La traición del olvido' *Pueblo* (28 December), n.p.

Castro de Paz, J. L. (2002) *El cine herido*, Barcelona: Paidós.

Delgado, J. F. (1991) *Alfredo Landa, el artista cotidiano*, Huelva: Festival de cine iberoamericano.

Díez, A. (1974) 'Gracita Morales rueda con Landa', *ABC*, 96 (April), n.p.

García de León. M. A. (1993) 'Los personajes rurales en el cine español; historia y sociología de un arquetipo rural: la figure del paleto', *Actas del IV Congreso de la A.E.H.C.*, Madrid: Editorial Complutense, pp. 321–32.

Georgakopoulou, A. (2000) 'On the Sociolinguistics of Popular Films: Funny Characers, Funny Voices', *Journal of Modern Greek Studies*, 18, 119–33.

'Gracita Morales, gente honrada' (1985) *Ya*, 6 December, n.p.

Gubern, R. and K. M. Vernon (2013) 'Soundtrack', in J. Labanyi and T. Pavlovic (eds), *A Companion to Spanish Cinema*, Malden, MA: Wiley-Blackwell, pp. 370–88.

Jenkins, H. (1992) *What Made Pistachio Nuts?* New York: Columbia University Press.

Karush, M. B. (2012) *Culture of Clash. Radio and Cinema in the Making of a Divided Argentina, 1920–1946*, Durham: Duke University Press.

Lowe, L. (2003) '"If the Country's Going Gracie, So Can You": Gender Representation in Gracie Allen's Comedy', in S. M Squire (ed.), *Communities of the Air. Radio Century, Radio Culture*. Durham: Duke University Press, pp. 237–50.

Marías Cadenas, S. (2010) 'Las empleadas de hogar durante el franquismo y la transición democrática: entre el paternalismo y la marginación', in A. Antón-Pacheco Bravo *et al.* (eds), *Estudios de mujeres, Vol. 7, Diferencia, (des)igualdad y justicia*, Madrid: Editorial Fundamentos, pp. 297–307.

Marsh, S. (2005) *Popular Spanish Film Under Franco: Comedy and the Weakening of the State*, New York: Palgrave Macmillan.

Mellencamp, P. (1986) 'Situation Comedy, Feminism and Freud: Discourses of Gracie and Lucy, in T. Modleski (ed.), *Studies in Entertainment*. Bloomington: Indiana University Press, pp. 81–95.

'Muere Gracita Morales, "chacha" del cine' (1995) *El Periódico*, 4 April, 119.

Mulvey, L. (2000) 'Visual Pleasure and Narrative Cinema', in E.A. Kaplan (ed.), *Feminism and Film*, Oxford: Oxford University Press, pp. 34–47.

Ordoñez, M. (1999) *Tony Leblanc, genio y figura*, Malaga: Festival de cine español de Malaga.

Ordoñez, P. (1983) 'La tenura de una "anti-diva"', *Garbo*, 13 June, n.p.

Ortiz, R. (1982) 'Gracita Morales en "Atraco a las tres"', *Tele-Radio*, 21–7 June, n.p.

Otero, N. (1992) 'Gracita Morales', *Mía*, 5–11 October, n.p.

Pérez Perucha, J. (ed.) (1984) *El cine de José Isbert*, Valencia: Ayuntamiento de Valencia.

Perriam, C. and N. Triana-Toribio (2013) 'The Politics of Stardom and Celebrity', in J. Labanyi and T. Pavlovic (eds), *A Companion to Spanish Cinema*, Malden, MA: Wiley-Blackwell, pp. 326–42.

'Los plazos de la vida' (1995) *ABC*, 4 April, 104–6.

Richardson, N. (2002) *Postmodern Paletos. Immigration, Democracy and Globalization in Spanish Narrative and Film*. Lewisburg, PA: Bucknell University Press.

Ríos Carratala, J. A. (1997) *Lo sainetesco en el cine español*. Alicante: Universidad de Alicante.

Rodriguez, E. (1989) *José Luis López Vázquez: Los disfraces de la melancolía*, Valladolid: 34 Semana de cine.

Rowe, K. (1995) *The Unruly Woman: Gender and the Genres of Laughter*, Austin: University of Texas Press.

Ruíz de Villalobos (1995) 'Muere la "chacha" más entrañable del cine español', *El Mundo*, 123.

Serna, G. de la (1958) 'La voz de Emma Penella', *Radiocinema* 407, 10 May, n.p.

'La sinceridad de una actriz olvidada' (1977) *Garbo*, 12 October, n.p.

Tasker, Y. (1998) *Working Girls. Gender and Sexuality in Popular Cinema*, London: Routledge.

Tusell, J. (2012) *Historia de España en el siglo XX*, Vol. 3 *La dictadura de Franco*. Madrid: Taurus.

Villán, J. (1995) 'La chaca respondona', *El Mundo*, 4 April, 127.

Wagner, K. A. (2011) '"Have Women a Sense of Humor?" Comedy and Femininity in Early Twentieth Century Film', *Velvet Light Trap*, 68 (Fall), 35–46.

Wojcik, P. R. (2010) 'Judy Holliday: The Hungry Star', in R. B. Palmer (ed.), *Larger than Life. Movie Stars of the 1950s*, New Brunswick: Rutgers University Press, 205–19.

Wolfe, C. (2011) '"Cross-Talk": Language, Space and the Burns and Allen Comedy Film Short', *Film History*, 23, 300–12.

Zunzunegui, S. (1999) *El extraño viaje. El celuloide atrapado por la cola o la crítca norteamericana ante el cine español*, Valencia: Episteme.

5

The sounds of José Luis López Vázquez: vocal performance, gesture and technology in Spanish film

Tom Whittaker

To speak of the late actor José Luis López Vázquez is to speak of the history of Spanish sound acting. Alongside his characteristically manic gestures, López Vázquez' was widely known for his distinctive style of vocal performance. Indeed, his last dramatic role in 2009 was that of a disembodied voice. López Vázquez was originally commissioned to provide the voice-over for Pedro Olea's theatrical adaptation of the film *El pisito/The Little Apartment* (Marco Ferreri, 1959), a celebrated black comedy in which the actor had famously appeared fifty years before, but sadly died before his voice was recorded. It was a fitting sonic homage. As with the vast majority of comedies in which López Vázquez starred until the 1970s, the film *El pisito* was recorded entirely in post-synch sound, a practice which required actors to dub their own voices (as well as occasionally be dubbed by others) in post-production. Yet, as this chapter explores, López Vázquez's vocal delivery would dramatically begin to change in the 1970s, when he was famously cast 'against type' in more challenging and artistically ambitious dramatic films, namely those of Carlos Saura, Antonio Mercero, Manuel Gutiérrez Aragón, Jaime de Armiñán and Pedro Olea. His performances in Saura's films were the very first in Spain to use direct sound recording, a crucial technological change which, as I will show, contributed towards an evolution of a different style of screen performance in Spanish cinema.

While long neglected within studies of Spanish film, the voice has in more recent years begun to receive the critical attention it deserves. Hart (2007), Gubern and Vernon (2013), Wright (2013), as well as myself (Whittaker 2012), have each addressed the importance of the voice in Spanish cinema, thereby providing a reassessment of the commonly held relationship between sound and image in film. This chapter contributes to this growing field of scholarship by specifically exploring the relationship between various stages of sound technology in Spanish film, and their subsequent impact in the development of screen acting, a crucial relationship which is vividly illuminated through the career of López Vázquez. Taking as its premise Pamela Robertson Wojcik's assertion that 'screen acting is constructed as much by sound design as by labour' (2006: 73), the chapter aims to show how López Vázquez's varied vocal performances illuminated the shifting location of the voice in Spanish film between these periods. In particular, it aims to show how sound design – namely the use of the microphone, whether within the dubbing studio or on location – not only influenced his various idioms and idiolects of vocal performance, but also crucially shaped the actor's mastery of bodily movement and gesture.

José Luis López Vázquez requires little by way of introduction to Spanish audiences. He was a staggeringly prolific actor, who over a period of 60 years appeared in 240 films. A self-confessed workaholic, López Vázquez lived in perpetual fear of returning to the poverty of his childhood, and in the 1960s and 1970s could be found working on two or three films at any given time. Although his output spanned a period of some sixty years, his body forever appeared to be locked in a timeless middle age: balding, moustachioed and unflatteringly short, he embodied the Spanish everyman oppressed by surroundings that were not of his making. Amongst some of his most popular comedic performances were as Gabino Quintanilla in *Plácido* (Luis García Berlanga, 1961), Fernando Galindo in *Atraco a las tres/Robbery at 3 O'Clock* (José María Forqué, 1962) and Padrino Búfalo in the films of the *La gran familia/The Great Family* (Fernando Palacios), as well as countless others with Pedro Lazaga and Mariano Ozores (also see Vernon, chapter 4 this volume). While he was largely unknown outside of Spain, the distinctiveness of his performances was nevertheless admired by the likes of Charlie Chaplin and George Cukor, to the extent that the latter cast the actor in a minor role in the 1972 MGM film *Travels with My Aunt*. His trademark comic style combined hysterical excess with a measured control, an anarchic disorder played out with fastidious precision. Correspondingly, López Vázquez has referred to his approach towards acting as 'correcta, meticulosa, perfeccionista' [correct, meticulous, perfectionist] (Cruz 2005). His characteristic fastidiousness would often carry over into the performance of his characters, like that of Gabino in *Plácido*, for instance, who repeatedly dons and doffs his hat and with the most delicate of hand gestures. Expansive and exaggerated, his body movements would often turn and twist, threatening to explode into fits of fury and rage, a characteristic of his performance that Berlanga would refer to as 'la revolera' [the whirlwind] (Galán 20). His vocal performances were equally distinctive. Most often crisp and clipped, his delivery frequently enunciated each consonant with staccato-like precision. In emphasising the nuance and texture of each and every syllable, his sentences acquired a both a distinctive rhythm and syntax – a delivery that was not only unique, but would also crucially point to the sonic materiality of vocal performance.

Polyphony and populism: vocal performance and post-synch sound

A significant number of comedies in which López Vázquez appeared in the 1950s and 1960s, namely those directed by Luis García Berlanga, Marco Ferreri and José María Forqué, bore the influence of the *sainete*. A Spanish theatrical form that first emerged at the end of the eighteenth century, the *sainete* was later more famously popularised by the Madrid-based comedies of Carlos Arniches in the early decades of the twentieth century.[1] Much like their theatrical counterparts, the films centred on everyday lives and locations, whereby characterisation was primarily articulated through external means – accentuated gesturality, iconographic costumes and settings, recognisable or stereotypical 'types' of characters – rather than by means of inner psychology. Of all their formal characteristics, however, their use of sound was arguably amongst the most striking. Vernon (chapter 4 of this volume), for instance, shows how comic actors such as José Isbert, Rafaela Aparicio and Gracita Morales, who like López Vázquez began their careers in the stage, each developed their own unique modes of speaking. Dialogue subsequently featured heavily in the films, to the extent that it most often raucously drowned out other ambient and sound effects. The *sainete* is thus an exaggerated expression of what Michel Chion terms 'vococentric' or 'verbocentric' cinema, in which the voice – or rather, in this case, *voices* – are privileged and foregrounded in the final sound mix (1999). Gubern and Vernon have shown how, in Berlanga's and Bardem's directorial début *Esa pareja feliz/That Happy Couple*, voices were most often presented in scenes of overlapping dialogue (2013: 383). Indeed, the *sainete* features fast-paced dialogues that constantly interject and interrupt one other, weaving together a rich cacophony of voices and words that is often disorientating to the listener. Spatial cues of closeness and farness, moreover, are often conveyed in the same volume, thereby adding to the general confusion and aural disarray. In the cinema of Ferreri and Berlanga, in particular, the sobbing of children and the guttural gasps and grunts of the ageing actor José Isbert added to the mix. As a strident cinema of voices and interruptions, the *sainete* throws into relief the musical origin of the term '*cine coral*'. The polyphonic soundtrack of these films therefore conveyed the importance of the popular, where the crowd is privileged over the individual, and the external over the internal.[2]

In his comedy roles, López Vázquez was known for delivering his lines at an urgent pace and thunderous volume. Yet, as we have seen, at the same time, his vocal performances were always strikingly intelligible and crisp – polished even. When asked in an interview how he managed to retain such clarity during his energetic performances, López Vázquez attributed it to the practice of dubbing, further adding – if a little nostalgically – that the practice of dubbing was far better during the early years of his career (Valencia 2002: 13). Berlanga has similarly lamented what he perceives as a decline in standards of Spanish film performance, praising the 1950s as the decade when actors vocalised the most clearly and sound quality was at its best (cited in García Berlanga 1998: 56). Moreover, Antonio Ozores (brother of the director Mariano Ozores), too, has more recently spoken of how the rhythm and intelligibility of dialogue in Spanish film were sacrificed for naturalism when direct sound would later become industry practice (Ozores 2004: 57). The clipped legibility of López Vázquez's performance was thus in part made possible by the use of post-synchronised dubbing, thereby illustrating Gianluca Sergi's argument that 'in movies actors do not just speak, they are recorded', and who further suggests that we should devote our attention to two of its consequences: 'there are people who record them and there is the technology to do so' (1999: 126). If the dubbing studio afforded actors such as López Vázquez far greater elocutionary control, it also allowed them to move their bodies and gesticulate with heightened spontaneity and physicality during production – an effect that, in the many of these comedies, was further facilitated through the persistent use of long-distance framing and extended takes. Unencumbered by the constricting presence of sound recordists, directional microphones and boom operators, much of the free-flowing fluidity and energy of the *sainete* comedy was thus arguably made possible through the technique of post-synch sound.

In spite of their intelligibility, many of these films were nevertheless poorly synched and, despite the efforts of the most significant dubbing studios of the time – Exa, Fono España and Sevilla Films, for instance – they rarely managed to conceal the split between voice and body. The synching often presented the films with an awkward fit between sound and image, creating a clumsiness wherein the body appears to be continually in search of a voice, and the voice is lacking a body. This mismatching recalls Henri Bergson's writing on comedy, which famously points to the incongruity of the body and soul as one of the causes of laughter (1980: 64). While Bergson does not specifically mention the importance of vocal performance, the human voice has long been associated with the soul. Jonathan Rée, for instance, has shown in the philosophy of Hegel that the voice 'was the most perfect instrument for giving expression to the inwardness of the soul' (1999: 61). For Bergson, moreover, the human subject is fundamentally split, and the comic moment can often derive from the 'body taking precedence of the soul' (1980: 64). Unmoored from the voice, the body in the *sainete* similarly appears to possess its own autonomy. The lack of synch often served to accentuate the corporeality of the body in all its unruly awkwardness, its manic movement and gestures driven by inner compulsion rather than by rational design. This division also arguably illuminates a series of tensions which are culturally specific to the *sainete*, and which, according to Ruis Román, can be clearly pinpointed in the theatre of Carlos Arniches. For Román, its humour derives from following: 'la simultaneidad de lo cómico y lo trágico ... el juego de comicidad externa y gravedad profunda, *el contraste entre la apariencia social y física y el ser íntimo y profundo*, es decir entre la máscara y el rostro' [the simultaneity of the comic and the tragic ... the play of external comedy and profound gravity, *the contrast between social and physical appearance and one's very intimate being*, that is to say between the mask and the face] (cited in Heredero 1993: 235, my emphasis).

Not only does López Vázquez embody this contrast between the comic and the tragic – a tension duly noted by Eduardo Rodríguez, whose book-length interview with the actor is pertinently subtitled *Los disfraces de la melancolía/The Disguises of Melancholy* (1989) – but the post-synch sound in these films throws into critical relief the anomalous relationship between social self and inner world, body and soul. For if, in the words of Mladen Dolar, the voice is the 'intimate kernel of subjectivity' (2006: 14), the sound design of the films reveals a selfhood that is continually displaced and deferred, one that is strikingly out of synch with both the body and its broader social milieu.

As Michel Chion has observed, synchronisation alerts us to the temporal dimension of film; the etymology of the word 'synchronisation', he shows, consists of the Greek for 'together' and 'time' (1999: 128–9). Intriguingly, the humour in several of López Vázquez's later comedies in the late 1960s and 1970s would hinge on the collision of tradition and modernity, thereby presenting a collision of rhythms and temporalities that were strikingly out of synch with one other. In several films directed by Pedro Lazaga, Mariano Ozores and Vicente Escrivá, his ageing body is set against the backdrop of a nation caught in the grip of accelerated modernisation. Otherwise known as the 'miracle years' or *desarrollismo*, Spain witnessed unparalleled economic growth during this period, in which its population would attempt to adapt to the temporality of rapidly urbanising, consumerist and increasingly mobile society. López Vázquez's performance in *Operación Secretaria/Operation Secretary* (Mariano Ozores, 1966) as Adolfo, a libidinous, skirt-chasing businessman, is typical of the period: clad in a snugly-fitting collar and tie, and wearing thick-bottled prescription glasses, his initial appearance at a youthful *ye-ye* party is strikingly incongruous. As he hopelessly pursues his younger secretary during the film, his histrionic register of acting becomes increasingly emphatic. Punctuated by jittery gestures and jolting body movement, clenched fists and lascivious curls of the lip, his performance points to a sexual repression continually bubbling to the surface. A recurring *mise-en-scène* in these films – especially in Mariano Ozores' *Operación Mata Hari/Operation Mata Hari* (1968), *Objetivo Bi-ki-ni/Objective Bi-ki-ni* (1968), *En un lugar de La Manga/In Some Place in the Manga* (1970) and Lazaga's *El turismo es un gran invento/ Tourism is a Great Invention* (1968) – was the rapidly transforming Mediterranean coastline, a site which was opening up to post-*apertura* investment and global tourism. Frequently held in long shots, López Vázquez's stunted, middle-aged physique appears ironically out of place within this landscape, as he unsuccessfully lusts after bikini-clad tourists. His performance in these films was a grotesque reminder of the superficiality of Spain's *desarrollismo*, in which the social and sexual mores of everyday Spain were dramatically out of synch with the modern narrative of the nation that Franco's technocrats endeavoured to project.

To this effect, López Vázquez's star persona has frequently come to embody a Spanishness that is insular and unenlightened, a *casticismo* which, like most of the comedies in which he appeared, cannot be easily translated or transplanted into other languages and cultures. In a recent homage to López Vázquez, the director Santiago Segura wrote that 'él y nadie como él ha representado el español medio, ese español tipo, típico y atípico, bajito y con bigote, miserable y entrañable, soñador y conformista, apocado y *echao palante*' [He and no one else like him has represented the average Spaniard, the Spanish type that is both typical and atypical, short with a moustache, wretched yet cheerful, idealistic yet conformist, meek yet determined to get ahead] (2007: 47). Like his counterpart Alfredo Landa, it is his performance as an unattractive Spanish everyman which provided the humour for many of these comedies. His physical indices of 'ordinary' Spanishness – the moustache, short stature, ever-expanding waistline – were often heightened to grotesque effect in these comedies, particularly by means of costume and the illustrations featured on their promotional material. In *Objetivo Bi-ki-ni*, for instance, his white skimpy shorts and tight red top comically accentuate his ageing physicality, as he tries and fails to win the affection of bikini-clad tourists on the beach. The disjuncture between sound and image only serves to emphasise the broad corporeality of his performances in these films, an unruly excess which appears to run away from his voice. Many years later, López Vázquez would appear in a self-conscious parody of these earlier roles in El oro de Moscú/The Moscow Gold (Jesús Bonilla, 2003) and Torrente 2: Misión en Marbella/Torrente 2: Mission en Marbella (Santiago Segura, 2001). If Segura's comedies, as Triana Toribio and others have observed, signalled a postmodern return to the sleazy *subproductos* [subproducts] of Lazaga and Ozores (2004: 151–2), they also often playfully embraced the post-synch sound design with which these films were associated. Indeed, Santiago Segura famously worked as a dubbing artist before becoming a film director, performing the soundtrack of porn films.

Disciplining the voice: vocalising 'against type'

While in the early 1970s López Vázquez continued to perform in similar comedies, he also began to feature in several artistically ambitious, *auteur*-led films, in which he was cast against type. During this period, his performances in films directed by Carlos Saura, Pedro Olea, Manuel Gutiérrez Aragon and Jaime de Armiñán signalled a dramatic shift in direction for the actor. As well as often demanding a radical transformation in the actor's physical appearance, these roles also required a very different approach to vocal performance, one that would appear to place his characteristically masterful possession of the voice in question. In the horror film *El bosque del lobo/The Ancines Woods* (Pedro Olea, 1971), he plays Benito Freire, a travelling salesman in the nineteenth century whom villagers believe to be a werewolf. In dramatically reshaping his usual intonation and diction for the role, López Vázquez's voice becomes snarling and inarticulate. His ramshackle appearance was as much of a radical departure as his vocal performance, where he wore ill-fitting false teeth and nails caked with dirt for the role. Even more dramatic was his transformation into a forty-three-year-old Galician spinster in *Mi querida Señorita/My Dearest Señorita* (Jaime de Armiñan, 1971), in which López Vázquez wears a full dress, wig and make-up. During the first half of the film, his 'female' voice was dubbed by Irene Guerrero de Luna (an actress who incidentally also dubbed the role of Sophia in the American comedy series *The Golden Girls*). In centring on narratives of bodily transformation – lycanthropy and gender change, respectively – the films also served to showcase the process of actorly transformation, thereby allowing López Vázquez to exhibit the craftsmanship and dedication required for these kinds of 'serious' roles. The dispossession of his voice in these roles, which in turn helped him to forge characters whose identities were incomplete and decentred, was similarly crucial to this transformation.

The dispossession of López Vázquez's voice was used to terrifying effect in *La cabina/The Telephone Box* (Antonio Mercero, 1973), a surreal horror film made for television in which the actor becomes inexplicably trapped in a red telephone box. Set for the most part on location in a square in an outer suburb of Madrid, the film captures the city in rapid flux and expansion, with its endless rows of new identikit apartments shielding the sky.[3] Unable to open the telephone door, López Vázquez enlists the help of passers-by and policemen; crowds slowly begin to gather, looking on in bemusement at their failed attempts. The film's opening location of the square – a site which, as Steven Marsh has observed, is a recurrent scenario of the *sainete* (2006: 25) – is not without irony, especially given López Vázquez's status as a comic actor at the time. But if, as we have seen, the sound design of the *sainete* evoked community and conviviality, here it establishes an alienating contrast between outside and inside: we can clearly hear the noisy chatter and laughter of the crowd, yet the actor's terrified gestures are nevertheless registered in silence. Trapped behind glass, the audience sees his screams for help but cannot hear them. In a recent interview, the director Mercero has commented that he cast López Vázquez in the role because wanted an actor whose performance style approximated mime (cited in Anon. 2011). As an acting style communicated through body movement rather than words, mime is composed of broad stage gestures that can be recognised instantly by audiences. Indeed, within the phone booth, López Vázquez's performance in the film emulates one of its most famous moves: that of pretending to be trapped within an invisible box. Yet here the gestural register of acting with which he was usually associated in earlier roles appears both heightened and defamiliarised, a dynamic which is compounded by the strategic use of silence in the film, and his spatial confinement to a claustrophobic telephone box (and which, according to the actor, was a source of fear during the shoot) (cited in Lloret 2010: 172–4). Most striking, though, is the film's horrific final sequence, in which, in a possible nod to the shower scene in *Psycho* (Alfred Hitchcock, 1960), a close-up shot condenses and fragments his performance into one single, terrifying gesture: an exhausted, trembling hand pressed against glass.

Vocal performance and possession – or, rather, the problem thereof – explicitly emerges as a theme in other films of this period, alerting us both to the materiality of López Vázquez's voice while also drawing thematically on its absence. In the rural drama *Habla, mudita/Speak, Little Mute* (Manuel Gutiérrez Aragón, 1973), he plays a professor of linguistics who becomes ensnared in an *amour fou* with an unobtainable mute girl. In attempting to teach her how to speak, he gradually loses his own mental and verbal faculties, and is driven out of the village by its protective inhabitants. In *Zorrita Martínez* (Vicente Escrivá, 1975), he plays 'Finito', a ventriloquist whose unruly puppets – dubbed by the actor José Martínez Blanco – would quite literally appear to have a life of their own. One of the puppets persistently makes lecherous remarks about women, thereby serving as a conduit for articulating what 'Finito', as a professional entertainer, is not permitted to say. The film brings to mind Rick Altman's writing on sound cinema, who famously draws on the analogy of ventriloquism to explain the illusory nature of sound in film. For Altman, the image serves as a 'ventriloquist dummy' whose 'voice' conceals the illusion of the real source of the sound, which emanates from the speakers from behind the screen (1980: 67). Yet the history of post-synch sound in Spain would appear to bear out Altman's analogy in a rather more literal expression: the Spanish actors *themselves* served as ventriloquist dummies, actors whose uncanny voices severed the supposedly organic link between body and voice. Ironically, the case of *Zorrita Martínez*, which in some sequences is markedly out of synch, constituted a particularly poor act of ventriloquism in more ways than one.

In synch: direct sound and vocal performance

Most critically acclaimed were López Vázquez's performances in Carlos Saura's films, which were produced by Elías Querejeta, in particular *El jardín de las delicias/The Garden of Delights* (1970) and *La prima Angélica/Cousin Angélica* (1974). Instead of his trademark expansiveness, López Vázquez here delivers performances which are far more minimalist in register – a style of acting with a far lesser degree of 'ostensiveness', to use James Naremore's term, in which gesture is contained rather than exhibited.[4] In the former, *El jardín de las delicias*, López Vázquez plays Antonio Cano, a wealthy industrialist, who has lost both his memory and his ability to speak properly. Bound to a wheelchair, López Vázquez's performance is one in which movement is heavily constricted, communicated mainly through facial expression rather than bodily gesture. His style of acting is thus more nuanced and finely modulated, shaped as much by the construction of his character as by the formal apparatus of the film. By means of static close-up shots, zooms and eyeline matches, the film lays a great degree of formal emphasis on López Vázquez's eyes – and, by extension, the broader thematic of seeing or watching. The actor repeatedly casts his large, childlike eyes slowly downwards, lost in a melancholy haze of half-forgotten memories. He watches impassively as his character's family re-enact key events of his life, in the desperate hope that he regains his memory and discloses the hidden whereabouts of the family's fortune. Yet it is only towards the end of the film, when listening to his *own* voice, that his memory begins to come into focus. As he is played an audio recording of a speech he gave before his accident, Antonio suddenly jolts upright and becomes animated, slowly and deliberately repeating the each word of the speech after he hears it. Here, the superimposition of two vocal performances – one pre-recorded and invisible, the other synchronised and visualised – creates a complex and uncanny soundscape. Michel Chion has referred to a voice whose source is unseen as 'acousmatic', writing that its presence in film brings disequilibrium and tension (1999: 24). For Chion, the location of the acousmatic voice is highly ambiguous: 'wandering the surface of the screen without entering it', he writes, it is both nowhere yet everywhere, often suggesting an all-seeing and all-knowing power in film (1999: 24). The acousmatic voice of Antonio's rousing and eloquent speech, whose ghostly echoes can be heard to reverberate throughout the room, provides a compelling contrast to his present-day voice. López Vázquez's characteristically crisp and staccato diction is used to brilliant effect in this sequence, painstakingly slowing down and stretching out each and every syllable, as if he were learning to vocalise the words for the very first time. The weaknesses of his body and vocal delivery in the present are eclipsed by the disembodied voice of his powerful past, providing a glimpse into the omnipotent figure he once was: an 'all-seeing' man whose unparalleled knowledge into the affairs of the family business has, until this moment, all but been erased.

As well as illuminating the crucial relationship between performance and sound, this scene also serves to showcase the expressive potential of synchronised sound. As Marvin D'Lugo, Kathleen Vernon and Roman Gubern have pointed out, *El jardín de las delicias* was the very first film to use direct sound in Spain (D'Lugo 1991: 104; Gubern and Vernon 2013: 382), and subsequently provided a radical departure in sound design in Spanish film. Elías Querejeta's sound technicians in the 1970s, Luis Rodriguez (1970–5) and Bernardo Menz (1975–82), would also go on to record the sound for Saura's other films, as well as other oppositional films of the period such as *El espíritu de la colmena/The Spirit of the Beehive* (Víctor Erice, 1973), *Pascual Duarte* (Ricardo Franco, 1976) and *Las palabras de Max/ Max's Words* (Emilio Martínez-Lázaro, 1978). Patricia Hart further notes that in the late 1970s and early 1980s the arrival of the sound technicians Gilles and Bernard Ortion, Pierre Gamet and James Willis in Spain further helped to standardise the practice of direct sound (2007: 133–46). In Saura's films of this period, dialogue is just one component of a far richer, crisper acoustic landscape in which the ambient sounds, echoes, resonances and other accidental sounds are palpably present. For instance, we often hear the creaking wheels of the wheelchair and the rustling of leaves as neatly as we hear the voice. By way of contrast, in post-synch recording, ambient sounds are not always realistically conveyed, and are most often reproduced by means of foley sound effects.

Most crucially, this new technology radically reshaped vocal perfor-mance in Spanish film, allowing for a style of acting would be one of the central tenets of Carlos Saura's authorial style from this moment onwards. In an interview from the 1970s, Saura enthused about the advantages of direct sound, commenting that it not only allows for a far greater nuance in the tone of the actor's voice, but that it also informs their style of gesticulating. To this effect, he argues: 'Porque si el tono es falso el gesto es falso también. Es algo que tengo comprobado. Mi obsesión siempre en el cine español son dos cosas: una, eliminar el gesto inútil, y otra, conseguir el tono correcto de los actores' [Because if the tone of voice is false, gestures are false too. This is something I've dem-onstrated. I have two obsessions in Spanish cinema: one is to eliminate useless gestures, and the other to achieve the correct tone of voice in the actors] (cited in Brasó 1974). Saura further says that direct sound brings a particular kind of tension to a shoot which cannot be created with post-synch sound, adding that: 'es un clima un poco especial. Y para mí es totalmente necesario' [it's a particular kind of atmosphere. And for me, it's totally necessary] (cited in Brasó 1974). Saura adds that Spanish film production has historically found it difficult to achieve the necessary silence during the film (Brasó 1974), a logistical challenge that largely depends on the discipline of the cast and crew, as well on as camera movement and other technology making the minimal degree of sound.

Saura's approach to sound here reveals the extent to which synchro-nisation forges an intimate link between voice and gesture, whereby one mutually reinforces the other's ability to communicate meaning. Yet, in speaking of post-synch sound in terms of its falsehood and excess, Saura reveals a discomfort towards dubbing that is shared by many of his gen-eration, for whom dubbing has long been associated with the Franco years, during which the dubbing of all foreign films was made compul-sory by law. Saura has long spoken out against the practice of dubbing, describing it as 'el mayor error cometido por el cine español' [the biggest error committed by Spanish cinema] (Anon. 2009). Whether actors are dubbing their own voice (which, as we have seen, was the case in Spanish film until the 1970s) or that of a foreign actor, their vocal performance in both cases is shaped by the closeness to the microphone and the space of the anechoic chamber in which they perform. The result is that Spanish film dialogue has sounded dry and depthless, often divorced from the physical environment in which it is supposed to be located. The post-synch voice therefore has its own sonic texture that deserves more critical attention. The overall effect is one which is sensorially heightened – a heightenedness which, in the case of the Spanish comedies discussed in this chapter, often works against the spatial construction of the film.

Yet, while direct sound created greater sense of spatial realism in Spanish cinema, it would be too simplistic to say that the sound design that preceded it was always inferior or primitive. As Gubern and Vernon show, the sheer inventiveness of the sound worlds of *Esa pareja feliz/ That Happy Couple* (Berlanga and Bardem, 1951) and *El cochecito/The Wheelchair* (Marco Ferreri, 1960) 'provides reasons to question the doctrine of direct sound and the assumption that technology always moves forward' (2013: 382–3). Correspondingly, the same could be said of gesture. If, for Saura, José Luis López Vázquez's expansive gestures in comedic films constituted an excess, for Berlanga his performances in serious cinema have constituted precisely the opposite. As García Berlanga acerbically comments: 'Cuando [José Luis López Vázquez y Alfredo Landa] hacen películas dramáticas no hacen más que quedarse quietos con una mirada perdida y abrir la boca' [When (José Luis López Vázquez and Alfredo Landa) make dramatic films, all they do is stay still with a lost look and an open mouth] (1998: 12). While it is most probably unfair to say that López Vázquez's dramatic performances are inexpressive, Berlanga's observation here nevertheless crucially raises the question of agency in the discussion of acting. In the films of Carlos Saura, in particular, screen performance is not solely the work of the actor. As we have seen in *El jardín de las delicias*, performance is constructed as another element of film form: a product not only of the actor's labour and skill, but also equally of the distinctive camerawork of Luis Cuadrado, the elliptical editing of Pablo del Amo and, of course, the sound recording of Luis Rodríguez. In contrast, in common with many Spanish comedies, Berlanga's filmmaking brings the process of acting upstage, thereby attributing the actors with a greater degree of autonomy and movement. Whereas direct sound brought a clearer alignment between voice and body in Spanish film, this did not necessarily equate to bringing a clearer *directness* to performance style. If it brought discipline and rigour to the craft of acting, it also curtailed its flow and trammelled its movement, often both regulating and reducing the unruly body to another element of *mise-en-scène*.

José Luis López Vázquez would continue to appear in both comedic and serious roles into the 1980s and 1990s, when direct sound would begin to become standard in Spanish film. In his performances of Luis José de Leguiniche in Berlanga's *Patrimonio nacional/National Heritage* (1981) and *Nacional III/National III* (1982), films which for the most part use synchronised sound, his acting style was markedly more muted and contained than his earlier comedies with the director. Pavlović, Perriam and Triana-Toribio have alerted attention to a recent article by Carlos Boyero, who suggests that Spanish critical establishment only recognised López Vázquez as a 'proper' actor after he had been forced 'to get rid of his characteristic pitch when speaking, show restraint, or at least show inner turmoil and express dark feelings and other similar signs of a superior sensitivity' (cited in Pavlović, Perriam and Triana-Toribio 2013: 330–1). I would argue that developments in sound design and technology – in particular, the shift from post-synch to direct sound – clearly played a role in this critical repositioning. As I have shown, the voice in both its presence and absence was an integral component of López Vázquez's performance style and star persona. Whether dubbed or synchronised, López Vázquez's vocal performance thus provides a crucial means of illuminating the shifting location of the voice in Spanish film during a period of great technological change.

Notes

1 For excellent introductions to the *sainete* in Spanish cinema, see Marsh (2006), Buse, Triana-Toribio and Willis (2007) and Carlos Heredero (1993).
2 For a discussion of the popular in Spanish popular cinema of this period, see Marsh (2006).
3 The square in *La cabina* was shot on location in Plaza de Arapiles, Madrid. The film's final sequences were shot in Madrid's Barajas Airport.
4 See his groundbreaking book, *Acting in the Cinema* (Naremore 1988).

References

Altman, R. (1980) 'Moving Lips: Cinema as Ventriloquism', *Yale French Studies*, 60 (Cinema/Sound), 67–79.
Anon. (2009) 'Carlos Saura carga contra el doblaje de películas', *Público*, 16 December.
Anon. (2011) '"La cabina" de Antonio Mercero', *La Mitad Invisible*, Televisión Española, 8 October.
Bergson, H. (1980) 'Laughter', in Wylie Sypher (ed.), *Comedy*, Baltimore, MD: Johns Hopkins University Press.
Brasó, E. (1974) *Carlos Saura*, Madrid: Taller de Ediciones Josefina Betancor.
Buse, P., N. Triana-Toribio and A. Willis (2007) *The Cinema of Álex de la Iglesia*, Manchester: Manchester University Press.
Chion, M. (1999) *The Voice in Cinema*, New York: Columbia University Press.

Cruz, J (2005) 'El actor inquieto: Entrevista: Goya de Honor: José Luis López Vázquez', *El País*, 30 January.

D'Lugo, M. (1991) *The Films of Carlos Saura: the Practice of Seeing*, Princeton, NJ: Princeton University Press.

Dolar, M. (2006) *A Voice and Nothing More*, Cambridge, MA: MIT Press.

Galán, D (2009) 'El gran versátil', *El País*, 2 November.

García Berlanga, F. (1998) *¡Con Mariano Ozores hemos topado!*, Festival Internacional de Cine de Comedia de Peñíscola.

Gubern, R. and K. M. Vernon (2013) 'Soundtrack', in J. Labanyi and T. Pavlovic (eds), *A Companion to Spanish Cinema*, Malden, MA: Wiley-Blackwell, pp. 370–88.

Hart, P. (2007) 'Sound Ideas or Unsound Practices?: Listening for "Spanishness" in Peninsular Film', in C. S. Conejero (ed.), *Spanishness in the Spanish Novel and Cinema of the 20th–21st Century*, Newcastle, UK: Cambridge Scholars, pp. 133–46.

Heredero, C.F. (1993) *Las huellas del tiempo: Cine español, 1951–1961*, Madrid: Archivo de la Filmoteca Española.

Lloret, L. (2010) *¿Para qué te cuento?: Biografía autorizada de José Luis López Vázquez*, Madrid: Ediciones Akal.

Marsh, S. (2006) *Popular Spanish Film under Franco: Comedy and the Weakening of the State*, Houndmills, Basingstoke: Palgrave Macmillan.

Naremore, J. (1988) *Acting in the Cinema*, Berkeley: University of California Press.

Ozores, A. (2004) *La profesión más antigua del mundo*, Barcelona: Belacqva de Ediciones y Publicaciones.

Pavlović, Tatjana, Chris Perriam and Núria Triana-Toribio (2013) 'Stars, Modernity, and Celebrity Culture', in J. Labanyi and T. Pavlović (eds), *A Companion to Spanish Cinema*, Oxford: Blackwell, pp. 319–44.

Rée, J. (1999) *I See a Voice: A Philosophical History of Language, Deafness and the Senses*, London: HarperCollins.

Rodríguez, E. (1989) *José Luis López Vázquez: Los disfraces de la melancolía*, Valladolid: 34 Semana de Cine.

Segura, S. (2007) '¡Viva José Luis López Vázquez!', *Fotogramas*, 1961, 46–7.

Sergi, G. (1999) 'Actors and the Sound Gang', in A. Lovell and P. Krämer (eds), *Screen Acting*, London: Routledge, pp. 126–37.

Valencia, M. (2002) *José Luis López Vázquez: Confesiones de un pícaro*, Valencia: Fundació Municipal de Cine, Mostra de Valencia.

Whittaker, T. (2012) 'Locating la *Voz*: The Space and Sound of Spanish Dubbing', *Journal of Spanish Cultural Studies*, 13.3, 292–305.

Wojcik, P. R. (2006) 'The Sound of Film Acting', *Journal of Film and Video*, 58.1–2, 71–83.

Wright, S (2013) *The Child in Spanish Cinema*, Manchester: Manchester University Press.

6

The influence of Argentinian acting schools in Spain from the 1980s

Carmen Ciller

During the 1970s, the Spanish film and television industry welcomed Argentinian actors and actresses, who were escaping from General Jorge Rafael Videla's dictatorship, which had started with the coup of 1976 and coincided with the Spanish transition to democracy. The first wave consisted of actors such as Hector Alterio, Hector Colomé, Norma Aleandro and Marilina Ross; the second wave followed soon after, with Ricardo Darín, Daniel Freire and Federico Luppi. Decades afterwards, Argentinian performers are regularly cast in Spanish productions and international co-productions of film and television, such as Leonardo Sbaraglia, Miguel Ángel Solá and Natalia Verbeke. This is what Manuel Palacio has called 'la transnacionalización del trabajo y los lazos de solidaridad con el exilio latinomaericano' [the transnationalisation of work and the links of solidarity with Latin American exile] (2012: 287). During the 1980s, not only did the presence and influence of Argentinian actors increase, but also Argentinian teachers, and schools of performing arts were established in Spain. Cristina Rota arrived during the late 1970s and Juan Carlos Corazza in 1990. They created two of the most influential acting schools in Spain, where some of the most relevant Spanish actors have studied, including Penélope Cruz, Javier Bardem and Paz Vega, to name but a few.

This chapter analyses the importance and influence of Argentinian acting schools in contemporary Spanish cinema. I will look at the more relevant acting schools in Madrid after the 1980s, and take the case of Cecilia Roth as an example of the impact of Argentinian acting in Spanish film. At the same time, I will examine the relationship between Spanish and Argentinian acting schools and methods in order to study how the two countries have influenced each other, through different waves of immigration that have resulted in fluid and varied collaborations.

Before studying Argentinian teaching of performing arts, it is important to look at the most relevant traditions in Spanish acting schools. The Real Escuela Superior de Arte Dramático/Royal School of Dramatic

Arts, or RESAD, opened in 1831, as part of the Real Conservatorio de Música [Royal School of Music]. It became an independent school in 1911, changing its name in 1952, and remains Madrid's most important centre for the study of performing arts. The Centro Dramático Nacional [National Centre of Dramatic Arts], also based in Madrid, was founded in 1978 and has several campuses in other parts of Spain, including the Centro Dramático Galego in Santiago de Compostela, Centro Andaluz de Teatro and Teatre Nacional de Cataluña. All of these schools aim to explore and support Spanish contemporary playwriting and favour the use of Spanish texts.

Beside these national acting schools, Spanish theatre companies have traveled and performed internationally, contributing to the education and recognition of Spanish plays and actors. At the beginning of the twentieth century, several Spanish theatre companies travelled all over Latin America, with a special interest in Argentina. As a result, virtually all of the more famous actors of Spanish theatre had a career in Buenos Aires, including María Guerrero, Margarita Xirgú, Imperio Argentina and Francisco Tressols. Xirgú is a very particular case: after General Francisco Franco's victory in the Spanish Civil War, she became an exile in Chile, Uruguay and Argentina, where she took part in productions of plays by Federico García Lorca, the Álvarez Quintero Brothers and Rafael Alberti. In Argentina, Xirgú starred in the film adaptation of Lorca's *Bodas de sangre/Blood Wedding* (Edmundo Guibourg, 1938). Eventually, she became a teacher in the Escuela Municipal de Arte Dramático [School of Dramatic Arts] in Montevideo, in 1949. There, Alberto Closas, Cándida Losada and other important actors of Spanish cinema and theatre received their education. Enrique Diosdado studied there as well, long before his daughter Ana Diosdado became one of the most important playwrights and actresses in Spain during the 1980s, with successful works such as *Anillos de oro/Golden Rings* (1983) and *Segunda enseñanza/High School* (1986).

The exchange of professionals of the film industry between Argentina and Spain has left some interesting testimonies that highlight the differences in approaches both to acting and directing actors in both countries. For instance, in his autobiography, Luis García Berlanga remembers how working with Argentinian actors was one of the most difficult experiences he had in the country:

'El primer escollo importante fue el reparto. Aquellos actores eran buenos – Rodolfo Beban, Ana María Campoy – pero no eran mi gente. Ya no era un film de Berlanga… perdía esa condición esperpéntica que mis personajes necesitan … los diálogos que en boca de López Vázquez, Julia Caba o

Elvira Quintillá habrían sonado a pura delicia, perdían su gracia y fuerza con otro tipo de actores. Puse en evidencia mi torpeza para comunicarme y mi incapacidad para llevar a todo un plantel de buenos profesionales a mi mundo … No basta que sean buenos: deben estar 'clavados' en los papeles. [The first difficulty was the casting. They were good actors – Rodolfo Beban, Ana María Campoy – but they were not my people. It was not a Berlanga film any more … it lost that *esperpento*-like quality that my characters needed … the dialogues said by López Vázquez, Julia Caba or Elvira Quintillá would have been pure bliss. But with those [Argentinian] actors they lost their humour and strength. I displayed my incapacity to communicate and bring that great cast to my world … It is not enough that they are good: they must fit their roles perfectly.] (Franco 2005: 138)

Those communication problems were not the only obstacles. Later, Berlanga mentions another difficulty: 'hubo que doblarla de nuevo para que todos aquellos porteños hablaran con acento de Valladolid, como era norma en la España de aquel tiempo' [we had to dub the film so that all those Argentinians spoke with accents from Valladolid, as was the norm in Spain at that time] (2005: 141). Berlanga's testimony is a reminder of the fact that, even as Spanish cinema welcomed Latin American actors, the final performance was determined by the voices of native speakers who used to dub foreign actors.

One of the first scholars who approached the study of acting in Spanish cinema was Julio Pérez Perucha (1984). He analysed the work of Pepe Isbert in order to study the legacy of the *sainete* in different generations of actors of popular cinema. Pérez Perucha believed that there were some features and body language that had been incorporated into the cinema from the *sainete*. In the case of Isbert, Pérez Perucha noted that 'discurso de medias palabras, gruñidos, suspiros, movimientos crispados y gestos indicativos, síntoma aterrador de una indescifrable angustia' [unfinished sentences, grunts, sighs, tense movements, pointing at several directions, all of them symptoms of an undecipherable anguish] (1984: 74) were the main characteristics of his style. Later, I will go back to Pérez Perucha's work to question the relevance of the influence of *sainete* on Spanish actors after the arrival of Argentinian schools.

Unfortunately, academic literature has long neglected a study of the cultural links between Spain and Argentina. For instance, there is no study on the representations of Argentinian stereotypes in Spanish cinema, despite their popularity. In November 2010, a conference was held in Buenos Aires in which film specialists gathered to compare both industries. This resulted in the book *Imágenes compartidas: Cine argentino-cine español* (Torreiro 2011), which explores the uninterrupted links between Spanish and Argentinian cinema, and the exchange of producers, scriptwriters and directors that resulted in countless collaborations. Mirito Torreiro claims that there are 'hasta 52 películas producidas en Buenos Aires [que] adaptan obras de actores españoles o se hacen eco de biografías más o menos reales, más o menos imaginarias de ciudadanos hispanos' [up to 52 films produced in Buenos Aires adapted from plays by Spanish authors, or that use biographies of (real or imaginary) Spanish people] (2011: 54). The book also looks at the contemporary relationship between both industries, paying attention to the Ibermedia programme, which, after 1998, has helped in the production, distribution and exhibition of Spain–Argentina co-productions. An example of the productivity of this relationship is found in the testimony of Spanish film director Agustín Díaz Yanes, who, after directing *Nadie hablará de nosotras cuando hayamos muerto*/*No One Will Talk About Us When We Are Dead* (1995) and *Sólo quiero caminar*/*I Just Want to Walk* (2008), supports the connection between Spanish and Argentinian film industries and invites filmmakers to explore the possibilities of our common language. According to him,

> Hay idiomas que están hechos para el cine y otros no, igual que la música pop. Los acentos latinoamericanos son muy buenos para el cine español. Son muy suaves, no parecen enfadados aunque en la escena te vayan a matar. También es porque creo que una de las oportunidades que hemos perdido es la de habernos unido todos. Nunca he entendido por qué los americanos y los ingleses o los franceses sí que lo hacen y nosotros no. [Some languages are made for the cinema, and some are not, just like pop music. Latin American accents are very good for Spanish cinema. They are soft, they don't make the character look angry even if he is about to kill someone. I believe it is a possibility we have not used, to be together. I have never understood why Americans and British and French people do it and we don't.] (quoted in Romero Santos 2014: 66)

Another work that explores the relationship between both film industries is the book *Che, qué bueno que vinisteis: El cine argentino que cruzó el charco* (González 2005). In it, six Argentinian actors (Héctor Alterio, Ricardo Darín, Federico Luppi, Miguel Ángel Solá, Leonardo Sbaraglia and Cecilia Roth) recall their experiences in Spain and how they have managed to work and live in both countries. They also pay tribute to the previous generations of Argentinians who worked in Spain, such as film directors Luis César Amadori and León Klimovsky and actress Analía Gadé.

In *Ché, qué bueno que vinisteis*, two of the more relevant Argentinian actors working in Spain are examined: Alterio, who arrived in 1974, and

Roth, in 1976, both of them as exiles. Alterio is the father of Malena and Ernesto Alterio, who are also recognised actors in Spain. It was in 1974, during his attendance at the San Sebastian Film Festival, that he decided not to go back to Argentina. He talks about his education at the Method School in Buenos Aires, and his connection to the Actor's Studio in New York, where he attended a masterclass given by Lee Strasberg (González Acevedo 2005: 68).

Roth arrived in Spain with her family; her father, Abrasha Rotemberg, was one of the owners of *La Opinión*, a newspaper that was expropriated by the Argentinian military in 1977. Between 1976 and 1985, Roth took part in sixteen Spanish films, working with recognised filmmakers, including Pedro Almodóvar, Jaime Chávarri, Fernando Colomo, José Luis Garci and Iván Zulueta. Her acceptance in the film industry seemed unproblematic. However, a close look at her works suggests that her contribution both as a woman and a foreigner helped to expand the representation of stereotypes in Spanish films.[1]

Despite the fact that she worked with different directors and in both popular and *auteur* cinema, some continuity can be found in the roles that Roth played during the 1980s. She occasionally played the role of the foreign woman, sometimes Argentinian, sometimes not; when she was playing a Spanish character, she had to be dubbed. More interestingly, though, most of her roles were as sexually liberated women, presented as a comparison to the more prudish Spanish counterparts. In order to help Roth's performance, the distinction between foreignness and Spanishness used in these films was often introduced through an unproblematic relationship with her naked body. Let us take her performance in the film *Pepe, no me des tormento/Pepe, Stop Bothering Me* (Jose M. Gutiérrez, 1981) as an example. It tells the story of two scriptwriters, Pepe (Luis Varela) and Mario (Emilio Gutiérrez Caba). Mario is married to Barbara (Roth), an American woman who owns her business, is very irresponsible and refuses to let her husband work. Barbara has divorced three times and is mother to three children. She is presented as a modern, independent worker, and representative of the sexually liberated non-Spanish woman. All she thinks of is going to parties, dancing and showing off her naked body as soon as she can. When we first see her, she is drinking alcohol while she takes a bath in a jacuzzi. Moreover, her children are providing her with the alcohol she seems to enjoy so much, reinforcing the idea that she is not a traditional mother. Later, she organises a party in which she is the star of a striptease number. The following sequences show her completely naked, with an American flag painted on her thighs. The film stresses Barbara's nakedness as much as her foreignness, while linking both characteristics. The stereotype of the sensual foreigner, which was so popular in the Spanish films of the Franco regime, is expanded here, and confirmed when Mario explains to Pepe that Barbara 'en la cama funciona estupendamente' [she works perfectly under the sheets], as if to explain why he still loves her despite her being so extravagant. It must be remarked that Barbara speaks with an accent that is clearly foreign. Everything in Barbara is presented as different to the traditions Spaniards are used to, including the fact that she has her own business and does not need her husband for financial security. Roth's creation of this character, including her unproblematic representation of nakedness, coincided with the novelty of these representations in the Spanish films of the time. It was her generation of actresses that opened the floodgates for future performances of sex on screen.

Roth's performance as Barbara can be compared to that of her most famous role of the same period, in Zulueta's *Arrebato/Rapture* (1979). In it, she plays another Barbara, also a foreigner, with a Latin American accent. This Barbara is fragile, beautiful, and the first time we meet her she is semi naked, on her bed. She is naked or semi-naked in almost all her scenes and, once more, this is all done unproblematically. An example of this is the scene when she is kneeling between Jose's (Eusebio Poncela) legs. Roth's use of her fully exposed body is absolutely under control, her movements are the result of precise emotional management and her strength as an actress contributes to make Barbara a strong female character. It could be argued that the characters that Roth played in the early 1980s lack psychological depth, including emblematic roles such as in *Laberinto de pasiones/Labyrinth of Passions* (Pedro Almodóvar, 1982). The female characters have little dialogue as compared to the male characters of the films, and spectators may be left to wonder about the relevance of the female characters to the plot. But, despite that, Roth's controlled use of her often-naked body makes these characters seem powerful, and their presence felt at every moment. Roth returned to Argentina in the mid-1980s, and it was later when, back in Spain again, she worked in her most acclaimed roles, such as *Un lugar en el mundo/A Place in the World* (Adolfo Aristarain, 1992), *Martín H* (Adolfo Aristarain, 1997) and *Todo sobre mi madre/All About My Mother* (Pedro Almodóvar, 1999), for which she received her second Goya Award for Best Actress. In these roles, she did not have to be concerned about hiding her Argentinian accent.

Roth's arrivals in Spain in the 1970s and 1990s coincided with the birth of Madrid's most important acting schools, Cristina Rota's and Juan Carlos Corazza's. The former was opened in 1978, one year after Rota's arrival, and since then the purpose of the school has been to 'crear un centro donde el actor obtenga una formación integral que le permita generar su propio trabajo, sabiendo abarcar todos los aspectos de la actividad teatral desde la gestión, la promoción, cuestiones técnicas, la dirección, la dramaturgia y la interpretación' [create a place where actors obtain a full education so that they can generate their own work and learn how to cope with all aspects of theatre life, including paperwork, publicity, technical aspects, direction, playwriting and acting] (CNC 2015). From 1979, the school has worked with the Centro de Nuevos Creadores [Centre of New Creators] to produce original plays, which are performed at CNC-Sala Mirador. Since its inception, a total of over 1,400 students have graduated from the school, including Juan Diego and María Botto (Rota's son and daughter) and Ernesto and Malena Alterio (Alterio's son and daughter). For her work as a teacher of performing arts, Rota was awarded with the Medalla de Oro al Mérito en las Bellas Artes 2010 en Teatro. This is the most important official award of the arts, given by the Ministerio de Educación, Cultura y Deporte [Ministry of Education, Culture and Sports]. The legacy of Rota's school can be seen in the career of her most internationally successful student, Penélope Cruz.

Cruz's début in *Jamón, jamón* (Bigas Luna, 1992) made her one of the most important young actresses of the 1990s in Spain. She first achieved international recognition in Almodóvar's *Todo sobre mi madre* and, following its success, she appeared in more US and international films, returning to Spain to work again with Almodóvar in *Volver* (2006). In 2009, she received the Oscar for Best Supporting Role by an Actress for her work in Woody Allen's *Vicky Cristina Barcelona* (2008). Cruz is attentive to the shape of her body, so that it illustrates certain aspects of the character she is performing. We see this, for instance, in *Volver*, where she famously used padding to augment Raimunda's thighs, which altered the way she walked and moved. Something similar happens in *Non ti muovere/Do Not Move* (Sergio Castellitto, 2004), in which Cruz used several types of body padding, make-up and hair extensions. For this role, Cruz was awarded with a European Film Award and the David di Donatello Award. Cruz's tendency to carefully work the physical aspects of her performances has been noticed by scholars such as Chris Perriam, who, in analysing her work in *Vanilla Sky* (Cameron Crowe, 2002), argued that 'she is also, through the idolization of her eyes, hair, face and body movements by the camera, made more than [herself], and becomes raised to the status of classic, fiction-film angel' (2005: 41). There is no doubt that Cruz's successful career owes much to her talent to choose the right roles, as much as her capacity to provide her characters with a unique physicality.

Juan Carlos Corazza arrived in Spain in 1990 and opened his school that same year. He had previous experience as both an actor and a teacher of performing arts in the school of Carlos Gandolfo, in Buenos Aires. Since then, he has formed several generations of Spanish actors, such as Elena Anaya, Raúl Arévalo, Jordi Mollà and he became the main figure of the Method Acting School in Spain. The list of his students is long, but no one is as important as Javier Bardem. Like Cruz (his wife), Bardem's work has been internationally recognised, especially since winning the Oscar for Best Supporting Role by an Actor for *No Country for Old Men* (Joel and Ethan Coen, 2007). Miguel Fernández and Vicente Rodríguez have studied Bardem's work with Corazza and explain:

> Corazza is a follower of the Argentinean approach to Stanislavski whose work marks a shift toward the institutionalization and professionalization of local acting. Of course, this comes hand in hand with the rigor and discipline associated with the Method, as well as with its realistic take on acting. In Bardem's case, his stress on learning and improving, and his growing attention toward impersonation and behavioral transformation, garner him a reputation of being a knowledgeable professional. Interestingly, Bardem's methodology, rooted in great performing accuracy, incorporates traditional clichés of first Method actors such as rebellion and psychic and sentimental instability. (2013: 170)

There are many similarities between the filmographies and work of Cruz and Bardem. Like Roth, both of them started their careers with films that demanded strong physical preparation and full control of their (again) normally naked bodies. Bardem's first role of relevance was in *Las edades de Lulú/The Ages of Lulu* (Bigas Luna, 1990), in which he played the role of a hypersexual man. This was followed by *Éxtasis/Extasis* (Mariano Barroso, 1996), which contained a famous scene in which Bardem had to climb up a rope. It is only after his role in *El detective y la muerte/The Detective and the Death* (Gonzalo Suárez, 1994) that Bardem started to explore characters with more psychological depth, which held greater interest for him. Perriam noticed this when analysing his performance in that film and the importance of it in the development of his career. According to Perriam, it is here where spectators could first see 'una composición interior, de miradas más que de palabras ... un tono diferente de interpretación al que estaba acostumbrado' [an internalised composition of feeling, made up of looks rather than words ... a different tone of acting from what I had been used to] (2003: 100). Afterwards, Bardem could explore limiting his physical ability in films such as *Carne trémula/Live Flesh* (Pedro Almodóvar, 1997), where his character had to use a wheelchair, and *Mar adentro/The*

Sea Inside (Alejandro Amenábar, 2004), in which he played a tetraplegic person. As Fouz-Hernández and Allbritton also note (see chapters 12 and 13 in this volume), physical control is a key to understanding the success of Bardem's performances. Only when he started working under Corazza's influence (with whom Bardem still works today) did he limit the excessive performances of previous roles, such as *Perdita Durango* (Álex de la Iglesia, 1997). Paul Julian Smith noticed this when he claimed that, in *Carne trémula*, 'Bardem, who is perhaps Spain's most versatile male star, displays a dignity and endurance at the hands of fate which is more moving than the emotional excesses of Almodóvar's earlier films' (2000: 183). The relevance of Bardem's career and the importance of his physicality has been profusely analysed by Santiago Fouz-Hernández and Alfredo Martínez-Expósito. According to them, 'Bardem has struggled to be disassociated from the muscular heterosexuality and overt physicality that characterised much of his early work' (2007: 9). Like Smith, they remark how relevant it has been for him to take control over his body: 'the malleability and adaptability of Bardem's body is a good illustration of the evolution of the representation of masculinity in Spanish cinema' (Fouz-Hernández and Martínez-Expósito 2007: 9).

Bardem and Cruz have no doubt contributed to the success of Argentinean acting schools in Spain, and it is not surprising that these are the first choice for young students of dramatic arts. In Madrid, it is not rare that actors discuss the differences between Rota and Corazza, comparing one with the other as if they were football teams, and sometimes a rivalry can be perceived. Nevertheless, it is generally admitted that no schools have been so influential in the world of Spanish film, theatre and television as those of Rota and Corazza. In my own experience as a student at Corazza's, I learned how acting is presented as a very demanding discipline that includes many areas that must be explored by the end of the course; these areas include physical, emotional and theoretical work. Students participate in the so-called 'preparación corporal' [physical preparation], which includes different exercises and games. The names of these are revealing: 'estiramiento' [stretching], 'desbloqueo muscular' [muscular unblocking], 'reubicación espacial' [spatial reordering] and 'relajación verbal' [verbal relaxation]. After this, students move on to a series of improvisations, the main purpose of which is to make the actor face her or his own limitations. The teachers guide the students in exercises to find themselves in unexpected situations that force them to find tools to solve given conflicts. This makes the student unlearn wrong strategies, break taboos and explore new and/or hidden aspects of their personalities. Finally, the students perform theatre plays, usually from contemporary authors. The work is mainly focused on what they call the 'objetivo psicológico' (psychological objective) of the character: the actors are asked what their characters want more than anything else at that particular time or in that scene. Then, they are invited to think of the actions that that character would do to achieve that goal. The question of 'actions' is of vital importance, as they are asked to go as far as ignoring the dialogue and make their characters use their bodies to obtain what they want. By doing this, actors are able to look for the right movements and strategies to perform their roles. Then, the concept of 'motivación' (motivation) is introduced, in order to study what makes that character perform those actions in order to achieve her or his 'psychological objective'. The Corazza Method is often seen as a long creative process, intense and even sometimes violent.

Hundreds of actors and actresses have received their education in Madrid's Argentinian schools of dramatic arts, sometimes attending more than one of them (for instance, the Alterio family has regularly attended both Corazza's and Rota's schools). It could be argued that there are as many acting styles as actors, but it seems very clear that today's acting styles are far from those of the previous generations of Spanish film actors, such as Isbert. Let us take, as an example, the extremely successful film *Ocho apellidos vascos/A Spanish Affair* (Emilio Martínez Lázaro, 2014). This comedy became the most profitable Spanish film of all time, with nearly ten million spectators.[2] It could be thought that this film follows the tradition of Spanish national comedy, in the line of the comedies of first Isbert, then Alfredo Landa (whose film *No desearás al vecino del quinto/Thou Shall Not Covert Thy Neighbour* [Ramón Fernández, 1970] was the most profitable Spanish film in its time), and later Santiago Segura (whose *Torrente, el brazo tonto de la ley/Torrente* [1999] later became the most profitable). In this sense, one could expect that Julio Pérez Perucha's analysis of the acting styles in Spanish comedy could be applied to *Ocho apellidos vascos*. However, it is easily perceived that the new generations of actors that appear in this and similar films are far from the traditions of *sainete* studied by Perucha and presented at the beginning of this chapter. The main characters are played by Dani Rovira (who received the Goya Award for this performance) and Clara Lago, who both studied at Argentinian acting schools – Rovira at Osqui Guzmán's and Lago at Corazza's. The impact of these schools in popular cinema is clearly seen today.

The cultural exchange between Spanish and Argentinian performers is an important aspect of Spanish film history that still needs to be researched and analysed in depth. The success of the collaborations between professionals of both industries is an invitation for teachers, actors and all members of the film industry to continue establishing links. The common language is perhaps the most obvious connection, but other issues unite Spain and Argentina ever more strongly: familiar bonds, long friendships, professional links, and solidarity in times of political difficulties. Spanish cinema owes a great deal to Argentinian actors and teachers. The consolidation of acting schools in Spain during the 1980s is nothing but the confirmation that the legacy of Argentinian culture is of vital relevance for the Spanish cinema of the present and of the future.

Notes

This work has been written as a part of the research project I+D+i 'El cine y la televisión en la España de la post-Transición (1979–1992)', financed by the Spanish Ministry of Economy and Competitiveness of Spain. Ref. CSO2011-15708-E.

1 For more on Cecilia Roth's performance style, see Ciller and Palacio (2011: 335–58).

2 According to the film database on the website of the Ministerio de Cultura, Educación y Deporte, *Ocho apellidos vascos* had garnered a total of 9.4 million spectators and made €55.2 million upon completion of its theatrical run.

References

Ciller, Carmen and Manuel Palacio (2011) 'Cecilia Roth en España (1976–1985)', *Signa: Revista de la Asociación Española de Semiótica*, 20, 335–58.

CNC, Centro de Nuevos Creadores (2015) 'Historia de la escuela', www.fcnc. es/escuela-historia, accessed 26 May 2015.

Fernández Labayen, Miguel and Vicente Rodríguez Ortega (2013) '(Almost) Everybody Loves Javier Bardem … "For he is a Good Actor": Critical Reception in the Spanish and US Media´, in Russell Meeuf and Raphael Raphael, *Transnational Stardom. International Celebrity in Film and Popular Culture*, New York: Palgrave Macmillan, pp. 165–86.

Fouz-Hernández, Santiago and Alfredo Martínez-Expósito (2007) *Live Flesh: The Male Body in Contemporary Spanish Cinema*, London: I. B. Tauris.

Franco, Jesús (2005) *Bienvenido Míster Cagada. Memorias caóticas de Luis García Berlanga*, Madrid: Aguilar.

González Acevedo, Juan Carlos (2005) *Che, qué bueno que vinisteis. El cine argentino que cruzó el charco*, Barcelona: Editorial Diëresis.

Palacio, Manuel (2012) *La televisión durante la Transición Española*, Madrid: Cátedra.

Pérez Perucha, Julio (1984) 'Deudas con Isbert´, in Julio Pérez Perucha (ed.), *El cine de José Isbert*, Valencia: Ayuntamiento de Valencia, pp. 71–9.

Perriam, Chris (2003) *Stars and Masculinities in Spanish Cinema: From Banderas to Bardem*, Oxford: Oxford University Press.

Perriam, Chris (2005) `Two Transnational Spanish Stars: Antonio Banderas and Penélope Cruz´, in *Studies in Hispanic Cinemas*, 2.1, 41.

Romero Santos, Rubén (2014) *La pistola y el corazón. Conversaciones con Agustín Díaz Yanes*, Madrid: Tecmerin.

Smith, Paul Julian (2000) *Desire Unlimited: The Cinema of Pedro Almodóvar*, London: Verso.

Torreiro, Mirito (2011) `Desde un observador distante´, in Centro Cultural Español de España en Buenos Aires (ed.), *Imágenes compartidas: cine argentino- cine español*, Buenos Aires: Centro Cultural de España en Buenos Aires, pp. 50–71.

7

Askance, athwart, aside: the queer plays of actors, *auteurs* and machines

Brad Epps

Overacting in *Thou Shalt Not Covet Thy Fifth Floor Neighbour*

He prances, minces and sashays; prattles, purrs and hisses; his wrists dangle, flop and twirl; his lips purse, pucker and pout; his eyes twinkle; his lashes flutter; his entire body frolics and furls. And Fifí, his adorable, snow-white toy poodle, he cradles and snuggles, cuddles and smooches as if the pup were a newborn baby – the child that presumably he will never have. For it is *all too clear* that he is not the reproducing kind, though he may be given, or so the story goes, to a certain fondness for proselytising, for converting and perverting. In any case, from the other side of the street one can see him for what he is: a pansy, a Nancy boy, a molly, a poof, a flamer, easily flustered, perhaps, yet steadfastly fey. Light in the loafers, he is also heavy with desire, hot to trot and saddled with a one-track mind. He is obsessed, that is, with sexual seduction: not of men, as would *all too clearly appear* to be the case, but rather, more deviously, of women, blushing or buxom, petite or plump, married or single, local or foreign, it matters little as long as they are relatively young and white – though he evidently has a predilection, well-trained mid-twentieth-century consumer that he is, for Hollywood pinups, blonde-headed Barbies and, a bit closer to his European home, Swedish flight attendants, all of whom appear to have a predilection, in turn, for middle-aged Spanish ham.

Such are some of the more flamboyantly stylised attributes of Alfredo Landa's character Antón Gutiérrez in Ramón Fernández's *No desearás al vecino del quinto*, known – or rather unknown – in English as *Thou Shalt Not Covet Thy Fifth Floor Neighbour*, a massively successful Spanish comedy from 1970 that Alejandro Melero has called 'la madre de todas las "comedias de mariquitas" españolas' [the mother of all Spanish 'poofter comedies'] (2010: 129).[1] In its reliance on *easily recognisable* figures and situations, the film that rankled a generation of gay activists (Melero 2010: 130) is nonetheless useful, as Alberto Mira points out, to understanding Spanish attitudes towards gender and sexuality (2004). It is just this reliance on easily recognisable figures and situations that I shall be querying in what follows by way of a deliberately disjunctive pairing of the actor-driven *Thou Shalt Not Covet* and, in the final section of this chapter, Lucrecia Martel's *La niña santa* (*The Holy Girl*, 2004), in which recognition is anything but easy. In so doing, I hope to bring to the fore, and perhaps to complicate, some longstanding tensions between actors and *auteurs*, commerce and art, frivolity and seriousness, overstatement and understatement, the popular and the personal, and the anthropomorphic and the mechanical. For it is my contention that, while the earlier film showcases, at once straightforwardly and deceptively, themes and identities, the later film deals in approaches and styles; in both films, moreover, heterosexual desire is dominant, but in both, for all their many differences, something queer is afoot.

Set in a provincial capital, Toledo, *Thou Shalt Not Covet* centres on the misadventures of a young gynaecologist, Pedro Andreu, played by French heartthrob Jean Sorel, who is too handsome for his own business. The husbands, fathers and brothers of Andreu's would-be patients refuse to let 'their' women avail themselves of the young doctor's services for the simple reason that they cannot believe that his gaze could really be clinical, that his speculum could be anything but prurient. As the gynaecologist's long-suffering girlfriend tells a more venerable doctor in Madrid: 'Somos demasiado provincianos para ser modernos y demasiado modernos para ser provincianos. Estamos acomplejados, ¿comprende?' [We're too provincial to be modern and too modern to be provincial. We've quite a complex, you see?]. Enter the aforementioned Antón, a local fashion consultant who, unlike Pedro, has managed to carve out a commercially and socially viable place for himself, paradoxically, by passing himself off as *visibly* homosexual. Thus, while the men of the town aggressively refuse to allow their wives, daughters and sisters to take off their clothes in front of the dreamy doctor, they shrug their shoulders when it comes to them doing the same in front of the ever-so-average-looking, dyed-blond fashion consultant, whose highly coded non-normative appearance renders him, in the predominantly feminine and relatively public space of the boutique, as much asexual as homosexual.

In more private spaces, especially when home alone with men, it would seem, however, that the asexual threatens to morph into the hypersexual, the symbolic eunuch into the predator. The phrase 'it would seem' is, as it were, essential, for while Landa plays Antón who plays the socially scripted part of the poof, there is, in fact, no evidence that he has actually acted on the desire that his highly conspicuous public act has led his fellow citizens to *imagine* as forever potential. So, along with the threat of trans-formation, indeed as its very condition of possibility, there is the imagi-nation. This imagined, imaginary transformation in private, dependent on the public perception of acts and appearances as signifying something essential, is just what Pedro's doting mother all but takes as an article of faith when her son, who still lives with her, goes to Antón's apartment to treat his neighbour for a toothache, an area of medicine – and of the body – beyond his explicit expertise. The nocturnal visit from one neigh-bour to another not only provides the film its title but also fills Pedro's mother with anxiety that a longstanding prohibition with the force of a commandment – 'thou shalt not' – will prove no match for the wiles and enticements of 'unnatural' desire. For she too knows Antón, knows what she sees, and imagines, it would seem, what she has not seen. But she also knows her son, the attractive, fatherless bachelor with a flair for fashion, and imagines, it would seem, that he might be less the ladies' man than the husbands, fathers and brothers of his would-be patients take him to be.

Beneath all the comic poses and light-hearted banter, lurks, *it would seem*, something darkly dramatic, some barely signalled carnal possibil-ity that the proverbial 'pecado nefando' or 'abominable sin' of sodomy might actually take place, just upstairs, ever so close to home. Comedy, of course, has long relied on the spectre of its opposite, tragedy, for its piquancy, its verve, its narrative drive; it dangles before its spectators, over and again, the risk of an infelicitous resolution in which errors become irrecoverable; confusion, cataclysmic; and silliness, sombre indeed. Farce is not infrequently the outcome, especially when same-sex desire is stuffed into the mix, but violence, both verbal and physical, also lies in wait. Farce has traditionally relied on aggression, mockery, cruelty and hyperbole, and supposedly funny situations involving the effemi-nacy of men have meant that these same men become the butt of deri-sion, parody and even brutality (Melero 2010: 129). And yet, inasmuch as the film mobilises images of the 'average fellow' that collide with images of the quintessential queer, these same images become at times – or, better yet, *over time* – mixed and confused. Cinema is a time-based medium, but the spectator is a time-based being, and a multifarious one to boot, so much so that the very notion of 'the spectator' is notoriously deceptive, perhaps as much as the notion, held by a number of critics, that the humour in *Thou Shalt Not Covet*, farcical and aggressive, *tar-gets* gay men and, through them, all women. For humour, in the sense of dampness, seepage and flow, cannot always be controlled or contained, policed or judged, regularised or normalised.

Offensive as the film may be, it is hardly a celebration of normative masculinity, which it presents as adolescent, prone to violence, easily distracted and deceived, unproductive and even downright stupid. The men in the film are almost invariably hot-tempered, lackadaisical and given to drink; they lie, cheat, dissemble, huff and puff; their much-touted strength is shot through with a lack of self-control; their much-ballyhooed decency, with hypocrisy. Pedro's colleagues, for instance, smirk at the academic conference that brings them to Madrid and only care about having fun; the ambulance attendants drop the patient for whom they are responsible – Andreu, who has been beaten by the men of Toledo after being publicly 'outed' as straight at the close of the film – to fight over his fiancée's pretty legs. The film is peppered, moreover, with criticisms of the provinciality, backwardness and dopiness that sup-posedly characterise the nation's capital, criticisms that, like Poe's pur-loined letter, are so obvious as to go unnoticed. As one male character says: 'qué asco de país' [what a disgusting country]. If the film is offen-sive, it is so, then, in a curiously equal-opportunity manner, one in which the *lack* of equal opportunity – for women, for gay men – is shadowed forth in all the shenanigans, simulations and seductions. The film is thus an exercise, perhaps in spite of itself, in the sly, slippery, unstable nature of gender and sexual orientation, in which nature itself is denaturalised and performed, in part, for laughs. But it is also an exercise in the force of standardised phrases, hackneyed images and rote gestures that remit to, and derive from, well-rehearsed social scripts and their actors. For in the clichés that constitute what might be called its normative non-normativity, same-sex desire swings farcically between the comic and the tragic, the piffling and the momentous, the frivolous and the monstrous, and finds itself caught in a play of appearances in which the presumably involuntary arching of an eyebrow, the drop of a hand, the quiver of a lip, the crossing of a leg are freighted with meaning – and meaning with any number of performative tricks and turns.

Retracting acting: a theoretical bender

The preceding paragraphs are an attempt to put into words a particu-larly charged instance of acting by one of Spain's most popular actors, Alfredo Landa, whose incursion into the subgenre colloquially known as the *comedia de mariquitas* is notable because Landa is tightly asso-ciated with the 'common man', the 'regular guy', the 'ordinary bloke', in short, with the incarnation of middlebrow normativity. So popular and prolific was Landa that his name gave rise to an entire current, *el landismo*, which Francisco Umbral considered to be an unintended social document critical to understanding Spain under and shortly after Franco (cited in Recio 1992: 30). The 'screen presence' of an actor as

encumbered with normalcy as Landa playing 'against type' is so imposing that both the director and the apparatus are all but pushed to the
sidelines. What comes deceptively to the fore, frontally and forcefully,
in *Thou Shalt Not Covet* is thus what Starr A. Marcello presents as the
'three areas of an actor's performance style: his or her gestures, facial
expressions, and vocal qualities' (2006: 59). It is in the light of the primacy of the actor – as star, but also as displaced author – in such a commercially orientated venture as *Thou Shalt Not Covet* that I have strived
to 'describe' what flits and flashes across the screen in the person of
Antón Gutiérrez. Such transposition from sounds and images to printed
words is fraught, for, as Carole Zucker notes in an anthology on film
acting, 'the project of describing and articulating an aural characteristic or a gestural trait can be daunting' (1990: viii). Pamela Robertson
Wojcik, in another anthology, makes a similar point: 'it can be very difficult to describe acting – to characterise what an actor does with his or
her hands, voice, or smile' (2004: 1). Arguing that viewers 'feel' that they
'know a good performance from a bad' and 'are either convinced by it
or not,' Wojcik declares that 'much film acting – at least in Hollywood
– tends to favor "invisible" naturalistic styles' (2004: 1–2), part and parcel of what Taylor calls 'acting's captivating elusiveness' (2012: 1). As a
result, 'film acting can seem transparent and resistant to description or
analysis' (Wojcik 2004: 1).

It is telling that something deemed to be so elusive, resistant, difficult and daunting to describe and analyse as acting is in the same blush
deemed to be so available and anecdotal, so impressionistic and casual,
bound more to 'feeling' than to 'thought'. For Taylor, summarising trends
and tendencies, the 'captivating elusiveness' of screen acting is linked to
a 'surfeit of trivia about the lives of film actors' and a 'concomitant def-
icit of theorizations about their work' (2012: 1). Zucker, for her part,
remarks that, 'to discuss acting is to align oneself with the "ordinary" (i.e.
untrained) moviegoer or the "everyday critical talking" cited by [Richard]
Dyer' or 'with "popular" television/radio style criticism' (1990: viii). The
'scholarly disinclination to concentrate on acting', which separates specialist from 'non-specialist viewers', leads Aaron Taylor, among others, to
refuse the division and to shuttle ambivalently between what he calls the
casual and the theoretical (2012: 1). Taylor's ambivalence is evident in the
following: 'in spite of the relative paucity of writing that gives an account
of what performers are actually doing on screen and why their creative
efforts excite our interest, non-academic viewers frequently extemporise
confidently about acting' (Taylor 2012: 1). With respect to the actor-cum-
star, Christine Geraghty similarly notes a 'contrast between the public and
the private, the ordinary and the extraordinary' that 'is made available

through a wide range of texts which go beyond the films into newspapers, fan magazines, television shows and exchanges of information and rumour between fans' (2000: 185).

The shuttling between the ordinary and the extraordinary, the popular and the specialised, the trivial and the theoretical in, around, beside and beyond the figure of the actor undergirds what I have presented as my deliberately disjunctive pairing of *Thou Shalt Not Covet* and *The Holy Girl*. It also suggests a mode of doubleness, if not a duplicity, that dovetails, interestingly, the performance and perception of appearances in such an otherwise 'obvious' and 'insignificant' film as *Thou Shalt Not Covet*, in which the then private 'sin' and 'crime' of adultery work, counterintuitively, under the cover of the public perception of the 'sin' and 'crime' of homosexuality. Shadowed by his on- and off-screen persona as a modern-day everyman, Landa's role as the deceitfully showy Antón Gutiérrez, in which performance is inseparable from parody, makes him a compelling candidate for reflections on the relations not just between actor and character but also, and more generally, between human embodiment and mechanical reproduction, talent and technology, authenticity and automation, spontaneity and simulation. But Landa's performance, in which the 'invisible naturalism' that Wojcik mentions is entangled in both the editorial mechanics of mediation and a highly histrionic and culturally overdetermined stylisation of gender, sexuality and desire, also raises questions about the status of the *queer* as a putatively radical interrogation of identity and reality in which performativity and parody are critical.

Although by no means immune to identitarian consolidations, *queer* is a complex figure, one that twists and turns, bending into a figure that is not one and that, in its very instability, contradictorily stabilises itself as a figure devoid of essence, that is to say, as a figure of process, in process. As Eve Kosofsky Sedgwick rather famously put it in a text published in the early 1990s, 'queer' constitutes 'a continuing moment, movement, motive – recurrent, eddying, *troublant* … "queer" itself means *across* – it comes from the Indo-European root -twerkw, which also yields the German *quer* (transverse), Latin *torquere* (to twist), English *athwart*' (1993: xii). Intensely implicated in the history of sexuality, *queer* has a genealogical affinity with gay, lesbian, bisexual and transgendered identities and commemorates, in its affirmative reclamation or resemantisation, a negative heritage of injury and offence. As such, *queer* signals a shuttling and a doubling that may be likened to what Taylor, in the realm of screen acting, presents as a tension between the casual and the theoretical. Decades after its defiant reclamation, Dana Luciano and Mel Y. Chen, in the introduction to a special issue of *GLQ* on 'queer inhumanisms', reiterate 'the divergent senses of the reclaimed term *queer* ... as primarily a tool of incessant unsettling, restless refusal of all forms of identity, or as an extensible collection or assemblage of overlapping and mutually imbricated forms of gendered, sexual and other corporealized dissidence' (2015: 192).

It is just this twisted, twisting, transversal sense of 'queer' as trope, turn and turning, as a restless, restive device that queries identity in general, that I would mine for a consideration of an elliptical drama – if the generic marker is even valid here – like *The Holy Girl* and for a reconsideration of a 'comedia de mariquitas' like *Thou Shalt Not Covet*, in which something queer *would seem* to declare itself *straight on* and to come at the audience *straight on* in the stereotyped guise of male homosexual 'overacting'. The caginess of the phrase 'something queer' is not incidental. For as important as actors, acts and actions undeniably are in and out of both these films, what Luciano and Chen also signal, after Sedgwick, is a 'nonhuman turn' or 'inhuman turn' that 'expands the term *queer* past its conventional resonances as a container for human sexual nonnormativities' (2015: 189) and that moves from the twists and turns of a film like *Thou Shalt Not Covet* to embrace the oblique approaches and multisensorial charge of a film like *The Holy Girl*. Far from being novel, the nonhuman or inhuman turn is, in many respects, a paradoxically foundational feature of the cinema. Walter Benjamin's much-cited claim that 'the audience's identification with the actor is really an identification with the camera' (1968: 228) is arguably its most succinct expression, one that reverberates, to differing degrees and effects, in discussions of cyborgs and simulacra, surveillance and hypermediation, object-orientated ontology and speculative realism. In the area of cinema studies and, more particularly, film acting studies, Benjamin's observation, which grapples with the 'withering' of the authenticity and aura of bodily presence, has been echoed and amplified, among others, by Philip Drake, who argues that 'presence' is 'a discourse produced *by* performance during its reception; it does not precede it' (2006: 86).

What thus comes to the fore is precisely what is conventionally discounted: the *mediated nature* of *all* film acting, no matter how hysterical and histrionic or unassuming and subdued, no matter how overstated or understated, theatrical or natural. In the words of Drake, 'mediated forms of performance, including screen performance, draw upon many other signifying elements in order to become meaningful, elements such as systems of editing, cinematic framing, and conventions of genre' (2006: 87). Similarly, Wojcik stresses that 'film acting does not exist prior to mediation' and that '[a] fissure between sound and image and the subsequent manipulation of both sound and image, together and apart, is constitutive' of it (2006: 75). The bodily presence of the film actor-character is indeed enmeshed in mediation, but so too, interestingly, is the much-adduced mechanical presence of the camera, which is likewise available to the *spectator* only in the form of the immaterial images that issue from projectors, screens and so on. So, while Drake is right to note that '[m]uch discussion of screen performance … assumes that the ontological ground from which the performance grows is the body of the performer' (2006: 87), it is also the case that a not insignificant amount of discussion, especially in more specialised venues, tends to pay little heed to actors and acting and to set its sights on cameras and camerawork and on those who presumably 'authorise' them, often from a remove, that is to say, directors as *auteurs*. Wojcik, who insists that 'discussions of film acting must find a way to account for the role of technology in performance', also notes that 'most auteurist critics, blind perhaps to actor labor, focus on … visual style' (2006: 80, 73), as is the case with Martel's *The Holy Girl*.

With respect to *Thou Shalt Not Covet*, however, it is arguably as difficult to be blind to actor labour – which Landa appears to deliver so easily – as it is to be attentive to either the role of the director or of technology. For in this technically conventional film what most memorably marks – or 'authorises' – the film is the actor, not the director as *auteur*, let alone the camera as cinematic principle, and to such a degree that it is more convincing to speak of Landa's film than Fernández's film. Be that as it may, Landa's Antón is a creature not entirely of nature made. The performance – by an exemplar of the everyman – of a figure seemingly *contra natura* exists, that is, because it has been recorded, mechanically 'massaged', as Wojcik puts it with respect to the 'synthetic quality of sound design and its effacement' (2006: 80). For Wojcik, '[a]bsent such technological information … an analysis of film acting would have to account for the representation through careful description, without resorting to guesswork or assumptions about origin'; and yet, as she well knows, such information is 'rarely made readily available except in anecdotal examples' (2006: 80) and description, no matter how 'careful', is inevitably partial. Not surprisingly, then, '[m]ost analyses of screen performance tend to scrutinize performances as texts and actors in terms of … their relationship to dominant discourses of gender, sexuality, or ethnicity' (Drake 2006: 84). This is precisely what I have done in the previous section and precisely why I have interrupted that analysis, that reading, with the present theoretical excursus, formulated, furthermore, under the (in)human sign of the queer.

Theory has its limits, of course. For if it is true, as Cynthia Baron contends, that film 'performances are not grounded in some noncinematic principle' (2007: 33), it is also true that they are often perceived, and performed, as if they were, as if the theatricality of Landa's performance captured something 'true' about gay men more generally or, for that matter, as if the (deliberate) tentativeness of María Alché's performance of Amalia, the 'holy girl', captured something 'true' about adolescent girls. For all their undeniable differences, both Landa and Alché, Antón and Amalia, no less than the directors, the crew, the other actors and the spectators, are preceded and exceeded by ideas and images that tend to efface their status *as* ideas and images and that cast perception, often imperceptibly, as misperception and performance, no matter how 'sincere' or 'natural', as performance. In other words, along with the mechanical 'nature' of cinema that remits to cameras and other inanimate instruments, there is its ideological 'nature' that remits to human ideas and images that include, to loop the loop, the dehumanised and the inhuman. Together, they serve to denaturalise nature even as they retain it as trace, effect or ungraspable horizon. Accordingly, while 'the fragmentary and highly mediated, collaborative nature of film performance is, like other technologically based aspects of cinema, effaced' (Wojcik 2006: 78), particularly in mainstream, commercial cinema, the pre-scripted, non-volitional nature of film performance is, like other ideologically structured aspects of cinema, also effaced. The ensuing double effacement of technology and ideology, of the mediated nature of nature itself, is, of course, one of the hallmarks of the aforementioned mainstream, commercial cinema, an effacement that distinguishes it from its more minoritarian, arthouse counterpart, in which the effacement is itself effaced, that is to say, laid bare.[2] The distinction has long acquired the force of a binary opposition that rivals, *toutes proportions gardées*, that of masculinity and femininity or heterosexuality and homosexuality. Put too axiomatically, any queering of the latter (which refuses to equate queerness with homosexuality or even with LGBT formations more amply, however insistent the overlaps) must also include, in the realm of cinema, a queering of the former.

It is at this juncture – after having signalled the contortions of the queer, both identitarian and inhuman; the double effacement of technology and ideology; and the fissured, manipulable relations between the performative and the real – that I shall move to consider some images and sounds that turn *aside* and run *athwart* of the spectator, diverting attention from the 'easily recognisable' situations and figures of gendered and sexual identity that come at the spectator *head-on*, all flashy and brash in the guise of Landa's Antón Gutiérrez. That these situations and figures endure as recognisable leads Chris Perriam, drawing on Melero, to note how the generally regressive charge of films like *Thou Shalt Not Covet* returns in a mode of retro-branding in 'commercially oriented gay- and, less often, lesbian-themed feature films that continue to be popular into the twenty-first century' (2013: 43). Although he admits that the 'effect of these entertainments is not unequivocally pernicious', Perriam goes on to state that this retro-inflected 'mobilisation is matched or exacerbated, at the extra-filmic level, by a commercial aversion to risk and innovation' (2013: 43). Taking Perriam's reference to risk and innovation as an implicit invitation to a remobilisation of the queer in a manner that *troubles* the framework of human sexual non-normativities, I will, as promised, supplement and complicate my reading of *Thou Shalt Not Covet* by bringing into play a diametrically different film, Martel's *The Holy Girl*.

The pairing, which I have already styled as deliberately disjunctive, borders, admittedly, on the extravagant. But disjunction and extravagance are very much to the point. For to pair an anodyne mid-twentieth-century comedy from dictatorial Spain in which verbal and gestural expression is 'overstated' or 'overacted' and a critically celebrated late-twentieth-century drama from post-dictatorial Argentina in which expression is so 'understated' or 'underacted' as to verge on the expressionless, is to cross, perhaps indeed to twist, longstanding binaries whose crossing and twisting are crucial to the very sense of queerness that I have so fitfully been deploying. My aim in doing so is to insist on the bent of queer, to resist its ironic straightening into something always already gay, lesbian, bisexual or transgendered, that is to say, to thwart normative expectations – including, critically, newly normative anti-normative expectations by which the queer would be styled, always already, as anything *but* heterosexual. Like Luciano and Chen, I am 'wary of divorcing "queer" thought entirely from located histories of precarity, of reducing "queerness" to simply a movement of thought, or of affirmation or negation' (2015: 194–5). But, also like them, I am interested in attending to what is at stake in a proliferation of signs not only of identity, but also of positionality, not only of agency, actoring and subjectivity, but also of situation, stance and style: those of the camera as well as of the body, of the machine as well as of the flesh.

Underacting in *The Holy Girl*

She stands stationary amidst other adolescent girls, her brow slightly furrowed, her eyes slightly glaring and her mouth slightly downturned, somewhere between a frown and a pout. At first, she is barely distinguishable from the others, only the normative centrality of her position and the deep red of her jumper marking her, ever so subtly, as a point of attention. Centrally positioned, her head is nonetheless slightly cropped, out of the frame, as if something about her resisted full representation, as if she could not quite fit in. She is silent, though the sound of a song fills the space, a song that is sung, as a cut reveals, by a young woman who struggles for breath because she is struggling to keep from crying. The scene takes place in a classroom, though sounds from other parts of the building and from the street, muted footfalls and muffled conversations, penetrate it, opening it to other voices, other spaces, and punctuating if not puncturing both the singing and the audition of the song. Within the room, the song is also interspersed, if not interrupted, by murmurs, as the girls pass around what appears to be a photocopied image and speak, in hushed tones, of breath and desire. The girl at the centre of the frame, the one who appears right after the letters of the title float down across a blue background, is Amalia, the young protagonist and 'holy girl' of the title. She is flanked by a number of other girls, but one, who turns out to be her most intimate companion, Josefina (Julieta Zylberberg), her face partially obscured in shadow, stands closest to her and whispers in her ear, first about how the singer lacks air and does not know how to breathe and then, in a scene that occurs a bit later, about how she saw the singer kissing a man older than she and trembling as if riven with epilepsy.

The characters, the actors, the situations, the performances in *The Holy Girl* could scarcely be further removed from those of *Thou Shalt Not Covet*. In that film, a well-known actor pulls out the stops in a boisterous, glossy, multicolour romp; in this film, a little-known actress provides a restrained, at times barely audible study in subtlety. In that film, the actor all but runs away with the script, overshadowing the director; in this film, the director, clearly in control of the nuances of cinematic technique, overshadows – at least in the critical pieces published on the film – not only the young, relatively inexperienced actresses who appear in the opening scene but also the more established professional actors: Mercedes Morán, who plays Amalia's attention-starved mother Helena, Carlos Belloso, who plays the languidly lecherous Dr. Jano, and Alejandro Urdapilleta, who plays Amalia's rather feckless uncle, Freddy. Critics almost unanimously praise Martel for her command of the cinematic craft. Leila Gómez, for instance, refers to Martel's 'extrema sutileza' [extreme subtlety] and her 'cuidado obsesivo en cada toma' [obsessive care with each shot] (2005: 1); Marcos Vieytes declares Martel to be 'una cineaste elegante' [an elegant filmmaker] who avoids 'la vulgaridad de imponerle un sentido único a las imágenes' [the vulgarity of imposing only one meaning to the images (2009: 131). Whatever the play of appearances in the 'Landa vehicle', however unstable its mobilisation of stereotypes, however raucous its humour over time, however slippery its rehearsal of injurious images and situations, in many respects it remains, paradoxically, more constrained than Martel's controlled work, which Pedro Lange-Churión deems an exercise in 'masterful cinematic obliqueness' (2012: 470), but which is in fact so oblique as to skew control and mastery, opening the film up to something *beyond* the grasp of any single subject, that of the *auteur* included.

The dramatic minimalism that for Ana Amado (2006: 51) marks *La ciénaga/The Swamp* (2001), and that also marks *The Holy Girl* and *La mujer sin cabeza/The Headless Woman* (2008), does not mean, however, that singular subjects and identities are not operant. In her three feature films to date, Martel presents a welter of non-normative desires and practices, including insinuated incest, inter-ethnic and inter-generational lesbianism and adolescent heterosexual anal sex. A few critics, notably Deborah Martin, Rosalind Galt and B. Ruby Rich, read Martel's works in relation to queerness or, as Galt puts it, a 'queer sensibility' and a 'queer worldliness' (2013: 63). While Rich, despite making important references to style, tends to focus on identifiable characters and character-driven situations, claiming, in an overview of cinematic production that is not limited to Martel's works, that '[k]idnapping, inchoate lust, rural transgressions, bourgeois accommodations and even street hustling figure in these new films as strong as the shadow figure of *la reina* (the queen) [sic] and the limits of social norms so haunted an earlier generation' (2013: xxvii), Galt and Martin push beyond identitarian categories even as they replay them. Martin, after unrolling stock images of the adolescent as awkward, misfit, weird, uncanny and even monstrous, comes to insist not on full-bodied personages or even their shadows, but on something else, something missing, 'a kind of sensory "gap", the interruption of the normal processes of sending and receiving touch or sound' (2011: 73). Galt, in turn, insists on a 'cinematic queerness that links sexuality and gender both to textual transgression and to a radical politics' and that 'rejects the dominant narrative economies of gay identity in favour of evoking queerness as a question of style' (2013: 64).

Aware that what she presents – rightly, I think – as a liberal view according to which 'the emphasis on style over representation' risks making the queer 'a rhetorical placeholder without material weight' (Galt 2013: 64), Galt argues 'that cinematic style is what enables queer default cinema' (2013: 64). By default cinema, she signals a 'refusal to play by the rules of the game [of neoliberalism] that carries a cultural charge as much as an economic one' (2013: 63). Galt explicitly references Martel's films, along with those of Apichatpong Weerasethakul, as endeavours that 'might not be legible as queer' (2013: 64) within a liberal identitarian framework. For her, 'Martel's films stage queerness obliquely in terms of inchoate opposition and tentative connection. They are not ebullient love stories, coming-out dramas or other such positives narrations of sexual identity' (2013: 66). Nor, for that matter, are they farcical comedies like *Thou Shalt Not Covet* in which offence and injury might be 'reclaimed', over time and with no small dose of spectatorial retro-perversity. Instead, Galt contends, 'they unsettle temporality, identity and relationality, positing hard-to-read possibilities and ambiguous familial relations' (2013: 66). Galt's 'take', with its insistence on the bend, is strikingly similar to what I have been striving to argue by way of a self-consciously circuitous reading shot through with extravagant comparisons and speculative interruptions. But if what Galt takes to be queer about Martel's films 'is their refusal to make sense, their jamming of the gears of social productivity' (2013: 66), it is precisely because they invite us, perhaps in fact compel us, to look askance, not merely in the prominent sense of 'with an attitude or look of suspicion or disapproval' but also in the etymological sense of 'sideways', 'asquint', 'oblique', 'slanting' and 'askew'.

In her film *La ciénaga* (2013), the recurrence of beds in which the members of a family sprawl about in various states of undress, males with females, adults with adolescents and children, suggests something promiscuously domestic, as do the images of indigenous servants, one of whom also lolls about in bed. As in *The Holy Girl*, camera angle and *mise-en-scène* are marshalled to queer effect – the otherwise dominant heterosexual dynamics of the storylines notwithstanding. In the words of Lange-Churión, *La ciénaga*, '[r]ather than featuring directly traditional images of the marginalised other in Argentine society', presents them 'askance, obliquely, through the point of view of her main characters: white women who belong to the decadent upper classes of provincial Argentina' (2012: 468). Adrián Veaute also notes the tendency for something off-kilter or 'sesgado' in Martel's films (2005), a tendency that is accentuated by her use of acousmatic sound, that is to say, a sound whose source remains obscured. Developed by Michel Chion as a special sort of off-screen sound, the function of the acousmatic has been sounded out, at least in part, by Gonzalo Aguilar (2006), María José Punte (2011), Martin (2011) and others in relation to Martel's film. Special and unsettling as it may be, the acousmatic is uncannily *common* in cinema; indeed, as Wojcik persuasively notes, 'virtually all sound is technically acousmatic in production and postproduction' (2006: 75). In *The Holy Girl*, the acousmatic is rendered reticular by way of a musical instrument that is played – or in Spanish 'touched' – in a manner that is at once physical and imaginary. The instrument in question is a thereminvox or etherphone, an electronic musical instrument that is activated without direct physical contact; the fingers move as if on air. As such, the thereminvox plays with the more established sense of the acousmatic: once the instrument is finally 'shown' on the street, the source of its strange sound remains at once visible and invisible. But the thereminvox also plays with the sense of the haptic, constituting, in the words of Hugo Ríos, a 'tacto que no toca', a touch that does not touch (2008: 21).

Attentive to the play of the senses in *The Holy Girl*, Ríos recognises that the paradoxes that here proliferate – the visible invisible, the touch that does not touch – conjure forth something mystical (2008: 21), in the double guise of a sensorial immersion and a sensorial transcendence. Not dissimilarly, María José Punte refers to a voice without body that surpasses the screen, the frame and circumscribed space more generally (2011: 9) and that recalls, for her, the voice of the mother, the sonorous, permeable envelope that Kaja Silverman has explored as the acoustic mirror (1998). The resultant space, sonorously surpassed but often cramped and crowded, recalls, in turn, for Cécile François, a metaphorically uterine space (2009–10: 3). Amanda Holmes, for her part, declares that the sound of the thereminvox 'evokes an other-worldliness that has made it attractive for use in science fiction films' (2011: 141). Together, what these various readings point to is a movement across genres, bodies, times, spaces and the senses, the visual sense of 'askance' being supplemented by more tactile senses of 'athwart' and more auditory senses of 'aside'. In its investment in what Forcinito calls a rethinking of the gaze (2006: 109) and in what Ríos presents as a questioning of the 'imperio de la mirada' [the empire of the gaze] (2008: 11), *The Holy Girl*, like Martel's other films, privileges ruptured stories (Lange-Churión 2012: 469) and fragmented montage (François 2009–10: 6). It also disjoins image from sound, which is often saturated, as Martin so beautifully puts it, 'with strange tappings, murmurings, and whispers, often coming from the building itself or from peripheral conversations, with the result that the domestic is perpetually constructed as the site of the unknown' (2011: 62). Though intensely stylised, the strangeness of sounds and the uncanny roil of rumour are amplified on a thematic level, most notably in the form of disturbances such as Ménière's disease or tinnitus – a ringing or tinkling in the ear in the absence of external sound; in other words, a sort of internal acousmatic sound – that affects Amalia's mother, sending her into the troubled care of Dr. Jano, the man quite literally behind the 'holy girl'.

It is not incidental that in *The Holy Girl* ears are often presented in close-up, or that bodies are often clipped, their component parts (heads, limbs, necks) unsettlingly framed and foregrounded, or that backs and backsides are favoured sites for approach and contact. If Amalia first appears in a frontal shot in an attentive attitude of listening that is interrupted by Josefina's whispers, she is later approached from behind, by Dr. Jano *and* the camera, as she listens attentively to the previously mentioned thereminvox that a man plays in the street. Tellingly, the thereminvox first makes its absent presence known in the space of the catechism, right after the instructor who has earlier sung her tearful song of spiritual (and sensual) submission, tells the girls that 'lo importante es estar alertas al llamado de Dios. Esto es la vocación' [the important thing is to be on the alert for the call of God. This is vocation]. Mystified by the eerie, electronic sound, the girls ask what it is and receive as their only answer that it comes from the street. There, in the street, in an open public space that contrasts with the enclosed, relatively private space of the classroom but that is no less crowded, Amalia hears the sound again and, drawn to it, siren-like, watches its invisible activation. It is then that Dr. Jano approaches her from behind and, standing quite still, barely brushes his crotch across her buttocks. Amalia's face is once more a study in understatement. With her head lowered and her brow again furrowed, her face, bathed in intermittent light, suggests what might be read as surprise and confusion mixed with wonder and curiosity. In this critical scene, Amalia appears to experience her calling, her vocation, but, as with so much else in *The Holy Girl*, it comes to her in a synaesthetic manner, an aural annunciation manifested as an anal approximation. The spectre of an anal or pineal eye, so dear to Georges Bataille and part of what Allan Stoekl (1985) has called a vision of excess, imposes itself, ever so suggestively. Excessive speculation aside, as Martin notes, what is clear is that 'Jano watches and approaches Amalia *from behind*, a positioning which she attempts to mimic when approaching him' (2011: 68, emphasis original). Heterosexual as the encounter may be understood to be the approach, the positioning, if styled ever so queerly.

The point is important, for, while Martin, focusing on a long kiss between Amalia and Josefina, writes of 'a lesbian *aporia* in the straight narrative, telling of the further "dangers" to the social order in uncontained, unchannelled adolescent female sexuality' (2011: 64), she also writes that '[t]he relationship between Amalia and Jose like others in the film, is characterised by its tactility' (2011: 64). This tactility is not bound to touch alone, but implicates, in Laura Marks' influential formulation, 'the eyes themselves', which 'function like organs of touch' and which tend 'to move over the surface of [their] object rather than to plunge into illusionistic depth' (2000: 162). As cunning and cowardly as Jano's approach may be in normative terms (Jano's name recalls, as critics have noted, Janus, the mythical two-faced guardian of gates, doorways and thresholds and other points of passage), Amalia experiences it as something extraordinary, as a calling that, far from cancelling the kiss with Josefina, buttresses it. For Jano, two-faced, backsliding being though he is, does not penetrate Amalia; instead, he *grazes* her. The graze, in turn, is what is conveyed to the gaze, and in a way that heightens its textural, ever so lightly tactile, charge. The gendered and sexual identity of the actors, the characters, is no doubt significant here, as significant as are the connections between lesbianism and queerness, but what *The Holy Girl* suggests is that they may be supplemented with other connections, other contacts, that range from the heterosexual and the same-sexual or lesbian to the object-orientated and the non-human. With respect to Martel's film, this means including, within the arc of queerness, the acts of heterosexual anal penetration between Josefina and her boyfriend (whose discovery leads Josefina to disclose Amalia's 'secret' with Jano) as well as the more general and formally inflected penchant for shots of bodies approached from behind, rear-viewed in a deliberate skewing of the conventional predisposition for the face.

Amalia's mother, Helena, with whom Amalia is locked in an unacknowledged sexual rivalry for Jano's attention, is also approached from behind, by the camera and hence by the spectator. This posterior approach, or rear view, is a positional leitmotiv in the film, and further undercuts the primacy of the gaze: by way of a turning away from the face, as site of normative identity, and by way of an emphasis on the graze, the caress, the touch. The fixation on identity, frontally and facially, is part and parcel of what Judith Butler calls 'regulatory regimes' and why she balks at being interpellated as a lesbian, being a lesbian, being 'anything, even for pay' (1991: 13). It is here, as I hurtle towards an impossible conclusion, that I would revisit the tropes of humour, once more in the sense of a flow, seepage or non-containment that raises some serious questions about the solidity or integrity of acting and actors, being and beings. For humour need not be *fixed* as comic or farcical, but may wax and wane melancholy and peevish and apathetic and angry. Humour, flowing into and as humours, may also be mixed, respecting neither laws of gender nor of genre, neither principles of discreteness nor of discretion, according to which, for instance, thou shalt not mix a lowbrow Hollywood-style narrative comedy with a highbrow meditative art piece, the work of a comic actor with the work of a serious *auteur*, or the exploits of a duplicitous middle-aged man with the travails of an ingenuous adolescent girl. Keeping things apart, keeping them straight, misses the *promiscuity of perversion*, that kissing cousin of queerness; it misses, that is, the myriad ways in which queerness dos not stop at some heterosexual limit or even at some human limit, but crosses them, crisscrosses them, with dizzying insistence. As bizarre as it may seem, as contrary to all that is high and low, theoretical and casual, *The Holy Girl* and *Thou Shalt Not Covet Thy Fifth Floor Neighbour*, so undeniably different the one from the other, nonetheless share a querying of the human. For all their differences, they share an engagement in the stylised utterances, gestures and glances, the mediatised objects, stances and situations, by which more subjects than one might think are implicated in something prolifically, promiscuously, perversely queer.

Notes

1 *Thou Shalt Not Covet* and similar films may be purchased in 'specialised' bookshops and websites and have been included in, for instance, the 'Cinema Oh-culto' film festival in Madrid, in which a young gay audience revisits the past; see: http://cinemaohculto.tumblr.com/. I would like to thank the editors for their suggestions.
2 *Thou Shalt Not Covet*, which stands as one of the biggest box office hits of Spanish cinematic history, is unquestionably a mainstream film, whatever problems it reportedly had with Francoist censorship. With its ostensible flouting of norms and its ostentatious flaunting of stereotypes, its complexity, such as it is, is decidedly more of a narrative and thematic than a formal and technical order. *Thou Shalt Not Covet* effaces, that is, both technological fissures and ideological gaps, a double effacement that may help to account for its popularity, but only in part. For its popularity is also bound up, *it would seem*, in exploiting the play across – and with – other fissures and gaps, significantly, those of the actor or performer and character. As Drake observes, '[n]ot all screen performance is as committed to closing the gap between performer and character. Some forms of performance are designed to disturb or put aside questions of narrative coherence and motivation, in order to concentrate on spectacle – the ostentatious presentation of performance' (2006: 93). Drake makes this observation not in relation to avant-garde experimentation or arthouse innovation but in relation to comedy, which he presents as other than naturalistic: '[q]uestions of authenticity – so important to acting discourses – may have little relevance to a comedic performance, or a spectacular stunt, or a song-and-dance routine' (2006: 93). For Drake, it bears noting, authenticity is part of 'journalistic discourse',

one of a number of 'vernacular critical terms' that include believability and sincerity (2006: 85). And yet, it is just the vernacular, popular and non-specialised that *Thou Shalt Not Covet*, a non-naturalistic, mainstream comedy suffused with camp theatricality, most intensely engages. At least two contradictions ensue: the film effaces technological fissures and ideological gaps, but exploits the gap between performer and character and, indeed, *within* a character; it addresses the spectator directly, straightforwardly, by way of stereotypes and easily recognisable referents, but partakes in an 'ostentatious presentation of performance' in which identity, twisted and troubled, is played to comic, or farcical, effect.

References

Aguilar, Gonzalo (2006) *Otros mundos: Ensayo sobre el nuevo cine argentino*, Buenos Aires: Santiago Arcos Editor.

Amado, Ana (2006) 'Velocidades, generaciones y utopías: A propósito de *La ciénaga*, de Lucrecia Martel', *ALCEU*, 6.12: 48–56.

Baron, Cynthia (2007) 'Acting Choice/Filmic Choices: Rethinking Montage and Performance', *Journal of Film and Video*, 59.2: 32–40.

Benjamin, Walter (1968) 'The Work of Art in the Age of Mechanical Reproduction', in *Illuminations*, trans. Harry Zohn, New York: Schocken, pp. 217–51.

Butler, Judith (1991) 'Imitation and Gender Insubordination', in *Inside/Out: Lesbian Theories, Gay Theories*. New York: Routledge, pp. 13–31.

Drake, Philip (2006) 'Reconceptualizing Screen Performance', *Journal of Film and Video* 58.1–2, 84–94.

Dyer, Richard (1979) *Stars*, London: British Film Institute.

Forcinito, Ana (2006) 'Mirada cinematográfica y género sexual: Mímica, erotismo y ambigüedad en Lucrecia Martel', *Chasqui: Revista de Literatura Latinoamericana*, 35.2, 109–30.

François, Cécile (2009–10) 'El cine de Lucrecia Martel: Una estética de la opacidad', *Espéculo: Revista de Estudios Literarios*, 43, 1–14, https://pendientedemigracion.ucm.es/info/especulo/numero43/lucmarte/html, accessed 15 June 2015.

Galt, Rosalind (2013) 'Default Cinema: Queering Economic Crisis in Argentina and Beyond', *Screen* 54.1, 62–81.

Geraghty, Christine (2000) 'Re-examining Stardom: Questions of Texts, Bodies and Performance', in Christine Gledhill and Linda Williams (eds), *Reinventing Film Studies*, London: Arnold, pp. 183–201.

Gómez, Leila (2005) 'El cine de Lucrecia Martel: La Medusa en lo recóndito', *Ciberletras: Revista De Crítica Literaria y de Cultura*, 7, n.p., www.lehman.edu/faculty/guinazu/ciberletras/v13/gomez.htm, accessed 17 June 2015.

Holmes, Amanda (2011) 'Landscape and the Artist's Frame in Lucrecia Martel's *La ciénaga/The Swamp* and *La niña santa/The Holy Girl*', in Carolina Rocha and Cacilda Rêgo (eds), *New Trends in Argentine and Brazilian Cinema*, Bristol: Intellect, pp. 131–46.

Lange-Churión, Pedro (2012) 'The Salta Trilogy: The Civilised Barbarism in Lucrecia Martel's Films', *Contemporary Theatre Review*, 22.4, 467–84.

Luciano, Dana and Mel Y. Chen (2015) 'Introduction: Has the Queer Ever Been Human?', *GLQ: A Journal of Lesbian and Gay Studies*, 21.2–3, 183–207.

Marks, Laura U. (2000) *The Skin of the Film: Intercultural Cinema, Embodiment, and the Senses*, Durham: Duke Univerity Press.

Martin, Deborah (2011) 'Wholly Ambivalent Demon-Girl: Horror, the Uncanny and the Representation of Feminine Adolescence in Lucrecia Martel's *La niña santa*', *Tesserae: Journal of Iberian and Latin American Studies* 17.1, 59–76.

Marcello, Starr A. (2006) 'Performance Design: An Analysis of Film Acting and Sound Design', *Journal of Film and Video*, 58.1–2, 59–70.

Melero, Alejandro (2010) *Placeres ocultos: Gays y lesbianas en el cine español de la transición*, Madrid: Notorious Ediciones.

Mira, Alberto (2004) *De Sodoma a Chueca: Una historia cultural de la homosexualidad en España en el siglo XX*, Barcelona: Editorial Egales.

Perriam, Chris (2013) *Spanish Queer Cinema*, Edinburgh: Edinburgh University Press.

Punte, María José (2011) 'Mirada y voz en el cine de Lucrecia Martel. Aportes desde la teoría crítica feminista', *Letras: Revista de la Facultad de Filosofía y Letras de la Pontificia Universidad Católica Argentina*, 63–4, 101–13.

Recio, José Manuel (1992) *Biografía y películas de Alfredo Landa*, Barcelona: Centro de Investigaciones Españolas e Hispanoamericanas.

Rich, B. Ruby (2013) *New Queer Cinema: The Director's Cut*, Durham: Duke University Press.

Ríos, Hugo (2008) 'La poética de los sentidos en los filmes de Lucrecia Martel', *Atenea*, 28, 9–22.

Sedgwick, Eve Kosofsky (1993) *Tendencies*, Durham: Duke University Press.

Silverman, Kaja (1988) *The Acoustic Mirror: The Female Voice in Psychoanalysis and Cinema*, Bloomington: Indiana University Press.

Stoekl, Allan (ed.) (1985) *Visions of Excess; Selected Writings, 1927–1939*, by Georges Bataille, trans. Allan Stoekl, Carl R. Lovitt and Donald M. Leslie, Jr, Minneapolis: University of Minnesota Press.

Taylor, Aaron (2012) 'Introduction: Acting, Casually and Theoretically Speaking', in Aaron Taylor (ed.), *Theorizing Film Acting*, New York: Routledge, pp. 1–16.

Veaute, Adrián (2005) 'Sesgar el discurso civilizado: Una aproximación a la idea de barbarie en el cine argentino', in Ana Laura Lusnich (ed.), *Civilización y barbarie en el cine argentino y latinoamericano*, Buenos Aires: Editorial Biblos, pp. 99–110.

Vieytes, Marcos (2009) 'Lucrecia Martel: La mujer del cuadro', in Jaime Peña Pérez (ed.), *Historias extraordinarias: Nuevo cine argentino (1999–2008)*, Madrid: T&B, pp. 129–38.

Wojcik, Pamela Robertson (ed.) (2004) *Movie Acting: The Film Reader*, New York and London: Routledge.
Wojcik, Pamela Robertson (2006) 'The Sound of Film Acting', *Journal of Film and Video*, 58.1–2, 71–83.
Zucker, Carole, (1990) *Making Visible the Invisible: An Anthology of Original Essays on Film Acting*, Metuchen, NJ and London: The Scarecrow Press.

8

The future of nostalgia: revindicating Spanish actors and acting in and through *Cine de barrio*

Duncan Wheeler

In the list of the most-watched films on Spanish television in 2011, only two from the top hundred emerged from within the national cinema industry: *Fuga de cerebros/Brain Drain* (Fernando González Molina, 2009) and *Agora* (Alejandro Amenábar, 2009). If we carry on down the list, the next five most popular domestic films were all over forty years old and broadcast as part of the *Cine de barrio* [neighbourhood cinema] slot: *La ciudad no es para mí/The City is Not For Me* (Pedro Lazaga, 1966), *Abuelo, made in Spain/Old Man Made in Spain* (Pedro Lazaga, 1969), *Esa voz es una mina/That Voice Is a Goldmine* (Luis Lucia, 1956), *Ha llegado un ángel/An Angel Has Appeared* (Luis Lucia, 1961) and *La hermana San Sulpicio/Sister Saint Sulpicio* (Luis Lucia, 1952) – all achieved higher viewing figures than *Volver* (Pedro Almodovár, 2006) (Telemanía, 2012). This has been a recurrent pattern since 1995, when Televisión Española (TVE) – the state broadcasting channel – first introduced the slot, which complements the screening of a classic national film, almost exclusively made between the 1950s and the death of General Francisco Franco, with an introductory section, comprising archival footage and/or a discussion with a practitioner. According to a letter sent in by one viewer, 'hacen ustedes un programa necesario; … hay una labor de recuperación de nuestros CÓMICOS, de esa gente que estaba hecha de otra pasta y que no tienen nada que envidiar a los grandes actores británicos' [You make a necessary programme; … there is a labour of recuperation, of our ACTORS, of those people who were made from a different mould and who have nothing to be envious of British actors for].[1]

As Annette Kuhn notes in a statement on British cinema, 'for an understanding of cultural memory, it is important to attend to the ways in which memory is produced in the activity of telling stories about the past, personal or shared; to the construction and narration of these memory stories; and in the present instance to the ways in which cinema figures in and shapes these memories' (2002: 9). In a manner akin to the way that Spaniards sometimes describe a situation as being 'de Almodóvar' [straight out of Almodóvar], it is a symptom of the programme's ubiquity and popularity that 'es de *Cine de barrio*' [straight out of *Cine de barrio*] has now entered the popular lexicon. While the original demographic for the programme was middle-aged and elderly viewers, the shows and the films it encompasses have become increasingly popular among younger viewers: hipsters in the Malasaña area of Madrid or El Raval in Barcelona can be seen wearing T-shirts of Paco Martínez Soria – the grandfather figure who specialised in *paleto* [country bumpkin] characters – alongside the names of some of his iconic film titles: *Abuelo, Made in Spain* and *La ciudad no es para mí*; a contestant in the second series of Spanish *Big Brother* claimed that another of Martínez Soria's star vehicles, *El turismo es un gran invento/Tourism is a Great Invention* (Pedro Lazaga, 1968), was his favourite film. This is both a product and cause of a marked nostalgic turn in Spanish cultural production: in a democratic habitus that has traditionally fetishised all that is modern, new and European, the mnemonic ethics and aesthetics of *Cine de barrio* clearly warrants explanation and contextualisation.

Building upon my previous work that has sought to demonstrate how and why the blanket dismissal of Francoist popular culture has been instrumental in the fetishisation of the *auteur* (coded as male) and the denigration of the star (coded as female) (see Wheeler 2014), my aim in this chapter is to locate *Cine de barrio* materially, ideologically and culturally within both a changing media-scape and a critical heterodoxy that has systematically sidelined the discussion and appreciation of performance in film. This discussion will provide the framework to then probe two major issues: the specific nature of the relationship between actors and their audiences; and the way in which this is forged through a myriad of forms not always clearly visible to critics working outside of Spain. My contention is that the programme forges a meaningful and sustained discourse on performance in the national cinema, while also undertaking an archaeological task of rediscovering the kind of popular films rarely included in retrospectives or film festivals.

Towards a genealogy of *Cine de barrio*

In July 1995, *Cine de barrio*, hosted and directed by José Manuel Parada, was aired for the first time on TVE2.[2] Viewing figures were better than anticipated and the programme was promoted to TVE1 in October of the same year. The films selected for inclusion did not encompass the canonical *auteur*-films that emerged from the Nuevo Cine Español [New Spanish Cinema] but were, rather, examples of the so-called Viejo Cine

Español [Old Spanish Cinema], commercial comedies and light dramas that dominated the domestic box office for virtually the duration of the dictatorship but rarely travelled abroad or gained prominence in written accounts of the national cinema. Parada continued a tradition whereby the closest approximation to a discourse on acting and performance in Spain has come predominantly from journalists rather than academics. In 1974, Antonio D. Olano published *Estrellas y stars*, which comprised studies of individual actresses that complemented interviews with analyses that combined industrial and artistic considerations; more recently, Marcos Ordóñez – arguably Spain's most knowledgeable and articulate theatre critic – published two books on Tony Leblanc and Alfredo Landa respectively (1999, 2008). Although actors in Spain had not traditionally penned autobiographies, there has been a post-1975 boom (see Ríos Carratalá 2001), with most being either officially co-authored or ghostwritten by authors frequently with a background in journalism.

As early as 1962, an official state publication lamented the kind of films promoted by prior legislation as being somewhat 'increíblemente el tipo de cine ramplón y provinciano que más en desacuerdo estaba con el patrón vigente en el mundo' [incredibly the type of coarse and provincial cinema that could not be more distant from dominant global trends] (Vizcaíno Casas 1962: 31); a book published in 1976, and sardonically titled *30 años de cine al alcance de todos los españoles/30 Years of Cinema in Reach of All Spaniards*,[3] effectively provided a blueprint for most subsequent scholarship on Spanish cinema, focussing almost exclusively on dissident films and dedicating just three pages to the purportedly anachronistic popular cinema (Hernández and Revuelta 1976: 76–8). Mariano Ozores, a prolific director of over one hundred films of the type frequently included in *Cine de barrio*, claims that, following her appointment as Director-General of Cinema, Pilar Miró vowed that he should be prohibited from receiving state subsidies because he made 'cine para fontaneros' [cinema for plumbers] (Ozores 2002: 278). The films chosen for *Cine de barrio* are, as we will see, far more heterogeneous than the detractors of this 'cine ramplón y provinciano' would have us believe, while the choice of programme title can be interpreted as a pre-emptive retort against those who decry the popular: the *cines de barrio* were a natural habitat for plumbers, and programmed with their tastes in mind.

In the later decades of the Franco regime, there was greater variation in prices in different cinemas than there is today, with tickets costing anywhere between 5 and 20 pesetas in 1965 (Barreiro 1999: 45). Popular films had sufficient commercial clout to premiere in city-centre cinemas before being transferred to the kind of fleapit or neighbourhood cinemas that Almodóvar has paid homage to in *¿Qué he hecho yo para* *merecer esto!!/What Have I Done to Deserve This?* (1984) and *La mala educación/Bad Education* (2004), where they would reach the masses of lower-income and frequently semi-literate Spaniards; as the iconic image of Sara Montiel from *Esa mujer/That Woman* (Mario Camus, 1969) in the latter Almodóvar film suggests (see D'Lugo 2009), it was actors that generally functioned as the star attractions to bring audiences into the cinematic auditoriums. Alberto Elena (2001) has, for example, examined how vehicles for Joselito – a child star and singing sensation of the 1950s and 1960s, whose 'films negotiated the passage between the moral tones of *cine religioso* [religious cinema] and the colour and light ushered in by Marisol's films later that decade' (cited in Wright 2013: 10–11) – premiered in major Madrid cinemas, but would find their main audience in rural or local cinemas.

Following contractual and personal arguments between José Parada and TVE, he was replaced at the end of 2003 by Carmen Sevilla (b. 1930), the actress formerly known as 'la novia de España' [Spain's bride]. According to José Aguilar and Miguel Losada, 'Carmen era de ese tipo de estrellas que conectaban inmediatamente con el gran público por su frescura, su alegría, su capacidad para transportar a otros mundos más agridulces que el gris y plano que en él que [sic] les tocaba vivir' [Carmen was one of those kind of stars who immediately connects with the general public through her freshness, her happiness, and her ability to transport them to more bittersweet worlds than the grey and plain one they inhabited] (Aguilar and Losada 2008: 9). As Terenci Moix notes, 'no hubo tómbola, festival benéfico, sopa para el pobre o cocido para huérfanos que no contase con la copla de Carmencita' [no prize draw, benefit concert, soup kitchen or stew for orphans was complete without a *copla* from little Carmen] (1993: 138); hence, the bathos of *Plácido/Placido* (Luis García Berlanga, 1961) is encapsulated by the fact that the promised appearance of Sevilla at a gala dinner for the 'Sienta un pobre en tu mesa' [Sit a poor person at your table] campaign never materialises.

Having previously appeared as a guest on *Cine de barrio*, her arrival as host led to an immediate increase in viewing figures: by early 2004, the programme was regularly attracting around four million viewers and approximately 38 per cent of the screen share (*El País* 2004). Although the show has been attentive to the role of performance from the outset, Sevilla's participation paved the way for actors to take on a more prominent role, commenting that 'es más cinematográfico, le demos más *chance*, más potencia a los actores, actrices, a los que han hecho, a lo que han sido sus vidas, aunque sean viejitos, como yo' [it's more cinematographic, and we've left more to chance, giving more potency to the actors, to the actresses, and to what their lives have been comprised, even if they are now oldies like me] (Sevilla and Herrera 2005: 203). Although consistently popular among audiences, the star's presence was not to everyone's taste. Carlos Boyero, the iconoclastic film critic for *El País*, responded to an intervention by Joselito in the following caustic terms:

> I also feel longing and a deep emotional memory for the neighbourhood cinema, for the now obsolete double bills, of entering into that wonderful refuge at four in the afternoon and coming out at ten, of the first films that I saw in solitude. They were titled *The Horse Soldiers* and *The Man Who Knew Too Much*. That love at first sight has stayed with me ever since, even though I didn't know at the time that it was the directors who make these films and, in these cases, their names were John Ford and Alfred Hitchcock. Although I was just a kid and not discerning in the least, I could never fall in love with those abandoned boys and girls who sang, and wound up finding their place in the sun, of that sentimental kitsch, nor could I with the tastes dictated by the common and popular wisdom for a kind of cinema that was made to measure according to the ethics and aesthetics of that undesirable Spain forged by Franco. (Boyero 2006: 45)[4]

I have cited this critique at length because it takes us to the crux of many of the debates surrounding both *Cine de barrio* and the type of cinema it showcases.

As Núria Triana-Toribio remarks, 'while the VCE [Viejo Cine Español] could operate blissfully unaware of the NCE [Nuevo Cine Español], the latter defines itself against the former' (2006: 93). Boyero's remarks are in fact something of a cliché, as he simply translates this opposition to the international arena, foregrounding his ethical and aesthetic discernment through the Manichean opposition of masculine *auteur* cinema with its feminised 'other', commercial Spanish cinema which, as Sally Faulkner has convincingly argued, was less director-driven and revealed the 'plural nature of authorship' (2006: 2). The most serious and troubling point raised by Boyero is to what extent *Cine de barrio* is guilty of historical revisionism through the celebration of a popular cinema that was, at the very least, often passively compliant with an authoritarian regime. In this regard, a special edition of the programme dedicated to Rocío Durcal following her death in 2006 is seriously problematic in a number of respects. First, the footage of her funeral voyeuristically intrudes on the fragile emotions of her bereaved friends and family in a manner more habitually associated with private as opposed to state television channels. Second, the presence of a voice-over accompanying archive footage of the singer and actress from the 1960s refers to it as 'un tiempo bello' [a beautiful time]. This impression is bolstered by the fact that *Cine de barrio* frequently incorporates archive footage from NO-DO – the official Spanish newsreel service, projected in cinemas before the commencement of the main feature – while pursuing an editorial policy reminiscent of celebrity and/or women's magazines of the late dictatorship period, which removes any comments by interviewees that might be construed as critical or cause offence.

Although this image of the film community – and, by implication, the nation – as one big happy family is clearly tendentious and misleading, neither does the Nuevo Cine Español nor the critical discourse that surrounds it provide an accurate corrective: 'conventional accounts of the political opposition to the regime tend to exaggerate both the presence and the impact of dissenting students, workers, and so on' (Townson 2007: 17). It is, of course, possible to interpret ostensible apoliticism as one of Francoism's most calculated political triumphs; this has been the line developed by a number of scholars in relation to Spain's tourist boom and nascent mass culture in the years following Manuel Fraga's appointment as Minister of Tourism and Information in 1962. Justin Crumbaugh has, for example, written extensively on how and why, 'by the late 1960s, Spanish mass culture had laid the symbolic grounds for citizens to be, similarly, at once blindly obedient and sadistically hedonistic' (2009: 93). According to this vision, commercial cinema of the 1960s and 1970s both documented and shaped this incipient form of surreptitious authoritarianism. While it is possible, and even desirable, to read these commercial narratives against the grain to locate potentially albeit frequently unwitting subversive content,[5] there can be no doubt that filmmakers' prime intention was to make a living: they were hardly likely to overtly bite the hands that feed, and they were at least passively complicit with new forms of governance.

This does not, however, imply that the films necessarily concur with this paradigm in a monolithic or uniform fashion. *En un lugar de la Manga/In a Place in La Manga* (Mariano Ozores, 1970) has, for example, many of the hallmarks of a typical Manolo Escobar star vehicle, with a self-consciously folkloric contrast between the traditional *galán* [leading man] and the onslaught of Northern European tourists. There are, however, darker undertones, as the protagonist is the only one of his neighbours unwilling to sell his plot to developers, not only because he suspects that modernisation will mercilessly sweep away the place he loves alongside his memories, but also due to fears that digging it up will reveal family secrets about his grandfather's actions in the Civil War. From a twenty-first-century perspective, the most problematic aspect of *En un lugar de la Manga* is in fact its gender politics: the lead female protagonist played by the young, bubbly and attractive Concha Velasco is desperate to marry an unattractive middle-aged man. Asymmetrical pairings of this kind would be repeated *ad nauseam* in films such as *El arte de casarse/The Art of Getting Married* (Jorge Feliu and José María Font, 1966), in which the actress was cast alongside Alfredo Landa, 'the unofficial symbol of the average Spaniard' (Vivancos 2012: 44; see also Delgado and Epps, chapters 7 and 15 in this volume). It is perhaps not surprising that objections of this kind have only been intermittently aired given that the repudiation and feminisation of the Viejo Cine Español have been frequent bedfellows. In more general terms, although we ought to reserve the right to censure *Cine de barrio* for its generally anodyne depictions of a dictatorial past, it also presents us with an excellent opportunity to reassess the sociological and aesthetic values of a popular cinema, the existence of which has often been lamented more frequently than it has been studied.

Actors and audiences, then and now

The combination of the ongoing financial crisis and the loss of revenue from advertising – which José Luis Rodríguez Zapatero's Socialist government banned from the state broadcasting channels in 2009 – has meant that *Cine de Barrio* is now more reliant than ever on the presence of actors and in-house archive footage. The set, designed to resemble a brightly lit and somewhat kitsch living room, is assembled on Monday afternoons, where the episode for the following week is shot generally in the two-hour slot between 4.00 p.m. and 6.00 p.m. Francisco Quintanar, the director of the programme since 2005, prepares a script in advance for the presenter, and provides briefing notes for the invited guests. Concha Velasco's verbal articulacy, alongside her popularity amongst colleagues, made her an ideal replacement for Sevilla, from whom she took over in early 2011. Although Quintanar can speak into her earpiece during filming, his interventions are far less frequent than they were during her predecessor's tenure, and her recruitment has ensured that a number of Spain's most respected actors, such as Sacristán, who had previously been reluctant to be interviewed for *Cine de Barrio*, have now become frequent visitors to the studio in Prado del Rey (Figure 9). This is in spite of the fact that guests are no longer paid, helping to explain why so many appear when they have a new product to promote.

In contrast to many of her contemporaries, Velasco is accustomed to direct sound as a result of her work in theatre and live television, a habit that has been lost or, in some cases, never learned amongst many Spanish stars. Alfredo Landa claims in his autobiography that Velasco and he broke with prevailing conventions in *Historias de la televisión/*

Figure 9 Concha Velasco discusses *Amor bajo cero* with Tony Leblanc on *Cine be barrio* (14 January 2012). RTVE.

Television Stories (José Luis Sáenz de Heredia, 1965) by physically and orally responding to each other in shot/reverse-shot dialogues, at a time whereby post-synch sound allowed actors to disappear to the bar while their interlocutor was filmed delivering their lines: 'Si te fijas, en muchas películas de entonces parece que los cómicos, de repente, se quedasen alelados, con mirada soñadora' [If you pay close attention, in many films from that time, it looks as if the actors suddenly come over all stupid with a dreamy expression] (cited in Ordóñez 2008: 128). Although this anecdote, which provides one explanation for the almost amateur-like nature of a number of *cine de barrio* films, hardly provides a flattering portrait of the acting profession in 1960s Spain, it does nevertheless bear further testament to the fact that, even though she might be reading from someone else's script, be it in a film or on television, Velasco is no mere puppet on a string and that her professionalism and talent come to bear on the final product.

One explanation for the excessive comic physicality of the *cine de barrio* films is that the use of non-direct sound and engagement with autochthonous theatrical traditions both encouraged actors and stars to perform at least as much through their bodies as through their words (see Whittaker, chapter 5 in this volume). If this is the case, then it seems logical to employ corporeal analysis as a means by which to detect and describe the delight taken in the physical rotundity of actors such as Antonio Garisa or Rafaela Aparicio. Lina Morgan's appearance in revue-like films such as *La tonta del bote/The Girl is a Complete Fool* (Juan de Orduña, 1970) and *Dos chicas de revista/Two Revue Girls* (Mariano Ozores, 1972) similarly exploits a combination of dextrous physical and verbal tomfoolery through which she self-consciously distances herself from the role of the traditional voluptuous vedette. Landa undoubtedly construes his craft in physical terms:

> Excess doesn't bother me, because I always think there's a way to tone it down, especially if there is a good director. In contrast, if I enter in a more muted tone, I find it terribly difficult to then raise it. Look at virtually any of my comedies and you'll see I always have a moment in which I lose my temper completely. Losing it completely and eating enthusiastically are two things that I do bloody well. (Cited in Ordóñez 2008: 126).[6]

In fact, what unites ostensibly disparate performance styles and star personas from Morgan to Landa is that actors are constantly making a spectacle of themselves.

On the one hand, an irrepressible physicality and ostensible lack of restraint has been the source of much of the ridicule to which *cine de barrio* has been subjected. Conversely, however, this excessive acting style is also at the root of a very popular form of pathos and tragicomedy which is artfully deployed in a number of performances and films. In *Vente a Alemania, Pepe/Come to Germany, Pepe* (Pedro Lazaga, 1971), the character played by Landa is tempted away from Spain because he thinks he will be able to make his fortunes abroad. The quixotic nature of this belief is frequently enacted through the humiliation of physical labour culminating in his hairy stout body literally being displayed in a shop window alongside an Apollonian Germanic figure as the 'before and after' advertisement for a shaving product. The frequently undiagnosed spectres of modernisation are also presciently depicted in *Historias de la televisión*, which reunited Velasco and Tony Leblanc – following their frequent pairing up in earlier films such as *Amor bajo cero/Love Below Zero* (Ricardo Blasco, 1960) and *Las chicas de la Cruz Roja/ Red Cross Girls* (Rafael J. Salvia, 1958) – on a new dating programme in which they have to ensure a number of challenges and humiliations in order to procure prized consumer goods; Leblanc's character being severely injured as he is forced to dive into a shallow swimming pool from increasingly greater heights is as apt a metaphor for the frustrated desire to physically and psychically transcend the shackles of Francoism as the repeatedly thwarted attempts by the character played by López Vázquez in *La cabina/The Telephone Box* (Antonio Mecero, 1972).

As Joan Ramón Resina notes, during the Transition, 'the past became a country where old people had once lived: an irrelevance' (2000: 92); as a result, celebrated performers either had to reinvent themselves or they were rendered invisible. Leblanc, arguably Spain's finest comic actor, disappeared from cinema screens for decades before making his return as the eponymous anti-hero's father in *Torrente, el brazo tonto de la ley/ Torrente, the Dumb Arm of the Law* (Santiago Segura, 1998). If nothing else, *Cine de barrio* has punctured this historical amnesia and reverted a linear chronology – by which films and actors from the dictatorship disappeared from view – in an act of historical revisionism, which has gained momentum since the mid-1990s. With the very occasional exception, such as Mario Camus, actors have moved with far greater ease than directors between popular and reified traditions of Spanish filmmaking. The traditional narrative in Spanish cinema history is that comic *cine de barrio* actors have been redeemed by their subsequent serious roles.[7] *Cine de barrio* provides us with the raw materials to begin to flesh out alternative historiographies of Spanish cinema, which might, for example, develop a methodological approach capable of reversing (pre-)existing hierarchies to suggest that celebrated films of the nascent democracy such as *La colmena/The Beehive* (Mario Camus, 1982) and *Los santos inocentes/The Holy Innocents* (Mario Camus, 1984) do not so much redeem actors such as José Sacristan and Alfredo Landa as they tap into an enviable and ready-prepared talent pool.[8]

A paradigm shift of this kind is beyond the remit of this chapter, but I would nevertheless like to employ *Cine de barrio* as a means to establish some preliminary remarks about acting and stardom that might provide the impetus for such studies in the future. On being invited onto the programme in October 2011 to discuss *Abuelo, made in Spain* with Velasco, Mónica Radall made the following distinctions between appearing in film and television:

> The audience changes a lot. That is to say that, when people see you in the cinema, and you must be aware of this, the screen creates something of a distance in a dark auditorium, and I don't know what. But then on the television you have people that are watching you right now at home, and as such we form part of the family. They think that they know us and that we know them, and they don't realise that we don't know each other.[9]

The fact that the current *Cine de barrio* set is deliberately designed to resemble a living room – and was, for example, even adorned with Christmas decorations and a tree for a screening of *La gran familia/The Great Family* (Fernando Palacios, 1962) on 28 December 2013 – bears testament to this observation, as does the way in which Almodóvar repeatedly returns to watching and discussing television as a form of developing intimate relations in his films (see Smith 2009).

A vital caveat is nevertheless in order. Radall's comments map on more readily to viewing habits of the late as opposed to the mid-twentieth century. Drawing on ethnographic research with cinemagoers from the 1940s and 1950s from the Maravillas (now Malasaña) area of Madrid, Esther Gómez-Sierra notes how 'the space of the *cine de barrio* becomes a gigantic games room, an impossible extension of the home and at the same time an affordable alternative to it' (2004: 95), while even in the 1960s, many Spaniards, especially in rural areas, watched television in the collective environment of *teleclubs* rather than in the privacy of their own homes (see Llorca 1971). A common characteristic of most of the guests invited onto the set of *Cine de barrio* is that their public personas were forged through a myriad of roles in different media; and one of the principal merits of the programme is that it invites us to consider the intertextual nature of their performances.

In an episode broadcast on 10 July 2011 with María José Goyanes – the daughter of the Svengali figure who catapulted Marisol to fame – a montage of clips from television, film and the stage shows how she and Emilio Gutiérrez Caba were repeatedly framed as a hip and passionate young couple over the course of the 1960s. Her male counterpart is best known to Hispanists as the brooding student from *Nueve cartas a Berta/Nine Letters to Bertha* (Basilio Martín Patino, 1966) or as the youngster amongst the embittered veterans of *La caza/The Hunt* (Carlos Saura, 1966), but these hardly exhaust his connotative associations for Spaniards, and neither are they his most representative performances for generations who have grown up with the actor: he appeared as the smiling sexy embodiment of contained adolescent bravura and insecurity in romantic comedies such as *Los chicos del PREU/The Pre-University Kids* (Pedro Lazaga, 1967) and *Las cuatro bodas de Marisol/Marisol's Four Weddings* (Luis Lucia, 1967); pioneered the limits of sexual frankness and nudity – inadvertently providing a prototype for the *destape* films – in *La petición/The Request* (Pilar Miró, 1976) while appearing in *La saga dels Rius/The Rius Saga* (TVE, 1976–77), a historical epic about the amorous and economic interests of a dynasty of industrialists from Barcelona, and one of the first major series to be made in Catalan; and has continued to command attention in prestigious and popular productions such as *La comunidad/Common Wealth* (Álex de la Iglesia, 2000) or as Sabino Fernández Campo, head of the royal household, in the TV mini-series *23-F: el día más difícil del rey/February 23: The King's Toughest Day* (Sílvia Quer, 2009).

Comments made by Dorothy Hobson about the audience's response to William Roache's performance as Ken Barlow since the first episode of Britain's *Coronation Street* (Granada, 1960–) are, I would suggest, in large part, translatable to the career of Gutiérrez-Caba:

> The ability to follow a character from teenage years is unique to the soap opera. It enables the characters to reflect a longer period of development – which also relates to the period known to the audience. It is again the intimate familiarity with both the characters and the period – running contemporaneously with the experiences of the audience – which heightens the unique relationship which the audience has with the form. (2003: 34)

The weekly living-room format of *Cine de barrio*, alongside its invited guests and the film it screens, is redolent of that of a soap opera and what Abigail De Kosnik terms its 'lifelong characters' (2013: 356). The traditional absence of long-running serials in Spain does, admittedly, change the dynamic somewhat: rather than lifelong characters, we have lifelong actors, whose characters frequently maintain continuity albeit under radically different circumstances and across different media. While not stars in the manner of Carmen Sevilla or Marisol, actors such as Gutiérrez Caba are familiar amongst most Spaniards, and have accompanied them throughout their lives, with each performance entering into a symbiotic relationship with both their previous roles and the socio-cultural context in which it is delivered.

According to Paul Julian Smith, '[i]n Spain, unlike in the UK, there is no popular television narrative which has lasted as long as Almodóvar's consistently successful cinematic serial' (2006: 152). As he goes on to say, this ubiquitous serialisation more akin to radio or television than the traditional stand-alone feature film is one of the reasons why the Manchegan director has been critically sidelined at home. It is symptomatic of a common aesthetic idiom that the current theme tune to *Cine de barrio* – Miguel de Molina's 'La bien pagá' – also appears in *¿Qué he hecho yo para mercer esto!!*, and Almodóvar's self-aware engagement with both the aesthetics and actors of *cine de barrio* is fundamental to his forging of an unfolding yet cyclical narrative for multiple generations of Spaniards. *Entre tinieblas/Dark Habits* (1983) can, for example, be seen as a remake of *Sor Citroen/Sister Citroen* (Pedro Lazaga, 1967) filtered through the ethics and aesthetics of *la movida*; Sister Rosa in *Todo sobre mi madre/All About My Mother* (1999) going to El Salvador as a missionary while pregnant and HIV-positive is a similarly postmodern spin on Marisol's escapades as a glamorous nun in *Las cuatro bodas de Marisol*; and Swiss Katia Loritz's appearance as Ingrid Muller, the German pseudo-aristocrat with whom the proletarian husband is besotted in *¿Qué he hecho yo para merecer esto!!* gains additional poignancy and significance for audiences who recall her earlier appearances as an exotic blonde beauty in films such as *Amor bajo cero* and *Las chicas de la cruz roja*. As with soap opera, Almodóvar and *cine de barrio* films rely both on familiarity and intimacy for their affect; their return to perennial themes, stock characters and a stable of actors can be construed as both (self-)plagiarism and a lack of originality or, alternatively, the edifice upon which engagement with specific audiences is built.

Conclusion

Cine de barrio reveals how and why actors have provided an affective link for domestic audiences not always predisposed to embrace their national cinema: its films and stars have supplied the most popular form of national cinematic entertainment for over fifty years. That is not to say that audiences are necessarily undiscriminating in their tastes: viewing figures are highest for comedies starring Manuel Escobar and Paco Martínez Soria, while star vehicles for Raphael and Julio Iglesias – e.g. *Cuando tú no estás/When You Aren't Here* (Mario Camus, 1966) and *La vida sigue igual/Life Remains the Same* (Eugenio Martín, 1969) – which feature risible lead performances, have seen a dip in audience numbers despite the continued popularity of these pop icons. In relation to the films he made in the 1960s, José Sacristán has adopted an intelligent and strategic ambivalence: 'No voy a ser tan estúpido para decir: Oh, todo maravilloso, ni tan hijoputa para decir: ¡Qué bochorno!' [I'm not going to be as stupid as to say: Oh, it was all marvellous, but neither am I going to be such a bastard as to say: How embarrassing!] (cited in Bayón 1995: 36). My intention in this chapter has not been to make any grand claims about the majority of the films featured in *Cine de barrio*: the quality is variable, and I would only voluntarily watch around 10 per cent of the films for a second time. This conclusion can, nevertheless, be seen to reflect positively as well as negatively on the actors who feature in them; as José Luis López Vázquez remarks, '¡También hay que saber "bailar con la más fea"... y salir indemne!' [You also have to know how to dance with the ugliest girl and escape unscathed] (cited in Valencia 2002: 42). The historical precariousness of Spanish cinema at the industrial level also ensures that popular Spanish actors have more mitigating circumstances than, say, Michael Caine or Nicolas Cage, when it comes to participating in films that are not always worthy of their talents.

One collateral benefit of the sheer volume of films in which many *cine de barrio* actors have appeared is that it has facilitated a performative function of affect, which is paramount to take into account in any overarching discussion of Spanish cinema. As the programme transports its audience and hosts back to a time when Spaniards were amongst the most regular cinemagoers in the world, then the translation of a less-*auteur*-driven and more collaborative mode of filmmaking has facilitated a certain degree of reconciliation between national films and their audiences; at the time of writing, *Ocho apellidos vascos/Spanish Affair* (Emilio Martínez Lázaro, 2014) – whose scriptwriters have noted how they were inspired by *Vente a Alemanía, Pepe* (cited in Cobeaga 2014: 56) – has just overtaken *Torrente 2: Misión en Marbella/Torrente 2: Mission in Marbella* (Santiago Segura, 2001) to become the most popular Spanish film of all time in terms of spectators at the domestic box office. The legacy of *cine de barrio* films can be discerned not only in the diegeses of recent successful Spanish comedies such as *La gran familia española/Family United* (Daniel Sánchez Arévalo, 2013) and *Vivir es fácil con los ojos cerrados/ Living is Easy with Eyes Closed* (David Trueba, 2013), but also in a new generation of actors such as Mario Casas, Carmen Machi and Hugo Silva, who have forged multimedia careers and in the process replaced directors as the star attractions for domestic audiences. *Perdiendo el norte/ Losing the Plot* (Nacho G. Velilla, 2015), about young Spaniards emigrating to Germany in search of better standards of living, be they real or perceived, showcases this conflation of traditions and generations: a number of popular twentysomething actors best known from the television share the screen with Almodóvar favourites Machi and Javier Cámara alongside José Sacristán, who effectively reprises and updates his character from *Vente a Pepe, Alemania* in the guise of an irascible but not unlovable emigrant from the 1960s who never returned home and is now suffering the onset of Alzheimer's disease. In other words, discussion in and about *Cine de barrio* not only engages with ongoing debates surrounding historical memory, but also formulates a series of questions that suggest the need to re-evaluate the role of actors and acting in our accounts of the past, present and future of Spanish cinema.

Notes

1 Letter from a viewer to *Cine de barrio* sent on 20 July 2011. I would like to express my gratitude to Francisco Quintanar, the director of *Cine de barrio* for sending me copies of letters sent in by viewers, as well as for inviting me to Prado de Rey on Monday 21 June 2014 to watch an episode being recorded. This visit was invaluable for the preparation of this chapter, while all unreferenced comments about the making of the programme come from my observations, alongside the conversation I had with Quintanar afterwards.

2 For a succinct and balanced overview of *Cine de barrio* during the Parada years, see Smith (2006: 73–9).

3 This is a reference to the fact that 'al alcance de todos los españoles' [within reach of all Spaniards] was the description used to describe the Francoist NO-DO, the official Spanish newsreel service, projected in cinemas before the commencement of the main feature.

4 'Yo también siento añoranza y profunda memoria sentimental de los cines de barrio, de los ya inexistentes programas dobles, de entrar en ese maravilloso refugio a los cuatro de la tarde y salir a las diez, de las primeras películas que vi en soledad. Se titulaban *Misión de audaces* y *El hombre que sabía demasiado*. Aquel flechazo fue para toda la vida, aunque no supiera que los que hacían las películas eran los directores y que en este caso se llamaban John Ford y Alfred Hitchcock. Pero aunque fuera un crío con escaso discernimiento nunca pude enamorarme de los abandonados niños y niñas cantores que acaban encontrando su lugar en el sol, de la caspa sensiblera, de los sabios gustos populares, de un cine concebido a la medida estética y ética de la indeseable España forjada por el Caudillo' (Boyero 2006: 45).

5 Future studies would do well to follow the precedent set by Barry Jordan (2003), in his detailed analysis of Landa's gay masquerade in *No desearás al vecino del quinto/Thou Shalt Not Covet Thy Fifth Floor Neighbour* (Ramón Fernández, 1970), or by Peter Evans (2000) and Sally Faulkner (2006: 27–48) in their respective analyses of *La gran familia*, a perennial Christmas favourite.

6 'No me preocupa el exceso porque pienso que siempre habrá posibilidad de bajarlo, sobre todo si tengo un buen director. En cambio, si entro bajo de tono, me cuesta horrores subirlo. Fíjate que en casi todas mis comedias siempre tengo un momento de cabreo explosivo. Cabrearme a lo grande y comer con ganas son dos cosas que hago cojonudamente' (cited in Ordóñez 2008: 126).

7 Berlanga has, however, interestingly, disputed this belief, which, he claims, has even been internalised by many of the actors themselves (cited in Valencia 2002: 67).

8 From an earlier generation, similar remarks could also be made as regards the acting skills and performance intertextuality associated with Alfredo Mayo and Aurora Bautista – both renowned for their roles in overtly patriotic and propagandistic films of the 1940s and 1950s – that are instrumental to the artistic and political credentials of *La caza/The Hunt* (Carlos Saura, 1966) and *La tía Tula/Aunt Tula* (Miguel Picazo, 1964) respectively.

9 'Cambia mucho el público, eh. Es decir, cuando la gente te ve en el cine, y esto tienes que saberlo, la pantalla hace como una distancia, es una sala oscura y no sé qué. Y entonces lo de la tele son personas que ahora mismo nos están viendo en su casa con lo cual formamos parte de la familia. Se creen que nos conocen y que los conocemos y no se dan cuenta que no nos conocemos' (Mónica Radall, n.p.).

References

Aguilar, José and Miguel Losada (2008) *Carmen Sevilla*, Madrid: I. and B. Ediciones.

Barreiro, Javier (1999) *Marisol frente a Pepa Flores*, Barcelona: Plaza & Janes.

Bayón, Miguel (1995) *José Sacristán: La memoria de la tribu*, Huelva: XXI Festival de Cine Iberoamericano.

Boyero, Carlos (2006) 'El voyeur: Nostalgia de saldo', *El Mundo*, 8 May, 45.

Cobeaga, Borja (2014) 'Los nuevos reyes de la comedia', *El País Semanal*, 23 November, 50–9.

Crumbaugh, Justin (2009) *Destination Dictatorship: The Spectacle of Spain's Tourist Boom and the Reinvention of Difference*, Albany: SUNY Press.

D'Lugo, Marvin (2009) 'Postnostalgia in *Bad Education*: Written on the Body of Sara Montiel', in Brad Epps and Despina Kakoudaki (eds), *All About Almodóvar: A Passion for Cinema*, Minneapolis: University of Minnesota Press, pp. 357–85.

De Kosnik, Abigail (2013) '*One Life to Live*: Soap Opera Storytelling', in Ethan Thompson and Jason Mittell (eds), *How to Watch Television*, New York: New York University Press, pp. 355–63.

Elena, Alberto (2001) 'El cantor del cine Rex. Una revisión del cine de Joselito', *Archivos de la Filmoteca*, 38, 49–61.

Evans, Peter W. (2000) 'Cheaper by the Dozen: *La gran familia*, Francoism and Spanish Family Comedy', in Diana Holmes and Alison Smith (eds), *100 Years of European Cinema: Entertainment or Ideology?*, Manchester: Manchester University Press, pp. 77–8.

Faulkner, Sally (2006) *A Cinema of Contradiction: Spanish Film in the 1960s*, Edinburgh: Edinburgh University Press.

Gómez-Sierra, Esther (2004) '"Palace of Seeds": From an Experience of Local Cinemas in Post-war Madrid to a Suggested Approach to Film Audiences', in Antonio Lázaro Reboll and Andrew Willis (eds), *Spanish Popular Cinema*, Manchester: Manchester University Press, pp. 92–112.

Hernández, Marta and Manolo Revuelta (1976) *30 años de cine al alcance de todos los españoles*, Bilbao: Zero.

Hobson, Dorothy (2003) *Soap Opera*, Cambridge: Polity Press.

Jordan, Barry (2003) 'Revisiting the "comedia sexy ibérica": *No desearás al vecino del quinto* (Ramón Fernández, 1971)', *International Journal of Iberian Studies*, 15.3, 167–86.

Kuhn, Annette (2002) *An Everyday Magic: Cinema and Cultural Memory*, New York: I. B. Tauris.

Llorca, Carmen (1971) *Los teleclubs en España*, Madrid: Publicaciones Españolas.

Moix, Terenci (1993) *Suspiros de España: La copla y el cine de nuestro recuerdo*, Barcelona: Plaza & Janes.

Olano, Antonio D. (1974) *Estrellas y stars*, Barcelona: Dopesa.

Ordóñez, Marcos (1999) *Tony Leblanc: Genio y figura*, Malaga: Festival de Cine de Málaga.

Ordóñez, Marcos (2008) *Alfredo el grande, vida de un cómico: Landa lo cuenta todo*, Madrid: Aguilar.

Ozores, Mariano (2002) *Respetable público: Cómo hice casi cien películas*, Barcelona: Planeta.

El País (2004) 'Record de audiencia de *cine de barrio*', *El País*, 27 January, 61.

Ramón Resina, Joan (2000) 'Short of Memory: The Reclamation of the Past Since the Spanish Transition to Democracy', in Joan Ramón Resina (ed.), *Disremembering the Dictatorship: The Politics of Memory in the Spanish Transition to Democracy*, Amsterdam: Editions Rodopi B.V., pp. 83–126.

Ríos Carratalá, Juan Antonio (2001) *Cómicos ante el espejo: Los actores españoles y la autobiografía*, Alicante: Publicaciones de la Universidad de Alicante.

Sevilla, Carmen and Carlos Herrera (2005) *Memorias*, Barcelona: Belacqua.

Smith, Paul Julian (2006) *Television in Spain: From Franco to Almodóvar*, Woodbridge: Tamesis.

Smith, Paul Julian (2009) 'Almodóvar on Television: Industry and Thematics', in Brad Epps and Despina Kakoudaki (eds), *All About Almodóvar: A Passion for Cinema*, Minneapolis: University of Minnesota Press, pp. 37–50.

Telemanía (2012) 'Almodóvar sucumbe ante Paco Martíez Soria en TVE', 5 January, www.telecinco.es/telemania/audiencias/ranking-peliculas-espanolas-television_0_1344525243.html, accessed 8 July 2014.

Townson, Nigel (2007) 'Introduction', in Nigel Townson (ed.), *Spain Transformed: The Late Franco Dictatorship, 1959–75*, Houndmills: Palgrave Macmillan, pp. 1–29.

Triana-Toribio, Núria (2003) *Spanish National Cinema*, London: Routledge.

Valencia, Manuel (2002) *José Luis López Vázquez: Confesiones de un pícaro*, Valencia: Mostra de Valencia y Fundació Municipal de Cine.

Vivancos, Anna (2012) 'Failure to Deliver: Alfredo Landa in the Wonderland of Spanish Development', *Post Script*, 31.3, 44–57.

Vizcaíno Casas, Fernando (1962) *Suma de legislación del espectáculo*, Madrid: Ediciones Santillana.

Wheeler, Duncan (2014) 'Acting and Directing in Spain: Historicising Stardom and the Author-Function', in Duncan Wheeler and Fernando Canet (eds), *(Re)viewing Creative, Critical and Commercial Practices in Contemporary Spanish Cinema*, Bristol: Intellect, pp. 273–90.

Wright, Sarah (2013) *The Child in Spanish Cinema*, Manchester: Manchester University Press.

9

Performing the nation: mannerism and mourning in Spanish heritage cinema

Sally Faulkner

The development of Film Studies as an autonomous academic discipline was characterised by stressing the differences between cinema and established arts, especially literature and theatre, and the area of the discipline that relates to acting on screen proves no exception. For example, in the chapter 'Remarks on the Actor', in *Theory of Film: The Redemption of Physical Reality* of 1960, Siegfried Kracauer bases his argument about movie-acting on the differences between theatre performance and film performance (1968: 93–4). In theatre, Kracauer argues, the actor uses 'theatrical devices … make-up, appropriate gestures and voice inflections' (1968: 93); in film, he or she 'must act as if he did not act at all but were a real-life person caught in the act by the camera. He must seem to *be* his character' (1968: 94–5). A logical extension of this stress on 'real life', which 'redeems physical reality', would be to prize the untaintedness of non-professional actors or, better still, the spontaneity of children (1968: 98). Spanish art cinema of the years immediately preceding and following Kracauer's time of writing illustrates these shifts perfectly. Take the send-up of 'theatrical device' in Juan Antonio Bardem and Luis García Berlanga's feature début: *Esa pareja feliz/That Happy Pair* (1953). The protagonist Juan (Fernando Fernán Gómez)'s occupation as a runner at a Madrid film studio allows co-directors to include a cameo by Lola Gaos that satirises the exaggerated theatrical acting-style particularly associated with Aurora Bautista in features such as *Locura de amor/The Mad Queen* (Juan de Orduña, 1948) and *Agustina de Aragón/Agustina of Aragon* (Juan de Orduña, 1950).[1] Gaos, face-painted and decked out in the bejewelled black shawl and headpiece that Bautista wore in *Locura de amor*, belts out a 'vuela conmigo el honor de Valencia' [honour of Valencia flies with me] with histrionic relish and gestural flourish before crashing through the phony setting – the set, it is implied, is as phony as her costume, make-up and performance style. Ten years later, Miguel Picazo, who was taught by Berlanga at the Madrid Escuela Oficial de Cine (EOC),[2] casts Bautista herself in *La tía Tula/Aunt*

Tula (1964) and draws from her a performance designed to repress and contain the excessive style associated with her earlier career – a mode of repression and containment that conveys her character Tula, the unfulfilled provincial spinster, particularly well (Faulkner 2006: 101–24). A decade later, Víctor Erice, who was also trained at the EOC, made the iconic child-protagonist art movie, *El espíritu de la colmena/The Spirit of the Beehive* (1973). While Fernán Gómez or Bautista, directed by Bardem, Berlanga or Picazo, may act like 'a real-life person caught in the act by the camera' and may 'seem to *be* [their] character', this quest for authenticity apparently culminates in the performance of six-year-old Ana Torrent. She appears to '*be*' the character Ana in Erice's film, rather than act as her, an interpretation confirmed by interviews with Torrent as an adult in which she recalls simply playing in front of the camera, rather than acting (Smith 1999: 106).

This neat argument allows film to emerge as a pure form, untainted by the other arts that might compromise its autonomy (like theatre) or the pleasures of popular culture that might compromise its seriousness (like excessive performance): thus Film Studies may take its solemn place as the seventh art in the academy. One problem with this argument about difference is that it is based on a caricature of theatre performance; fifty years on, its championing of realism also appears of its time. In Film Studies, recent work in Adaptation Studies also explodes the distinctions on which the argument insists. From its early connections to popular theatre and fairground attractions, to the longstanding cross-fertilisation with literature through film adaptations of novels and novelisations of films, to its economic and aesthetic entanglements with television,[3] and now the internet, film is about as impure an art form as you can get. And, just as films do not exist in isolation from other media, neither may they be understood in isolation from each other, thus the art movies of Bardem, Berlanga and Picazo mentioned above are intertextually meshed with popular cinemas, both domestic and international. Gaos may be adopting a hyperbolic performance style in *Esa pareja feliz* to spoof popular historical melodramas against the foil of the naturalistic style of Fernán Gómez's earthy working-class protagonist, but both performances exist on a continuum of different styles, and, considered as a whole, the film is in fact respectful of the pleasures provided by popular spectacle. Cross-fertilisation between popular and art cinemas is especially clear when Picazo casts Bautista against type in *La tía Tula*. Her shift from overstatement to understatement is only meaningful if understood as connected to, rather than divorced from, the earlier performance. Similarly, Manuel Palacio and Paul Julian Smith have shown the constructedness of some of the myths that have grown up around

Torrent's performance in *El espíritu de la colmena*. While Erice insisted on her 'innocence', Torrent has revealed that, for all the 'playing' in front of the camera, for Erice, unlike for Carlos Saura (*Cría cuervos/Raise Ravens* [1976]), she learned her lines (Elsa Fernández Santos, cited in Smith 1999: 108) and press coverage on the film's release stressed her 'precocious ambition and professionalism' (Smith 2012: 138).

The film subdiscipline of Star Studies, usually dated as beginning with Richard Dyer's publication of *Stars* (1979), is predicated on film's intermediality and intertextuality, accounting for the pertinence to a given film of a star's involvement in other media, and for the pertinence to a given film of a star's involvement in other films. Likewise, Audience Studies address both hybridity and impurity, because a film attracts fans or otherwise based on its location within plural cultural consumption choices. In Spanish film scholarship it was the conjunction of Star and Audience Studies, along with the example of feminist work in British film, that allowed Jo Labanyi (2000a) and others to perform an important act of feminist cultural rehabilitation by stressing the importance and pleasures of performances precisely like Bautista's in *Locura de amor*.[4] Labanyi adapted to the contemporary Spanish case Sue Harper (1994) and Pam Cook (1996)'s arguments that Gainsborough's British costume dramas of the 1940s offered female audiences the pleasurable and empowering spectacle of female stars on screen. 'Bautista's hyperbolic acting style', Labanyi suggests, 'turns history into pure performance. In [*Locura de amor* and *Agustina de Aragón*], it also provides female spectators (the majority audience) with the pleasurable spectacle of female agency, at a time when the dictatorship had rescinded all women's rights' (2012: 244–5).

In this chapter I explore performance in a genre that also links British and Spanish cinemas: heritage film. In this shift from the 1940s historical costume dramas that were especially prominent in Anglophone cinema, to the heritage genre that has been especially prominent in European cinema from the 1980s onwards (sometimes termed 'post-classical', 'postmodern' or 'post-1989' cinema), new contexts must be taken into account, in particular the question of national cinemas and the transnational. If, as I have suggested, films are embedded within intermedial and intertextual networks, so too they are embedded in transnational ones. It can of course be argued that all the films I have already mentioned from the 'classical' (Orduña's work) and 'modern' eras (Bardem, Berlanga, Picazo and Erice's work) may be labelled transnational. *Locura de amor* forms part of the 1940s costume-drama cycle that included the Anglophone Hollywood and British examples dubbed and screened in Spain contemporaneously to great popular acclaim. *Esa pareja feliz*, on the other hand, could be described as a version of Italian Neorealism made-in-Spain.[5] *La tía Tula*, which co-starred the Argentine Carlos Estrada, similarly exhibits the influence of Neorealism, and found its most appreciative audience at a film festival which, although located in Spain, stressed its internationality by adopting the adjective in its title from 1954: the 'San Sebastián International Film Festival' (Gubern 2012: 443) awarded Picazo best director in 1964.[6] 'Heritage film' may similarly be described as transnational at these levels of aesthetic choices (including casting) and audience reception (both foreign audiences of Spanish films, and Spanish audiences that enjoyed Spanish films because they imitated foreign films). In the contemporary era, we need also to acknowledge that many films are also transnational in the sense that they are backed by international finance.[7] Above and beyond these questions, though, heritage cinema is transnational in a different way. A genre both identified and named by academics rather than the industry (unlike the standard emergence of generic labels), 'heritage film' is always and already transnational – there was no 'national' heritage genre from which 'transnational' heritage developed. Established as a key term in British Film Studies by Andrew Higson (1993) and Claire Monk (1995) (though the term was actually coined by Charles Barr to refer to Laurence Olivier's *Henry V* [1944] in 1986), the films thus named, like Merchant-Ivory's *A Room With a View* (1986), can scarcely be termed 'British' without qualifications. Made by international creative teams both in front of and behind the camera ('Merchant-Ivory' famously refers to a team of Indian producer Ismail Merchant, American director James Ivory, and German screenwriter Ruth Prawer Jhabvala), and backed by multinational finance, it is perhaps in reception that heritage cinema's transnationality is clearest, for, in order to recoup costs, the films must be successful at the international box office. In the US, for example, association with a particular distributor meant that the European heritage movie became popularly known as 'a "Miramax" film' (Galt 2006: 29). Heritage films thus exemplify the wider shift of contemporary European cinemas away from the national to the transnational. The successful heritage film will, then, strike a balance for audiences; in Rosalind Galt's summary, it must 'negotiate the requirement to produce a national cultural discourse for audiences and producers at home, and the sometimes contradictory need for that discourse to be legible – and, indeed, pleasurable – for a less knowledgeable global audience' (2006: 86).

Galt notes that these successes with audiences may not necessarily occur in that order – national, then international. For example, in the case of Italian heritage (*Cinema Paradiso* [Giuseppe Tornatore, 1988]; *Mediterraneo* [Gabriele Salvatores, 1991]; *Il Postino* [Michael Radford,

1994]), films that were initially unsuccessful with domestic audiences gained popularity only after international acclaim (2006: 86). However, the Spanish heritage examples I discuss here, *El perro del hortelano/The Dog in the Manger* (Pilar Miró, 1997) and *Alatriste/Captain Alatriste: The Spanish Musketeer* (Agustín Díaz Yanes, 2006), show the reverse: they were popular domestically but failed abroad (Wheeler 2012: 173 on *El perro del hortelano*; Wheeler 2014: 220 on *Alatriste*; see also Smith [2006: 110] on the similar case of Vicente Aranda's 2001 *Juana la Loca/ Mad Love*). I explore the perplexing case of transnational performance in two films that succeeded in producing 'a national cultural discourse for audiences and producers at home', but which, despite the adoption of foreign aesthetics, failed to be 'legible' or 'pleasurable' to the foreign audiences familiar with those very aesthetics.[8] Perhaps it is this odd mismatch between legibility at home and illegibility abroad that has led the few critics who do pay attention to the undoubtedly 'modest' Spanish heritage (Perriam 2003: 85) to describe it as 'mediocre' (Smith 2006: 112) and 'nascent and unconsecrated' (Wheeler 2014).[9] In the rest of this study I will therefore explore, first, foreign-influenced performance style in two Spanish films and propose that local audiences, who were fans of foreign heritage dubbed into Spanish, enjoyed these knowingly derivative or mannerist performances (in concert with other aspects such as *mise-en-scène*), which pleasurably repeated the films they had already enjoyed.[10] Next, I will locate these acting styles within historical contexts to explore them as 'haunted' by earlier performances, and argue that Spanish heritage, for all its transnational aesthetics, provides a particularly national opportunity for audiences to experience their own history as part of a process of mourning.

ImpersoNation

Although the 1940s historical costume dramas and the 1980s heritage films are connected – it seems significant that Barr should coin 'heritage' in relation to the 1944 *Henry V* precisely in 1986, when films that would come to be known as 'heritage' were in ascendance – the new transnational context of contemporary heritage means we must update Labanyi's comment on 1940s acting style. If, for her, theatrical acting style 'turn[ed] history into pure performance', my argument here is that the mannerist acting style in contemporary Spanish heritage turns nation, Spanishness, into performance; it becomes, in Thomas Elsaesser's neologism, 'ImpersoNation' (2005: 57–81).

Since 'heritage' was coined within British Film Studies to refer to transnational films associated with Britain, and since many of these films dubbed into Spanish attract high audiences figures in Spain (for example, nearly 900,000 saw *Much Ado About Nothing* [Branagh, 1993]; nearly 3,000,000, *Shakespeare in Love* [Madden, 1998]; and over 250,000, *Elizabeth* [Kapur 1998]),[11] I frame my argument about performance in Spanish heritage within performance in British heritage. British heritage directors and casting directors may take advantage of cross-fertilisation between the Shakespearian actor, especially those associated with the Royal Shakespeare Company, and the cinema. The films named above, for example, borrow the prestige and audiences of RSC actors Kenneth Branagh, Judi Dench and Joseph Fiennes (*Elizabeth*'s star, Cate Blanchett, trained at the National Institute of Dramatic Art in Sydney), to the acclaim of British and American audiences, but also, as we have seen, non-Anglophone ones such as Spain's and Italy's (Wheeler 2012: 173), who enjoyed dubbed versions of the originals.

Turning to Spain, the comparison is unflattering. Spain's equivalent of the RSC, the Compañía Nacional de Teatro Clásico [CNTC; National Company of Classic Theatre], was established only in 1986, and examples of similar cross-fertilisation are rare. They do include, nonetheless, the domestically successful 1997 adaptation of Félix Lope de Vega's *El perro del hortelano*, whose director (Pilar Miró), costume designer (Pedro Moreno) and cinematographer (Javier Aguirresarobe) had all worked for the CNTC (Wheeler 2012: 170–1). The actors Carmelo Gómez (Teodoro) and Ana Duato (Marcela) also brought the prestige, training and audiences of classical theatre with them, and if the female lead Emma Suárez (Diana) had in fact failed a CNTC audition, this was made up for by her training, alongside Gómez and the rest of the cast, by the company's Alicia Hermida (Wheeler 2012: 171). Despite the involvement of this team, the afterlife of *El perro del hortelano* unfortunately proves the centrality of the occasionally unfashionable idea of the director as *auteur*. The cycle of CNTC/film collaboration that *El perro del hortelano* inaugurated proved to depend principally on Miró, and thus ended with her untimely death, with the two further Golden Age Lope adaptations on her books, *El castigo sin venganza/Punishment without Revenge* and *El caballero de Olmedo/The Gentleman from Olmedo* never made.

In celebrating this cross-fertilisation between cinema and theatre we are overlooking, however, other sources of influence, and Duncan Wheeler's excellent reading of *El perro del hortelano* is careful to stress that, in addition to her work for the CNTC, Miró also brought many years of experience adapting literary texts to television (2012: 170). This is also true of the actors. Gómez's mannerist performance as the lovelorn secretary in *El perro del hortelano* is born of his previous experience on stage, film, and TV. His performance as the sexually-obsessed priest Fermín de Pas in Fernando Méndez-Leite's lavish and much-loved 1995 three-part TVE adaptation of Leopoldo Alas's 1884–85 novel *La Regenta/The Judge's Wife* is particularly relevant. Although in the shift from *La Regenta* to *El perro del hortelano* Gómez's characters shift from economically and socially omnipotent Magistral, with darkly swirling cassock and cinematic low-angle shots to match, to the social and economic underdog secretary Teodoro, often shot in now appropriately cinematic high-angle, the thwarting of, then triumph of, sexual desire he performs is shared by both characters. In mainstream TV and film, it is the portrayal of the thwarting of desire that may be more erotically charged than the portrayal of its satisfaction, and Gómez draws on a range of brooding silences and meaningful frowns efficaciously – and non-linguistically – to convey it.

The theatrical and televisual layers of Gómez's performance do not fully account for its mannerism, however. Its postmodern edge is brought about by knowing imitation, in particular his evocation of the performance of Gérard Depardieu in *Cyrano de Bergerac* (Jean-Paul Rappeneau, 1990), complemented by make-up and costume design (Perriam 2003: 85). Ginette Vincendeau's description of Depardieu's performance style as a mixture of 'theatricality and naturalism' (2001: 31) also describes the mixture of flourish and familiarity that Gómez brings to the Teodoro role, even appealing to the audience by addressing the camera directly. Suárez's Diana, too, in her coquettish enjoyment of word-play and clasping of love letters to the breast in a swoon, recalls Anne Brochet's Roxanne, Cyrano's muse in the Rappeneau precedent. In a film that is all about fantasy wish-fulfilment and make-believe, these knowingly make-believe performances are especially satisfying. When Gómez's Teodoro all but winks at the audience in the boat scene, it is a self-conscious reminder of these complicit pleasures of mannerism. Here, then, a Spanish actor, playing a Spanish role for a Spanish audience – though international audiences were also hoped for – does so through a performance style derived from foreign models: he plays the national through the aesthetics of the international. Miró, for her part, made much of the film's inspiration in contemporary British and French heritage in the Spanish press before and after the film's release (Fernández Soto and Checa y Olmos 2010: 86).

In the years immediately following *El perro del hortelano*, British heritage hits *Shakepeare in Love* and *Elizabeth* would continue to prove that RSC and classically trained actors could be deployed to great advantage in films that were not strictly theatre adaptations, but were set in the Elizabethan era, when much of Britain's most-loved drama was penned.

Part of the global appeal of both films, Julianne Pidduck pointed out in 2001, was the fusion of international stars with these British theatrically trained actors, plus a mix of actors popular on small and large screens: 'this mélange of accents, star personas and acting styles suggests the pleasures of make-believe so central to costume drama and historical fiction' (2001: 133). The 'ImpersoNations' that I have suggested enjoyably occur in Miró's *El perro del hortelano*, whereby Gómez and Suárez offer mannerist performances of Spanish roles by imitating foreign models, therefore look forward to these blockbuster heritage hits in which American, Australian and French actors perform Britishness. While Vicente Aranda's *Juana la Loca* (2001) shares some characteristics of *Elizabeth*, and Brazilian director Andrucha Waddington offers a Spanish *Shakespeare in Love* with a teaming of youthful romance with writer's block in *Lope/Lope: The Outlaw* (2010), it was Agustín Díaz Yanes's *Alatriste* (2006), based on Arturo Pérez Reverte's ongoing series of enormously popular 'Captain Alatriste' historical novels, which would provide Spain's high-budget answer to this transnational post-heritage trend in the new millennium.

While *El perro del hortelano* proves that romantic comedy is especially hospitable to the postmodern play of mannerist performances, *Alatriste* reveals that this style can be more challenging in historical drama. Eduardo Noriega, for example, who plays Count Guadalmedina, is partially successful in basing his performance on British actor Jeremy Irons's heritage roles, as he was encouraged to do by director Díaz Yanes (Perriam 2012: 58). The English middle-class stiffness often undercut by eroticism that Irons has honed in a career that includes heritage hits like TV series *Brideshead Revisited* (Sturridge and Lindsay-Hogg, 1981) and film *The Merchant of Venice* (Radford, 2004) is tricky to transfer as it is rooted in a particularly English obsession with class, reinforced by the public-school system. Nonetheless, Noriega is able to profitably redeploy what is the nearest version of this in Spain. In 2003, Chris Perriam described the 'posh qualities' Noriega brought to his early roles: 'a preppy, safe-looking sexiness, a rich-kid aura, and a crystalline received punctuation' (2003: 174–5). Crucially it was the rough edge provided by sinister roles such as Jacinto in *El espinazo del diablo/ The Devil's Backbone* (Guillermo del Toro, 2001) that allowed him to nuance his style. He replicates Irons's brooding impassivity, for example, in the scene in *Alatriste* in which he admonishes his protectee for his role in sparing the lives of two English noblemen. However, Viggo Mortensen's casual delivery of lines and gruff gestures as Alatriste occasionally render Noriega's performance as Guadalmedina wooden, surely not because the Spanish star is in awe of the American, given his own successful transnational career, but nonetheless giving something of this impression.

For a film that has been praised for its deployment of non-cinematic visual arts (especially the *mise-en-scène* of Velázquez's paintings) and criticised for its failure in cinematic storytelling (especially disjointed script and editing), the decision to cast Mortensen is a success in cinematic terms. If Pidduck praises Gwyneth Paltrow's accentless English in her various transnational roles (she '"pass[es]" in British drama, while remaining Pure Hollywood' [2001: 133]), it is precisely Mortensen's accent that works so well. A North American actor, Mortensen spent part of his childhood in Argentina, where he learned his South American-accented Castilian. Visually reminding the audience of his previous roles in *The Lord of the Rings* trilogy (Peter Jackson, 2001–3), acoustically, the accentedness of his spoken speech suggests a space in between North America, South America and the peninsula. Whereas a non-national accent might be considered to interrupt a national narrative, the multiple geographic echoes contained in Mortensen's spoken Castilian in fact effectively convey his character's ambiguous relation to Spanish king and country.

Take, for example, the productive interplay between sight (especially *mise-en-scène*) and sound (especially accent) in mercenary soldier Alatriste's meetings with representatives of the state in key scenes that establish the narrative: with Blanca Portillo in her transgender turn as Fray Emilio Bocanegra, Head of the Inquisition; and with Javier Cámara, cast against type as the powerful, scheming royal favourite Count-Duke of Olivares. As is typical in the heritage genre, *mise-en-scène* is carefully – and expensively – deployed to establish characterisation: Portillo and Cámara's dress, hair and make-up, as well as the settings in which we find them, imitate contemporary portraits of the characters (for example, Velázquez's 1624 portrait of Olivares). Their characters' central roles in the centralised imperial state are also underscored acoustically, for, just as the male voice-over of the prologue describes the Spanish empire in a Castilian spoken without traces of the many accents available to this world language, both Portillo and Cámara also deliver their lines in accentless Castilian spoken by a supposedly male voice. Penniless soldier-turned-occasional-mercenary Alatriste's scepticism of their power is presented through striking visual contrast, and the tatty soldier's attire throws into relief the candle-lit and creepy chamber of the Inquisitor, and the polished opulence of Olivares's El Escorial study. The old soldier's boots Alatriste wears in the latter scene even find their way into the narrative through a conversation regarding their suitability with Guadalmedina, which is stressed in the subsequent scene by a

Figure 10 The presence of Alatriste (Viggo Mortensen) undermines the opulent settings surrounding him (Agustín Díaz Yanes, 2006). Estudios Picasso, Origen Producciones Cinematogáficas S.A., NBC Universal Global Networks.

showy close-up. Alatriste's suspicion of both worlds, religious and political, is underscored by an acting style that punctures the pomposity of the period recreations in which Portillo and Cámara are imprisoned. Through gesture, Mortensen brings the swagger of the twentieth-century cowboy (in the *Alatriste* DVD extras, director and scriptwriter Díaz Yanes cites the western as a key influence in interview) and, though Mortensen's dialogue is penned by the director-scriptwriter, he delivers it with a brevity and directness that further deflate period rhetoric (Figure 10). Also, traces of both North and South American accents may be detected in the actor's spoken Spanish, in contrast to the Spaniards Portillo and Cámara's received pronunciation. In these scenes, which echo throughout the film in Mortensen's interactions with a cast of well-known peninsular actors,[12] Díaz Yanes deploys multiple aspects of film form to work in concert to underscore the narrative of the lone hero. It should be noted, however, that, while overall such individual moments of the film are impressive, they fail to cohere collectively, amounting to a picture that is less than a sum of these parts.

Haunting and mourning

In addition to the postmodern pleasures provided by these mannerist performances, or 'ImpersoNations', these transnational styles also enact a particularly national process of 'haunting' in which domestic spectators engage. I take this term from Theatre Studies, and propose that Marvin Carlson's use of 'haunting' to describe the experience of audiences seeing repeated theatrical productions of the same play (2001) offers a suggestive model for describing the layering of performance on screen.[13] Writing at around the same time in the field of Spanish Cultural Studies, Jo Labanyi also uses this metaphor to discuss the ways Spain's repressed twentieth-century history of Civil War and dictatorship 'haunts' contemporary culture (2000b, 2002), and investigates charged symbols like ghosts, werewolves, vampires, monsters and the *desapareci-dos* [disappeared] in post-Franco film and literature (2000). By combining Carlson and Labanyi's insights, I argue that Spanish heritage movies like *Alatriste* stage not ghostly symbols, but 'haunted' performances that allow audiences to mourn not Spain's twentieth-century horrors, but her earlier imperial decline. While these 'haunted' performances were especially resonant for national audiences, they did not translate to the international audiences that the films failed to attract.

In the not identical, but similar, case of popular Italian heritage films, Rosalind Galt counters the critical dismissal of their pretty, spectacular landscapes as nostalgic and touristic by adducing the Italian national historical contexts of loss to construct an interpretation based on mourning. In particular, these Italian heritage examples hold in tension the loss experienced by the Italian left in 1945 in creating a new Italian Republic (the temporal era of the films' settings) and the nation in the 1990s witnessing its collapse (the temporal era of the films' release). 'The spectacular images that could be perceived as merely touristic or beautiful', Galt argues, 'are, rather, imbricated with the social logic of Italian political loss and thus interpellate the spectator not as a tourist but as a subject of mourning' (2006: 67–8).

While the narratives and settings of Spanish heritage cinema like *El perro del hortelano* and *Alatriste* may consolingly return audiences to a national 'Golden Age' of literary achievement and empire, it is the mannerist performances of the actors, haunted by British and French precedents, rather than Galt's landscapes, which disrupt this return with the reminder of Spain's decline in relation to its Northern neighbours. The casting of Mortensen, while obviously commercial in motivation, is nonetheless especially significant. Mortensen plays the familiar Spanish character of the underdog (which has made frequent cultural appearances from *Lazarillo de Tormes* [Anon. 1554] onwards), yet his every word, gesture and action return the audience to Spain's colonial past. The plot of *Alatriste* may revolve – with much-criticised digression – around Spanish imperial decline, but this decline is a trigger for action and is thus contained within the narrative. It is the performances of the actors that provide the living, breathing bridges between the past depicted and the present of the 2006 Spanish audience. Mortensen acoustically encodes the former colony of Argentina that Spain lost in 1816 and, as a Hollywood star, physically encodes the North America to whom the country infamously lost her last colonies Cuba and the Philippines in 1898.

This acoustic encoding in fact occurs despite Mortensen's efforts to mask the non-peninsular traces of his Spanish accent. When a non-national actor embodies a treasured national fictional character, the press and social media can be expected to seize on the question of authenticity (Renée Zellwegger's portrayal of British-beloved Bridget Jones is a famous example from the Anglophone world, with Sharon Maguire's adaptation [*Bridget Jones's Diary*, 2001]). Thus Mortensen's fit with the author of the original and ongoing 'Alatriste' historical novels Arturo Pérez Reverte's character was also much debated.[14] The question of accent was a particular focus. The press reported Mortensen's preparatory stay in León prior to filming (Hernández 2007), in part to eradicate non-peninsular accent traces, but many viewers remained sceptical with what they heard in the final version of the film. In fact, the only partially successful masking of accent conveys the sense of haunting particularly well. Rather than an obvious accent disrupting a national narrative, in *Alatriste* we have a partial masking that suggests a more insidious, and therefore more troubling, kind of ghostly unsettling, or haunting. Mortensen's western genre-influenced performance as the cowboy-loner of the Spanish empire thus makes on the one hand for an effective and cinematically appropriate contribution to Díaz Yanes's vision of Spanish empire. On the other hand, Mortensen's performance is also haunted by contemporary North and South American acoustic traces that convey Spanish imperial decline, and their nonetheless pleasurable presence in the person of a popular actor allows the audience to mourn this decline.

Performances haunted by foreign precedents may thus play a positive role in connecting past and present in contemporary Spanish heritage, allowing audiences to work through national loss. Another haunting occurs in these films, however, which still resists this working-through. It is curious that, on the one hand, directors and actors of Spanish heritage alike cheerfully cite the transnational models they imitate in media articles and interviews,[15] yet, on the other, the major domestic precedent of contemporary heritage, the 1940s historical melodramas, is only ever mentioned to accuse contemporary film of a lack of originality (e.g. Pérez Gómez 2010). For commentaries in the national press regarding performances in contemporary Spanish heritage films, Aurora Bautista is, so to speak, the elephant in the room.

If contemporary Spanish heritage is layered with transnational performances that are present in derivative, mannerist gestures or delivery of lines, it is also haunted by 1940s 'Francoist' aesthetics that are pointedly absent, but paradoxically present through their pointed avoidance. Spanish audiences reject Spanish heritage films that do engage with this legacy. Manuel Iborra's Lope adaptation *La dama boba/The Foolish Lady* (2006), for example, despite shrewd casting (Wheeler 2012: 186), failed owing to what Elaine Canning described as 'theatrical acting' (cited in Wheeler 2012: 186), which, for domestic audiences at least, is forever associated with 1940s 'Francoist' historical melodramas. As Wheeler stresses, this acting style is problematic 'because it is seen to represent an anachronistic style of film-making that has specific negative temporal and political implications' (2012: 86). Unlike *La dama boba*, heritage examples *El perro del hortelano* and *Alatriste* were successful with national audiences, thanks in part to the mannerist performances that carefully follow contemporary foreign heritage precedents rather than theatrical acting styles that recall 1940s domestic ones. It is possible to argue that these mannerist performances, which are enthusiastically emphasised and praised in the Spanish press, may provide a smokescreen that hides any association with the 1940s historical melodramas still popularly considered only to be Francoist.

Conclusion

The layers of cultural meaning contained within every film performance thus cluster around questions of nation and history in Spanish heritage cinema. Far from dismissing the derivative, mannerist performances discussed as empty signifiers, a position adopted by early dismissals of postmodern culture,[16] I have argued that the traces of the performances of British, French, North American and Australian actors in Spanish heritage film mean that, even though Spanish actors play often key national roles for Spanish audiences (e.g. Noriega's Spanish grandee), they do so through transnational aesthetics coded as foreign rather than Spanish. This knowing imitation of foreign models in performances of the nation, which is particularly successful in the case of Miró's *El perro del hortelano*, looks forward to casting choices in British turn-of-the-century heritage blockbusters, *Shakespeare in Love* and *Elizabeth*, where non-British actors pleasurably perform Britishness.

Every Spanish heritage picture set in the Golden Age, however celebratory, must necessarily also remind audiences of decline. A further level of engagement between Spanish audiences and these films was, then, the possibility they offered for mourning, a possibility that would not translate to non-Spanish audiences. If Spanish imperial decline, at a safe distance of four hundred years, may be mourned through the visible and audible textures of actors' performances – with simultaneously North yet South American Mortensen as the familiar Spanish underdog Alatriste particularly representative of this – the more recent, traumatic, past of dictatorship haunts the present even in its absence. Bardem and Berlanga may have been able to satirise a performance style that in the popular imagination was politically tainted as Francoist, and Picazo may have been able to reverse it through casting against type, but mainstream Spanish heritage today, while celebrating its non-Spanish influences, still dares not speak the name of the 1940s Spanish historical melodramas that are its most obvious national precedent. While Spanish Film Studies may be recovering the empowerment offered to audiences by the theatrical performances in these films, this recovery has yet to occur in Spanish heritage cinema.

Notes

1 Juan de Orduña cast Bautista in *Locura de amor* after seeing her perform at the Teatro Español. Bautista recalls in interview that she débuted with Shakespeare's *A Midsummer Night's Dream* in 1947, but Orduña saw her in Friedrich Schiller's historical drama *Fiesco, or the Genoese Conspiracy* (Castillejo 1998: 13–14).

2 Established as the Instituto de Investigaciones y Experiences Cinematográficas in 1947 and attended by Bardem and Berlanga, it changed its name to the Escuela Oficial de Cine in 1962 as part of José María García Escudero's reforms, and closed in 1976. My sincere thanks to Asier Aranzubia Cob, who advised me on access to film books at the Escuela when Picazo and Erice attended, and Berlanga taught, in the 1960s. Their reading included Kracauer's earlier classic, *From Caligari to Hitler* (1947), translated into Spanish in 1961, but not *Theory of Film* (1968).

3 For a summary of this intermedial traffic in Spanish cinema, see Faulkner, Sánchez-Biosca and Smith (2012).

4 These acts of recuperation continue with, for example, the collaborative project 'An Oral History of Cinema-Going in 1940s and 1950s Spain' that Labanyi leads.

5 There is a venerable critical tradition that aligns Spanish dissident cinema under Franco with Italian Neorealism, following the Italian Film Week in Madrid in 1951, which many of the students of the EOC attended, including Bardem and Berlanga. See Kinder (1993, 18–53) and, for a revision and dismissal of Neorealism's dominance, Castro de Paz and Cerdán (2011, 43–81).

6 In 2007, Triana-Toribio expressed scepticism about retrospectively assigning the adjective 'transnational' to cycles such as 1960s Spanish art cinema or the Nuevo Cine Español, but, as Gerard Dapena notes, it provides an immensely useful framework in which to unsettle critical readings – for example, those surrounding the Nuevo Cine Español as a 'National Cinema' (2012: 23).

7 Though co-productions are not unique to contemporary cinema: almost all of Bardem's films from the 1950s and 1960s were co-produced (Dapena 2012: 23).

8 Earlier attempts to satisfy simultaneously both national and international audiences by the adoption of transnational aesthetics had also been mixed, like some of the Nuevo Cine Español films: rewarding as art movies to audiences on the foreign festival circuit, yet less rewarding at home (Dapena 2012: 23).

9 The failure of the films in countries where the term 'heritage' is used also explains why there is no equivalent of this word in Spain. It is not used in Monterde, Selva Masoliver and Solà Arguimbau's 2001 volume *La representación cinematográfica de la historia*, nor does Vicente Rodríguez Ortega use it in his 2012 summary of 'The Historical Film'. I use 'heritage' in this chapter in order to connect the Spanish films with transnational trends.

10 Belén Vidal names the aesthetics of period film 'mannerist', in the sense of a self-conscious deployment of recognisable aspects of film form (2012).

11 Audience figures are taken from the 'Base de datos de películas calificadas', 'Cine y audiovisuales' at www.mcu.es, accessed 3 October 2014.

12 Unknown English actor Simon Cohen plays Philip IV, but this role includes no spoken dialogue, an absence that efficaciously conveys aloof royal power.

13 My thanks to Pascale Aebischer for alerting me to this reference.

14 See, for example, www.foroseldoblaje.com/foro/viewtopic.php?f=18&t=3164, accessed 3 October 2014.

15 Wheeler notes that *La dama boba*'s creative team also claimed inspiration in international films (2012: 188).

16 See Barry Jordan and Rikki Morgan-Tamosunas's quotation of Fredric Jameson's critique of postmodernism's 'pseudo-historical depth' to criticise films like Mario Camus's *La colmena* (1982) and *Los santos inocentes* (1984) (1998: 37), or Paul Julian Smith's use of Baudrillard's 'History: A Retro Scenario' to critique *Belle Epoque* (Trueba, 1992) (2000: 42), for example.

References

Barr, Charles (1986) 'Introduction: Amnesia and Schizophrenia', in C. Barr (ed.), *All Our Yesterdays: Ninety Years of British Cinema*, London: British Film Institute, 1–30.

Carlson, Marvin (2001) *The Haunted Stage: The Theatre as Memory Machine*, Ann Arbor: University of Michigan Press.

Castillejo, Jorge (1998) *Las películas de Aurora Bautista*, Valencia: Fundació municipal de cine.

Castro de Paz, José Luis and Josetxo Cerdán (2011) *Del sainete al esperpento. Relecturas del cine español de los años 50*, Madrid: Cátedra.

Cook, Pam (1996) *Fashioning the Nation: Costume and Identity in British Cinema*, London: British Film Institute.

Dapena, Gerard (2012) 'War, Isolation, and New Transnational Openings', in Jo Labanyi and Tatjana Pavlovic (eds), *A Companion to Spanish Cinema*, Oxford: Wiley-Blackwell, pp. 21–6.

Elsaesser, Thomas (2005) *European Cinema: Face to Face with Hollywood*, Amsterdam: Amsterdam University Press.

Faulkner, Sally (2006) *A Cinema of Contradiction: Spanish Film in the 1960s*, Edinburgh: Edinburgh University Press.

Faulkner, Sally, Vicente Sánchez-Biosca and Paul Julian Smith (2012) 'Cinema, Popular Entertainment, Literature, and Television', in Jo Labanyi and Tatjana Pavlovic (eds), *A Companion to Spanish Cinema*, Oxford: Wiley-Blackwell, pp. 504–17.

Fernández Soto, Concepción and Francisco Checa y Olmos (2010) 'El cine de Pilar Miró. Homenaje ypuente hacia la literatura', *Arbor* 186.741, 79–88.

Galt, Rosalind (2006) *The New European Cinema: Redrawing the Map*, New York: Columbia University Press.

Gubern, Román (2012) 'Film Festivals', in Jo Labanyi and Tatjana Pavlovic (eds), *A Companion to Spanish Cinema*, Oxford: Wiley-Blackwell, pp. 442–6.

Harper, Sue (1994) *Picturing the Past: The Rise and Fall of the British Costume Film*, London: British Film Institute.

Hernández, María Jesús (2007) 'Viggo Mortensen. Nominación: mejor actor por *Alatriste*', www.elmundo.es/especiales/2007/01/cultura/goya/nominados/mortensen.html, accessed 3 October 2014.

Higson, Andrew (1993) 'Re-presenting the National Past: Nostalgia and Pastiche in the Heritage Film', in L. Friedman (ed.), *British Cinema and Thatcherism: Fires Were Started*, London: UCL Press, pp. 109–29.

Higson, Andrew (2003) *English Heritage, English Cinema: Costume Drama since 1980*, Oxford: Oxford University Press.

Jordan, Barry and Rikki Morgan-Tamosunas (1998) *Contemporary Spanish Cinema*, Manchester: Manchester University Press.

Kinder, Marsha (1993) *Blood Cinema: The Reconstruction of National Identity in Spain*, Berkeley: University of California Press.

Kracauer, Siegried (1968) *Theory of Film: The Redemption of Physical Reality*, Oxford: Oxford University Press. Originally published 1960.

Labanyi, Jo (2000a) 'Feminizing the Nation: Women, Subordination and Subversion in Post-Civil War Spanish Cinema', in U. Sieglohr (ed.), *Heroines without Heroes: Reconstructing Female and National Identities in European Cinema 1945–51*, London: Cassell, pp. 163–84.

Labanyi, Jo (2000b) 'History and Hauntology; or, What Does One Do with the Ghosts of the Past? Reflections on Spanish Film and Fiction of the Post-Franco Period', in J. R. Resina (ed.), *Disremembering the Dictatorship: The Politics of Memory in the Spanish Transition to Democracy*, Amsterdam: Rodopi, pp. 65–82.

Labanyi, Jo (2002) 'Engaging with Ghosts; or, Theorizing Culture in Modern Spain', in J. Labanyi (ed.), *Constructing Identity in Contemporary Spain: Theoretical Debates and Cultural Practice*, Oxford: Oxford University Press, pp. 1–14.

Labanyi, Jo (2012) 'The Ambivalent Attractions of the Past: Historical Film of the Early Franco Period', in J. Labanyi and T. Pavlovic (eds), *A Companion to Spanish Cinema*, Oxford: Wiley-Blackwell, pp. 241–8.

Monk, Claire (1995) 'Sexuality and the Heritage', *Sight and Sound*, 5.10, 32–4.

Monterde, José Enrique, Marta Selva Masoliver and Anna Solà Arguimbau (2001) *La representación cinematográfica de la historia*, Madrid: Akal.

Pidduck, Julianne (2001) '*Elizabeth* and *Shakespeare in Love*: Screening the Elizabethans', in Ginette Vincendeau (ed.), *Film/Literature/Heritage: A Sight and Sound Reader*, London: British Film Institute, pp. 130–4.

Pérez Gómez, Ángel (2010) (n.d., 2010?), '*Alatriste*' Cine para leer, www.cineparaleer.com/archivo/item/190, accessed 3 October 2014.

Perriam, Chris (2003) *Stars and Masculinities in Spanish Cinema*, Oxford: Oxford University Press.

Perriam, Chris (2012) 'Eduardo Noriega's Transnational Projections', in L. Nagib, C. Perriam and R. Dudrah (eds), *Theorizing World Cinema*, London: I. B. Tauris, pp. 77–92.

Rodríguez Ortega, Vicente (2012) 'The Historical Film: Genre and Legibility', in Jo Labanyi and Tatjana Pavlovic (eds), *A Companion to Spanish Cinema*, Oxford: Wiley-Blackwell, pp. 240–1.

Smith, Paul Julian (1999) 'Between Metaphysics and Scientism: Rehistoricizing Víctor Erice's *El espíritu de la colmena*', in Peter W. Evans (ed.), *Spanish Cinema: The Auteurist Tradition*, Oxford: Oxford University Press, pp. 93–114.

Smith, Paul Julian (2000) *The Moderns: Time, Space and Subjectivity in Contemporary Spanish Culture*, Oxford: Oxford University Press.

Smith, Paul Julian (2006) *Spanish Visual Culture: Cinema, Television, Internet*, Manchester: Manchester University Press.

Smith, Paul Julian (2012) 'Víctor Erice', in J. Labanyi and T. Pavlovic (eds), *A Companion to Spanish Cinema*, Oxford: Wiley-Blackwell, pp. 136–40.

Triana-Toribio, Nuria (2007) 'Journeys of Deseo between the Nation and the Transnational in Spanish Cinema', *Studies in Hispanic Cinemas*, 4.3, 151–63.

Vidal, Belén (2012) *Figuring the Past: Period Film and the Mannerist Aesthetic*, Amsterdam: Amsterdam University Press.

Vincendeau, Ginette (2001) 'Unsettling Memories', in G. Vincendeau (ed.), *Film/Literature/Heritage: A Sight and Sound Reader*, London: British Film Institute, pp. 27–32.

Wheeler, Duncan (2012) *Golden Age Drama in Contemporary Spain: The comedia on Page, Stage and Screen*, Cardiff: University of Wales Press.

Wheeler, Duncan (2014) 'Back to the Future: Re-Packaging Spain's Troublesome Past for Local and Global Audiences', in Fernando Canet and Duncan Wheeler (eds), *(Re)viewing Creative, Critical and Commercial Practices in Contemporary Spanish Cinema*, Bristol: Intellect, pp. 205–33.

10

Performing sex in Spanish erotic films of the 1980s

Alejandro Melero

Spanish films are known for their graphic representation of nudity and sex. While Pedro Almodóvar, Julio Medem and Bigas Luna are most widely known for screening sex, it in fact has a longer tradition in Spanish cinema. From the first illegal pornographic films of the silent era, to the so-called *destape* [uncovering] trend of the 1970s, Spanish cinema has found many ways to explore the representation of sexual acts. However, the contemporary success of Porn Studies in Anglophone academia has not yet reached Spain, and a deep study of the complexities of performing sex on screen is still needed.

This chapter studies the performance of sex in Spanish films of the early 1980s, a crucial time for the understanding of visual representations of sexuality in Spain. In the last years of Franco's dictatorship, the *destape* shaped the production of all film genres. Sexual scenes and motifs were expected in comedies such as those of the '*landismo*' trend, or horror films such as *La noche de Walpurgis/The Night of Walpurgis* (León Klimovsky, 1971). In the years after Franco's death, this tendency increased to the extent that even adventure films, traditionally targeted for children, included erotic scenes, as we can see, for instance, in *Kilma, reina de las amazonas/Kilma, Queen of the Amazons* (Miguel Iglesias Bonn, 1975). In 1978, the so-called 'S' rating was invented for the distribution and production of films with sexual content. After 1982, the 'S' label disappeared, and the more international 'X' was introduced. This chapter will discuss *Con las bragas en la mano/Panties in the Hands* (Julio Pérez Tabernero, 1981), which was made during the last years of the 'S' period, a time when the frontiers between erotic and pornographic cinema were blurred. The move from one rating to the other exemplifies the difficulties in measuring the immeasurable: the explicitness of sex in X films is not necessarily bigger than it was in the previous 'S', as this chapter will go on to show. This confusion was felt at the time, as we can see when one film reviewer, unable to find the right word, simply wrote: 'una película de vídeo fuerte, (S), (X) o porno' [a hardcore film, (S), (X) or porn] (Anon. 1983: 11).

Hispanists and film scholars have analysed Spanish cinema's interest in the representation of explicit sex. Barry Jordan and Rikki Morgan-Tamosunas, with their chapter on 'Gender and Sexuality on Post-Franco Cinema', were possibly the first to note how 'Spanish cinema is known for producing explicit images (of both sex and violence) more than most other contemporary European countries' (1998: 112). During the 1980s and 1990s, the popularity and international recognition of filmmakers such as Vicente Aranda and Pedro Almodóvar cemented the association of Spanish cinema with sex. The successful international distribution of films such as *Amantes/Lovers* (Vicente Aranda, 1991) and *Jamón, jamón* (Bigas Luna, 1992) is part of this trend. The following generation of directors continued the tradition, as we can see when we look at the international reviews of *Lucía y el sexo/Sex and Lucia* (Julio Medem, 2001). This reveals how the blatant sex scenes (which included the close-up of an erection) were the film's most intriguing aspect. For instance, film critic Chris Tookey noted Medem's 'fascination with erect penises' (2002: n.p.). BBC critic Simon Wardwell also remarked on the film's 'pornography, portrayed in [a] sort of unembarrassed, explicit detail' (2002: n.p.). International critics and spectators know that screening erotic sex is, or can be, part of the content of a Spanish film of all genres, something that would be more surprising in, for example, a Hollywood production.

The origin of explicit images of sex in Spanish films must be located in the times of the Transition to democracy. After the disappearance of the code of censorship in 1976, Spanish audiences rushed to see the films that had been banned before. As one film review of the time remarked, 'se diría que todo lo que queremos ver hoy en día es sexo, sexo, y más sexo. Una buena historia no importa. Unos buenos actores no interesan. La fotografía, el sonido, los decorados ... nada importa con tal de que haya escenas de sexo' [it looks like all we want to see nowadays is sex, sex, sex. Good plots are irrelevant. Good performers are of no interest. Cinematography, sound, settings ... nothing matters as long as the sex scenes are there] (Martalay 1976: n.p.). One of the pioneer actresses to perform simulated sex in Spanish cinema was Susana Estrada, who starred in very popular films such as *La trastienda/The Room Behind the Shop* (Jorge Grau, 1975) and *Pepito Piscina* (Luis María Delgado, 1978). Decades after her stardom, she complained that 'lo que nosotras hacíamos no era más de lo que hacen las actrices de hoy en día ... pero a nosotras se nos insultaba y no se nos respetaba nunca, cuando fuimos las que abrimos las puertas para que las gentes del cine que vinieron después pudieran expresarse libremente' [what we used to do was no more than what actresses do today ... but we were insulted and never respected when, in fact, we were the ones who opened the floodgates for future filmmakers to express themselves freely] (*Qué tiempo tan feliz*, 13 November 2010). Estrada sees her acting as an act of freedom, almost something revolutionary, as well as a precedent for contemporary actors and actresses who perform sex scenes in Spanish cinema.

The relatively recent popularity of Sex and Porn Studies has provided scholars with new theories to analyse the mechanisms of performing sex in front of a camera. One of the most significant debates of Porn Studies is that of the importance of film techniques and devices in order to fully understand the chronological (albeit unstable and fluctuating) advances in the portrayal of sex in cinema. Linda Williams noticed this in her seminal book *Screening Sex*, which is based on the premise that 'sex is an act and more or less of "it" may be revealed but ... it is not a stable truth that cameras and microphones either "catch" or don't catch. It is a constructed, mediated, performed act and every revelation is also a concealment that leaves something to the imagination' (2008: 2). Williams' study of the performance of sex is a reminder that sexual acts on screen are as much a recreation as any other aspect of performance. Lighting, sound, make-up and, most crucially, acting are part of the process of capturing sex for the cinema. In this sense, Martalay's complaint about the Spanish audiences of the 1970s and their indifference to 'cinematography, sound, [and] settings' (1976: n.p.) is inaccurate, as those elements are part of the performance of sex on screen, too. In the following paragraphs, I will analyse how sex was performed in the Spanish erotic films of the 1980s. First, I will look at the difficulties presented by the representation of the erection, and problematise the traditional debate between pornography versus eroticism. For this, I will focus on the film *Con las bragas en la mano*. Later, I look at the career of its leading actor, Emilio Línder, in order to analyse the question of the legitimisation of the performances of sex and the careers of the actors and actresses who participated in 'Cine S'.

Spanish erotic films made between 1981 and 1984 offer a good contribution to the study of the blurred lines between eroticism and pornography. After some decades of Porn Studies, it seems that still the more valid definition of pornography is the one provided by the Supreme Court Justice Potter Stewart who, back in the 1960s, famously claimed about porn: 'I don't know what it is but I know it when I see it' (Williams 2008: 328). This non-definition shows how the consideration of what is or is not pornographic depends on a series of variable features difficult to apprehend and sometimes left to the imprecise and swinging moods of commonsensical approaches.

The testimony of director Julio Pérez Tabernero, who specialised in erotic cinema during the 1980s, confirms how difficult it is to locate the thin border that separates eroticism from pornography. In a personal interview (unpublished), he explained: 'la única indicación que se nos dijo fue que no podíamos mostrar pollas duras. Consoladores, todos los que quisiéramos, cualquier clase de objeto, candelabros, peluches … pero que ni se nos ocurriera poner una polla dura. Eso era todavía censura. La única indicación de la censura que quedó' [the only indication that we were given was that we could not show hard cocks. There could be dildos galore, any kind of objects from candlesticks to stuffed dolls … but we could not even think about showing a hard cock. That was still censorship. That was the only remaining indication of censorship]. Pérez Tabernero's words indicate that penetration was not problematic as long as it did not involve an erect penis. Indeed, penetration was favoured by these filmmakers, to the extent that it can be considered one of the characteristics of the first erotic films of the democracy. Penetration or even the suggestion of it is not present in the erotic films of late Francoism (for instance, *El erotismo y la informática/Eroticism and Computers*, 1975). Penetration is not performed in Pérez Tabernero's erotic films made under Franco's regime, such as *Sexy Cat* (1973), but is a constant feature in his films of the democratic period. What is more interesting, however, is that Tabernero's testimony contradicts his own works and the work of many of his colleagues, for Spanish actors have been showing their erect penises in many non-pornographic films (or, at least, in films which were not labelled as pornographic).

Con las bragas en la mano is one of those films, as well as one of the most successful 'S' movies. It was seen by more than half a million spectators and roared its way to a stellar 94 million pesetas at the box office.[1] In it, Emilio Línder plays Sergio, a man in his twenties who suffers from impotence. The film starts with a sex scene in which we see Sergio enjoying sex with his wife, Marta, while she shows her dissatisfaction. Close-ups of Sergio's body (legs, chest, face, biting lips) are followed by close-ups of Marta's face, with obvious signs of boredom. When she complains to Sergio, he decides to start a series of sexual encounters in order to find a solution to his problem. The narrative structure of the film is not dissimilar from many other 'S' films, as it presents one sexual encounter after the other. In this sense, *Con las bragas en la mano* follows the pattern detected by Linda Williams when she claimed that 'hard core's narrative form has a link with that of the musical in that the narrative is shaped by each of the numbers "performed"' (1990: 130). Thus, Sergio has encounters with a male transvestite, then takes part in a ménage-à-trois, then an orgy, while his wife has an affair with a woman, providing the requisite lesbian sex scene. The narrative structure of this film follows the Aristotelian traditional pattern of the hero pursuing an objective and surpassing a number of obstacles in order to get it; only, instead of seeing Indiana Jones looking for the Holy Grail, what we see here is Sergio looking for an erection, which he gets after his many encounters. What interests me is that, as in a Hollywood happy end, Sergio gets an erection and the spectators have the chance to see it in a close-up.

A number of cinematic transgressions operate when we see Sergio's erection. According to Tanya Krzywinska, 'the inclusion of real sex in legitimate cinema pushes at regulatory and generic boundaries. While simulated sex acknowledges normative "appropriateness" of purpose, the act of putting real sex on camera disturbs normative rhetorics of sex as an intimate and private affair' (2006: 222). Krzywinska believes that 'when characters have "real" sex onscreen, spectators are to some extent taken out of the frame of fictional representation, focus shifting perhaps from character to actor. A modal ambiguity is created between the real and the fiction' (2006: 222). The erection that spectators see is both the actor's and the character's, and this process breaks the line that separates them. Considering that *Con las bragas en la mano* is pre-Viagra, spectators would or could assume that when we see Sergio's erection (that is, Emilio Línder's erection), the performer must have been sexually aroused himself. But it is much more complex than this. First of all, a spectator familiar with film technique could consider the fact that there are no scenes in which Linder's face and his erect penis are captured within the same frame. A stunt double could have been used, although it is indeed unlikely that this low-budget film would have used stunt doubles for actors who were not stars.

The presence of the character's (that is, the actor's) erection disrupts traditional performances of sex in cinema. The performance of sex in Hollywood cinema has always been allowed as long as it was presented as a suggestion of sex, but not a confirmation of it. According to Linda Williams, 'a physical relation can be suggested as long as it is also possible to deny it' (Williams 2008: 41). Williams has analysed several examples of Hollywood films to explain how a number of sex acts (kissing, caressing, licking) could work as metaphors or substitutes of other, more conclusive, acts. However, in *Con las bragas en la mano* the close-up of an erection obliterates the possibility of suggesting a performance of sex. On the contrary, an on-screen erection is the corroboration of a sexual act that transcends the limits of suggestion. When spectators see Sergio's erect penis, the possibility of denying the confirmation of sex is no more. Thus, the representation of sex as a performance is denied by the presence of the ultimate contribution of the 'Cine S': the erect penis.

Understanding the presence of an erection as the key to discern real from fake sex limits the complexity of human sexual experience, as it presumes that an actor or actress is not sexually aroused when kissing or caressing (because one does not need to be aroused in real life to do that) but is necessarily not performing if he has an erection (because one needs to be aroused to get it). Admittedly, although an erection means arousal, it does not mean that the arousal comes from the action carried out by the actor at that particular time (and therefore he could still be performing an attraction to the actor/actress he is having sex with). The presence of an erect penis invites and complicates the question of what is and is not indeed real and performed sex on screen. An actor could be more aroused when kissing before the camera, only that the size of the shot does not show his potential erection. This is a phallocentric distinction between eroticism and pornography, for it is based solely not on the presence but on the revealing of the penis. Moreover, it ignores sex scenes between two or more women, which were actually extremely popular during the 1970s and 1980s.

The problems of performing sex determine the film's reception and rating as much as they affect the performer's persona and career. Emilio Línder's personal webpage reveals his concern to legitimise his career as an actor. Under the section 'trabajos' [works] he includes his, admittedly, 'selected' filmography. It is meaningful that the only roles he does not include are precisely those he made for erotic and pornographic films. Thus, after his début in *La mano negra/The Black Hand* (Fernando Colomo, 1980), an adventure film directed by a filmmaker who was already perceived as an *auteur*, there is a gap of five years in which it seems as if Línder had not been working. As a matter of fact, those were the years in which he worked more profusely, with over seven titles in 1982, all of them pornographic. The pictures that illustrate this section of his webpage show Línder with Milos Forman, Vicente Aranda, Benito Zambrano and other filmmakers who directed him during the 1990s and 2000s. There is even a picture of him with Woody Allen, with whom he has never worked in a film. Intriguingly, in his section 'Gracias por su visita' [Thanks for your visit] he presents a text in which he apologises for not updating his web with more frequency and writes that he intends to create a blog in which he will talk about 'recuerdos y aventuras' [memories and adventures]. He continues: 'podría ser un suicidio (*a buen entendedor*)' [it could be a suicide].[2] It is difficult to conclude what he is referring to by '*a buen entendedor*', but the fact remains that Línder is proud of some parts of his biography, while he ignores or conceals others. This is something that surely applies to most actors of all genres, but, in the case of Línder, it just so happens that the genres he deliberately ignores are the erotic and pornographic. His personal webpage also displays Línder's work as a professional theatre actor. He seems to be particularly proud of his collaborations with William Layton's theatre company and of his attendance to Juan Carlos Corazza's acting school in 1989, sometime before Corazza became one of Spain's most prestigious acting teachers, especially thanks to his work with stars such as Javier Bardem and Penélope Cruz.

The question of legitimation is of relevance for scholars of performance studies. The processes of legitimation of the careers of some actors and acting schools are not far from the processes of legitimation of cinema itself as a high art, which took place during the first part of the twentieth century. According to Ivo Blom, during the period 1905–20, 'motion-picture theatres were modelled on large dramatic theatres and opera houses. Film began to compete with established culture, seeking to legitimise itself by adapting its visual narrative forms to traditional dramatic structures, by accepting and applying censorship, by throwing open sumptuous theatres with fashionably dressed front-of-house staff and by getting itself talked about in the quality newspapers' (2003: 32–3). In order to be legitimate as an art form, cinema first tried to escape from its own specificity and struggled to incorporate or reinforce elements of other arts that already had cultural legitimacy, mainly theatre. Mirabelle Ordinaire, who has studied theatricality in the cinema, believes that the association of theatre with film endows the latter 'with the cultural legitimacy that theatre possesses by simple virtue of its "age"' (2001: 3). For other film historians, such as Shyon Baumann, 'the legitimation of Hollywood film as art occurred mainly during the 1960s and involved … changes in acting techniques' (2007: 3). These changes included the elimination of theatricality in performance and settings, and are best exemplified by the Hollywood musicals which, after 1960, were filmed in locations (and not in the studios, as was the tradition).

The tensions between acting for the theatre and for the cinema, and the resulting cultural prestige, are present in Emilio Línder's career. Interestingly, the necessity to move far from the theatricality that cinema had experienced in the 1960s is the opposite to what Línder attempts on his webpage. For him, it is precisely his work in the theatre that starts his career as a legitimate actor. It seems that Línder's career confirms Krzywinska's thesis, for whom 'when an actor takes part in a sex scene in a film they are, in a sense, committing a form of transgression by making sex public, and the viewer too, by virtue of being a viewer, becomes complicit in that transgression' (2006: 38). A particularly interesting case is that of the socialist deputy and activist Carla Antonelli, who is now one of Madrid's most visible politicians but refuses to recognise her past as an erotic actress in films such as *El higo mágico/The Magic Fig* (Julio Pastor, 1983). Línder is one of the few cases of success, but this has involved the negation of his past as an actor of 'S' films. The performers of Spanish erotic and pornographic films during the 1970s and 1980s have not had solid filmographies in non-erotic cinema. After the disappearance of the 'S' trend, most of them had to change careers.

Critical approaches to the performances of actors who work on erotic and pornographic cinema have traditionally been negative. Linda Williams herself, when she analyses the pornographic film *Pirates* (Joone, 2005), and after remarking on its importance in the history of the industry of porn, writes that 'it fell short of being a "real" movie: atrocious acting, mispronounced lines' (2008: 5). Of course, by 'acting' she refers to the moments in which the performers are not involved in sexual intercourse. What makes their acting work deficient is not specified, but the reader may infer that it is perhaps their bad diction or inability to deliver their lines clearly. However, earlier on in her book, Williams had praised the adequacy of the performers of *Pirates* when she describes how one of the female characters 'has the patented porn female body complete with enhanced breasts, slim waist, long, bleached blond hair'. The same is said of the male counterpart, who 'has the patented male body complete with big pecs and a long, frequently erect penis' (2008: 4). Williams' appraisal of the actors is based on their physicality, while she considers equally successful the way that these actors and actresses do their jobs in the sex scenes and praises, with particular emphasis, their acrobatics, which make possible that 'penetration [is] staged for maximum visibility' (2008: 5). However, for Williams, those skills are not sufficient to consider their performances not 'atrocious', as if sex acts are not part of the acting repertoire of the film.

The critical reception of the performances of the actors of 'S' films was extremely negative, and sometimes very aggressive. This explains Susana Estrada's regret for her unrecognised work. The reviews of these films are full of derogatory words and insults. For instance, one film critic lamented the absence of real actresses in Spanish cinema: '¿Qué fue de nuestras buenas actrices? ¿Dónde están Montiel, Bautista, Gadé? Si quieres actuar en la actualidad, tienes que estar desnuda, y parece que nuestras grandes figures han preferido una jubilación temprana antes que caer en esta trampa' [Whatever happened to our good actresses? Where are Montiel, Bautista, Gadé? If you want to act nowadays, you have to do it naked, and it seems that our big names have preferred to opt for a premature retirement than to fall into this trap] (Rodríguez 1977: 22). Later, Rodríguez makes his point clearer: 'hoy en día *no hace falta ser una actriz* para actuar, el único talento que se pide es estar dispuesta a desnudarse' [in order to act, *you don't have to be an actress* today, the only talent required is a willingness to get naked] (1977: 22, emphasis mine). For Rodríguez, as well as for many critics, performers of sex scenes are not actors or, at least, they are not when they are compared to 'good' (his words) actors. The erotic magazine *Machos* was one of the first publications which paid significant attention to 'S' films, with reviews, photographs and interviews with actors and directors. The interest of this magazine in erotic cinema was confirmed after volume 4, issue 8, when the film review section 'Video macho' was introduced and later expanded. Very often, there were articles about casting sessions, information about shootings and forthcoming projects, and even job vacancies for people who aspired to be erotic and porn film stars. The article 'The Oscars of Porn Cinema' covered the awards of 1983 for best performances in the American porn industry. Interestingly, even in this piece, which was about the best performers, the writing was patronising and highly denigrating. In order to legitimise the value of the performer who won the Best Actress Award, the writer said: 'she has performed in important films with Toni [sic] Curtis and Burt Reynolds' (Anon. 1983: 23). The actress's success is confirmed not by the award that proclaimed her the best actress of that year, but by her collaboration with well-established actors of non-erotic cinema.

One of the explanations for the demeaning attitude towards these performers might be the limited conventions of acting in the sexploitation cinemas, which Linda Williams has listed as 'frenzied dancing, writhing, drinking, and close-ups of ecstatic female faces' (2008: 90). These were the result of the need to indicate 'sexual activity without necessarily revealing more of the act of sex than in Hollywood' (2008: 90). Spanish 'S' films were no exception, and, although Williams finds these conventions in the sexploitation global cinemas of the 1970s, we can find them in Spanish 'S' and 'X' films of the 1980s, too. For instance, if we take the films scripted and directed by Ignacio F. Iquino, such as *La desnuda chica del relax/The Naked Masseuse* (1981) or *Jóvenes amiguitas buscan placer/Young Friends Looking for Pleasure* (1982), and look at the repertoire of gestures of the actresses in the sex scenes, we see that in order to insinuate sexual excitement they sensually bite their lips, roll their eyes over, close their eyes while their mouths are wide open, suck their own or each others' fingers, etc. The list is short and the gestures and positions are repetitive, and maintained in long shots. If we look at the original scripts for these films, we can see that most of the sexual positions and gestures were explicitly instructed by Iquino. In the script for *Liliana. Los increíbles vicios/Liliana. The Unbelievable Vices*,

Iquino detailed each shot of the lesbian scene, and the performers' tasks in them:

> Plano 3; Plano medio. Marion le acaricia el pelo. Plano 4a: Primer plano. Liliana se chupa un dedo. Plano 5a; Primer plano. Marion chupa un dedo a Liliana. Plano 4b; Plano medio. Liliana se chupa un dedo y chupa otro a Marion. Plano 5b; Marion besa a Liliana apasionadamente [Shot 3; Medium shot. Marion caresses her hair. Shot 4a: Close-up. Liliana sucks her finger. Shot 5a; Close-up. Marion sucks Liliana's finger. Shot 4b; Medium close-up. Liliana sucks her finger and Marion's. Shot 5b; Marion kisses Liliana passionately]. (Iquino 1978: 5)

This excerpt from the script reveals that the performance of sex was based on a list of sexual acts, each shot contributing to the creation of the final scene. By fragmenting sex into a series of shots and countershots, each one being a sexual act (a kiss, a caress), the performance of sex was reduced to a catalogue of positions and gestures. This implied that other acting possibilities such as improvisation were not an option, and Iquino's detailed scripts do nothing but confirm this. The performance of sexual acts in most of the erotic and pornographic films of the early years of the transition to democracy was very far from portraying the fluidity, variety and complexity of human sexuality. Cinematic conventions, legal restrictions and directorial choices limited the actors' performance of sex.

Con las bragas en la mano's last sex scene complicates further recent porn film theory. Marta is satisfied with extramarital and lesbian sex, but still unhappy with Sergio, and later is raped by a man and a woman. Although at the beginning she screams and shows panic, she eventually comes to enjoy it and is willing to participate, arguably converting the rape into an act of consensual sex. This scene can be very problematic when analysed in the light of Linda Williams' disagreement with Bazin's comparison between the representation of sex and violence on screen. Williams uses Bazin, for whom, 'if you can show me on the screen a man and a woman whose dress and position are such that at least the beginnings of sexual consummation undoubtedly accompanied the action, then I would have the right to demand, in crime film, that you really kill the victim. Or at least wound him pretty badly' (Bazin 1971: 173). According to Williams, 'to go all the way in the depiction of sex – not just the kiss but the consummation to which the kiss tends – would also require going all the way in the depiction of violence: not using the dummy's head but, for consistency's sake, a real decapitation. To Bazin, these are true obscenities that the cinema simply should not show' (2008: 65). The equation between real sex and violence on screen seems to ignore that, as far as an act is filmed, it is always a performance, no matter whether the effects of those acts (pleasure in sex, pain in violence) are achieved or not. Maybe the problem resides in the word 'real', which is insufficient to cover the complexities of the cinematic experience. When we are watching Marta being raped, we assume that she is not being a victim of violence. It is, however, more difficult to know if the actress was actually enjoying the sex she was performing. *Con las bragas en la mano* is asking the spectators to believe that the violence they are contemplating is not real while, at the same time, spectators are asked to believe that the actors and actresses are *having* sex, and not *performing* it. Thus, conventions of spectatorship guarantee that the experience of watching violence is safe, as we know that what we are watching is not real violence, but a performance of it. On the other hand, the experience of watching the performance of sex acts (including rape) is more complex, for no matter how real they may seem onscreen (the erection being the most extreme case of realism in a sex act), cinematic conventions are inviting the spectator to believe in the performance they are watching.

Film theorist Ralph Blumenthal famously coined the term 'porno chic' (1973: 28) to refer to this brief period of upper- to medium-class interest in explicit pornography, which he framed between 1972 and 1979. It could be argued that the 'Cine S' (1978–83) is the Spanish equivalent of this popular interest in explicit representations of sex. Actress Susana Estrada was right to claim that her generation of actors was the one 'who opened the floodgates for future filmmakers to express themselves freely' (*Qué tiempo tan feliz*, 13 November 2010). In the process of opening those floodgates, they had to refigure the lines that limited the representation of sex and the suggestion of it. The legacy of their performances, which is so often ignored or despised, should in fact be seen as a very relevant and unique contribution to the history of film and performing arts. Those men and women who, through their talent and courage, brought this about deserve much credit. Perhaps it will be accorded to them in time.

Notes

This chapter is the result of the research funded and developed within the academic group TECMERIN (Universidad Carlos III de Madrid) and the proyect I+D+i CSO2012-31895, 'El cine y la televisión en la España de la post-transición (1979–1992)', Ministry of Culture and Education, Spain.

1 Another example of a very popular 'S' film is *La caliente niña Julietta/Julietta, the Hot Girl* (Ignacio F. Iquino, 1980), with similar results (98,000,000 pesetas and 578,000 spectators). This is more than what successful American

films of the same time made such as *An American Werewolf in London* (John Landis, 1981), which had 514,000 spectators; *Bronco Billy* (Clint Eastwood, 1980), with 458,000; and *Buddy Buddy* (Billy Wilder, 1981), which totalled 348,000 spectators. Pedro Almodóvar's *Pepi, Luci, Bom y otras chicas del montón/Pepi, Luci, Bom* was seen by 216,000 spectators. All information taken from the film database on the website of the Ministerio de Cultura, Educación y Deporte.

2 *A buen entendedor, pocas palabras* (sometimes, *A buen entendedor, pocas palabras bastan*) could be translated as 'A word to the wise is sufficient' and is used when the writer or speaker assumes that the reader or listener knows something that the writer or speaker prefers to ignore or hide.

References

Anon. (1983) 'Vídeo macho', *Machos*, 4.11, 21–4.

Baumann, S. (2007) *Hollywood Highbrow: From Entertainment to Art*, Princeton: Princeton University Press.

Bazin, A. (1971) *What Is Cinema?*, Berkeley: University of California Press.

Blom, I. (2003) *Jean Desmet and the Early Dutch Film Trade*, Amsterdam: Amsterdam University Press.

Blumenthal, R. (1973) 'Porno Chic: "Hard-core" Grows Fashionable and Very Profitable', *New York Times*, 21 January, 28–34.

Iquino, I. (1978) *Liliana. Los increíbles vicios*, Barcelona: IFI Producciones.

Jordan, B. and Rikki Morgan-Tamosunas (1998) *Contemporary Spanish Cinema*, Manchester: Manchester University Press.

Krzywinska, T. (2006) *Sex and the Cinema*, London: Wallflower Press.

Martalay, F. (1976) 'Más que nada, escaparate', *El Alcázar*, 1 May, n.p.

Ordinaire, M. (2001) *'The Stage on Screen: The Representation of Theatre in Film'*, Ph.D. thesis, Columbia University.

Rodríguez, F. (1977) 'Cine de la semana', *Cinespectáculo*, 12, 22.

Tookey, C. (2002) *'Sex and Lucia/Lucia y el sexo'*, *Movie-Film-Review*, www.movie-film-review.com/devFilm.asp?ID=13396.

Wardwell, S., *'Sex and Lucia/Lucia y el sexo'*, *Movie-Film-Review*, www.movie-film-review.com/devfilm.asp?rtype=1&id=13396

Williams, Linda (1990) *Hard Core*, London: Pandora Press.

Williams, Linda (2008) *Screening Sex*, Durham: Duke University Press.

11

Becoming Mario: performance and persona adaptation in Mario Casas's career

Alberto Mira

For the 2007–13 period, Mario Casas was his generation's most popular actor in Spain. A home run in the box office that included such mega-hits as *Mentiras y gordas/Sex, Parties and Lies* (Alfonso Albacete and David Menkes, 2009), *Fuga de cerebros/Brain Drain* (Fernando González Molina, 2009), *Tres metros sobre el cielo/Three Steps Above Heaven* (Fernando González Molina, 2010) (also known as *3MSC*), *Tengo ganas de ti/I Want You* (Fernando González Molina, 2012) and *Las brujas de Zugarramurdi/Witching and Bitching* (Álex de la Iglesia, 2013). Each of these films was among the most popular in their season, and in this period he was one of the top box office attractions in Spain. In 2012, both *ABC* and the magazine *Tiempo* ran features coincidentally labelling Casas 'La gran esperanza del cine español' [The Great Hope of Spanish Cinema]. The fact that certain audiences become obsessed by certain stars carries specific meanings which are the result of a series of roles, career design and some particular traits (physique, behaviour, cultural type) that go beyond simple attributes. We can consider these factors as a carefully constructed performance. Casas is important for reasons that go beyond acting, which are linked specifically to the dynamics of stardom. Between 2009 and 2013 he became an icon, his image gracing covers of magazines ranging from *El país semanal* to *Men's Health*, *Fotogramas* and *GQ*. Always an object of adoration for the female teen demographic, his exposure in those years suggests that there's more to Casas than the simple appeal of the female teen idol.

This chapter is about what Mario Casas represents, and how the meaning of Mario Casas is conveyed through performance in a wider sense, including personal appearances, body image and career choices in terms of persona. The term *persona* comes from the Latin, where it referred to a theatrical mask symbolising character *type*. Sociologist Ervin Goffman (1959) adapted the concept to account, more broadly, for the presentation of self in life, and in Performance Studies it merges both ideas to refer to the way actors present themselves to audiences beyond acting particular roles.[1] An actor's persona is a public adaptation of his or her individual identity; the mask has cultural repercussions that go beyond individual psychology, and brings the individual closer to an established cultural type. Certain personae affect powerfully our perception of each individual performance. Hollywood actors like Marlene Dietrich, Charlie Chaplin, Bette Davis or Humphrey Bogart, or Spanish actors like Lola Flores, Sara Montiel, José Luis López Vázquez or Carmen Machi, developed solid, strong personae that helped audiences connect with them. Far from being just natural attributes of the performers, the mask needs to be carefully and consistently put together.

A performer's persona can shift depending on new contexts or the need to address new audiences. I will argue that, in spite of a clear shift in type regarding his roles around 2010, Casas provided coherence between the type he represented during his early years in teen soaps and film on the one hand and the highly successful Hugo ('Hache') of *3MSC* and its sequel *Tengo ganas de ti*, and his part as Ulises in the Antena 3 hit adventure series *El barco/The Boat* (2011–13). The evolution was both a necessity (the transition from adolescence to young maturity) and a constructed performance put together by the actor, the creative teams of the vehicles he appeared in and his managers. The range of performances between these two points covers two key cultural types: the geeky, soft, sensitive Casas incarnated in his breakthrough role in teen soap *SMS, Sin miedo a soñar/SMS* (2006–7), in *Mentiras y gordas* or in *Fuga de cerebros*; from around 2010, Casas's image shifts to the hard, muscle-bound, assertive stud of *El barco*, *Tres metros sobre el cielo*, *Tengo ganas de ti* or, less precisely, the tough, increasingly cynical cop of *Grupo 7/ Unit 7* (Alberto Rodríguez, 2012).[2] Although such types are markedly different from each other, Casas has managed a smooth transition that worked very well for his fan base. I will focus on the continuities and discontinuities of these two types through key roles representing the earlier type (*Mentiras y gordas*, *Fuga de cerebros*) and the second, his iconic Hache in *Tres metros sobre el cielo* and *Tengo ganas de ti*.

Notwithstanding his big screen successes, Casas's impact cannot be understood only in terms of the film industry, and it is easy to see in his early career the tensions between specific kinds of popularity in different media: very broadly, TV success is about repetition; for critics, success in film acting tends to entail versatility. The arc of his career is easy to summarise. His first important part was in the hit teen show *Sin miedo a soñar* (airing on La Sexta and popularly known as SMS). As Javi, the alternative, slightly grungey musician in a posh high school, he became a favourite of the series' target audience and was widely featured in magazines like *Bravo!* and *Super Pop*. He was discovered by the masses in the more widely appealing *Los hombres de Paco/Paco's Men* (2005–10), an Antena 3 cop-cum-comedy show into which he came in 2007. Casas's film career took off in 2006 with a small part in Antonio Banderas's film *El camino de los ingleses/Summer Rain*, as the least substantial character in the group of friends whose story it told, but his real breakthrough on film would be the critically panned box office hit *Mentiras y gordas*, in which he played a timid gay teen. The comedy *Fuga de cerebros*, another huge hit in which he also played a sensitive guy (and was also universally panned by the critics) followed the same year. These teen roles constitute the first cycle in Casas's career.

When *Los hombres de Paco* ended in 2010, he signed a contract with the same producers (Globomedia) to star in Antena 3's science fiction adventure series *El barco*, which started broadcasting in 2011 and would last for three seasons. Mario Casas was huge in 2009 for his niche audience, but this was only the beginning in comparison to the fame and significance he acquired after starring in *Tres metros sobre el cielo*, a Spanish adaptation of Federico Moccia´s bestselling *Romeo and Juliet*-themed novel of young urban passion.

If previous roles struck a chord with the female teen erotic and sentimental imagination, his part as Hache had a broader cultural impact. The combination between the previous 'Mario Casas persona' and these new characters overcame all expectations: intense, bold, prone to violence, rebellious, brimming with emotional pain, Hache seemed to capture a certain type of teen fantasy exactly right, and his audience responded by attending in droves. The shift included a change in his looks and his demeanour. He bulked up, his jaw became clenched, as if withholding an explosion, his characters tended to display outbursts of physical violence. His acting in this film is close to the approach James Naremore (1988) refers to as Delsartean:[3] excessive, superficial, even facile (each emotion or thought is accompanied by a standard gesture). This second phase extended to the film's sequel and to *El barco*, and dominated perception of the actor, as evidenced in a number of TV appearances between 2010 and 2013. Such appearances are the key to contextualising performances and to reminding audiences of the more sensitive aspects of the Casas persona.

In discussing the Casas persona and the types he played, we need to keep well in mind the constituency addressed. The mention of Mario Casas in Spain immediately brings to mind his main niche audience between the start of his acting career and 2013, although this focus is not exclusive and there is an attempt to introduce 'alternative traits' for alternative audiences.[4] As we shall see, in interviews Casas explicitly acknowledges his fan base but also claims to be overwhelmed by his success among them. Although we could argue there was more to Casas than his role as a teen fantasy, it is this type that remained at the core of the phenomenon until 2013. In fact, as we shall see, both versions of Mario Casas were equally successful and capitalised on different sets of expectations from his fan base.

Casas's body has been central in the construction of both the teen fantasy he represents and his broader persona. His body performance is based both on the typical and the individual: first, as a general phenomenon, his is a very particular type of body that represents very well current trends in young male performers[5] and which also carries connotations of the cultural type of the 'cani' [chav] or 'poligonero' [mallrat[6]] in Spain; and second, and more specific to Casas's case, although clearly objectified in films, TV appearances and magazine features, he has counterbalanced the charges of being simply an object.

In tracing this evolution and placing Casas within it, I draw from the work of Susan Bordo in her collection *The Male Body* (1999), particularly the chapter 'Beauty (Re)discovers the Male Body'. Bordo was among the first to discuss a shift in the representation of the male body that took place from the mid-1980s, and how a new way of bodily performance became prominent in acting and modelling. Her work focuses on advertising, and clearly it was in this area that the new images and their implications were first rehearsed. The trend she discussed spread to film and television, and the impulse to objectify the male body has become more noticeable in the past decade. There is indeed a new enthusiasm for displaying pecs, delts, lats, groin muscles and abs both for actors and models. A neat six-pack, in particular, has become something of a holy grail for many young actors, some magical object that gets them photo opportunities and hits on Google. Such actors have made taking the shirt off a cultural commonplace, to the extent that it is now expected of them. Casas is a typical instance of this trend in Spanish film and TV. Such display is not always linked to plot needs, and exceeds the limits of actual film texts into numerous magazine features and photo sessions. Iván Escolar, one of the producers of *El barco*, acknowledged that physical display was one of the series's *raisons d'être*: 'Si tenemos a Mario Casas, si tenemos a Blanca y tenemos unos chavales guapísimos… evidentemente es parte de la geografía de nuestra serie' [As long as we have Mario Casas, or Blanca and we have a bunch of very handsome kids … this becomes part of the series' geography] (quoted in Montes 2014: 184).

Casas took advantage of the new set of cultural expectations for his 2010 makeover. It could be argued that the degree of success he achieved would have been impossible without the new trends surrounding masculine bodies and the new permission men have to exhibit them. One distinction proposed by Bordo in her discussion of advertising is particularly relevant to Casas's body performance. In her work, Bordo still follows the general idea proposed by Dyer that somehow the suspicion of narcissism needs to be compensated through body posture, glances, imagery, etc (1992: 103–20). In her analysis of body representation in advertising, she identifies two distinct types. On the one hand, there's 'the leaner', a young, soft model, sometimes sulky, often casting a shy, mistrustful glance or even looking off-field, who is typically represented leaning on a wall or other hard surface. The second type is what she calls 'the rock': hard and phallic, the model looks towards the camera as if challenging viewers. As we shall see, the implications of both types are relevant when discussing the two stages of Casas career.

Casas the leaner

In a 2006 promotional photo shot for the actors of *Sin miedo a soñar*, Mario Casas posed with the rest of the male cast, shirtless, barefoot and wearing jeans, in what seemed like a barn. Surrounded by ropes and a tyre, and lying on a heap of straw, he represents Bordo's leaner type: the body is presented as a passive object, almost offering itself up to the spectator, but lacking in agency; it acknowledges the beauty of the body but implies that the model is not completely aware of the gaze or saves the model from conveying awareness of being objectified.

Two key points are apparent in this image. First, in the spread, Casas's body is ostensibly objectified in a way that would have not fitted on the conventions for the representation of masculinity only a couple of decades ago. Such objectification was, at the time, an understated part of his persona, and is also evident in his TV work. Episode 24 of the second season of *Sin miedo a soñar* featured his character having his clothes stolen while he was having a shower at the school's gym, therefore being forced to wander the corridors lost, vulnerable, completely naked and gazed at by two female students. Such vulnerability was a character trait, which was demonstrated through the way he carried his body and the way his naked body was exposed to the desiring gaze of the female students. Similarly, the first episode of the fourth season of *Los hombres de Paco* has a skinny, shirtless Casas wandering around with very slight justification. Given that the police station has been under attack and he is surrounded with the results of the explosion, vulnerability is also emphasised in the display of the naked body. The fact that the body is skinny and soft – as in the magazine feature described – contributes to this effect. In a way, these two moments represent very well the first

Mario Casas: an innocent boy surrounded by glances or unable to cope with external circumstances.

This leads to a second important point we can derive from these images. The body acquires meaning by fitting into certain cultural stereotypes. This Casas is perceived as a loner, a vulnerable teen, quietly rebellious and beautiful in a passive way. One central type that determined the perception of Casas at the time was the 'poligonero', a working-class youth whose habitat is the suburban shopping mall. While basically perceived in terms of class, it is associated with certain visual traits such as a mullet, jewellery, vests and tattoos, which suggest brashness but also hostility, macho posturing and violence. Some of these traits were incorporated into the Casas persona, but the negative implications were carefully avoided. For his character in *Los hombres de Paco*, he changed his look to shorter hair and soon did away with the earrings, but some class connotations of the 'poligonero' were still very much present.

The best instance on feature film of Casas the leaner is his performance in the film *Mentiras y gordas*. The film features a group of teens whose lives are tangled up in a turmoil of drugs and meaningless sex. The approach was sensationalist and critics were not kind. Casas played Tony following key traits from his TV roles so far – a sensitive, gentle boy. In the film, he was best friends with the assertive Nico (Yon González). It turns out Tony is gay and in love with Nico, but he feels unable to come out to him until late in the narrative. The arc of his character is linked to the way Casas uses his body.

The film opens with both boys lying on the beach. It is the start of the summer and they are making plans to spend time together. Casas's lingering glances at Nico show desire, which registers even on first viewing. Nico, on the other hand is harder: we don't get a clear idea of what he is thinking, and there is certainly less tension between what he thinks and the way he acts; González plays assertively and his eyes fixed on Tony suggest self-control. After a conversation pregnant with a subtext of power and desire, Nico suggests that they go swimming. Both peel off their jeans. Nico does so with a quick, sharp shake; Tony, more awkwardly, getting at one point tangled up in the trousers. We see them in long shot, from behind, walking towards the sea. The ways both move echo the personalities that came across in their short conversation. Whereas González strides cockily, Casas hesitates, hunches his shoulders, seems aware of his nakedness and soon starts running nervously, as if unable to stand the tension of being naked next to his friend.

Later in the film, Carmen (Elena de Frutos) proposes to have sex with both Tony and Nico. Tony is at first horrified, although he ends up succumbing to their advances. Again we have the contrast of both boys' nakedness. Although both bodies on display are slim, Casas seems more fragile and we are more aware of a hard, stereotypical masculinity in González's body (a stronger chest, more defined muscles). Holding hands, they come into the room where Carmen is waiting for them and sit together. When they strip, there is a certain nervousness in Tony, who holds his hand to the back of his head as if trying to keep it from wandering. The three of them start fondling each other and, although Carmen seems initially more interested in Tony than in Nico, the former shifts smoothly from kissing Carmen to kissing Nico passionately, at which point he is stopped in his tracks. This is a turning point in the scene and the film, the moment in which Tony stops lying to himself. In terms of Casas's performance, it is remarkable how straightforward he plays the scene and how believable the transition is. There are certainly no alibis, nothing to signal distance between the actor and the character's desire.

Coming out to Nico seems to liberate Tony's body. He spends the rest of the film in a despair- and drug-induced daze. For his final moments, he seems to become alive, stretching his arms and adopting a gestural repertoire that the directors and co-writers have linked to a *'via crucis'*, impregnated with religious imagery: arms stretched, head looking up as if asking heaven why. As Chris Perriam (2013: 87) points out, Tony's death at the end of *Mentiras y gordas* has irritated many gay commentators in Spain.[7] However, portraying Tony as a tragic victim worked well both in terms of the moralistic meaning of the plot and the teen audiences. In terms of Mario Casas, it makes a point about vulnerability and honesty. Like some other characters in the film, he overcomes his lies.

In the same vein, in *Fuga de cerebros* Casas played an awkward teenager so in love with the most beautiful girl in his class that he follows her to Oxford University with his friends. His performance is a companion piece to the one in *Mentiras y gordas*. Bespectacled and briefly seen in braces, the character's body is still central to the performance (there is, again, an unnecessary nude scene which, oddly, also involves corpses). Some commentators complained he was too attractive to play an ugly duckling (see Montes 2014: 49). Although this is in a way missing the point, it does point out a tension between the character and the actor's body. It looked as if he was trying to have it both ways. This tension will become exacerbated in the next stage of his career.

Casas the rock

Although he was born in 1986, Casas played teenagers in both of his 2009 roles; however, it soon became imperative to move on to a more mature persona that retained some of the previous formula but was more attuned to his actual age. The transition to this second Mario Casas took place a few minutes into *Tres metros sobre el cielo* in a series of shots that make the shift explicit. The film opens with a tight close-up of Hugo and a voice-over which interestingly describes 'that moment in life when everything changes' (presumably his). The film's characters are in a court-room and Casas's face is tense, eyes fixed on the judge. This shot already showed a side of Mario Casas that was, at that point, unfamiliar: the expression of the face on the screen is edgy, as if Hugo is deep in concentration; the gestures when he starts to move, sharp and brimming with energy. The transition between the old Mario and the new Mario is completed as he exits the courtroom: Hugo sheds his ironed, formal white shirt and shows off bulky, perfectly toned shoulders and arms, which are subsequently covered by a biker's jacket, and he walks out of the building with precise, determined strides and rides his motorcycle away (Figure 11). The transformation from 'Mario the leaner' into 'Mario the rock' was carried out especially through the unveiling of Casas's newly built-up muscles. Throughout this film, his body is very much on display. Well-intentioned commentators and interviewers had been asking him about going shirtless in the past, but now it was more than that. In *3MSC*, his body is always there, tanned and glistening, bulging through clothes even when it's not completely naked. Actually, everything about the new Casas is hard. The voice tends to have a hushed unemotional tone that belies the stuttering and inconclusive intonation of previous characters played by him, his gestures are short and decisive, and he always moves with determination, as if driven, whether riding his motor-cycle or striding towards the camera. When one compares the nervous

Figure 11 The emergence of Mario the rock in *Tres metros sobre el cielo* (Fernando González Molina, 2010). Antena 3 Films.

walk of Tony at the start of *Mentiras y gordas* to the way Hugo walks in this film, one is aware of a complete change in approach that points towards a shift in his persona and performance. In a very vivid way, he was impersonating a cultural type carefully avoided so far in his career, the 'chulo poligonero': an arrogant, assertive, and laconic working-class male who has a possessive relationship with women. The repertoire of gestures seems taken from some Delsartean manual that accounted with contemporary character types: the quick wink, the nod, the sharp chin-up, the cocky smirk. These make up the character of Hugo, and this Hugo is not very much beyond this collection of signs. In terms of acting styles, Casas avoids the introspective expressions of Tony, suggesting a less conflicted emotional life. Actually, the essence of the character seems to be achieved through the constant repetition of those gestures.

In the film he falls in love with Babi (María Valverde), the sheltered daughter of a conservative family, only to lose her when she is afraid of his unstable behaviour. In the film's narrative, Hugo is very much in love, but, much as he tries to dress more formally and give up death-defying motorbike races, he can't seem to channel his personality into something Babi might find acceptable. His excessive intensity keeps on preventing him from developing a steady relationship with the woman he loves. In spite of Valverde's appeal, it is Casas who becomes the difficult object of desire.

Ideologically, this is the kind of film that prefers fantasy and visceral emotions to logic, coherent narrative or common sense. An important part of the film's fantasy work is carried out through Casas's physique. Casas's body is very much on display throughout the film. And, as in *Mentiras y gordas*, the character's arc can be retold in terms of the way he presents his body. In an early scene, he takes his shirt off to engage in a push-up competition with his friends (which he wins). His macho posturing depends on his muscles. The scene is largely unnecessary in terms of plot and can be understood in terms of montage of attractions. On the other hand, it does have narrative function, as it strengthens characterisation through a display of physical strength and endurance. With very little justification, the push-ups recur later in the film when he is rejected by Babi.

The sex scene in *Tres metros sobre el cielo* with María Valverde seems to be more concerned about objectifying Casas' body than hers: as shot, it is all about his rippling muscles catching the moonlight (Figure 12). The contrived lighting in the film has a way of falling on the dimples in his back, in between his abdominal muscles, in his glutes. The point of his trim physique is not health or action, the usual alibis for aesthetic male bodies in classical cinema; it's not even about 'going to the gym'

Figure 12 Hache (Mario Casas) and Babi (María Valverde) in the moonlight. *Tres metros sobre el cielo* (Fernando González Molina, 2010). Antena 3 Films.

(although the sequel had him boxing to justify the bulk in narrative terms) – it's about having aesthetic muscles, muscles that *look* good on screen. The new approach to the male body discussed by Bordo (1999) had found one of its outstanding representatives in Spanish visual media in Casas.

Hache is a morally problematic character, and his impact made it essential to negotiate Casas's persona. Identification between persona and roles is both somewhat necessary but also a sensitive area in the case of characters with antisocial behaviour. Although Hache himself comes from a wealthy family, he keeps company with 'poligoneros' (like his best friend Pollo, played by Alvaro Cervantes) and is impulsive and prone to violence. Although almost a polar opposite of the first type, the film needed to remind audiences that there was something of the old Mario in the new. One flashback in the film seems intended to bridge the change. At one point we see Hugo before he discovered his mother's infidelity as a studious, soft teenager that would not have been out of place played by pre-Hache Casas. Briefly, the teen Mario is back, and somehow the link between the two Marios is made explicit narratively: in terms of persona, it's as if teen Mario Casas had evolved into young adult Casas due to Hugo's trauma when discovering his mother was having an extramarital affair. Teen Mario and the new Mario are juxtaposed by means of a simple cut (across which one seems to be looking at the other), and such juxtaposition can help us understand the way the Casas's image was now being produced and consumed. Even when teen girls fell for the hot, sweaty, nervy stud of *3MSC*, loyal audiences had in mind the more sensitive boy of previous films. Some of this comes across in internet fora where fans (gay and straight) insist on the combination between sensitiveness, hotness and macho posturing.[8] Mario Casas is, after all, a fantasy, and a fantasy can reconcile apparently contradictory traits.

Bridging the gap: Casas's persona and the two Marios

Actors can incorporate unsavoury traits into their personae. Mel Gibson, Leonardo DiCaprio or Russell Crowe are just some examples of the kind of actors whose reputation survives and thrives on such bad boy antics: there is a pretence that beyond playing dangerous, rough characters, they are actually rough and dangerous. What certain audiences love in actors is the fantasy that, no matter how dangerous, it doesn't hurt their acceptability if some traits of the fantasy become part of their personae. Although Casas insisted Hugo was a character very close to himself (Montes 2014: 84), the fact is that he steered away from incorporating such rebellious traits into his public image.

He has not succumbed to the temptation to be dismissive in order to boost his reputation among critics. In interviews, Casas is courteous and respectful towards his teen audiences, even when telling anecdotes like the one about the girl pressing her naked breasts to his car window or the one about two young women conspiring to pluck out some of his hair and then proceeding to attempt it.[9] On TV, he describes these situations calmly, almost puzzled, and never winking at more cynical audiences, but still comments on the downside of being a teen idol abound. A typical statement runs something like this:

> Las fans son personas que te siguen y te apoyan. Uno está ahí porque ellas lo deciden. Si alguna vez me he sentido violento porque me esperaban a la puerta de mi casa, mi madre siempre me ha dicho que esté tranquilo, que hay que tomárselo bien. Pero sé que no están ahí por mí sino por mis personajes. El cine te lleva a idealizar ciertos papeles. Ellas, en realidad, no me conocen. [Female fans are people who follow you and support you. It is their decision that I'm here. If I have ever felt a bit uncomfortable because they were waiting at my door, my mother has always insisted that I should not worry, that I should take it easy. But I know they are not there because of me, but because of my characters. Because of films, people idealise certain roles. Actually they don't know me.] (Montes 2014: 33)

Another aspect that Mario Casas has had to contend with in his personal appearances was the charge of objectification. In the case of Casas, as suggested in several examples above, objectification is a fact that is impossible to dismiss and has extended to his work as model in magazine features. Casas's cover for issue 71 of *Revista 40* in 2011,[10] illustrates this attitude: slim, naked, toned, holding a shaving razor, slightly nonchalant, the image draws attention towards his abs (which have the phrase 'Yo me afeito a navaja' [I shave with a razor] written across them) and well-defined groin muscles. Whereas such body display in previous instances seemed to demand a certain shyness on his part, now he is allowed to show joy in his tight body, to welcome the objectifying gaze. Still, accusations of 'mere' passivity as result of objectification do need to be dismissed if the persona is to work. In the previous example, the reference to the razor seems to counterbalance such passivity with a hint of violence. In an interview for *El Mundo* the headline was 'No me siento un hombre objeto' [I don't feel objectified] (Polo 2013: n.p.). Elsewhere he claims to be in control: 'A veces la prensa da a entender que nos están obligando a enseñar carne, cuando yo sé muy bien lo que estoy haciendo. Nadie me miente ni me utiliza. Me lo preguntan mucho: ¿te parece bien?¿Está justificado? Me quito la camiseta porque me da la gana' [Sometimes the media suggest that we are being forced to show some skin when I know very well what I'm doing. Nobody lies to me, nobody is using me. I get asked that all the time: how do you feel? Is it justified? I go shirtless because I feel like it] (Montes 2014: 185).

Female performers might have thought twice before such statements, as objectification of women is politicised territory that most actresses feel uncomfortable entering. Acknowledging objectification means taking a position vis-à-vis old debates on the feminine body on display. One occasion in which we can see a clash between the old and the new approach happened in the first programme of the Nieves Herrero show, *Hola Nieves!*, which was largely devoted to an interview with Casas, who was then promoting *Las brujas de Zugarramurdi*. Even though this is one of the films in which Casas's body is less in evidence, the topic had to be broached. One of the programme's guests asked Casas about his body. The actor was apparently going to reply about training and how hard it was (following the new pattern of boasting about the process rather than concealing it), but was interrupted by Herrero, who, more traditionally, tried to make him say that no, he didn't try very hard, that his muscles were 'natural'. For someone in the mindset of Herrero (or of Herrero's audience), going on about the trials of diet and gym was simply not masculine enough for Casas. This blatantly contradicted Casas's stated agency (see above) in the way he controlled the meaning of his own body. My reading of the scene is that Herrero represents old attitudes towards men's bodies, whereas Casas plays the new script, according to which one is supposed to be unembarrassed by (and to willingly play into) objectification.

There is in the end a contradiction, which an old-fashioned talk show host like Herrero failed to see. The young male body is clearly objectified in the twenty-first century in TV, film and advertising. What Casas and other actors are resisting is the negative stigma attached to the objectification of the female body rather than the objectification itself. In order to do this, they need to create a discourse of 'active' objectification. So, yes, Casas accepts the fact that his body is treated as an object and an instrument for popularity but, like other young stars, he needs to explain how such objectification is something they had to work hard to achieve, through strict diet (which speaks for discipline) and physical exercise. So, Nieves Herrero had it wrong. The best way to present the new bodies is not by labelling them natural and effortless, but by having the performer becoming the agent of his body.

Finally, such conflicted readings of Casas's body and the way his persona works to shape the meanings of his body – which are very much in line with contemporary displays of the nude male body and central to changes in its perception of in advertising, music videos or magazine features – seem to be a very recent trend in Spanish cinema. It's true that, at least for a few decades, the male body has been a focus of Spanish cinema. As also noted by Dean Allbritton (chapter 13 this volume), Fouz-Hernández and Martínez-Expósito's analyses (2007: 17–27) show how there has been a clash between the stereotype and its contestation in a film like *Jamón, jamón* (Bigas Luna, 1992). In this film, Fouz-Hernández and Martínez-Expósito interpret Javier Bardem's body as being a site for Spanish cultural change, a tool Bigas Luna is using to tell his story. If the gaze lingered over Bardem's muscles, this was acceptable, but not necessarily something acknowledged either by the star or the director. This earnestness seems to have disappeared in the young TV generation, led by a strong contingent of young girls who are able to turn hormonal change into a cultural phenomenon. Unlike the Bardem–Mollá pairing in *Jamón, jamón*, bodies are not attempting to make a political or cultural point. Young performers offer their bodies as products or, even more cynically, as a means to an end. If it takes a six-pack to become a media celebrity, that is something one can work on. Also, Casas's body is not making a point on Spanishness or even on politics (although many reviewers accusing *3MSC* of being reactionary subtly referred to Casas's tight body), but it does gesture towards changes in the market that challenge old taboos that were constitutive of masculinity.

The end of 2013 brought another turning point in Mario Casas's career. For his role in *Las brujas de Zugarramurdi*, he presented an ironic combination of the Mario Casas image by mixing up all types he had played. He had the looks of a 'chulo poligonero', but a 'soft' one, and he played an innocent involved in a comedy plot, sidekick to the more 'active' character played by Hugo Silva. Even more surprising, his role in *Ismael* (Marcelo Piñeyro, 2013) presented him as a physically challenged teacher who survives a motorcycle accident. This may be a symbolic response to criticisms about his Hache in *3MSC* riding a bike without a helmet. But it is interesting to see how the persona keeps developing, as the film was not a hit. Indeed, without the body, Mario Casas's run of hits might be slacking. In interviews around that time, he insisted that for his next film he would be playing a starving labourer trapped in a mine. Whether the actor will be able to proceed with his career as he starts leaving behind such a crucial part of his persona is, at the time, anybody's guess. Still, his significance – in terms of offering the male body as a site for cultural change and relating to it in markedly different ways to those of traditional masculinity – cannot be denied.

Notes

1 Some accounts focus on the image conveyed by a series of performances. In this chapter I will work with a concept closer to Goffman: persona is the public mask of the actor, conveyed not just through character types but also through interviews, features and other public appearances.

2 Although these are the two more prominent images he projects, there is a third, less-discussed Mario Casas: the 'comedy Casas' of *Carne de neón/Neon Flesh* (Paco Cabezas, 2010) or *Las brujas de Zugarramurdi*. Some of the discussions in this chapter apply to this third type, and it is clearly a strand within his career, but for reasons of extension and focus I will be referring only to the other two strands.

3 The term 'Delsartean' derives from François Delsarte (1811–71), a popular writer on stage acting, author of one of the most influential manuals for actors that proposed standardised gestures to make communication of emotions easily understandable by audiences. See Naremore (1998).

4 Although not the focus of this chapter, Casas has also been a favourite of gay media, and received nominations for *Shangay* magazine and an award at the Festival de Cine Gay y Lésbico de Madrid. See Perriam (2013: 88).

5 See Dutton (1995) on the iconography of the male body as an object of beauty. It is interesting that the aesthetics and the implications of the new body type young actors represents were not yet completely established when the book was written. Although the new masculine body participates in some visual traits of what Dutton calls 'classical bodies', one key aspect distinctive about the new body is that it calls attention on itself as a locus of effort and manufacturing. The ideal classical body represented values. The bodies of actors such as Casas, Miguel Ángel Silvestre, Taylor Lautner or Zac Efron remind one of carefully planned workout plans.

6 One possible translation of 'poligonero' is 'mallrat', although arguably the connotations are different.

7 See, for instance, Fran Zurian (2014: 151–70).

8 See, for instance, http://clubmariocasas.blogspot.co.uk/, accessed 15 December 2014. Several Facebook pages cover Casas in different countries. Also, online magazines like *Superpop* have open threads on Casas.

9 See his interview in *El hormiguero*, 3 September 2012 (*fansdelhormiguero* 2012).

10 The caption read 'Vuelve el hombre' [The man is back]. One wonders whether the editors were being ironic.

References

Bordo, S. (1999) *The Male Body*, New York: Farrar, Straus and Giroux.

Dutton, K.R. (1995) *The Perfectible Body: The Western Ideal of Male Physical Development*, London: Cassell.

Dyer, R. (1992) 'Don't Look Now. The Instabilities of the Male Pinup', in *The Matter of Images*, London: Routledge, pp. 103–20.

fansdelhormiguero (2012) 'El Hormiguero 3.0 (03/09/2012) – Mario Casas y Clara Labo [sic]' YouTube, https://youtu.be/H2081-UdbEw, accessed 29 April 2015.

Fouz-Hernández, Santiago and A. Martínez-Expósito (2007) *Live Flesh: The Male Body in Contemporary Spanish Cinema*, London: I. B. Tauris.

Goffman, E. (1959) *The Presentation of Self in Everyday Life*, New York: Random House.

Montes, J. M. (2014) *Mario Casas en cuerpo y alma*, Barcelona: Quarentena ediciones.

Naremore, J. (1988) *Acting in Cinema*, Oakland: University of California Press.

Perriam, C. (2013) *Spanish Queer Cinema*, Edinburgh: Edinburgh University Press.

Polo, S. (2013) 'Mario Casas: "No me siento un hombre objeto"', *El Mundo*, 18 December, www.elmundo.es/cultura/2013/12/18/52b09def22601d163c8b458a.html, accessed 31 March 2015.

Zurian, F. (2014) 'Cuerpos masculinos, hormonas y sexo' in Fran Zurian (ed.) *Imagen, Cuerpo y sexualidad. Representaciones del cuerpo en la cultura audiovisual contemporánea*, Madrid: Ocho y medio.

12

Performing fatness: oversized male bodies in recent Spanish cinema

Santiago Fouz-Hernández

Every actor undergoes a certain degree of physical transformation in preparation for a role. This could be as simple as changing hairstyle or as drastic as completely altering body shape. Regardless of the complexity of the makeover, this very physical aspect of characterisation is undoubtedly a major part of any performance. Major body transformations are often highlighted in the advertising campaigns of some films as a means to attract audiences. In biopics, for example, the process might have resulted in an actor achieving a remarkable resemblance to the real-life character she or he is impersonating – the classic example is Robert De Niro, who gained around 30 kilograms to portray the older version of boxer Jake LaMotta in Scorsese's *Raging Bull* (1980). In an action movie, in an epic or a superhero film, physical changes usually involve packing up a lot of muscle bulk in a short period of time, such as Chris Hemsworth's recent transformation for his role in for *Thor* (Kenneth Branagh, 2011). Some roles require actors to lose a lot of weight, for instance, Christian Bale for *The Machinist* (Brad Anderson, 2004). There are also short cuts – Eddie Murphy wore a fat suit for *The Nutty Professor* (Tom Shadyac, 1996) and its sequel (Peter Segal, 2000).

The field of Fat Studies has gained critical momentum in recent years, and its impact on Film Studies is becoming increasingly evident. Yet, fat bodies are rarely discussed in the context of masculinities and Men's Studies. In *Fat Boys*, a pioneering book-length study on representations of fat men in art, literature and popular culture, Sander L. Gilman offers some answers as to why that may be. The title of his introduction, 'Fat is a Men's Issue' (2004: 1–35), is an explicit response to Orbach's much-critiqued argument in *Fat is a Feminist Issue* (first published in 1978).[1] He argues both that the cultural association of women and fat ignores the history of fat men in ancient Greece, nineteenth-century medical discourses and Western literary history. His examples demonstrate a persistent association of male obesity with failed masculinity, deviance and disability.[2]

There is now a well-established body of scholarship that reads actors' physiques as a tool to interpret and analyse films. Some recent studies discuss fat masculinities in cinema, but most of these have focused on well-known Hollywood actors, genres or Hollywood cinema more generally.[3] In *Transgressive Bodies*, Niall Richardson examines the representation of fatness in recent mainstream film and popular culture. His findings imply that contemporary representations of fatness follow the pattern described by Gilman: 'the suggestion of fat has always been that the character is lazy, undisciplined' (2010: 96). In his study of fat masculinities in film noir, Christopher Forth agrees that 'fat has been gendered as "feminine" in the Western cultural imagination' and argues that in film noir fat manhood is generally associated with 'looseness, immorality, weakness and cowardice', and thus a threat to patriarchy (2013: 389). In the context of Spanish cinema, Pavlović's groundbreaking *Despotic Bodies and Transgressive Bodies* (2002) lucidly explores the connections between national identity and visual depictions of the body during Franco's dictatorship and the Transition. My own work with Martínez-Expósito (2007) investigates the prominence of male bodies and male nudity in Spanish films of the democratic period. In both cases, fat male bodies are discussed, but not in much detail. This chapter aims to provide a better understanding, both of fat masculinities and how fatness might affect an actor's performance, in the context of contemporary Spanish cinema. I will start by exploring two stars whose performances of fat masculinities has fundamentally different meanings (Santiago Segura as Torrente for the famous saga, and Javier Bardem as Santa in León de Aranoa's *Los lunes al sol/Mondays in the Sun* (2002)), to then focus on *Gordos/Fat People* (Daniel Sánchez Arévalo, 2009), a film that confronts the issue of fatness directly and that usefully complements the other two cases.

Santiago Segura and the *Torrente* saga

The highly profitable *Torrente* saga (with five instalments so far – 1998, 2001, 2005, 2011, 2014) seems the ideal starting point for a discussion of fatness as performance in contemporary Spanish cinema. Santiago Segura, the saga's director and protagonist became famous for putting on inordinate amounts of weight for the role (an average of 30 kilos in the first four films – see Belategui 2012). A crucial aspect of the discussion here is the very public spectacle that Segura makes of his physical transformations for the role, including, in 2005, a regular weigh-in on national television in the run-up to the release of *Torrente 2* (see Fouz-Hernández and Martínez-Expósito 2007: 30). The *Torrente* films are among the clearest illustrations of what could be regarded as the 'performance' of fatness in Spanish cinema. Since the leading actor is also the director of the films, as well as the main orchestrator of the whole phenomenon – which sustains his production company 'Amiguetes Entertainment' – he has control over the character's performance on and off screen (as amply demonstrated by Triana-Toribio 2004). Although part of the appeal of the saga relies on relatively high-profile cameo roles by famous Spanish (and some international) celebrities, actors and television personalities, this is mostly a one-man show. The importance of fatness as an essential part of Torrente's persona is evident in the film, but Segura's constant promotion of this particular aspect of his performance as Torrente underscores its significance. In his numerous public appearances, he makes it very clear that becoming fat is an essential part of his preparation for the role, of the character's identity and, ultimately, of the films' refusal of dominant discourses of beauty. Performing fatness, in the case of *Torrente*, is as much a performance of abjection as it is a refusal to conform to what the films present as imposed and foreign models of physical and behavioural normalcy.

Torrente is an overweight middle-aged former policeman who, having been expelled from the police force, decides to continue working by himself, imposing his own, bigoted and outdated, vision of Spanish society on those around him, also taking on some very ambitious missions along the way. These missions are usually related to a controversial and embarrassing aspect of Spain's current affairs, such as the sovereignty of Gibraltar or, most recently, the failed Eurovegas project (for *Torrente 5*). The crucial importance of Torrente's obesity is perhaps best illustrated by the amount of press coverage generated when rumours of a 'slimmer' version of the infamous detective for the fifth instalment of the saga started to circulate at pre-production stage (see, for example, *Cinemanía* 2013). In interviews at that time, Segura claimed that, fifteen years since the start of the first film in the saga, his older self could not put up with the health consequences that come with this process. The reason he gave was that, while he really wanted Torrente the character to be an obese 'excessive' man, he (the actor) could not cope with that (Belategui 2012). The prospect of a slim Torrente was ultimately too unbearable: appropriate for the start of the film when Torrente has just completed a prison sentence, but unthinkable for the character. During the promotional campaign of *Torrente 5*, Segura argued that he felt so sorry for the character when he saw early footage of the film that he had to put on weight again (González-Alegre 2014). The actor and the character gradually gained 17 kilograms in three months of filming, further blurring the distinction between the two.

In her recent study of Phillip Seymour Hoffman, Benson-Allot argues that fat actors have been typecast as 'overgrown children', 'fools', 'grotesques', 'corporeally intuitive detectives', 'appetitive villains' and 'effeminate failures' (2013: 203). Most of these adjectives have indeed been used by reviewers and academics in their analyses of the Torrente character (see, for example, Esquirol and Fecé 2001). Torrente's awkward body language, his often-infantile facial expressions and a limited range of comical one-liners also point in that direction. Benson-Allot's words, however, refer to actors that are fat, not those who, like Segura, become fat for a role. Performing Torrente is, at least in part, performing fatness. A key aspect of the preparation for the role is to put on the weight, making a big spectacle out of it in order to build expectation for the release.

A considerable part of Torrente's comic value resides in the fact that he behaves like an action hero and seems blissfully unaware of his physical limitations. In his frequent erotic dreams, he is a *macho ibérico* (Iberian male) whom no young attractive woman of any nationality can resist. In reality, however, he seems more interested in masturbating in his car with his much younger and intellectually challenged male assistants. The visual absence of the protagonist's penis in the frustrated masturbation scenes and erotic dreams contrasts with his frequent phallic jokes and the inescapable phallic imagery that often surrounds him, thus drawing more attention to Torrente's sexual complexes. In his erotic dreams, his large stomach (often exaggerated through low camera angles and profile shots) overshadows the rest of his body, especially his genitals. Thus, fatness is visually associated with his sexual frustration, not only because the fat body makes the penis shrivel in comparison, but because it also creates an uncomfortably obvious physical contrast between Torrente and the sultry women who surround him in his dreams. This is also clear in the famous opening credit segments. The credits are elaborate parodies of Hollywood sagas led by global icons of masculinity, such as James Bond, Bruce Lee, Rambo or the *Lethal Weapon* and *Mission Impossible* films.[4] In those sequences, as well as in the absurd narratives and impossible scenarios elsewhere in the films, Torrente's farcical and excessive performance also questions imposed models of masculinity that are often uncritically accepted by film audiences around the world. Those models are usually excessive and very problematic in themselves (as argued by Susan Jeffords 1994), and yet somewhat credible for some mainstream audiences. Despite an implicit refusal of those foreign models of hegemonic masculinities, the carnivalesque atmosphere that characterises the *Torrente* films also contributes to perpetuate the Hollywood standard as the norm and Torrente's politically incorrect world-view as cathartic, but ultimately undesirable. Torrente's obese body is *itself* the cause of laughter, the butt of the joke, and intrinsically associated to his outdated and despicably prejudiced attitude.

The vision of an overweight, unkempt middle-aged Spaniard seems doomed to failure in contexts and settings that may seem suited only for Hollywood supermen. In the *Torrente* saga those (usually foreign) muscular men always play the role of villains. The Spaniard, of course, has the last laugh, as, against all odds, he often succeeds in his action-packed missions and defeats those intimidating opponents. Yet the triumph always comes as a result of coincidences and good luck, and not due to the former detective's competence or skills. On the contrary, his fatness is rendered the cause of all trouble. In *Torrente 4*, for example, he frustrates a plan to escape prison because the access to the undercover tunnel that had been built by other inmates was not big enough for him. The image of Torrente's behind – in close-up and at one point occupying most of the frame, as it gets stuck in the entrance hole – is meant to be one of the most hilarious moments of the film, especially since *Torrente 4* was also released in 3D, adding to the effect. In a scene which could be read as yet another metaphor for his sexual frustration and his obsession with penetrative sex, the whole tunnel collapses when he tries to release his body from the hole, thus frustrating the whole plan and accidentally killing his mates, who were already inside the tunnel.

As funny as this character might seem to be, then, and as much as we may interpret his racist and sexist behaviour as part of the joke (cancelled out by their very excessiveness), there is a sombre aspect to the way in which Segura's performance draws attention to Torrente's obesity. Fatness is used for laughs, but here it is also connected to a much more sinister side of Torrente's character. He is in the habit of stealing food from restaurant tables or bins, often tricking vulnerable people in order to achieve his goals. He seems to have little regard for anyone other than himself and shows no remorse or compassion of any kind. His insatiable appetite might be the cause of his obesity, but, as Forth has found in the context of film noir criminals (2013: 391), fatness can also signify the excessiveness and lack of control that define other areas of the character's life, including, in the case of Torrente, his troubled sexuality and his bigoted world-view. Benson-Allot found a similar pattern in some of the roles played by Seymour Hoffman: 'the cultural invisibility already associated with overweight bodies', she argues, can be used as a cover (2013: 205). In all its excessiveness, Torrente's abject and uncontrollable body creates the necessary distance to overlook the real ugliness that his character hides behind layers of fat and the laughter provoked by the endless absurdity it is meant to provoke.

Javier Bardem in *Los lunes al sol*

Together with Segura (and, more recently, Antonio de la Torre, as we will see later), Javier Bardem is perhaps *the* Spanish actor best known for his physical malleability. Achieving notoriety early on in his career for the '*macho ibérico*' roles in the 'Iberian Portraits' trilogy directed by José Juan Bigas Luna in the 1990s, he has since made an internationally successful career out of roles that have actively resisted that initial typecasting.

The first Spanish reviews of *Los lunes al sol* (Fernando León de Aranoa, 2002) referred to Bardem's expanding waistline and receding hairline as somewhat incompatible with the actor's reputation as a sex symbol: 'Da la impresión de que Javier Bardem ha desaparecido en la película y que otro, más gordo, calvo, más afeado, es decir, su personaje, se ha apropiado de él' [It would appear that Javier Bardem has disappeared in this film and that someone else, fatter, bald less attractive; in other words, his character, has taken over] (EFE 2002). The rather simplistic contrast established in this review between Bardem the actor (usually in very good shape and perceived as attractive) and Santa, his character in *Los lunes al sol* (fat, bald and perceived by this journalist as unattractive), is revealing. The statement shows how actor/real person and fictional character are mixed up in ways that highlight the value of Bardem's very physical performance in this role. It also illustrates the long-term impact that other iconic performances – in this case, the (by then) ten-year-old roles in the Bigas Luna trilogy – might have in an actor's career. This is a distinction usefully explained by Barry King, who differentiated between 'impersonation' (the actor's ability to transform his body and body language to take on different personas for each role) and 'personification' (the long-lasting effect of a specific performance in other roles played by the actor) (1985: 42). In the interview with Bardem included in the aforementioned article, the actor confessed that he gained weight for the role (around 10 kilograms) in part coincidentally as a result of giving up smoking, but also because the role required a certain physical build of someone who is always eating and drinking.[5] He added:

> Si a un actor le piden que sea guapo, debe luchar con uñas y dientes por ser guapo … Un actor es simplemente un vehículo para contar una historia, mejor dicho, es el vehículo para contar la historia. [If an actor is asked to appear handsome, she or he should fight tooth and nail to look handsome … An actor is a mere vehicle to tell a story, or more exactly, she or he is the vehicle to tell the story]. (EFE 2002)

In Bardem's case, then, 'telling the story', delivering a credible performance as a middle-aged unemployed former shipbuilder, in *Los lunes al sol* would rely, to some extent at least, on his ability to make audiences forget those past performances that had built his reputation as a muscular sex symbol. As I will argue, however, it was because of Bardem's personification that Santa's fatness acquires a radically different signification in this film compared to Segura's in the *Torrente* saga.

Santa can be immediately associated with Santa Claus, not only for his name but also for his appearance (namely, his large build and beard). Unlike in the case of Torrente, it could be argued that Santa's large build had been an asset for his former profession. Although, as Whittaker has pointed out, his body is now 'a body of consumption rather than production' (2011: 136), the narrative also suggests that Santa used and continues to use his larger size to legitimise his position as a leader: previously during the workers' revolts, and now as a sort of spokesperson for the group of former colleagues who, now mostly unemployed, meet regularly at the bar. As Bardem said in the interview with EFE (2002), his character is a *pícaro* [rascal]: constantly showing off about his travels and skills that he is supposed to have (but has not), he inhabits the space around him in ways that exude confidence. His use of space mirrors the kind of territorialism displayed by Raúl, Bardem's character in *Jamón, jamón* (Bigas Luna, 1992),[6] in sharp contrast with Torrente's farcical awkwardness and recklessness. Far from being a clownish figure or the object of laughter, Santa is the one in charge of the jokes. He is also highly respected by his former colleagues, who seem to accept his role as leader and even protector of the group unquestionably. This is visually emphasised in frequent medium shots where his profile occupies most of the frame. He often proudly directs attention to his paunch by resting his hands on top of it.

As mentioned earlier, profile shots of overweight characters can be used for comic effect, to highlight the protruding belly (as in the opening credits of *Torrente 2: Misión en Marbella*) (Figure 13). In Santa's case, however, the profile shot is used in climactic moments, such as when he is delivering one of his monologues about the shipyard and what he and his former workmates should do about their futures. The visual emphasis on his large body during these scenes highlights the fact that he carries the 'moral weight' of the story on his shoulders. In a panel discussion on Spanish television following the screening of *Los lunes al sol*, Bardem and León de Aranoa explained that Santa was meant to be centre of gravity, the character who is more grounded and who helps build a strong group mentality among his former co-workers (RTVE 2010). This aspect of the character relies very much on his size, his weight, but also on the way in which Bardem's performance qualifies his fatness as a tool to define his masculine identity.

Figure 13 Santiago Segura in the title credits of *Torrente 2: Misión en Marbella* (Santiago Segura, 2001). Amiguetes Entertainment and Lola Films.

Although Santa provides some comic relief in the midst of the tragic reality that surrounds him, his sizeable body and his swagger come across, not as laughable or pathetic (as they did with Torrente), but as commanding and even threatening.[7] In one scene he visits the old offices of the shipyard and challenges the only (male) administrator left in charge of the closing-down operation. Helping himself to an old welding mask that lay abandoned, he wears it and moves around defiantly, as if marking and reclaiming his former territory, occupying space in ways meant to intimidate the initially self-assured clerk, who grows increasingly defensive, slouching over his desk. The welding mask gives Santa the appearance of a frightening, cartoonish villain, reaffirming his power and giving credibility to his threat that 'como vaya a la central, salimos todos en los periódicos' [if I go to the headquarters, we will be in the papers], his way of saying that there will be blood. In other words, the mask perfectly complements Santa's fatness as part of his performance of defiant masculinity.

Santa's resourcefulness and sense of entitlement are played out elsewhere in the film. He helps himself to items in the supermarket that he does not pay for, he openly refuses to pay for his ferry ticket to cross the Ría de Vigo. He repeatedly disobeys a court order to pay the council for a lamppost he broke during a demonstration. Eventually, persuaded by his solicitor, he agrees to pay, only to break it again immediately after paying, right in front of his startled solicitor. His role as the leader of the pack is confirmed in the ultimate act of social defiance at the end of the film, when he takes the lead as the group breaks into the ferry *Lady España* and sails into the Ría.

When comparing Torrente and Santa, Richardson's distinction between 'bulk' and 'fat' is particularly useful. As he explains, bulk is crucial for men in some competitive sports, including rugby and body-building, denoting strength and power; fat, however, 'denotes inactivity, slothfulness and the ultimate feminine trait – passivity' (Richardson 2010: 94). In the *Torrente* saga and *Los lunes al sol*, there is a clearly gendered representation of fatness. Bardem's larger size for his role in *Los lunes al sol* could be read in terms of 'phallic swelling', as Hennen (2005: 35) has done in his reading of the gay 'bear' body. His size and his previous on- and off-screen history as a rugby-playing, muscular *macho* add to his performance of masculinity, which here comes across as phallic, as bulk. In contrast, Segura's self-deprecating public persona draws more attention to Torrente's fatness as incompatible with the old-fashioned understanding of Iberian masculinity that the delusional character strives to embody. Segura and Bardem are both clear examples of how iconic performances can, and do, impact an actor's career, regardless of how wide-ranging their roles might be.

Antonio de la Torre in *Gordos/Fat People*

The film *Gordos* (2009) offers a different perspective on fatness and, especially, fat masculinities. As is clear from the title, Sánchez Arévalo's second feature-length film takes fatness as its main theme. The whole narrative is structured around the weight-loss process of six main characters, staged in four 'acts': 'Honesty', 'Action', 'Perseverance' and 'Victory'. Although there is no space here to go into much detail for each of the main characters, it is worth pointing out that excess weight in the four women and the gay man is seen as a direct result of emotional problems: loneliness, instability, sexual dissatisfaction, low self-esteem and so on. Excess weight as a problem is gendered to the extent that it is even discussed in relation to pregnancy in two cases.

As was the case with *Torrente* and *Los lunes al sol*, press coverage at the time of the release of *Gordos* focused on the actors' physical transformation. This process was particularly important in this film, as actor Antonio de la Torre had to gain 33 kilograms and then lose them all over again *during* production, in a space of eight months: it took him half of that time to put the weight on and the same again to lose it. The publicity campaign for *Gordos* is a good example of how physical transformations add value to the performance and are often used to sell the film. In this case, the emphasis on the physical transformation of the actors was amply discussed in interviews (some of these are archived in RTVE 2013), and echoed in reviews. Writing for *El País*, Cuéllar starts his piece on *Gordos*, stating: 'Adelgazar más de 33 kilos en cuatro meses es posible' [It is possible to lose 33 kilos in four months]. Here, reality and fiction *do* overlap, since de la Torre's weight loss was real, but the comment had nothing to do with Enrique, the character played by de la Torre, and everything to do with the actor's performative potential, 'un actor de peso' [a weighty actor], as described in the headline (Cuéllar 2009). In ways that echo the contrast established between Bardem, the 'handsome' actor, and Santa, the overweight character, the article also describes de la Torre at his usual 69 kilograms as 'Espigado, pelo pajizo, ojos color mar, atractivo … con el poder mágico de encandilar' [Tall and slim, layered hair, blue eyes like the sea, attractive, with a magic ability to dazzle you].

Four months later, at 102 kilograms, the article continues, de la Torre is described as 'bruto, parecía más bajo, sus movimientos eran torpes, un tanto zafios, y su mirada ya no era la misma' [brutish, almost shorter, his body language was awkward and coarse, and he had a very different look in his eyes]. In press interviews, director and cast emphasised the role of specialist doctors and nutrionists (their names appear in the film credits), and also the methods used to gain and lose the weight.

The film starts with an extract of the American-style television show led by a very fit Enrique, where he promoted the miraculous fat-busting pills 'Kiloaway' using his own 'before and after' photographs as testimonial for the effectiveness of the product he is selling. The elaborate sets of the show are immediately juxtaposed with the bare surroundings of an after-hours bingo, where Enrique, who has now gained all the weight back, is watching what we assume is a rerun of his 'Kiloaway' show. The contrast that *El País* article established between the thin and obese versions of de la Torre, the actor, could well apply here to the visual juxtaposition established between Enrique, the dishy, smart, heroic television presenter, and Enrique, the reckless, lazy and morbidly obese casino patron who watches his previous self in that illusory mirror: the television set (Figure 14). Another obese casino patron recognises Enrique from the television and takes a photograph with his smart phone as *real* proof for his wife that, as he keeps telling her, the pills are a rip-off. Cut to a Weight Watchers-style meeting, where the thin, attractive team leader Abel (Roberto Enríquez) welcomes his new group of customers as he walks around the room tilting body-size mirrors towards each one of them and asks them to get undressed. The play with mirrors continues, then, but this time the emphasis is not on visual (mis)recognition, as in the previous scene, but on exposure of the group members' true selves and the reasons that have led them to become fat, and why they may want to change their bodies.

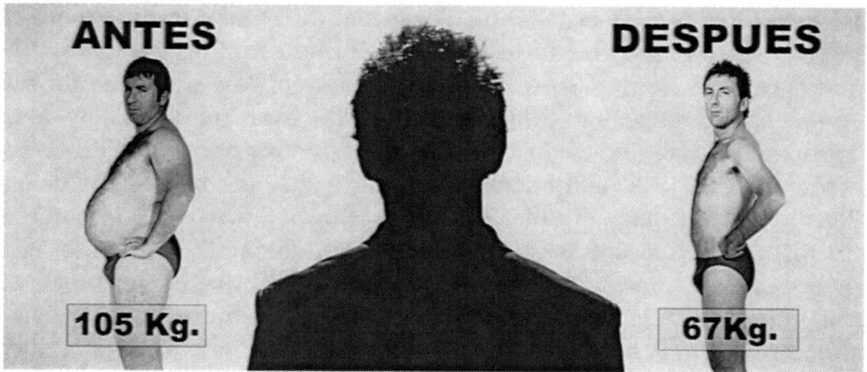

Figure 14 Antonio de la Torre in *Gordos* (Daniel Sánchez Arévalo, 2009). Canal + España, Filmanova, Gobierno de Cantabria, Instituto de Crédito Oficial (ICO), Instituto de la Cinematografia y de las Artes Audiovisuales (ICAA), Televisión espanola (TVE), Tesela Producciones Cinematográficas.

From the outset, then, *Gordos* deals with fatness as a mask, a cloak that, only in some cases, may be hiding something, be it an unplanned pregnancy, or something more abstract: loneliness or self-hatred. As in the previous case studies, fat is visually emphasised with profile shots and low angles that highlight the characters' shape. Sometimes the bodies almost fill the frame. In the casino scene, the man who takes Enrique's photograph remarks that he does not even fit into the frame. This is done partly for comic effect – the casino snap reverses the 'before' and 'after' promo shots by having obese Enrique positioned just in front of his thinner self on television – but elsewhere in the film the fat bodies are highly aestheticised. In some instances, such as in the 'before' and 'after' shots of Enrique in the opening credit sequence, the camera turns fat bodies into desirable commodities. Some of the images, including the 'before' shots of Enrique that open the film (inviting our gaze at the semi-nude fat male from the start of the film), or the lone male nude figure used for the poster and later as icon in DVD menu, resemble paintings by Fernando Botero or Lucian Freud, or the more classical beauty of Rubens.

As Stearns observes, 'until the twentieth century fatness was associated with prosperity' and plumpness with 'good health in times when many of the most troubling diseases were wasting diseases' (cited in Gilman 2004: 11). This same association applies to the popularity of more rounded bodies in the gay community around the time of the social panic caused by the first outbreaks of AIDS (see, for example, Llamas 1995). In *Gordos*, the use of medium-close-up and close-up shots of nude obese bodies throughout the film emphasises their haptic quality. The desirability of these bodies is perhaps best symbolised by the fact that a video recording of Andrés and his wife (also obese) having sex goes viral. The video had been secretly filmed and uploaded by their mischievous teenage children as a revenge for a family feud that ended with their parent's separation, but it ended up being instrumental in bringing the family back together. In watching the video online on their computers (another mirror), Andrés and his wife, separately, miss the fun that they used to have. The vision of their nude bodies engaged in sex also reignites their physical attraction for each other. Conversely, Abel's aversion towards fatness and large bodies, despite his profession, ends up breaking up his marriage, as he could not stand the vision of his pregnant and slightly rounder wife.

The performance of fat masculinities in this film, then, breaks some taboos and myths highlighted in the previous two case studies. Fatness is not solely depicted as comic or abject, as in the *Torrente* saga, nor as a symbol of phallic masculinities, as in *Los lunes al sol*. The emphasis on gazing at those large bodies as reflections of our inner selves is symbolised by the important role of the mirrors and the television or computer screens throughout the film. This rare invitation to gaze at large nude male bodies, be it those on the screen or our own reflection on the mirror, as a way to investigate what may hide behind the layers of fat, could be interpreted as judgemental, and yet some characters decide to stay fat and, as discussed, fat bodies are at times presented as desirable and explicitly sexual.

Two problematic aspects about the representation of fat bodies in this film remain: the gendered representation of fatness, and the link between fatness and Enrique's troubled sexual identity. These instances can be illustrated by briefly returning to the opening credit sequence and also his last scene as Enrique, the 'real' person, not the television presenter. The 'before' and 'after' shots of Enrique that open the film (part of his 'Kiloaway' presentation on TV) emphasise his fat/thin silhouettes against a plain white background. The 'before' shots seem to perpetuate the association of fatness with passivity through poses that could be described as emasculating: Enrique sits down on the floor, then on a chair with legs spread, in two of the images almost submissively averting his eyes; in others, he is shyly facing the camera with a certain look of shame in his eyes. In sharp contrast, the 'after' shots show Enrique staring directly at the camera, defiantly, in poses that emphasise his fitness and strength. In one of the shots he looks as if he were ready to punch the viewer, in the manner described by Dyer in his study of the male pin-up (1992).

Conclusion

The three case studies discussed here show how changes in an actor's body shape often attract significant attention from the media, and are proactively used to promote the films. While this is by no means exclusive to male actors, fatness in males destabilises and threatens traditional and hegemonic notions of 'masculinity'. As Gilman argues, 'being obese, fatter than fat, changes what the culture represents as male' (2004: 9). My examples have shown how the Spanish press draws significant attention to the way in which an actor's weight can drastically alter our perception of that actor in negative ways: they highlight how fatness makes actors unrecognisable, it changes their body language, makes them appear older, even shorter. Yet, despite a tendency in some of these films to use fatness in men as a means of emasculating the character and making him either a source of laughter or pity, fatness can also be used to hide something more serious (in the case of Torrente his bigoted world-view, for instance), and even to *reinforce* traditional notions of hegemonic masculinities (namely, Santa's bulk). The way in which we read fat in films can be influenced by an actor's public persona and off-screen performances of that fatness, but it can also be hugely influenced by her or his on-screen history. In Bardem's case, for example, his early roles as a stereotypical *macho* seem to have marked his acting style in ways that influence how his fatness is performed and perceived in *Los lunes al sol*. In the case of Santiago Segura, it works in the opposite direction: Torrente's version of farcical and excessive fat masculinity has become the actor's signature performance, affecting how we perceive the actor in other films, even when slim. Similarly, some spectators might think of Enrique's voracity in *Gordos* when watching Carlos (Antonio de la Torre) consume human flesh in *Caníbal/Cannibal* (Manuel Martín Cuenca, 2013). Benson-Allot argues that an actor's fat body shouldn't necessarily be read as abject and that, instead, it can imply 'that the body's representational contract is a social construction, just like any element of gender' (2013: 212). *Gordos* is an ideal illustration of this point, as fatness is portrayed as something transitory and changeable. Unlike race, for example, fat can be 'lost' or 'gained' and as such it is not necessarily an essential part of anyone's identity. Early in the film, a female character suggests that she might look fat, but she is not a 'fat person' (the distinction between 'estar gordo' and 'ser gordo' in Spanish makes this contrast more evident). In a film where mirrors play a crucial role, Enrique's changing shape *during* the film also works as a mirror in itself: just like his poses and attitude change noticeably in the 'before' and 'after' photographs of his 'Kiloaway' presentation, the radical ways in which his performance as thin or fat is gendered as more or less 'masculine' respectively during the film is very revealing. De la Torre's performance of fatness, then, goes hand-in-hand with his performance of masculinities. More importantly, Enrique's interaction with his television audience, encouraging them to lose weight with the pills that he advertises, is a constant reminder both of the fakeness of that television performance (in reality he didn't stay thin, he is nowhere near as confident as he pretends to be there) and of the fact that his role elsewhere in the film is also a performance. Finally, the film's emphasis on mirrors also reminds us of the important fact that a performance relies not only on an actor, but also, as Bial has argued, on the spectator (2004: 57). The performative spell is broken with Enrique's very final line: 'el triunfo es dejar de mirarme a mí y empezar a fijarte en ti' [victory is to stop looking at me and start looking at yourself].

Notes

1 See, for example Diamond (1985), who argues that Orbach's argument perpetuates fat as a problem and thinness as the solution.

2 In the USA the Federal Equal Opportunity Commission ruled in 1993 that the severely obese should be included in the statutes that protect the disabled against discrimination (Gilman 2004: 3).

3 I am referring to Benson-Allot's (2013) study of 'the queer fat' of Seymour Hoffman, Harris's work on Depardieu (2013), Richardson's discussion of gendered fatness in recent comedies (2010: 83–100), or Forth's study of fat men in film noir (2013). All of this work has been published since 2010.

4 The Bond-style credit sequence became a staple offering of the films from *Torrente 2: Misión en Marbella/Torrente 2: Mission in Marbella* (Santiago Segura, 2001) onwards, but the clearest example is perhaps *Torrente 3: El Protector/Torrente 3: The Protector* (Santiago Segura, 2005). The titles of the films are also parodies of Hollywood blockbusters featuring iconic males. *Torrente, el brazo tonto de la ley/Torrente, the Stupid Arm of the Law* (Santiago Segura, 1998) was a twist on George Pan Cosmatos' film *Cobra, The Strong Arm of the Law* (1986), starring Sylvester Stallone. The title of *Torrente 4: Lethal Crisis (Crisis Letal)* (Santiago Segura, 2011) is a spoof of the *Lethal Weapon* saga starring Mel Gibson, while the 'Missions' in both *Torrente 2* and *Torrente 5: Misión Eurovegas/ Torrente 5: Mission Eurovegas* (Santiago Segura, 2014) are clear references to the *Mission Impossible* saga, starring Tom Cruise.

5 In a round table with the director and co-protagonist Luis Tosar on Spanish television some eight years later, however, Bardem argued that it was his idea that Santa was fat. This was because he had already gained a few kilos after giving up smoking, but also because he and the director agreed that it would give the role the kind of 'heavy weight' that would bring the group of unemployed men together (RTVE 2010).

6 See Fouz-Hernández (2005) for more on the use of mirrors in *Jamón, jamón*.
7 Another character in the film, Lino (José Ángel Egido), embodies a more negative side of fatness. In his case, the emphasis on weight (pointed out by Santa
   on one occasion) is linked to the issue of ageing as an added handicap in a
   competitive job market. This is visually emphasised in close-up shots of his
   plump and wrinkling face, and his unsuccessful attempts to appear younger
   by wearing his son's clothes and even dyeing his greying hair black.

References

Belategui, Óscar (2012) 'Santiago Segura: "En España no me llaman para nin-
   guna película"', 'Hoy Cinema', *ABC*, 26 September, http://hoycinema.abc.
   es/noticias-cine/20120926/santiago-segura-espana-llaman-450401.html,
   accessed 17 August 2014.
Benson-Allot, Caetlin (2013) 'The Queer Fat of Philip Seymour Hoffman', in
   Timothy Shary (ed.), *Millennial Masculinity. Men in Contemporary American
   Cinema*, Detroit, MI: Wayne University Press, pp. 200–22.
Bial, Henry (ed.) (2004) *The Performance Studies Reader*, London and
   New York: Routledge.
Cinemanía (2013) 'Rumor: Santiago Segura ¿dejará de engordar para "Torrente
   5"?', *Cinemanía*, 16 November, www.cinemania.es/noticias/rumor-santiago-
   segura-dejara-de-engordar-para-torrente-5/, accessed 17 August 2014.
Cuéllar, Manuel (2009) 'Dos actores de peso', *El País*, 30 August, http://
   elpais.com/diario/2009/08/30/eps/1251613611_850215.html,   accessed   17
   August 2014.
Diamond, Nicky (1985) 'Thin is the feminist issue', *Feminist Review*, 19, 45–64.
Dyer, Richard (1992 [1982]) 'Don't Look Now: The Male Pin-Up', in Mandy
   Merck (ed.), *The Sexual Subject: A Screen Reader in Sexuality*, London and
   New York: Routledge, pp. 265–76.
EFE (2002) 'Bardem: "'Los lunes al sol' me ha servido de terapia tras los
   Oscar"', *El Mundo*, 24 September, www.elmundo.es/elmundo/2002/09/23/
   cine/1032791072.html, accessed 17 August 2014.
Esquirol, Meritxell and Josep Lluís Fecé (2001) 'Un freak en el parque de atrac-
   ciones: Torrente, el brazo tonto de la ley', *Archivos de la filmoteca*, 39, 26–39.
Forth, Christopher E. (2013) 'Nobody Loves a Fat Man: Masculinity and Food
   in Film Noir', *Men and Masculinities*, 16.4, 387–406.
Fouz-Hernández, Santiago (2005) 'Javier Bardem: Body and Space', in Wendy
   Everett and Axel Goodbody (eds), *Revisiting Space: Space and Place in
   European Cinema*, Oxford: Peter Lang, pp. 187–207.
Fouz-Hernández, Santiago and Alfredo Martínez-Expósito (2007) *Live Flesh:
   The Male Body in Contemporary Spanish Cinema*, London and New York:
   I. B. Tauris.
Gilman, Sander L. (2004) *Fat Boys: A Slim Book*, Lincoln: University of
   Nebraska Press.

González-Alegre, Mafalda (2014) 'Santiago Segura: "Cuando yo fallezca otro hará de Torrente"', *Antena*, 3, www.antena3.com/se-estrena/especiales/torrente-5/santiago-segura-cuando-fallezca-otro-hara-torrente_2014100300137.html, accessed 15 October 2014.

Harris, Sue (2013) 'Gérard Depardieu: The Ageing Star Body as a Site of Generational Crisis', conference paper, 12 June, 'Revisiting Star Studies', University of Newcastle.

Hennen, Peter (2005) 'Bear Bodies, Bear Masculinity: Recuperation, Resistance, or Retreat?', *Gender and Society*, 19.1, 25–43.

Jeffords, Susan (1994) *Hard Bodies: Hollywood Masculinity in the Reagan Era*, New Brunswick, NJ: Rutgers University Press.

King, Barry (1985) 'Articulating Stardom', *Screen*, 26.5, 27–50.

Llamas, Ricardo (1995) 'La reconstrucción del cuerpo homosexual en tiempos de Sida', in Ricardo Llamas (ed.), *Construyendo Sidentidades. Estudios desde el corazón de una pandemia*, Madrid: Siglo Veintiuno, pp. 153–89.

Orbach, Susie (1978) *Fat is a Feminist Issue: The Anti-Diet Guide for Permanent Weight Loss*, New York: Paddington.

Pavlović, Tatjana (2003) *Despotic Bodies and Transgressive Bodies: Spanish Culture from Francisco Franco to Jess Franco*, Albany: State University of New York Press.

Richardson, Niall (2010) *Transgressive Bodies. Representations in Film and Popular Culture*, Farnharm and Burlington, VT: Ashgate.

RTVE (2010) *Los lunes al sol*, 'Versión española', 2 October, www.rtve.es/alacarta/videos/version-espanola/version-coloquio/894308/, accessed 17 August 2014.

RTVE (2013) 'RTVE te ofrece *Gordos*', www.rtve.es/television/gordos-pelicula/, accessed 17 August 2014.

Triana-Toribio, Núria (2004) 'Santiago Segura: Just When You Thought Spanish Masculinities Were Getting Better ...' *Hispanic Research Journal*, 15.2, 147–56.

Whittaker, Tom (2011) *The Films of Elías Querejeta. A Producer of Landscapes*, Cardiff: University of Wales Press.

13

Disabling Bardem's body: the performance of disability and illness

Dean Allbritton

In many Western societies, the logic is as follows: our natural biological state is a healthy one. That is, health is who we are and illness and disability are the less desirable, temporary or inauthentic versions of ourselves; they represent roles that we must suffer through, or passing identities that must be endured until we return to good health. Clinging to the temporality of illness and disability – even when the problem is not so temporary, even when it sticks around as chronic illness or flares into disability, and even when it means death – imbues sickness with a performative aspect which is even further underscored in film and screen acting. There are myriad signals and movements of illness, within screen acting and without: tears that show suffering, a crinkled face and movement to block a sneeze, a hand stifling a hacking cough, or the gestures and grimaces that accompany stabbing pain.

If there is something performative about our relationships to illness and disability, what emerges in film acting, then, is a doubly wrought performance that attempts to express a natural event that is often believed to be wholly unnatural. An actor who plays sick highlights the performative nature of the illness or disability, and in doing so draws lines across cultural assumptions, the social conventions that make up their definitions, and deep-seated fears of what illness and disability may do to our bodies and selves. This chapter analyses treatment of illness and disability in the performances of Javier Bardem in *Mar adentro/The Sea Inside* (Alejandro Amenábar, 2004) and *Biutiful* (Alejandro González Iñárritu, 2010). The choice of Bardem is not casual: he is an actor who has been read as a healthy Spanish body *par excellence* as well as a figure that is emblematic of a range of Spanish masculinities. His performances in these two films, then, serve to showcase and spread widespread beliefs about what it means to be sick, in Spain and abroad. In analysing the emphasis placed on Bardem's sick body in these films, it becomes clear just how the borders between what is considered natural and unnatural for our bodies are blurred, and how the lines that separate illness and health have been thinned.[1]

In a fundamental way, illness, disability and acting hinge on perceptions of the natural. Illness and disability have been perceived alternately as aberrations of our purportedly natural, healthy states but also as normal manifestations of natural biological processes; likewise, a similar split in performance between recreating natural processes (what is known as the Stanislavskian Method) and the rejection of the natural as impossible to recreate (in broad terms, the Brechtian Method) has also influenced stage and screen performances worldwide for over a century. Describing the Stanislavskian Method, James Naremore writes that its iterations try to 'inculcate spontaneity, improvisation, and low-key psychological introspection; they devalue anything that looks stagy, and in their extreme form ... they lead to quasi-psychoanalytic rehearsal techniques, inviting the actor to delve into the unconscious, searching out "truthful" behavior' (1988: 2). The naturalistic Stanislavskian actor is often contrasted by the Brechtian actor, who is 'concerned less with emotional truth than with critical awareness' and who 'examines the relation between roles on the stage and roles in society, deliberately calling attention to the artificiality of performance, foregrounding the staginess of spectacle, and addressing the audience in didactic fashion' (Naremore 1998: 3).

In the search for the 'natural' performance – and there can be no question that much modern film acting looks to recreate naturalistic performances – there is nevertheless a fine line that divides the act of living a purely biological process from the act of representing it. That is to say, sex on screen is most often simulated, not actually carried out, just as actors rarely harm themselves or others physically on screen, get drunk on camera or contract or live with an illness they are meant to only portray. These examples of 'pure biological processes', as Naremore lists, have often been considered too extreme, too chaotic or too unpredictable to film; as such, the concept of the 'natural performance' is vexed, and vexes further the category of the 'natural' itself.[2] A spectator judges the performance of a biological event like illness or disability on whether it seems real, natural or without artifice (i.e. how well it represents a true experience); but in actuality there is always a performance being staged between illness, disability and health. Many spectators will cling to an imagined line, one that divides the purported authenticity of health from the temporality and inauthentic nature of illness and disability, and expect to see this reinforced on screen. This line is in reality never so firmly delineated, and the split between health and illness is not so easily made as divisible as many of us might wish. What occurs in on-screen performances of illness and disability, then, is often the re-performance of an expectation. Casting a healthy body (like that of Javier Bardem) in roles defined by their proximity to illness and disability requires a complex process that utilises stardom, health and a shared belief of the 'unnaturalness' of being and staying sick.[3]

Javier Bardem's physicality has long been appraised, admired and (albeit less frequently) critically called into question. Chris Perriam has noted that Bardem 'is an established sex symbol who to an unusual degree has … attracted commentary on his physical presence and the sensuality of both his everyday demeanour and his acting' (2003: 93). Here, Perriam is making reference to what has been described as Bardem's carnality and his 'brutishly passionate and sexual' demeanour (2003: 19). The performances of physicality and raw sexuality in Bardem's early films marked him as a bodily actor, or one whose body is of high importance in his acting, and the sexual charge apparent in many of these early roles has only fostered such an impression. Just a cursory review of these characters reveals a long list of masculinity in motion: bisexual prostitute Jimmy in *Las edades de Lulú/The Ages of Lulu* (Bigas Luna, 1990), dominant and domineering Raúl in *Jamón, jamón* (Bigas Luna, 1992) and Víctor Ventura, phone sex operator, in *Boca a Boca/Mouth to Mouth* (Manuel Gómez Pereira, 1995).[4] In their study on masculinities in Spanish cinema, Santiago Fouz-Hernández and Alfredo Martínez-Expósito note just how much Bardem's performances have saturated discussions of the Spanish cinematic male body. Bigas Lunas's 'Iberian trilogy', for Fouz-Hernández and Martínez-Expósito, presents a masculinity in performance that is 'excessive and in tune with the traditional traits of physicality, competitiveness and aggression' (2007: 19). And, in an interview with Frédéric Strauss, Pedro Almodóvar references the virility and power of Bardem and Liberto Rabal, the main actors in *Carne trémula/Live Flesh* (Pedro Almodóvar, 1997), and states that the film is ultimately about men and their relationships to each other (Strauss 2007: 173).

As often as Javier Bardem's body has been used to portray a potent type of Spanish masculinity in his early films, his later films have troubled this image. In this volume, Santiago Fouz-Hernández writes on Bardem's role as the overweight Santa in *Los lunes al sol/Mondays in the Sun* (Fernando León de Aranoa, 2011), and how this role may serve to reinscribe concepts of fatness in Spanish cinema; in their analyses of the same film, Sally Faulkner (2013) and Tom Whittaker (2011) also note the impact of Javier Bardem's changed physicality; and Madeline Conway (2000) and Julie Minich (2010) both deftly critique and analyse the thematic usage of disability in *Carne trémula* and *Mar adentro*. The literature on what Bardem's body 'means' is consequently wide-ranging and, naturally, hardly conclusive – except to surmise that it means something important. My purpose here is not to recreate these analyses or to simply say that Bardem's acting is important to Spanish cinema, but to shift attention to his performance of illness and disability and, in so doing, understand the ways that these concepts have been naturalised and made self-sufficient.

In *Mar adentro*, the incongruities between Bardem's healthy body and that of the person/character of Ramón Sampedro[5] have been remarked upon many times, including by the film's director, Alejandro Amenábar. Regarding this, Amenábar states that 'the casting of Bardem to play a man that renounces his body, his physique, of a different age and tetraplegic, could seem a complete mistake. Everything was against him' (cited in Fouz-Hernández 2007: 99). Bardem's own account of his transformation into Sampedro reveals the difficulties of inhabiting the role – after a five hour make-up session that aged the 33-year-old Bardem into the 55-year-old Sampedro, he would spend anywhere from four to ten additional hours immobile while filming (Bustamante 2004: n.p.). In an interview with Daisy Garnett for *The Telegraph*, Bardem lauded the film's make-up artist, Jo Allen: 'I owe 50% of my performance to her. Because once I had my make-up on, all I had to do was to fit what she created with veracity' (2005: 31). Amenábar dismissed the wholly transformative power of the make up, indicating instead that becoming the aged Sampedro was about 'a subtle delivery of energy' (Garnett 2005: 31) which Bardem was able to channel into his performance.

The subtle energy of Bardem's performance is owed, at least in part, to his training at the famed Juan Carlos Corazza Acting School in Madrid. As noted in Ciller's chapter in this volume, Corazza has developed a well-deserved reputation in Spain as one of the foremost acting coaches for stage and screen, and his students include a host of actors familiar to audiences: Carlos Amman, Elena Anaya, Angela Molina and Lola Dueñas, to name only a few. Developed from Corazza's studies of Stanislavskian Method acting, his training emphasises (among other things) naturalistic performances, the actor's interior search for emotion and the spontaneous potential of performance. In an interview with RT correspondent Francisco Guaita, Corazza discusses these traits, saying that 'trabajar con un actor es una fiesta, porque nunca se sabe todo lo que puede salir. No lo sabe el actor, no lo sabe uno – es una aventura' [working with an actor is a party, because one never knows what might emerge. The actor himself doesn't know, you don't know – it's an adventure] (Guaita 2011). For this reason, when Amenábar notes the challenges that Bardem faced in 'becoming' Sampedro and subsequently praises his subtle performance he is admiring not only the actor's considerable talent but the naturalistic performances that are characteristic of the Corazza School.

Uncovering the interiority of a character like Sampedro, whose emotions and physical pains were entirely foreign to Bardem, is fundamental to the actor's performance. Accordingly, and by Bardem's own admission, the make-up process that physically transformed him into Sampedro also produced a symbolic and 'involuntary' or accidental communion with Sampedro's pain. The 'low-key psychological techniques' that Naremore highlights in the Stanislavskian Method are a pronounced component of Corazza's adaptation of the Method, and they are fully evident in Bardem's acting process. That is to say that in *Mar adentro* the arduous combination of make-up and filming prodded Bardem further into the psychology of Sampedro, producing a sensation of impotence that he would liken to his character's paralysis:

> I went through many stages: rage, anger, denial ... All this helps you to understand ... the sensation of impotence, of being forced in an shameful situation for a long time. Evidently, I'm not paraplegic nor have I been so for 28 years. But to spend six hours a day in a bed produces an involuntary act of communion with what I was looking for. (Bustamante 2004: n.p.)[6]

But isn't such a communion also only temporary, something to endure while performing a body that doesn't align to one's own physicality? How could this performance, that of the rage and helplessness of immobility during a few hours, even come close to performing Sampedro's decades-long paralysis?

Perhaps the real question at stake is whether audiences demand such realism, or if it is instead preferable to keep illness or disability at bay and mediated through the lens of health. Certainly, Spanish audiences would have been intimately aware of *Mar adentro*'s story and outcome as they entered the cinema, thus shaping the cinematic encounter with the transformed body of Javier Bardem. That is, Sampedro's life and death had already been highly mediated: his court appearances had made nightly news reports, the video of his last will and testament was posted on a Spanish right-to-die website, and his final statement and death from cyanide were filmed and ultimately broadcast on Spanish television. The experience of watching the opening sequences of *Mar adentro* has a dual function, then: it overlays and negotiates the split between the specific (and culturally valorised) bodies of Sampedro and Bardem in familiar terms for the Spanish public while forcing them to recognise the differences between one body performed within the other. The filtering of this narrative through film is further emphasised by the opening scenes, which consciously mediate the spectator's experience with nature while underscoring and rupturing the taken-for-granted abilities of touch and uninhibited sight.[7]

What Fouz-Hernández and Martínez-Expósito term the 'fleshiness' of this film (and in the cinema of Alejandro Amenábar in general) (2007: 96) is then increasingly important for understanding the performance of Sampedro's disability. This cinematic 'fleshiness' is left undefined, but it presumably references a certain attention dedicated to the mechanics of the body, in which the flesh is made more apparent as it is mediated and fully revealed in its workings and failures. But it is also considerably evident just how much *Mar adentro* resists such fleshiness; or, at the very least, how much effort is expended in hiding and reducing the physicality of Bardem's acting. Pointing out the techniques used to 'cancel out the physical' in Bardem as Sampedro, Fouz-Hernández and Martínez-Expósito write of a harness that forced him to arch his back and tuck in his shoulders, a special bed that hid part of his body, and the digital reduction of his shoulders, arms and legs in other scenes (2007: 100). Bardem's own account of this process highlights the discomfort these techniques produced:

> I tried to adapt my body, which by itself is clumsy and a bit big, and very fleshy, to an atrophied, immobile and fairly deformed body. I spent quite a while with the patients of the hospital. I even got into a bed. There, a doctor moved me around for hours, except for cleaning me she did everything. I realised there was a big problem: the width of my shoulders. It was important to cover them up, and so I adopted a really uncomfortable posture … It produced an arching in my back and tension in my lumbar zone, in my neck and in my shoulder blades. And I said to myself: I can't do this every day, 10 hours a day. In the end I was able to, thanks to the doctor. And to my physical therapist, who made me a special pillow to mould my body. (Bustamante 2004: n.p.)[8]

The attempt to reconfigure Bardem's physicality and to reshape his physical acting style draws attention to the ways that physical presence and performance may be altered, distorted and covered up through techniques that are often considered unrelated to performance. The processes employed (digital effects, camera tricks, make-up, wardrobe), however, may have had an unintended side effect: disabling Bardem's always-apparent physicality highlights Sampedro's disability, but in a way that underscores the artificiality of the digital effects and make-up used to reduce or cover Bardem's body. For all the 'fleshiness' of Bardem's performance, Fouz-Hernández and Martínez-Expósito neglect to point out that, in Sampedro's stark bodily difference, Bardem's hidden body is instead made more apparent; the spectator knows it is there, perceives the shift and perhaps because of that is able to recognise Sampedro's disembodiment as affective loss. Ultimately, the artificial and hybridised body of Sampedro (a body that, in this film, can be read in its lack of Bardem) is a body twice removed, mediated by Bardem but by the audience's own perceptions of the unnaturalness of illness and disability.

The use of Bardem's head as Sampedro's avatar may similarly lend a certain complex symbolic weight that cannot be casually dismissed, and that is backed up by the filmography of the actor and the roles he has inhabited. This is not to suggest that the audience member sees Bardem's face in Sampedro and superimposes it with that of, say, the hypermasculine Raúl from Bigas Luna's *Jamón, jamón*, but that the residue of that character and knowledge of Bardem's past – for certain spectators – may serve to underscore Sampedro's disability while keeping it comfortably marked as acting. This is confirmed by Richard Maltby, who writes that 'the audience experiences the presence of the performer as well as – in the same body as – the presence of the character' (2003: 380). This effectually means that neither actor nor character is fully lost or found in the performance, and that both serve to promote, enhance and influence a film. The international marketing campaign for *Mar adentro*, for instance, so often relied on the youthful figure of Sampedro in flashback – that is, Bardem at his fleshiest – as a promotional tool for audiences, capitalising on Bardem's famed physicality and physical performances. This is markedly different from the theatrical posters for Spain, which used a full facial shot of Bardem/Sampedro that was a fairly faithful recreation of the cover to Sampedro's *Cartas desde el infierno/Letters from Hell* (1996), for audiences in the know. The theatrical poster and DVD cover image selected for its international release, nevertheless, were of a younger-looking and shirtless Bardem/Sampedro in his healthy prime.

For Barry Jordan, the limitations placed on Bardem's (stereo)typically physical acting style in *Mar adentro* meant that the actor had to 'find expressivity and performance from the neck up, mainly through the gaze, facial gestures (his smile) and in the tone and cadence of the voice in his dialogue' (2012: 197). Jordan's remarks call attention to the subtlety in Bardem's performance (admittedly, a trait that the actor was not particularly known for in his earlier films), and in doing so relies on the notion that '"visible" acting is bad acting, whereas "invisible" acting, because it is natural, can't be properly described because its properties of authenticity and inwardness are ineffable and can't be identified, much less interpreted' (Austin-Smith 2012: 20). Seeing Bardem recreate Sampedro's quickness to smile is one thing, but what does this mean for recreating Sampedro's paralysis, or his other invisible qualities? In an online interview, Bardem emphasises the need to perform patience in his recreation of Sampedro: 'I'm not patient, and he was patient. I mean, there was no other way for him – he was condemned to be on the bed for 30 years. So [I] try to be relaxed, and calm, and peaceful. And I'm not that. I'm anxious' (Bombarda 2011). The invisibility of patience, like the immobility of playing Sampedro, simultaneously calls for a new understanding of acting and defies what Austin-Smith believes to be a sort of spectatorial aphorism for many audiences: 'If you can see it, it isn't working; if it works, you can't really see it' (2012: 20).

The constraint of physical acting, and the challenge to see the 'invisible' choices of acting in *Mar adentro*, seem to crystallise most clearly in a scene between Ramón and Julia (Belén Rueda), a lawyer who wants to help bring Sampedro's case to the courts. In their first meeting, Julia questions Ramón's desire for assisted suicide. Ramón looks down at their hands, which are positioned close to each other. His hand is curled, a loose fist; hers is slightly open, her fingers vaguely extended but unmoving. He says: 'Tú estás ahí sentada a menos de 2 metros. ¿Qué son 2 metros? Un recorrido insignificante para cualquier ser humano. Pues para mí esos 2 metros necesarios para poder llegar hasta ti … para poder tocarte … es un viaje imposible' [You're sitting there three feet (sic) away. And what are three feet (sic)? An insignificant distance for any human being. But for me, those three feet (sic) that keep me from reaching you … touching you … is an impossible journey]. These impossible three feet are further underscored by the slight distance between their hands, which appear poised to join together but could never do so.

More precisely, it is Sampedro's hands that cannot move; Javier Bardem would have no difficulty in reaching out to grasp Belén Rueda's hand. This lack of movement, emphasised by the actor's necessary decision to be still and immobile in order to portray paralysis, dictates and reinforces the dramatic tension of the scene. In other words, if a known quadriplegic actor was playing this scene in the role of Sampedro, the loss of mobility would be a given factor and potentially understood as tragic in an extra-diegetic sense; knowing that Javier Bardem is willing his hand to stillness, however, vivifies the experience of disability for an able-bodied audience. This scene, then, contributes to the widely held assumption by spectators that acting is about 'the freedom of actors to make choices that result in visible performance signs' (Austin-Smith 2012: 21). What type of visible sign is stillness?

Bardem's hand can stretch, move and grasp, but it must not do so for the sake of this scene; and so the loss of Bardem's mobility – his freedom to perform visible performance signs that can be interpreted as acting – renders Sampedro's inability to do so as especially tragic for the film's audiences. This simplistic formula means that cinematic representations of illness and disability actually rely not on perceptions of naturalness but on artificiality, and that the actor's role is to shift the invisibility of our biological bodies into something lightly falsified, a replica that can approach – but must never truly be – illness.

Nevertheless, the role of the actor (in this case, that of Javier Bardem) in representing illness and disability will necessarily change as the social perceptions and beliefs surrounding certain illnesses and disabilities do. Taking on the role of Reinaldo Arenas in *Antes que anochezca/Before Night Falls* (Julian Schnabel, 2000), for example, meant that Bardem had to portray the complexities of a person living with HIV/AIDS in the late 1980s, an era that was only coming to grips with what the disease meant; in *Carne trémula*, Bardem's performance of a paralysed police officer dramatised the loss of sexual potency and fears of imperfect masculinity made real by disability. Surrounding these illnesses and disabilities are a range of social anxieties about contraction and contagion, interaction with the sick, and the fragility of health and life.

As has been noted, an actor's performance therefore usually attempts to negotiate these anxieties while producing something that seems like an 'authentic' experience of illness – an experience which is never really so authentic, or never really strives to be. In *Mar adentro*, we have seen that artificiality and stillness are key components of Bardem's performance of disability; in *Biutiful*, another film characterised by its profound exploration of its main character's sickness, the progressively visible physical deterioration of illness is juxtaposed with fantastic elements to underscore the (theoretically) otherworldly experience of getting and staying sick. Escaping the confines of Sampedro's bed, and now permitted to use the full physicality and interiorisation that the Corazza Method inclines towards, Bardem (as Uxbal in *Biutiful*) displays the pains of terminal illness and the darkness of dying, but can do so mainly through a performance that highlights the supernatural (read: wholly unreal) experience of death and loss.

Biutiful tells the story of Uxbal, a single father of two who provides for his children through odd jobs of suspect legality but only slightly murky ethics. At the beginning of the film, he is diagnosed with (already metastasised and therefore terminal) prostate cancer, and the remainder of the narrative finds him reconciling himself to his illness while searching for a way to ensure that his children are cared for after his death. After a brief dreamlike opening sequence, the audience is introduced to Uxbal *in medias res* – lying on his stomach grunting at the ignominy of a prostate exam. The initial frames are harsh and uncomfortably vivid: over a black screen, the audience hears the snap of rubber gloves being placed on hands, followed by a jump to Bardem's face presented in tight close-up, lying on his side. He swears under his breath as the examination begins, his brow knotted and his eyes opening and closing in discomfort and shock. The camera is too close to his face, forcing the audience to witness the intimacy of this experience. The cold blue tones of the film and the fluorescent lights above Uxbal give his face a waxy, ashen appearance.

From the lighting to the cinematography to the up-close facial performance of experiencing a prostate exam, the queasiness of this opening scene is meant to portray that something is very wrong. The invisibility of prostate cancer to the naked eye means that its consequences need to be made evident to the spectator somehow, that they must be forecast and felt through the film's on-screen effects and performances. To this end, lighting and cinematography play important roles in conveying Uxbal's illness and impending death, and the film gets increasingly dark and grainy as Uxbal succumbs slowly to his illness and fights to 'learn to let go', as he is advised to do by a spiritualist friend. Rodrigo Prieto, the film's cinematographer and longtime collaborator with director Gozález Iñárritu, discusses the film's usage of dusky settings and tones to highlight what he calls the impending 'dusk of Uxbal's life' (Benjamin B. 2011: n.p.). Prieto also makes special note of natural light sources, which were carefully stylised and heightened or dimmed to 'align the viewer with Uxbal's thoughts' (Benjamin B. 2011: n.p.).[9]

Working to present Uxbal's transition in demeanour and health as he accepts his fate (his death), Prieto also discusses the film's format change in aspect ratio from 1.85:1 to 2.40:1, and from spherical to anamorphic lenses.[10] The shift in a 1.85:1 aspect ratio (or, what is commonly known as 'letterbox' or 'widescreen' images) to a 2.40:1 (what has sometimes been known as 'super widescreen') would ostensibly allow for more images to appear on screen as the visible width of the shot is increased. The switch from a spherical lens, the standard for most filmmaking, to anamorphic lenses, which compress the image along the longer dimension and often require stretching post-production, also alters the perception of certain scenes and images. Prieto and González Iñárritu used these effects as a way to 'represent the transition from tight control to ultimate release' (Benjamin B. 2011: n.p.). Referencing Uxbal's controlling nature at the film's outset, Prieto uses these cinematic transitions to unravel his life and to help convey the isolating experience of illness.

Even if Prieto is quick to admit that these camera effects are 'subtle enough that the average viewer wouldn't notice it' (Benjamin B. 2011: n.p.), they nevertheless work closely with Bardem's own acting choices to contribute to the portrayal of illness in *Biutiful*. After a sequence that shows him receiving an MRI scan during a return trip to the clinic, it then cuts to a medium close-up of Uxbal with a furrowed brow. The look is complex: he seems angry, confused and perhaps a little stunned. It becomes apparent that he has been informed of his prostate cancer off screen. After a few seconds he cuts his eyes to the side, thinking of a way to bargain with the doctor. When he begins to speak, his voice is a gravelly whisper that is coarse with contained emotion. He trips over his words slightly, he drifts off in confusion, he swallows and licks his lips in what looks like a sudden, frightened, dryness of mouth. Bardem is lit from one side in this scene, the blacks and blues of his outfit and the background creating a dark template that foregrounds his facial expressions. The camera stays fixed on him, as it has in the prostate exam, registering his every emotion. Eventually, when he is given his final prognosis, the shot pulls in tighter and Bardem/Uxbal looks directly into the camera, where he can only repeat quietly '¿Meses?' [Months?].

In the camera's insistence that the spectator be present in this moment with Uxbal, that we sit across the table as he frantically digests and challenges this news, *Biutiful* seeks to harness the realism of this scene and experience. This impression of naturalism is reinforced on all sides of the film, including in Javier Bardem's own performance methods. As is common for both Method and Corazza actors, Bardem seeks to live, act and react as the character, becoming at one with him in order to provide an authentic exploration of the character's emotions. Discussing this process in an interview with David Poland, he initially likens this exploration as an experience akin to living with schizophrenia, although he is quick to search for another word. Nevertheless, this initial verbal slip is telling, as he goes on to say that it took him somewhere between six and seven months after the film's completion to distinguish between 'what was Uxbal's and what was mine' (Poland 2010), or the life that he leads and the life belonging to Uxbal. He finally states that 'leaving Uxbal' was, for him, 'a healing process' (Poland 2010). From this interview it becomes clear just how much Bardem's experiential method of acting is wrapped up in notions of good health and bad, and how the process of becoming Uxbal was an attempt to inhabit illness itself, to live with a life on its way out.

As with his performance in *Mar adentro*, Bardem attempts to faithfully recreate the experience of illness through his physicality, contorting his body and underscoring the visibility of performance. As he explains: 'In Uxbal ..., there's a weight in [his] back ... and there's a chest that is going inward, because he's not a man that is not really expressive himself. And the whole journey is for the chest to come up, and open, and back to feel[ing] more relaxed, because he has to give up' (Poland 2010). The emphasis on Uxbal's gait and general physical bearing under pain aim to make visible the invisibility of an illness like prostate cancer, thereby portraying illness as a natural and visually evident phenomenon; at the same time, the Method performance of *Biutiful* utilises sensations of pain and physical discomfort to 'inhabit' illness in a theoretically realistic and natural manner.

It is thus quite clear that *Biutiful* wants to portray this world that Uxbal inhabits – his pains, his life, his relationships and his eventual death – as wholly believable and natural. However, *Biutiful* has no real desire to live in such a believable world. González Iñárritu's purportedly naturalistic recreation of the world of Uxbal is shot through with fantasy, with magically stylised elements that proclaim the film's counterfeit reality: Uxbal communes routinely with the dead (a young boy, an old man and his dead father) in efforts to help them 'cross' into a higher plane and let go of life; he has haunting visions of the dead, who terrifyingly appear attached to ceilings; and his mirror image sometimes moves of its own accord. The resulting effect presents illness and death as otherworldly, experiences so mystical and personal that they can scarcely be comprehended. *Biutiful*, like *Mar adentro*, thus clings to artificiality as a distancing mechanism from the actualities of illness.

The representational distance between illness and health is about more than the excessive stylisation of cinema or the space between fictionalised melodrama and realistic documentary, and has everything to do with the performative recreation of illness and disability. So, although Bardem's performance of Sampedro in *Mar adentro* de-emphasised the actor's physicality in a bid to bring the spectator closer to Sampedro's experience of paralysis, the resulting effect is that the make-up, accented speech and digital and physical effects are underscored – and the spectator is no closer to understanding the realities of Sampedro's disability and lived experience, which is ostensibly what the movie hopes to convey. In *Biutiful*, the naturalistic hazes of light, the grainy texture of the film and unflinching camera record a life in its twilight moments while Bardem's Method performance physically bears the pain of cancer, but the stylisation that would highlight the otherworldly experience of living with an expiration date renders these techniques a controlled experiment. Death, illness and disability continually elude the camera. Performing the sick body is thus a lesson in temporality, a slipping into a body that one may ultimately slip right out of. That this confirms our hopes for illness, and the ways that we feverishly work to keep illness at bay, further demonstrates how performance and sickness are tied together in ways that are complex, poorly understood and so often lurking behind the fear of our very vulnerable bodies.

Notes

1 Although the film is referenced throughout the chapter, I have chosen not to analyse Bardem's performance in what is perhaps his most well-known 'disability film', *Carne trémula/Live Flesh* (Pedro Almodóvar, 1997). Whereas both *Mar adentro* and *Biutiful* deal squarely with the impact of illness and disability in the protagonist's life, the dense plot of *Carne trémula* tangles sex, mystery and murder freely into its story, so much so that the viewer may arguably be able to dismiss David's (Bardem) disability as a mere plot point.

2 This is clearly not to say that directors have never found ways to represent such biological processes. Naremore notes a whole host of film types and genres that have filmed such processes to both acclaim and infamy: animal deaths in films, pornography, snuff films and instructional cinema, to name a few (1998: 20). In Spanish film, similar exceptions can be found. For example, *Petit indi* (Marc Recha, 2009), *Furtivos/Poachers* (José Luis Borau, 1975), and *Hable con ella/Talk to Her* (Pedro Almodóvar, 2002) contain scenes of animal deaths and abuses; *Lucía y el sexo/Sex and Lucía* (Julio Medem, 2001) shows its female star (Paz Vega) giving a handjob to an erect penis; and many of the films of Jesús 'Jess' Franco shift between explicit pornography and horror, dancing around the representation of sex and gore and its enactment. For a more detailed analysis of the performance of sex between actors in Spanish cinema, see Alejandro Melero (chapter 10 this volume).

3 The complexity of representing illness and disability through acting necessarily becomes even further layered when the actor is her/himself ill or disabled, as Benjamin Fraser (2013), Ryan Prout (2008) and Raquel Medina (2013) have convincingly argued. As these performances necessarily differ from those of the purportedly purely healthy body taking on the role of illness and disability, they fall beyond the scope of this chapter. For further readings on the performances of disabled and ill actors, see the authors mentioned above.

4 Scholars and journalists have been writing for decades on the often-loaded symbology of Javier Bardem's body in his films, and every effort has been made to incorporate a variety of the most applicable thoughts and interpretations in this chapter. Perhaps most notably (and most relevant to the present study, as will be apparent) are *Live Flesh* (Fouz-Hernández and Martínez-Expósito 2007) and *Stars and Masculinities* (Perriam 2003), both of which discuss a variety of Bardem's films in detail.

5 Sampedro's story is a familiar one to Spanish audiences: as a young man, he was involved in a diving accident that left him quadriplegic. Refusing to recognise his paralytic state as a worthwhile life, Sampedro fought for the right to assisted suicide for over 29 years through a variety of legal venues (the regional courts of Galicia, the high court of Spain, the European Commission for Human Rights) and his case was routinely denied. In 1998, he devised a

method that sidestepped the supposed 'criminality' of his actions by dividing the administration of cyanide through small steps done by different people. Ramón's case and death drew national and international attention, and at the centre of it was the perception of his physicality and his (in)ability to move through the world.

6 'Pasé por muchos procesos: rabia, cabreo, negación ... Todo eso te ayuda a entender ... la sensación de impotencia, [el] estar obligado a una situación indigna durante mucho tiempo. Evidentemente, no soy tetrapléjico ni he estado así 28 años. Pero pasar en una cama seis horas diarias produce un acto involuntario de comunión con lo que yo estaba buscando' (Bustamante 2004: n.p.).

7 Victoria Rivera-Cordero (2013) also writes on the importance of the film's opening sequence, drawing attention to the contrast between the 'rainy Galicia' and the 'ideal space' of the beach, and the division between disabled body and able mind. Rightly arguing that this mind–body split dominates the film's thematic imagery, Rivera-Cordero nonetheless fails to note its potential to both challenge and reaffirm popular notions of what constitutes illness and disability.

8 'Intenté adaptar mi cuerpo, que de por sí es torpe y grandullón, y bien rellenito, a un cuerpo atrofiado, inmóvil y un tanto deforme. Pasé una larga temporada con los enfermos del hospital, hasta que me metí en la cama. Allí, una médico me manipulaba durante horas, menos limpiarme me hace de todo. Me doy cuenta de un problema grave: la anchura de mis hombros. Es importante que se tapen, y nace una postura realmente incómoda ... Produce un arqueamiento en la espalda y tensión en la zona lumbar, en el cuello y en los omóplatos. Y me digo: no puedo estar así jornadas de 10 horas diarias. Al final lo conseguí, gracias a la doctora. Y también a mi fisioterapeuta, que me hace una almohada especial, para que el cuerpo se amolde' (Bustamante 2004, n.p.).

9 In this same interview, Prieto discusses the film's grainy texture, which is used to contrast with the cleanliness and sterility of most modern digital films. Such references to clean, pristine film – and the contrasting notions of filth, contagion and disease – clearly motion towards *Biutiful*'s goals of presenting illness and death in its most raw forms.

10 The aspect ratio refers to the shape of the image area presented on screen, and is the width of the image divided by its height and expressed as a ratio.

References

Austin-Smith, Brenda (2012) 'Acting Matters: Noting Performance in Three Films', in Aaron Taylor (ed.), *Theorizing Film Acting*, New York: Routledge, pp. 19–32.

Benjamin, B. (2011) 'Letting Go: Rodrigo Prieto, ASC, AMC and Alejandro González Iñárritu Make Spiritual Connections on *Biutiful*', *American Cinematographer*, 92.1, www.theasc.com/ac_magazine/January2011/Biutiful/page1.php, accessed 18 September 2014.

Bombarda, Olivier (2011) 'Javier Bardem – Mar Adentro' for 'Novo Cinema' http://youtu.be/TR_kzci-C2I, accessed 16 September 2014.

Bustamante, José Manuel (2004) 'Entrevista Javier Bardem', *El Mundo Magazine* www.elmundo.es/magazine/2004/256/1093014690.html, 22 August, accessed 16 September 2014.

Conway, Madeline (2000) 'The Politics and Representation of Disability in Contemporary Spain', in Barry Jordan and Rikki Morgan-Tamosunas (eds), *Contemporary Spanish Cultural Studies*, London: Arnold, pp. 251–9.

Faulkner, Sally (2013) *A History of Spanish Film: Cinema and Society 1910–2010*, London: Bloomsbury.

Fouz-Hernández, Santiago and Alfredo Martínez-Expósito (2007) *Live Flesh: The Male Body in Contemporary Spanish Cinema*, London and New York: I. B. Tauris.

Fraser, Benjamin (2013) *Disability Studies and Spanish Culture: Films, Novels, the Comic and the Public Exhibition*, Liverpool: Liverpool University Press.

Garnett, Daisy (2005) 'Undercover Operative', *Telegraph*, 1 February, www.telegraph.co.uk/culture/4730545/Undercover-operative.html, accessed 16 September 2014.

Guaita, Fernando (2011) 'Entrevista con Juan Carlos Corazza, famoso director de teatro', *RT en Español*, 9 March, http://youtu.be/nxUyfTNFghE, accessed 1 December 2014.

Jordan, Barry (2012) *Alejandro Amenábar*, Manchester: Manchester University Press.

Maltby, Richard (2003) *Hollywood Cinema*, 2nd ed., Malden, MA: Blackwell.

Medina, Raquel (2013) 'Shifting Alzheimer's Paradigm in Spanish film: *¿Y tú quién eres?* and *Amanecer de un sueño*', *Hispanic Research Journal* 14.4, 356–72.

Minich, Julie A. (2010) 'Life on Wheels: Disability, Democracy, and Political Inclusion in *Live Flesh* and *The Sea Inside*', *Journal of Literary & Cultural Disability Studies*, 4.1, 17–32.

Naremore, James (1988) *Acting in the Cinema*, Berkeley: University of California Press.

Perriam, Chris (2003) *Stars and Masculinities in Spanish Cinema: From Banderas to Bardem*, Oxford: Oxford University Press.

Poland, David (2010) 'DP/30: *Biutiful*, actor Javier Bardem', *Movie City News*, www.youtube.com/watch?v=7cu8v3LMtIg, accessed 19 September 2014.

Prout, Ryan (2008) 'Cryptic Triptych: (Re)Reading Disability in Spanish Film 1960–2003: *El cochecito, El jardín de las delicias*, and *Planta cuarta*', *Arizona Journal of Hispanic Cultural Studies*, 12, 165–87.

Rivera-Cordero, Victoria (2013) 'The Self Inside and Out: Authenticity and Disability in *Mar adentro* and *Yo, también*', *Hispania*, 96.1, 62–70.
Whittaker, Tom (2011) *The Films of Elías Querejeta: A Producer of Landscapes*, Cardiff: University of Wales Press.

14

Body doubles: the performance of Basqueness by Carmelo Gómez and Silvia Munt

Rob Stone

Whereas regional stereotypes are often subject to parody, the construction of nationalist archetypes demands more formal analysis of the negotiations and compromises that feed into the performance of identity. Setting aside the eternal argument of whether Basque cinema actually exists,[1] yet also hitting it head on, this chapter explores one of many paradoxes that inform and complicate its definition, namely a reliance upon the non-Basque actors León-born Carmelo Gómez and the Catalan Silvia Munt to perform a masquerade of Basqueness that often emphasises physicality and eroticism. In several key Basque films, these actors seem to incarnate Basque archetypes that are enhanced by cinematography and other filmmaking procedures such as make-up and costume. However, the templates drawn from Basque mythology and informed by nationalist iconography fit inexactly over the performances of Gómez in *Vacas*/*Cows* (Julio Medem, 1992), *Días contados*/*Running out of Time* (Imanol Uribe, 1994), *La casa de mi padre*/*Black Listed* (Gorka Merchan, 2008) and *Baztán* (Iñaki Elizalde, 2012) and those of Munt in *Akelarre*/*Witches' Sabbath* (Pedro Olea, 1984), *Golfo de Vizcaya*/*Bay of Biscay* (Javier Rebollo, 1985), *Alas de mariposa*/*Butterfly Wings* (Juanma Bajo Ulloa, 1991), *Todo está oscuro*/*Everything is Dark* (Ana Díez, 1997) and *El viaje de Arián*/*Arián's Journey* (Eduard Bosch, 2000) respectively. By means of close readings of these performances and contextual and comparative analyses, this chapter exposes the screen personas of Gómez and Munt as false identities that complicate the articulation of desirable and desiring Basqueness.

Both the actors in question are classically trained. Gómez was born in 1962 and grew up working on his father's farm in Sahagún but moved to Salamanca to find work in the theatre, joining José Antonio Sayagués's Garufa group, which emphasised the teachings of Stanislavski and toured Salamanca and Castile and León. He then won a place to study acting at Madrid's state-funded Real Escuela Superior de Arte Dramático (RESAD), where his brooding handsomeness and dramatic intensity were yoked to classic theatre and soon claimed for leading roles by the Compañía Nacional de Teatro Clásico. Small film roles followed in *El viaje a ninguna parte/Voyage to Nowhere* (Fernando Fernán Gómez, 1986) and *Bajarse al moro/Going down to Morocco* (Fernando Colomo, 1988), an adaptation of the comic play by José Luis Alonso de Santos in which Gómez appears awkward and stilted. The move away from the stage to the more collective and technical process of filmmaking betrayed the training of the actor, who diagnosed his own discomfort during the filming of *Vacas* as a case of 'Stanislavsky on the brain and on my shoulders, thinking there's a method above all else and that the actor and his character are the most important thing' (cited in Stone 2007: 48). This training had inculcated the method of drawing out emotions to add depths to dialogue and was based in part upon the actor making connections between the character he played and emotional memories of his own. The methodology was established by Constantin Stanislavski of the Moscow Art Theatre and was adopted and transformed into the Method by tutors associated with the American theatre including Lee Strasberg and Stella Adler.[2] Method acting in American cinema was popularised by the emotional, sensorial and psychological performances of actors such as Marlon Brando and James Dean, but it was the angry young men of 1970s American cinema who wielded more direct influence on Gómez's generation. The spectacular examples on screen of a simmering or fit-to-burst Al Pacino, Dustin Hoffman or Robert De Niro prompted a psychological and physical commitment to a role that could dominate a stage but be ill served by blocking, cutting and retaking single shots for a performance on film that, as Walter Benjamin surmised, was 'composed of many separate performances' (1999: 223). Physical movement could differ from take to take, while a paucity of rehearsal only exacerbated the lack of preparation afforded by single shots played to an indifferent camera in comparison to the weeks of preparation usually set aside for honing performances intended to move a theatre audience. Naturalistic Stanislavskian techniques demanded long takes to evolve and gain effect, and therefore were opposed to the Kuleshov effect that underpins Eisensteinian montage. Given time, actors trained in Stanislavskian techniques tended to make thought, speech and their lack (for American Method actors at least were much given to brooding silences and mumbling) indicative of a troubled character struggling towards self-expression despite or through corporeal limitations and defects. The practice could also be exhausting for the actor, especially when physical transformation and even deliberate disfigurement concluded the mental process of building up a character from the inside out. The forcing of empathy that typifies Stanislavskian techniques is not exactly the same as the Method by which actors substitute their equivalent emotional responses for those of their character. Nevertheless, the recognition of initial physical and mental confinement in the words on the page prompts the search for inner truths. This culminates in an outer resemblance that can result in an actor both underplaying the dialogue and overthinking the physicality at the end of a process that emphasises psychological realism in its grounding of a role or myth.

Gómez fulfilled this commission in *Vacas*, whose spiralling narrative formed a critique of recycled Basque myths in which he explored a contradictory, even paradoxical, fusion of manliness and cowardice as the grandfather, father and son in three successive generations of the Irigibel family. *Vacas* begins with a celebration of his physical prowess as he chops wood behind the credits in the style of a Basque *aizkolari* [woodsman] standing barefoot on a log and striking the axe between his feet, yet the framing, myriad camera angles and editing fragment this display of masculinity until the temporal and spatial unity of the character is exploded. The sequence also evokes a violent divisiveness with every blow of the axe and concludes with a close-up of the vaginal 'V' that he hacks into the wood, thereby indicating the potential for aggression against the feminine. Gómez shoulders the complexity of this sequence with a mix of outward might and inner compulsion that is a common trait in his performances. Although admirable and even mythic in his bearing and strength, his impersonation of Basqueness as an actor matches the pretence of bravery of a character identified in the chapter heading as 'the cowardly *aizkolari*'. In *Días contados*, Gómez will convey a similarly hollow virility as a *gudari* [soldier] in the guise of an ETA terrorist, who moves from boyish recklessness at the beginning of the film via a passionate but self-deluding *amour fou* with a young Gypsy prostitute to suicidal compulsion at its end, while his delivery of dialogue gradually shifts from a controlled, laid-back tone to impulsive reactions that culminate in morbid introspection. The penultimate shot of him barrelling towards his death in slow motion exposes this violent masquerade at its most contradictory. He appears to embody the outward signs of a fanatic in the cause of Basque separatism but, while the slow motion and low-angle shot corroborate his martyrdom, his facial contortions emphasise his character's desperate and unequal human effort at embodying this mythic demise. Gómez returns to the Basque Country as Txomin in *La casa de mi padre*, whose homecoming after several years of exile in Argentina is met by the same enmities that expelled him. By this time, however, Gómez's identification with the performance of Basqueness was so established that the film cannot fail to echo former roles in this new character's ill-fated attempt at neutrality.

Most specifically, because his screen persona carried the baggage of playing characters who, albeit unwillingly, perform the stereotypes associated with the iconography of Basque nationalism such as the *aizkolari* and the *gudari*, so the nonpartisanship of Txomin, who completes the triptych of performances of Basque masculinity by being a champion *pelotari* (Basque ball player), seems a fragile pretence too. Richard Dyer uses this type of cultural studies framework to diagnose screen personas as an aspect of performance in roles in which 'elements may be to some degree in opposition or contradiction, in which case the difference between the star's image is characterised by attempts to negotiate, reconcile or mask the difference between the elements, or else simply hold them in tensions' (2000b: 124). Gómez's performance of Basque identity brings all these elements to bear in films that play on this aspect of his screen persona while obliging him to work through contradictions from the inside out. That is to say, in order to 'negotiate, reconcile or mask the difference' between his non-Basque self as actor and aspects of Basqueness, he must summon up a forced empathy with experience of the violent history of the Basque Country, which was racked by conflict between militant Basque separatists and Spanish security forces since 1968, from his memories of growing up in the comparatively more peaceful rural Castile and León.

This notion that Gómez might encounter and be unable to erase dissonance between his own nationality and that of his character may appear simplistic and even dismissive of the art of acting, but it gains importance in a cultural and political context where identity and its perception are key factors in the long-standing conflict over the status and formation of Basque Country. The most radical nationalists in this conflict (hope to) impose a criterion for Basque nationality that includes a bloodline that is sufficiently established, which may even result in a physiognomy that is recognisably Basque, and the ability to speak *Euskara* or a willingness to learn it. Looking and sounding Basque is as important for public office as it is for non-Basque film stars, at least for audiences who might assume from the frequency and prominence of Gómez's roles that the actor actually is *euskaldun* (Basque-speaking). On the other hand, more radical audiences may find this association of the actor with Basqueness amusing or even insulting and point to his accent, physiognomy and stocky build as discrepancies that betray his difference that, in turn, reinforces the assumption that only authentic(ated) Basques can play/be Basques. This censure of non-Basque actors playing Basque characters is demonstrated by the review of the culture-clash comedy *Ocho apellidos vascos/Spanish Affair* (Emilio Martínez Lázaro, 2014), the most successful Spanish film of all time, that was published in the Basque nationalist newspaper *Gara* [*We Are*]. Attacking not only the film's intrinsic farce of the Sevillian Rafa (Dani Rovira) pretending to be Basque in order to woo Amaia (Clara Lago), but also the extrinsic casting of Lago, a non-Basque actress, as the Basque object of desire, the critic Mikel Insausti declared that 'resulta un completo despropósito que dentro de la propia película intérpretes que no son vascos jueguen a hacer de vascos que imitan acentos de chiste, confundiéndose con los que en la ficción se hacen pasar por vascos de zarzuela' [it is complete nonsense that actors within the film itself who are not Basque play Basques with funny accents alongside fictional characters who also play Basque characters as if in a comic opera] (2014). Such criticism may be understood in Barthesian terms, because Gómez, like any actor, is a sign and his performances in the films under discussion are signifiers that point to an aspect of Basque identity as the signified, which is commonly masculine prowess, a potential for violence and a tender even tremulous heart. Yet for radical nationalist Basques this equation is invalid because, one might say, the pretend sign does not correspond to the one in *Euskara*. Nevertheless, the frequency of Gómez's roles as Basques does suggest that the equation has tended to become rigid. As Chris Perriam has noted, Gómez exudes nobility on screen:

> He appears, in many roles, to line up with an older type of Hollywood star, a 1930s hero [who] offered a manly and reassuring route to emotional identification with a perceived national destiny, who offered women a fantasy man ideal for his reliability rather than his capacity to thrill and to hurt, and offered men a fantasy role model. (2003: 71)

Perriam attributes this identification with a particular national destiny 'to "being Spanish" at a number of different levels' (2003: 72). However, the association of Gómez with key Basque archetypes – *aizkolari*, *gudari* and exile in *Vacas*; ETA terrorist and martyr in *Días contados*; returning exile in *La casa de mi padre* – also indicates what Dyer calls a 'problematic fit' (2000a: 126) with this and, indeed, with the perception of Basque national destiny too. This is because Gómez's forced empathy and physical appearance are not enough to assuage the problematic fit and cannot entirely erase dissonance and discrepancies between his performance of Basqueness and different, even opposing, ideas of Basqueness held by his audience. Nevertheless, his struggle to adjust the fit by drawing on empathetic memories as a spur to unquestionably vivid renditions may actually enhance awareness of conflict over Basque identity. This is because his stardom fulfils Dyer's notion of an actor's ability to hold such elements in tension being a determining factor in both the impact and affect of performance. In addition, to borrow theories of difference associated with gender and apply them to nationality allows for the application of Mary Ann Doane's idea that 'to masquerade is to manufacture a lack in the form of a certain distance between oneself and one's image' (2000: 253), which suggests that Gómez's performance of Basqueness both embodies this lack in the eyes of some audiences, such as the radical nationalists or *abertzaleak* represented by the afore-mentioned response of Mikel Insausti to *Ocho apellidos vascos*, and disavows it in the minds of others, such as those who see the Basque Country as part of Spain. Laura Mulvey states that actors are 'formative structures, mechanisms not meaning. In themselves they have no signification, they have to be attached to an idealization' (2000: 242). However, when Gómez is attached, as film stars are to films, to the idealisation of Basqueness demanded by his roles as champion *aizkolari* or martyred *gudari*, the contradictions described as a 'problematic fit' that suffer from 'lack' result in a complex, even dysfunctional, process of identification that is exacerbated when the character is eroticised.

There is significant pleasure in looking at Gómez and, as we shall see, Munt too; but there are also dangers in assuming a passive theoretical spectator. Both Munt and Gómez provide occasions to desire. Their performances invite a spectatorial gaze that indulges in the fetishisation of the martyr in the flames that engulf Gómez at the end of *Días contados*, for example, and the Bava-like scenes of torture inflicted on Munt in *Akelarre*. Their roles even contain moments of over-compensating excess of physical prowess and eroticism, such as in the wood-chopping that begins *Vacas* and Garazi (Munt) dancing half-naked around a bonfire in *Akelarre*. However, there remains a divide that these non-Basque actors cannot cross, even though their performances may resemble authentic Basqueness, and it is a conflict that complicates spectatorship too. This divide resembles a paradox that occurs in relation to performances that are subject to the 'overpresence of the image' (Mulvey 2000: 250) and result in the 'over-identification with the image' (Mulvey 2000: 252). This is not to say that either Gómez or Munt overact, but that their attempts at compensation will never abolish the distance that exists in their performances between them as non-Basques and their roles. At the same time, however, it is precisely this distance that adds eroticism to their performances because it creates the possibility of their being fetishised. Virile and attractive Basque actors who might be said to also look more Basque, such as Patxi Isbert or Elena Irureta, might play their roles too, but they would lack the difference or at least only demonstrate lesser differences in their relation to the scripted roles, such as contrary political ideas that do not show on camera. However, if we suppose that it is only because Gómez and Munt are non-Basque that their representations of Basqueness may be fetishised, then we encounter the corollary that authentic Basque identity is evicted from a cinematic discourse that is purportedly about it.

Rather than invalidate the performance, however, this may actually suit the nationalist view that informs many aspects of Basque culture, which has occasioned the representation of Basque identity as a void, as something as yet lacking adequate legal, territorial and political representation.[3] The sculpture of Basque artists Eduardo Chillida and Jorge Oteiza, for example, tends to suggest attempts at enclosing and defining spaces that are revealed as incomplete in *Oyarak/Echo* (1956) and *Construcción vacía/Empty Construction* (1957), respectively. Perhaps, in terms of radical nationalism, Basque identity is non-representable, at least until the imagined community is realised in place of the ideology that currently signals the void. Thus, non-Basque actors like Gómez and Munt are acceptable because they can embody a desired and fetishised Other that even the most militant nationalist can enjoy, perhaps more than most. Just as 'the paradox of phallocentrism in all its manifestations is that it depends on the image of the castrated woman to give order and meaning to its world' (Mulvey 2000: 239), so the non-Basque actor gives order and meaning to the representation of Basque nationalism. Following Mulvey, who references Christian Metz, what specifies Basque cinema is 'a further reduplication of the lack which prompts desire' (2000: 250). That is to say, it is Gómez's lack of Basqueness that allows him to embody an as yet unrealised Basque nation. He becomes a symbolic presence and his difference permits his fetishisation, while the function of Munt in relation to Basque identity is both duplicated and further doubled by reference to Mulvey and Doane because her roles are, of course, female.

Munt was born in Barcelona in 1957 and grew up in the privileged environment of the Catalan middle class, going on to study psychology, classical ballet and contemporary dance before taking a place at the Royal Ballet in London. Her slim, elegant physique and delicate but resolute young beauty, allied to the poise and precision of her training, led to lead roles in productions of classical ballet and her subsequent founding of the Ballet Contemporáneo de Barcelona dance company. However, her talent for the theatre diverted her career and in 1977 she appeared in *A Midsummer Night's Dream* in the role of Puck and began accumulating experience in television and film that began with her début in *L'orgia/ The Orgy* (Francesc Betriu, 1978), one of the first post-dictatorship films to feature explicit sexual themes and nudity, which was filmed in Catalan and then dubbed into Castilian by the same actors for general release. Munt graduated to leading roles in the Civil War melodrama *La plaça del diamant/The Time of the Doves* (Francesc Betriu, 1982) and her career has since been characterised by great fluidity between stage and screen, which includes her work as film and theatre director. Her enduring association with Basque cinema began with the role of Garazi in *Akelarre*, a seventeenth-century period drama in which she embodies a frail but sensual serving girl accused of witchcraft and then tortured, her martyrdom galvanising the Basques to revolution and inspiring in them the fight for independence. The role is a straitjacket of symbolism. Called on to represent the ideal and embattled Basque Country in need of rescue, Munt moves from sensual and libertine sprite to masochistic submission and from imperilled heroine to a Basque Marianne in blunt acts requiring both the exaltation and surrender of her sensuality to the cause of revolution. As Garazi undergoes fellatial waterboarding, being lynched up and dropped repeatedly, and having her naked body stretched to breaking point by four racks that pull her limbs apart, so Munt's litheness remains pliant and resolute, her endurance is eroticised and close-ups of her head hanging down as she gasps first 'no', then 'yes', to her inquisitor's demands for admission of guilt carry a sexual charge that is rare in Basque cinema, which otherwise tends towards a decisive rejection or abnegation of the sexual impulse. In part, this displacement of eroticism suggests a challenge that the more politicised Basque cinema sets itself to effectively remain celibate until the pre-eminent conflict over the Basque Country has concluded. Like a prize fighter who refrains from sex before a bout, the Basque cinema of radical nationalist sentiment seems to want to conserve its strength along with a sense of purity that deep-rooted Catholicism and Basque nationalism both demand. The sexual aspect of the roles played by non-Basques Munt and Gómez in films such as *Akelarre* and *Días contados* may therefore indicate a kind of surrogacy that allays the possibly damaging, even traumatic effect of succumbing to sexual impulses in Basque cinema, which generally withholds eroticism in order to appoint a more politicised role for the Basque body instead.

Ann Davies (2009) and others (Stone and Jones 2004; Stone and Rodríguez 2015) have criticised theories of Basque nationhood and its representation in the cinema for eliding matters of gender. As body doubles in Basque cinema, Munt and Gómez must conform in some way to the nationalist ideology and iconography of Basque myths of idealised gender, while at the same time including a sufficient indication of difference between themselves and Basqueness in their performances as to function as objects of more neutral desire for wider audiences. The slight Munt is physically distinct from the stereotypical physiognomy of Basque females, which can tend towards stockiness, and her sexualised victimhood in *Akelarre* thus retains a distance from actual victims of torture, which consequently allows her performance to remain symbolic and erotic. The film concludes with Garazi actively assuming the mantle of a witch-like spiritual leader for her rebellious countrymen and screaming like Mari, the cave-dwelling Basque goddess of popular myth.[4] The final freeze-frame captures her trauma and defiance, but it also transforms her doe-eyed beauty into a warrior's mask and thus hints at the masquerade.

Munt's performances in subsequent films retain this aspect of incarnating stereotypical females, but make such clichés a problem for the characters too. In *Golfo de Vizcaya*, for example, she plays the wife of an ETA terrorist in a seemingly frail but resolute manner, which recalls her training as a ballerina. In several scenes she is physically tentative and then suddenly decisive, her potential and its realisation recalling the pauses and sharp movements of ballet. By *Alas de mariposa*, however, this poise has become rigid, its potential curtailed. As Carmen, a young mother desperate to bear a son and neglectful of her infant daughter, Munt performs as if physically trapped within the strictures of phallocentric Basque society because she is psychologically bound to carry the responsibility of embodying the legacy of the fertile *ama lur*.[5] Carmen exploits her diminishing sexuality for procreative reasons, aiming to safeguard the myth by delivering its male heir, but she succumbs to delusions that reveal her ambition as madness. Her movements here are not tentative but stunted, unable to connect with those around her, and the desperation of this broken ballerina continues in *Todo está oscuro*, a dark tale of investigation into corruption that provides an unflattering comparison of contemporary terrorism in the Basque Country with the drug wars of Colombia, in which Munt's character concludes: 'el idealismo es una enfermedad que se cura pronto' [idealism is an illness that's quickly cured]. Perhaps inevitably, Munt essays the role of an ETA terrorist in *El viaje de Arián*, in which the sexuality of her character, Maite, is subsumed within the cause of the organisation and represented by the suppression of her femininity too. In contrast with her tresses in *Akelarre*, her tokenistically boyish haircut in this film is both symbolic and allusively concealed beneath the disguise of stereotypical femininity that her character performs by donning a long wig in order to function as assassin.

The coincidence of Munt and Gómez both playing terrorists, albeit in separate films, is rather banal in the context of Basque cinema, which has ETA as a recurring theme, but it still invites a comparative analysis of the male and female masquerade of such a potent symbol of Basqueness. Gómez and Munt still offer scopophilic pleasure, which 'arises in using another person as an object of sexual stimulation through sight' (Mulvey 2000: 242), but, whereas Gómez is a towering example of male strength and determination as a terrorist in *Días contados*, Munt has become more androgynous and neutered as Maite. Whereas his performance of overt and stereotypical masculinity fits (albeit problematically) the iconography relative to his character's cause and drives the plot, Munt's interpretation of a cliché of femininity occurs within the narrative and is donned and doffed for militant purposes. Gómez plays Antonio as cunning but clumsy, as if not quite aware or in control of his physical capacity until lust or fury take control. Munt, on the other hand, is contained and precise to the point of neurotic.

The differences in their performances comply with the idealisation of the soldier in the myths that inform the use of violence in the cause of Basque independence, because it sexualises the male terrorist and desexualises the female one. Gómez certainly approaches the role with a degree of animalism in such scenes as his face-off with Javier Bardem as a mercenary junkie-pimp, the previously mentioned race to final martyrdom, and the scene in which he consummates his desire for the prostitute Charo (Ruth Gabriel), whereby the film's allusions to the myth of Carmen cohere. The pretence of masculinity that informed *Vacas* is still being played in *Días contados*, in which Gómez plays Antonio as a testosterone-fuelled innocent who chokes on his first toke of marijuana and is tentative in his wooing of a prostitute, but it remains a valid referent for the mythology and iconography that inform radical Basque nationalism because it upholds the symbol of a warrior with a pure heart. Munt, on the other hand, embodies an eroticism that is withheld or postponed, which is also coded in a patriarchal system, but doubly so, in the Basque as well as the Spanish. That is to say, whereas Antonio only opposes the Spanish state, Maite opposes both the Spanish state and the imagined community of radical Basque nationalists, whose ideology tends towards sexism and does not allow for the terrorist to be female unless she renounces her femininity. This is all a question of stereotypes and archetypes, of course, but Jungian psychology attests that such things can at least be assumed to inform the unconscious structuring of performance by these actors. Gómez works from the inside out by accumulating memory triggers to empathetic emotions and embellishing them with adjustments to voice, posture and even body type. Munt, meanwhile, works from the outside in by projecting an idea of her character in her stance, movement or its lack and her bearing and then delivering an appropriate reading of the lines. Both build their characters via an assimilative approach that includes appropriation and reflection as well as exemplification and a concomitant repetition of symbolism. Both risk being enshrined in the semiology of Basque terrorism by which their screen personas, albeit unwittingly, can be associated with an ideological position. Indeed, the repetition of such roles, which has prefigured a degree of stereotyping of both Gómez and Munt, suggests that their performances might even constitute a fetish of representation, particularly for audiences that we might theorise for illustrative purposes as radical Basque nationalists and anti-Basque Spanish nationalists that are ironically united in 'watching, in an active controlling sense, an objectified other' (Mulvey 2000: 241).

The idea of these audiences peeping through these films to see Gómez and Munt offering glimpses of the desired but unreal Basque Country evokes a process of performance and reception that provides an audience with explicit pleasure and satisfies its curiosity. The way that both actors embody and articulate the Basque imaginary arguably responds to 'the position of the spectators in the cinema [which] is blatantly one of repression of their exhibitionism and projection of their repressed desire onto the performer' (Mulvey 2000: 241); but this has its ironic element too. Following Mulvey, we might presume that filmmakers and audiences seek out their reliable, even bankable performances because they create 'the imagised, eroticised concept of the world that forms the perception of the subject and makes a mockery of empirical objectivity' (2000: 242). This posits the Basque imaginary and its primary component, the imagined Basque community, as existing above and beyond any current reality, which suggests that the performances of Munt and Gómez realise a metaphysical function too for those who believe in a unique and independent Basque homeland, whether they campaign for or against it, whether they believe in it or not. However, this theorising of audiences also assumes an outdated reliance on positing the gaze as exclusively hegemonic. Whereas hegemony might, in Mulvey's much-refuted equation, be posited as simply heterosexual male, the hegemonic view of Munt and Gómez is infinitely more complex because it is subject not only to gendered responses but also to the troubled historical context and contested political arena to which their performances refer. On the one hand, as previously suggested, an audience steeped in Basque nationalism may feel their desire enabled by Gómez and Munt, as well as fetishised by these actors' differences from the archetype to which their characters aspire. On the other hand, however, audiences that do not share in the campaign, whether political, cultural or even violent, for an independent Basque Country, may discover that their performances, as Mulvey counsels, though 'pleasurable in form, can be threatening in content' (2000: 242). These performances, however complex and multilayered, are indebted to the Basque myths of difference that inspire separatism and even terrorists charged with the realisation of these myths in the real world after all. The irony is that the use of Gómez and Munt also alleviates the specificity of the threat, because their presence and their performances ultimately render the archetype non-Basque.

Other films and activities have extended the screen personas of Gómez and Munt beyond their association with Basque cinema. Munt has explored opportunities in film, theatre and television and directed productions in all three media, but her association with Basque cinema has largely been supplanted by her affiliation to the Catalan. Gómez explored estrangement from the Basque Country in *La ardilla roja/The Red Squirrel* (Julio Medem, 1993) and especially *Tierra/Earth* (Julio Medem, 1996) (see Santaolalla 1998; Stone and Rodríguez 2015) and has also continued to move between theatre and film, giving especially strong performances in an adaptation of the Golden Age play by Lope de Vega that preserved its verse, *El perro del hortelano/The Dog in the Manger* (Pilar Miró, 1996), and the rural noir *La noche de los girasoles/The Night of the Sunflowers* (Jorge Sánchez-Cabezudo, 2006) (see Whittaker 2013). However, the association with Basque cinema has never left him, to the extent that he engages in self-parody about this aspect of his career in the postmodern *Baztán*, in which he plays himself returning to the location where *Vacas* was filmed, the valley of Baztán in Navarre, which was itself a 'body double' for the Basque Country in that film. Approaching his destination, Gómez chances upon an *aizkolari* chopping wood in the manner he once essayed for *Vacas* and tells the man: 'hace tiempo hice yo también una apuesta de hacha, y soy de León, allí está la gracia' [a long time ago I took part in a wood-chopping competition, which is funny, because I'm from León]. Yet in a reunion with Basque actors from *Vacas* – Txema Blasco and Kandido Uranga, with whom he will make a film within the Basque film that is the postmodern *Baztán* – Gómez admits to 'un sentido de relajo, de estar a gusto por dentro, como volver a casa, y es que hace veinticinco años que no volvía desde que hicimos *Vacas*, ¿no?' [a feeling of relaxation, of feeling good inside, as if I were coming home, and I haven't been back here since we made *Vacas* twenty-five years ago, right?]. Blasco and Uranga good-humouredly tease him about his non-Basqueness in a way that also mocks the supposition of muscle memory that he brought to the previous role from growing up on a farm – '¡Le tienes que haber visto con el hacha!' [You should have seen him with an axe!] – and Gómez joins in the nostalgic chuckle: '¡Casi me llevo un pie por delante!' [I almost cut my foot off!].

The accumulation of Basque characters by Munt and Gómez has not defined their careers but has contributed to the formation of their screen

Figure 15 Tío (Carmelo Gómez) and Madre (Silvia Munt) toast their marriage in *Secretos del corazón* (Montxo Armendáriz, 1997). Aiete Films S.A., Ariane Films, Canal+ France, D.M.V.B. Films, Eurimages, Euskal Media, Fábrica de Imagens, Instituto de la Cinematografía y de las Artes Audiovisuales (ICAA), Sogepaq.

personas (Figure 15). This is not the same thing as acting, but one is certainly the lining of the other. Performances that presume to represent Basqueness might be expected to close all gaps between the non-Basque actor and the role, whether externally by make-up, costume and accent or by their lining, which in the case of Gómez is composed of an emotional equivalence and motivation found in his own memories for the actions and reactions required by the script, and in that of Munt is informed by posture, gesture and movement. Where these actors can be seen to meet, both physically and symbolically, is in their on-screen romantic union in *Secretos del corazón/Secrets of the Heart* (Montxo Armendáriz, 1997). Shot to represent the subjective view of life in the rural Basque Country enjoyed by nine-year-old Javi (Andoni Erburo), the film explicitly raises Gómez and Munt to the status of archetype by naming their characters Tío (uncle) and Madre (mother) respectively. In marriage, Tío assumes his rightful paternal and conjugal role, and his kind-hearted and virile demeanour wins both the love of Javi and the desire of his mother. Mulvey concludes that 'there are three different looks associated with cinema: that of the camera as it records the profilmic event, that of the audience as it watches the final product, and that of the characters at each other within the screen illusion' (2000: 248). However, there is a fourth, which is that which passes between the actors. What Gómez and Munt share during the happy event that ends this product may seem an illusion, but their look, if not of love, is certainly one of complicity in the performance of Basqueness.

Notes

1 For analyses and discussions of Basque cinema that contend with paradox and contradiction in the nature of its existence, see Santiago de Pablo (1996, 2012), Carlos Roldán Larreta (1999), Rob Stone (2001; 2007), Joseba Gabilondo (2002), Jaume Martí-Olivella (2003), María Pilar Rodríguez (2002), Joxean Fernández (2012) and Rob Stone and María Pilar Rodríguez (2015), amongst others.
2 For more on the development of Method acting in American cinema, see James Naremore (1988), David Krasner (2000) and Cynthia Baron, Diane Carson and Frank P. Tomasulo (2004).
3 For further information and discussion on the symbolism of the void in Basque culture in general, see César San Juan Guillén (1992) and Jon Etxeberria (2006). For analysis of the void as motif in the films of Julio Medem, see Rob Stone (2007).
4 Mari, who is also known as the lady of Anboto, was the wife of of the god Maju (a.k.a. Sugaar), whom she met at every *akelarre* [witches' Sabbath]. Said to control the weather, this mythical figure derives from the Basque word *Amari* meaning 'wife' (plus the suffix of her profession) and the closeness of the names Mari and Mary contributed to the ease with which the cult of the Virgin Mary helped establish Catholicism in the Basque Country.
5 'Ama lur' is the Basque name for Mother Earth and can also be translated as 'motherland'. This mythic, maternal figure carries strong associations with the landscape and nationalist beliefs. It is also the title of the key Basque film *Ama Lur/Motherland* (Néstor Basterretxea and Fernando Larruquert, 1968), which serves as a mnemonic and manifesto of Basqueness. For more on Ama Lur, see Rob Stone (2010) and Rob Stone and María Pilar Rodríguez (2015).

References

Baron, Cynthia, Diane Carson and Frank P. Tomasulo (2004) *More than a Method: Trends and Traditions in Contemporary Film Performance*, Detroit: Wayne State University Press.

Benjamin, Walter (1999) 'The Work of Art in the Age of Mechanical Reproduction', in *Illuminations*, London: Pimlico, 211–42.

Davies, Ann (2009) 'Woman and Home: Gender and the Theorisation of Basque (National) Cinema', *Journal of Spanish Cultural Studies*, 10.3, 359–72.

de Pablo, Santiago (1996) *Cien años de cine en el País Vasco (1896–1995)*, Vitoria-Gasteiz: Diputación Foral de Álava.

de Pablo, Santiago (2012) *The Basque Nation On-Screen: Cinema, Nationalism, and Political Violence*, Reno: Center for Basque Studies, University of Nevada.

Doane, Mary Ann (2000) 'Film and the Masquerade: Theorizing the Female Spectator', in J. Hollows, P. Hutchings and M. Jancovich (eds), *The Film Studies Reader*, London: Arnold, pp. 248–56.

Dyer, Richard (2000a) 'Stars and "Character"', in J. Hollows, P. Hutchings and M. Jancovich (eds), *The Film Studies Reader*, London: Arnold, pp. 124–8.

Dyer, Richard (2000b) 'Stars as Images', in J. Hollows, P. Hutchings and M. Jancovich (eds), *The Film Studies Reader*, London: Arnold, pp. 121–4.

Etxeberria, Jon (2006) 'Experiencia y vacío: Los componentes míticos y místicos en la obra de Jorge Oteiza', *Ondare*, 25, 327–35.

Fernández, Joxean (2012) *Euskal zinema/Cine vasco/Basque Film*, Donostia: Etxepare Basque Institute.

Gabilondo, Joseba (2002) 'Uncanny Identity: Violence, Gaze and Desire in Contemporary Basque Cinema', in Jo Labanyi (ed.), *Constructing Identity in Contemporary Spain: Theoretical Debates and Cultural Practice*, Oxford: Oxford University Press, pp. 262–79.

Insausti, Mikel (2014) 'La vuelta al humor regionalista de Chomin del Regato', *Gara*, 16 March, www.naiz.info/es/hemeroteca/gara/editions/gara_2014-03-16-06-00/hemeroteca_articles/la-vuelta-al-humor-regionalista-de-chomin-del-regato, accessed 17 March 2014.

Krasner, David (2000) *Method Acting Reconsidered: Theory, Practice, Future*, New York: St Martin's Press.

Martí-Olivella, Jaume (2003) *Basque Cinema: An Introduction*, Reno: Center for Basque Studies, University of Nevada.

Mulvey, Laura (2000) 'Visual Pleasure and Narrative Cinema', in J. Hollows, P. Hutchings and M. Jancovich (eds), *The Film Studies Reader*, London: Arnold, pp. 238–48.

Naremore, James (1988) *Acting in the Cinema*, Los Angeles: University of California Press.

Perriam, Chris (2003) *Stars and Masculinities in Spanish Cinema*, Oxford: Oxford University Press, 2003.

Rodríguez, María Pilar (2002) *Mundos en conflicto: Aproximaciones al cine vasco de los noventa*, San Sebastián: Universidad de Deusto-Filmoteca Vasca.

Roldán Larreta, Carlos (1999) *El cine del País Vasco: De Ama Lur (1968) a Airbag (1997)*, Donostia: Eusko Ikaskuntza.

San Juan Guillén, César (1992) 'El vacío y los vascos: Interpretación estética y psicodinámica', *Revista internacional de los estudios vascos*, 37.2, 383–92.

Santaolalla, Isabel (1998) 'Far from Home, Close to Desire; Julio Medem's Landscapes', *Bulletin of Hispanic Studies*, 75, 331–8.

Stone, Rob (2001) *Spanish Cinema*, Harlow: Longman.

Stone, Rob (2007) *Julio Medem*, Manchester: Manchester University Press.

Stone, Rob (2010) 'The Coding of Aesthetic and Thematic Discourse in a Cinematic Mnemonic: The Case of "Ama Lur" (1968)', *Journal of European Studies*, 40.3, 230–42.

Stone, Rob and Helen Jones (2004) 'Mapping the Gendered Space of the Basque Country', *Studies in European Cinema*, 1.1, 43–55.

Stone, Rob and María Pilar Rodríguez (2015) *Basque Cinema: A Cultural and Political History*, London: I. B. Tauris.

Whittaker, Tom (2013) '*La noche de los girasoles*', in M. Delgado and R. Fiddian (eds), *Spanish Cinema 1973–2010: Auteurism, Politics, Landscape and Memory*, Manchester: Manchester University Press.

15

Los amantes pasajeros/I'm So Excited! (2013): 'performing' *la crisis*

Maria M. Delgado

In 2013, Almodóvar released *Los amantes pasajeros/I'm So Excited!*, his nineteenth feature-length film. The film was not judged kindly by Spanish critics. Almodóvar was criticised for the misfiring comic tone of the film, an overwrought performance register and a plot that seemed to suggest the filmmaker had lost touch with 'reality'. *El País*'s lead film critic Carlos Boyero dismissed *Los amantes pasajeros* as 'una de las películas más tontas que he visto en mucho tiempo' [one of the silliest films that I have seen in a long time] (Boyero 2013), appropriating the headline of his 2009 review of *Los abrazos rotos/Broken Embraces* (2009) as well as one of Almodóvar's earlier films '¿Qué he hecho yo para merecer esto?' [What have I done to deserve this?], in cataloguing what he saw as the film's failures (Boyero 2009). And yet what Boyero didn't want, or was unable to see was the Manchegan filmmaker's deliberate deployment of theatrical tropes – from the recourse to the plot of *A Midsummer Night's Dream* to an acting style that referenced the work of Spain's most animated screen performers from the 1950s, 1960s and 1970s – positioning the film within a consciously 'staged' world. Described by Almodóvar as his most political film to date (Almodóvar 2013a), *Los amantes pasajeros* is a film about Spain's extra-ordinary social situation. At a time when he is categorised as a *bête noire* of the ruling Partido Popular or Should be People's Party, Almodóvar opts not for stylised realism or a plot that overtly comments on contemporary events but rather uses the mechanism of a screwball comedy set up in the air to supposedly provide 'an escape' from Spain's woes. The country's discontents, however, are like a series of skeletons rattling in the cupboard. Indeed, during Península's Flight 2549, making its way from Madrid's Barajas Airport to Mexico City, these skeletons tumble out one after another, providing a portrait of Spain as a corrupt and misgoverned nation that has lost its bearings. This chapter provides a reading of the film as a work that performs *la crisis*, offering a blistering portrait of a nation flying around in circles as it waits to be told where it can make an emergency landing.

Back to the 1980s: a drawing room farce in the air

> We need to work to make the world better. This film is a tribute to a time
> when the world was a better place. So there is a kind of nostalgia for my
> youth and for the early years of democracy in Spain. I was 33 years younger
> when I made my first comedies, and the film is a celebration of that time,
> of the culture of sex and drugs and pleasure. So it is related to Spain and
> to my life then.
>
> I don't know if it's nostalgia but the film is a homage to the decade of
> the 1980s and the way we lived in Spain at that time. There was an explo-
> sion that came with democracy. I don't like the word nostalgia but Madrid
> was more interesting than it is now. It was living through a moment of
> great euphoria. It's not just Spain that has changed, the world has changed,
> I have changed. We can't all live like we did in the 1980s. But I miss the
> liberty of that time. Madrid was a fiesta then 24/7, now it only parties 7
> hours a day. (Almodóvar 2013a)

The playful opening credits of Pedro Almodóvar's *Los amantes pasajeros*, designed by graphic designer and 1980s underground icon Javier
Mariscal, and underscored by the Los Destellos' jaunty rendition of 'Für
Elise', allege that the film that follows is fiction and fantasy and bears
no relation to reality. But this is an assertion that should be taken with
a pinch of salt. *Los amantes pasajeros* may be set almost entirely in the
bubble of a plane suspended up in the air but it is anything but escapist
entertainment. The film may ostensibly function as a screwball comedy
with nods to Luis García Berlanga's acerbic films of the 1950s, but it is a
feature grounded in Spain's political actualities. It offers a denouncement
of the empty rhetoric and opinionated posturing peddled by bankers and
politicians and adopted in the discursive language of wider Spanish society which has been documented by writer Antonio Muñoz Molina in
his 2013 book, *Todo lo que era sólido/All That Was Solid*. The vocabulary of performance has here been co-opted to deceptive ends: affirming
exploitative political values and a culture of game-play used to advance
blatantly material ends. The playful and creative pleasure promoted by
the three flight attendants, however, serves a different end. It is both
a challenge to the bland, uninspired and overly recited discourses of
austerity promoted by politicians and a mode of facilitating a process
of social reflection and self-analysis that is shown to have transformative effects during the course of the film. *Los amantes pasajeros* demonstrates the ways in which decision-making processes are best handled
from the bottom up; encouraging a participatory model of democracy
where diversity, difference and intuition are prioritised over uniformity
and rigidity, and where creativity is harnessed to public service.

Los amantes pasajeros brings together a group of characters cocooned in the Business Class cabin of a fictional airline, Península's Flight 2549, making its way from Madrid's Barajas Airport to Mexico City. When the aeroplane experiences a technical failure, the pilots realise that they have to perform an emergency landing. As there is a UN Security Summit at Barajas, returning to Madrid is no longer an option. Valencia is hosting a Formula 1 race and Seville a motorcycle championship, so neither of these airports presents alternative options. While the passengers wait for news from air traffic control on where they might bring the plane down to safety, a trio of male flight attendants in Business Class tries to keep the cockpit and cabin entertained.

Drawing on the conventions of the drawing-room farce, 80 per cent of the action is largely confined to a single interior location.[1] While the 'hermetically sealed apartment' of *Átame!/Tie Me Up! Tie Me Down!* (Pedro Almodóvar, 1989) may appear as the most discernible model for the confined cabin in *Los amantes pasajeros*, the film draws on the environmental configuration of *Mujeres al borde de un ataque de nervios/Women on the Verge of a Nervous Breakdown* (Pedro Almodóvar, 1988), where the action is similarly centred on a single interior space and draws on the dramatic structure of Georges Feydeau's fast-moving mannered comedies. In *Mujeres al borde de un ataque de nervios*, this is manifest in the comings and goings in and out of Pepa's stylised apartment: slamming doors, amorous infidelities, mistaken identities, rapid-fire dialogue. *Los amantes pasajeros* features a similarly artificial set dominated by the split stages of the cockpit and cabin: the latter segregated into Business Class and Economy. The cabin is styled in a more muted colour scheme than the primary colours that dominated in *Mujeres al borde de un ataque de nervios*. Red is here largely confined to the piping both on the seats and the trio of male flight attendants' baby-blue shirts, the theatrical curtains that separate out the Business and Economy Class cabins and the carmine lipstick of a wronged woman or scarlet summer dress of her dramatic nemesis. The dominant palette of pastels accord the film a retro feel that positions it in a mythical space hovering somewhere between the black humour, systematic distortion and disfiguring anti-naturalism of Spain's *esperpento* tradition, 1980s pop cinema and the classic comedy of transformation. The latter sees characters escaping conformity to find release, albeit temporarily, from outmoded modes of behaviour while learning something about themselves in the process.

All the characters in the film have something to hide. Norma Boss (Almodóvar regular Cecilia Roth) is a failed actress turned dominatrice with a powerful client list and an inflated sense of her own self-importance. There is something of Barbra Streisand meeting Carol Burnett in her self-conscious appearance – early on in the film she is spotted as if in disguise peering irately from her seat at the flight attendants. Norma's full lips, large eyes, and manicured persona also reference Bárbara Rey, the ex-beauty queen turned actress and TV presenter, alleged to have been King Juan Carlos's mistress, receiving a retainer from the state for her 'services' until 1996. Norma's clandestine videos further point to Rey as a possible model. Norma's Business Class companions include a shady businessman, Más (José Luis Torrijo) embroiled in a major financial scandal and trying to leave the country without drawing attention to himself. Más's name – *más* means 'more' in Spanish – is significant of excess and gluttony, pointing to an individual whose existence has been predicated on the desire for more than is necessary or desirable. A womanising actor Ricardo Galán (Guillermo Toledo) - *galán*, of course, is the Spanish term for a leading man in theatre and cinema – is travelling to Mexico to shoot a soap opera and escape responsibility for an emotionally disturbed girlfriend.[2] A recently married couple (Miguel Ángel Silvestre and Laya Martí) are carrying some illegal substances to spice up their honeymoon. A wistful psychic Bruna (Lola Dueñas) is heading to Mexico to help with the disappearance of some Spaniards involved in drug trafficking. The final cast member in Business is Infante (José María Yazpik), a hitman masking as a security advisor whose ostentatious urbanity, inky hair and slick suit allude to the macho men of *Reservoir Dogs* (Quentin Tarantino, 1992). His name is perhaps a nod to the scandals in which the Spanish royal family have been embroiled since 2011 – *infante* is the name of a Spanish prince – as well as a reference to the actor Pedro Infante (1917–57), a key figure in the Golden Age of Mexican cinema who died in a plane crash en route to Mexico City.

These are knowingly theatrical types, larger-than-life characters whose self-conscious performance register – associated with the *sainete* and other populist stage genres – owes much to the lively generation of 1960s actors deployed by two directors admired by Almodóvar, Berlanga and Fernando Fernán Gómez. Pedro Infante belongs to that same generation of performers and there is something of Spanish actors Alfredo Landa and José Luis López Vázquez in his comic timing, facial inflections and empty macho posturing. As Brad Epps also shows (chapter 7 this volume), Landa went on to give his name to a genre of films that offered a particular take on Spain's burgeoning tourist economy. He embodied the generation of Spaniards educated under Franco who found their Catholic values questioned by the progressive ideas and new culture of *apertura* that was introduced with the opening of Spain's borders to foreign visitors in search of cheap package holidays. According to the psychologist José Felix Rodríguez, the fiercely heterosexual, womanising, hypocritical macho males embodied by Landa in formulaic *Carry On*-like sexual comedies such as *No desearás al vecino del quinto/Thou Shalt Not Covet Thy Fifth Floor Neighbour* (Ramón Fernández, 1970) and *Los días de Cabirio/Cabirio's Days* (Fernando Merino, 1971) allowed Spaniards to approach motifs and mores that were stifled by censorship (Portalatín 2013). The social and sexual posturing of Landa's ordinary looking men struck a chord with the Spanish populace who identified with his mundane appearance but quick enterprising wit.

As was also the case with José Luis López Vázquez (see Whittaker, chapter 5 this volume), Alfredo Landa looked like a next-door neighbour. His ordinariness differed conspicuously from the debonair actors of the 1950s, like Alberto Closas and Paco Rabal, whose smouldering good looks offered a model closer to the French sophistication of Yves Montand and Alain Delon. Almodóvar may open *Los amantes pasajeros* with two of Spain's most glamorous stars, Antonio Banderas and Penélope Cruz, as a pair of lovesick ground staff whose absent-mindedness is responsible for the problems later experienced by the plane. Banderas and Cruz, however, are soon put to one side as the director opts for three male protagonists – Joserra (a svelte Javier Cámara), Ulloa (Raúl Arévalo) and Fajas, which translates as 'girdles' (Carlos Areces) – whose pedestrian looks hark back to Landa, López Vázquez and José Sacristan. In choosing, though, to queer the quotidian qualities of *landismo*, Almodóvar offers a new take on the battle between repression and desire, which clinical psychologist Esteban Cañamares sees as central to the protagonists personified by Landa. Landa's camp couturier Antón in *No desearás al vecino del quinto* offers his 'services' to the air hostesses in the neighbouring apartment; here, the three flight attendants proffer their services to those they perceive to be in need of their help. Only the needy here are not the ignored populace packed into Economy but the privileged few cocooned in Business Class whose criminal behaviour is responsible for the woeful state of Spain's economy. As the film progresses, the attendants come to question the both passengers' and their own behaviour. As Núria Triana-Toribio aptly observes, *No desearás al vecino del quinto* opts for a resolution which reinforces the need for moral rectitude, monogamy and conservatism (2003: 104). *Los amantes pasajeros*, however, as I will go on to demonstrate, argues for a rather different course of action. The overblown but repeatedly thwarted libido which Barry Jordan sees as a consistent feature of *landismo* (2003) is here given free rein in a Marx Brothers-cum-Tricicle[3]-like manner that lampoons the vanities of the political and social elite. Hierarchies have to be challenged, cycles of abuse have to be broken, extra-judicial murders have to be halted. The theatricality of play offers a way towards transformation, but it must necessarily be followed by recognition that not all excesses can be permitted in the name of the pleasure principle.

In his autobiography, when discussing *No deseáras*, Landa recalls his wife alluding to the characteristics of silent cinema that defined the actors' performances (cited in Ordóñez 2008: 181). The observation recalls Norma Desmond's declaration in Billy Wilder's *Sunset Boulevard* (1950) that before the talkies actors 'had faces then'. Agustín Almodóvar has referred to his brother's reliance on a regular troupe of actors as 'almost as if he has a repertory company' (cited in Dickson 2014). The familiar faces that feature in the film – Roth, Cámara, Cruz, Banderas, Dueñas – are cast in roles that comment on their off- and on-screen identities as forged through Almodóvar's oeuvre. This primarily involves the recourse to a comic vulgarity and verbal explicitness that visibly contrasts with the performance register of earlier roles. Javier Cámara's lean, animated tequila-swigging Joserra is a veritable contrast to the calm, plump Benigno of *Hable con ella/Talk to Her* (2002) and Cecilia Roth's cool, manicured Norma is similarly distanced from the fresh, unmannered warmth of Manuela in *Todo sobre mi madre/All About My Mother* (1999). Our first glance of Fajas shows him theatrically flicking his hair into place – a plastered-down hairstyle worthy of a silent cinema comedian. The impassive look that had characterised Antonio Banderas's suave surgeon in *La piel que habito/The Skin I Live in* (2011) has no place in *Los amantes pasajeros*. Rather, a swaggering exuberance, shameless carnality and lurid expressivity take the viewer back to the much-disdained shenanigans and *paletismo* of *landismo*. The three gay male flight attendants – this is arguably Almodóvar's most overtly gay film since *La mala educación/Bad Education* (2004)[4] – function as a flapping, animated chorus of sorts: a trio of picaresque adventurers commenting on the predicament of the passengers but throwing their own amorous intrigues and obsessions into the narrative mix. The indiscreet chief flight attendant Joserra, incapable of keeping a secret, is having an affair with the plane's pilot, Alex, a married father of two who is not prepared to go public about their relationship. Joserra's two deputies, purse-lipped Ulloa and plump, overly superstitious Fajas, offer little in the way of constructive advice, instead throwing their own mix of fear and paranoia into the air crew's attempts to keep the passengers distracted and entertained.

Almodóvar cultivates a topsy-turvy world – at times the camera work literally emulates the plane's movement to plunge the viewer into the cabin space – creating a space for revelry and fantasy where anything is possible. The baby-blue walls of the cabin interior suggest a child's nursery, and ideas of regression, infantilisation and play are evidently central

Figure 16 The three flight attendants Fajas (Carlos Areces), Ulloa (Rául Arévalo) and Joserra (Javier Cámara), entertain the passengers in Business Class with a perfectly choreographed dance routine that harks back to the Hollywood musical. *Los amantes pasajeros/I'm So Excited!* (Pedro Almodóvar, 2013). El Deseo.

to the director's handling of his skeletal plot. This is certainly a nod to the childish males of *landismo*, but also whereas the low-budget look of films like Fernando Merino's *No desearás la mujer de tu prójimo/Thou Shalt Not Covet Thy Neighbour's Wife* (1971) eschewed colour coordination and textured interiors, Almodóvar's eye for production décor offers an elegantly conceived stage for the action.

The trio of flight attendants perform an expertly choreographed safety routine, dancing to the donning of life jackets while the opening and closing of the red curtains that separate out the different parts of the cabin lend the action a theatrical sense of purpose. The visual language of this sequence may reference the gestural vocabulary of vaudeville but the verbal puns and *double entendres* that follow have more in common with the stage comedies of Miguel Mihura and Jardiel Poncela that Peter Evans has located as a palpable influence on Almodóvar's cinema (1996: 13). The film's narrative arc also harks back to what Almodóvar terms the 'rather theatrical dramatic structure' of *Mujeres al borde de un ataque de nervios*, whose script reads 'as if it were adapted from a play' (Strauss 1994: 79). Theatrical enterprise appears central to *Los amantes pasajeros* with the slapstick antics and *non sequiturs* of the trio of flight attendants recalling the Marx Brothers of *A Night at the Opera* (Sam Wood, 1935).

Key here is the appropriation of pivotal tropes from Shakespeare's *A Midsummer Night's Dream*, a play that similarly dismantles archaic models of authority in a fairyland setting where magical makeovers are matched by erotic gameplay. The love potion of Shakespeare's comedy is refashioned by Almodóvar in a mode that further acknowledges its earlier use in *Mujeres al borde de un ataque de nervios*. The Economy Class passengers and flight attendants have been given a tranquilliser to send them to sleep while the trio of enterprising flight attendants – the Rude Mechanicals of Shakespeare's piece – amuse Business Class passengers with their anecdotes and escapades. In *A Midsummer Night's Dream* the Mechanicals put on a play; here dominated by a similar creative impulse, they present a choreographed dance routine to the Pointer Sisters' 1984 hit 'I'm So Excited' – the English title of *Los amantes pasajeros* comes, of course, from this song – which Almodóvar films in a patterning worthy of Busby Berkeley as legs kick outwards, heads peer out, and curtains open and close with a boisterous sense of timing.

The magical elixir of Shakespeare's comedy, applied to the eyelids of the sleeping characters in *A Midsummer Night's Dream*, is here first tequila and then a cocktail, *Agua de Valencia*, composed of vodka, champagne and orange juice with synthetic mescaline – the illegal cargo of the honeymooning Groom – thrown in for good measure. (A popular beverage in the 1980s, it is one of Almodóvar's many nods to the hedonism of that decade.) As the intoxicating beverage is consumed by passengers and crew, confessions and revelations tumble. The hitman announces that he has been hired by the wife of one of Norma's high-profile customers to kill her; Norma exposes a list of clients that includes the highest echelons of royalty and business; Más discloses a tale of domestic dysfunction and estrangement where his wife's *opus Dei* conservatism has driven their daughter away from home.

Bacchanalian sexual encounters take over the cabin: the sleepy dishevelled Bride fellates the Groom; Joserra and Alex escape to the lavatory; Ulloa 'comforts' the unhappily married first officer Benito; while the wistful clairvoyant stalks the Economy cabin in search of a stud male with whom she can lose her virginity – a sequence scored by Alberto Iglesias's snake-charming soundtrack. Suspended in time, intoxicated and deprived of their mobile phones and social media, codes of decorum regulating the characters' behaviour effectively slip away. Their progressively dishevelled attire and hair testify to the pulling down of polished appearances, with the sexual orgy functioning as the most evident manifestation of this process.

Almodóvar has acknowledged his own deployment of this magical potion trope both in *Los amantes pasajeros* and in *Mujeres al borde de un ataque de nervios*: 'its something I've seen many times in classical theatre' (Almodóvar 2013a; Strauss 1994: 89). In *Mujeres al borde de un ataque de nervios*, the elixir is reconceived as an irresistible *gazpacho* laced with sleeping tablets that transforms Rossy de Palma's Marisa from an irritable, laced-up pesky virgin to a wiser and more considerate human being, able to enjoy and relax in the company of others. Following her erotic dream, she awakes as if from a fairy tale, with the clear sensation that she has lost her virginity. Her dour green coat has been removed to reveal a vibrant scarlet dress beneath; her fiancé, his new amour, two farcical policemen and a good-looking telephone repairman all litter the apartment in their slumbered state.[5]

Altered states generated by the consumption of drugs are present in a conspicuous number of Almodóvar's films from *Pepi, Luci, Bom y otras chicas del montón/Pepi, Luci, Bom* (1980) to *Los amantes pasajeros* (see Sánchez-Carbonell and Colomera 2003). In the former it offers release and pleasure, a new consciousness embodied by dynamism of *la movida*. In *Los amantes pasajeros*, the sleeping tablets that produced the transformation of Marisa are deployed to destructive effect as the passengers in Economy Class are placated into a drug-induced sleep. Even the legendary Pepa Charro, popularly known as 'La Terremoto de Alcorcón' [the Earthquake of Alcorcón], and a figure whose animated Andalusian-inflected cover performances of number such as 'It's Raining Men' and 'I Will Survive' has won her a loyal gay following, here cast as Piluca, a flight attendant in Economy Class, has conveniently been knocked out alongside the passengers she is nominally in charge of. The 'parte más lúdica y hedonista del carácter español' [most ludic and hedonistic part of the Spanish character] identified by Almodóvar as arriving with democracy (Martín Garzo 2011: 123), and embodied by Charro's post-*movida* performances, has been silenced by the abusive behaviour of the plane's two ostensibly 'nice guy' pilots (Almodovar 2013a).

Indeed, *Los amantes pasajeros* exposes the destructive games of a number of characters, pointing to a wider malaise with the execution of authority in contemporary Spain. The selfish womanising of actor Ricardo Galán is revealed through the public phone he utilises to ring his on–off girlfriend Alba (Paz Vega), only to find that she is contemplating suicide perched on the side of Madrid's Segovia Viaduct – an impressive theatrical backdrop, known as a site for suicides, this art deco bridge features also in *Matador* (1986), *Tacones lejanos/High Heels* (1991) and *Los abrazos rotos*.[6] In a coincidence worthy of the classic screwball comedy, the phone falls out of her hand into the basket of another of this Don Juan's ex's, Ruth (Blanca Suárez). Ruth's open face, short fringe and bouncy ponytail visibly references the freshness and fragility of Audrey Hepburn. This temporary foray away from the plane serves to highlight Ricardo's irresponsibility while offering a brilliant cameo to Carmen Machi in matching aqua outfit and eyeshadow as his inquisitive concierge: a mantle she has inherited from the iconic Chus Lampreave. And, while it is the elegant Ruth who greets Ricardo when the plane finally secures a landing strip at La Mancha Airport, she simply passes on his battered case and walks away from the culture of deception and untruths that had marked his past behaviour.

Politics and posturing

Los amantes pasajeros is, in so many ways, a film about the politics of deception, the culture of posturing and *apariencias*, or short-term gains and over-politicisation that Antonio Muñoz Molina (2013: 48–65) and Luisa Elena Delgado (2014: 33–97) see as partly responsible for Spain's economic woes. Alex and Benito have sham marriages; unbeknown to his new bride, the Groom is transporting recreational drugs; Norma protects herself by alleging ownership of a collection of videos implicating 600 of her clients in uncompromising behaviour – a further nod to the compromising videos of King Juan Carlos Bárbara Rey is rumoured to have stored. Más is a financier whose Guadiana Savings Bank has swindled millions of clients out of their savings. While Almodóvar wrote the film before Spain's former Bankia chairman, Rodrigo Rato, was called (alongside thirty-two current and former officials from the bank) to Spain's high court to answer questions on fraud and the falsification of accounts, this case, ongoing at the time the film was released, presents a potent off-screen backdrop to the action. Bankia is Spain's fourth largest bank, created by Spain's then Socialist government in December 2010 through a merging of seven ailing *cajas* [savings banks] hit badly by the toxic debts generated by the burst property bubble in 2008. The Spanish government's bailouts of the bank in May and September 2012 failed to curb the culture of haemorrhaging, with losses of €19 billion registered in 2012, six times those of 2011. *Los amantes pasajeros* went on general release in Spain on 7 March 2013 amidst press reports that Bankia shareholders stood to lose practically all their invested capital in what appeared to be a fraudulent exaggeration of the market value of its loans. So, while the shady Más decides to go back and face the music following his in-flight ordeal, there is no such prospect available for Bankia's unlucky investors. At the time of the film's cinematic release in Spain, domestic unemployment was hitting 26 per cent and painful austerity measures taking their toll – including savage cuts to culture which have seen VAT rise from 8 to 21 per cent on all cinema tickets – with little governmental appetite to tackle institutional corruption. The Bankia scandal continues to rumble, while the ruling People's Party is tainted by revelations that its former treasurer Luis Bárcenas amassed €22 million in Swiss bank accounts, overseeing a widespread culture of bribes to PP politicians from senior figures in the construction industry. The terms 'recession' or 'economic crisis' may conspicuously never feature in Almodóvar's film, but the Guadiana plotline offers a pertinent comment on a society where patronage, politics and public administration are indelibly interwoven. *Los amantes pasajeros* is a film that systematically highlights the abuse of power by those in authority, the culture of *pelotazo* denounced by Antonio Muñoz Molina in *Todo lo que era sólido*, published in Spain the same month as Almodóvar's film's domestic release (2013: 39).

The metaphor of a society flying around in circles without going anywhere is hugely pertinent to *Los amantes pasajeros*. The film, Almodóvar claims, 'is a reaction to the uncertainty and fear that Spain has been living through' as the austerity measures introduced to tackle its double-dip recession hit home: 'Passengers are flying around in circles; they know they have to make an emergency landing but they don't know where or when or how it is going to happen' (Almodóvar 2013a). The plane finally lands at La Mancha Airport, an empty ghostly space of pristine floors and mirrored surfaces that manifestly references the high-profile white elephant airports of Ciudad Real and Castellón. The former, 150 kilometres south of Madrid, closed down in 2012 after only three years in operation, while the latter was initially unable to secure a licence because its runway failed to meet EU regulations.[7] These derelict spaces are the public wastelands of a nation inebriated by the frenzy to construct at any expense. Almodóvar's decision to shoot at Ciudad Real, one of seventeen unused airports in Spain, according to the Minister of Works, and boasting the longest runway built on the Iberian Peninsula, is significant (Almodóvar 2013b): 'The immense areas inside the real airport' – here renamed Aeropuerto de Castilla la Mancha – 'are deserted, ghostly' and they 'become the best metaphor for the ghostly journey of Flight PE2549, a journey without destination that, after many difficulties, lands in the characters' present, an unavoidable present' (Almodóvar 2013a). They are also a pertinent embodiment of an observation made by Alfredo Landa in his autobiography that perhaps Spain is not 'un país de esfuerzos continuados sino de chispazos y abandonos' [a country of sustained effort but rather of sparks and states of abandon] (cited in Ordóñez 2008: 185). Almodóvar's airport shows the Spain of shiny surfaces signalled by Muñoz Molina in *Todo lo que era sólido*: 'el país de los simulacros y los espejismos, el de las candidaturas olímpicas y las exposiciones universales, el de las obras ingentes destinadas no a ningún uso real sino al exhibicionismo de los politicos que las inauguraban' [the Spain of simulacrum and mirrors, that of Olympic candidatures and universal expos, that of huge works designed not for any real use but rather to the exhibitionism of the politicians who inaugurated them] (2013: 53). In *Mujeres al borde de un ataque de nervios*, Pepa's dream visualises Iván dancing between shiny surfaces that reflect the ugly skyscrapers of Azca, the urban development in northern Madrid that Paul Julian Smith notes was conceived by urban planners 'to rival Manhattan' (2000: 94). A generation on, the empty, seductive rhetoric that defined Iván's amorous encounters has been reborn in the untruths peddled by the similarly irresponsible Ricardo. Almodóvar's intoxicated characters are potent similes for an irresponsible generation whose vanity and cronyism brought the country to the point of bankruptcy.

Los amantes pasajeros paints a society indelibly scarred by secrets and lies. Lola Dueñas' pensive psychic is en route to Mexico to try and locate the bodies of Spaniards who have disappeared in mysterious circumstances – a possible reference to Spain's own 'disappeared' from the Civil War and its aftermath that Almodóvar references in *Volver* (2006), *Los abrazos rotos* and *La piel que habito*. Javier Cámara's Joserra confesses his own involvement in a pact of silence that echoes that of the Spanish nation in relation to the crimes of the Franco era, when he recounts the tale of a man who was suffocated by his fellow passengers. The death was consequently hushed up as heart failure. To a greater or lesser degree, all the passengers are somehow implicated in a pact of silence and deception where the relationship between truth and lies cannot easily be prised apart.[8] As Luis Martínez perceptively observed in his review of the film: 'No se engañen, no es comedia, aunque lo parezca. Es Almodóvar devolviéndonos, para bien o para mal, la perfecta imagen de lo que somos. Brillante. Una provocación' [Don't deceive yourself, it isn't a comedy, even though it may appear to be. It's Almodóvar returning to us, for better or worse, the perfect image of what we are. Brilliant. A provocation] (2013: n.p.). The publically legitimised discourses of political performance, with their reliance on the playacting of flinches, grimaces, rolling eyes and sauntering moves, may have been criticised by critics such as Carlos Boyero (2013), Salvador Llopart (2013) and Oti Rodríguez Marchante (2013), but Almodóvar's skilful co-opting of this gestural language argues for the need to contemplate the relationship between levels of fiction endorsed by the state and those that are delegitimised for a series of political and social reasons. In a culture where identity is effectively performed across all areas of social and political life, can the relationship between fact and fiction ever be appropriately qualified?

Conclusion

Los amantes pasajeros offers a conscious move away from the lithe intertextuality and elegantly layered plotting of his most recent films, but I would argue that this is an extra-ordinary film for the extra-ordinary times *crisis* Spain is living through. In it Almodóvar consciously recycles elements, characters and lines of dialogue from his earliest work. Characters talk openly of desire and dicks, of fellatios and fucks. The uncompromising exchanges, sexual puns, vulgar one-liners and adoption of caricature hark back to his first film, *Pepi Luci, Bom* while also pointing to the verbal comedy of the Marx Brothers that is continuously alluded to throughout the film. There is a nod to the final sequence – again set on a plane – in *Laberinto de pasiones/Labyrinth of Passions* (1982) and the stylish reprocessing of camp, kitsch and Spanish 1950s cinema was previously evidenced in *Entre tinieblas/Dark Habits* (1983). The tone of *Los amantes pasajeros* owes more to the in-yer-face verbal excesses of these early films than the noirish melodrama of *Los abrazos rotos* or the narrative suppleness of *Volver*. As Carlos Losilla notes, observing the older more visibly worn Antonio Banderas and Penélope Cruz, whose absent-minded misadventures in love offer the film's prelude – 'time has passed, and the country of *la movida* and design has become an abandoned no man's land, misty and spectral, from which the only thing to do is run away' (2013: 97). The phantoms of Madrid's *movida* may run through *Los amantes pasajeros*, but they jostle for attention with those of late Francoism's *landismo* and the satirical energy of the Marx Brothers fusion of verbal wit and vaudeville. In *Los amantes pasajeros* Almodóvar shows *la movida* as a once bright spark currently in a state of abandon. *La movida* may have promised modernity but this once golden generation is shown in the film to have either now been put to sleep – like the passengers in Economy Class – or been allowed to run riot. Social responsibility has been eschewed in favour of a political *amiguismo* [cronyism] where, as Muñoz Molina observes, 'la fiesta era una forma de vida' [the *fiesta* was a way of life] funded in the post-Franco era by an unaccountable level of public subsidy that played a decisive role in bringing the country to its knees (2013: 61).

The film may have been accused of apoliticism and shallowness, but its promotion of the importance of civic values and joviality that Paul Julian Smith has identified as key to *la movida* underpins the behaviour of the trio of Business Class flight attendants (2006: 51–75). Joserra's confession (itself a theatrical device) acknowledges the dangerous complicity that underpinned the institutionally endorsed *pacto del silencio* [pact of silence] and found some sort of release in countercultural energy of *la movida*. Almodóvar may have been classified as a director more concerned with playfulness than politics,[9] but *Los amantes pasajeros* shows that discourses of performativity can be used to both expose and comment on the proliferation of empty rhetoric that underpinned the building frenzy embodied by the gleaming reflective floors of Richard Rogers' T4 extension to Madrid's Barajas Airport cleaned by Penélope Cruz's Raimunda in *Volver*. If, as Duncan Wheeler argues (see chapter 8 in this volume, p. 265), it is the idea of 'making a spectacle of themselves' that unites the 'ostensibly disparate performance styles and star personas' of Spanish actors, Almodóvar harnesses this effusive physicality and extreme emotion to potent effect. Even Banderas and Cruz, Spain's most glamorous acting exports, are here presented as clumsy *paletos*, cinematic siblings to Fajas – who prays piously before his makeshift altar – and the limp wrist and animated eyes of Ulloa. Almodóvar's recourse to the vaudeville and mime traditions of silent cinema creates no place for performative subtlety. As David Denby notes, 'in the silents, you have do something; you can't just *be* … Physical exuberance was so beautifully madcap, and so bizarrely beside the point in plot terms, that it became and end in itself; it couldn't be translated into mere words. And it was a product of silence' (2012). In a society where institutional corruption and pacts of forgetting have produced a culture of silence and injustice that Almodóvar has repeatedly criticised in interviews (see AFP 2009; Delgado 2009b: 40, 44; Gómez 2015), *Los amantes pasajeros* demonstrates the possibilities that a theatrical language of narrative and gestural excess offers to dramatise, and indeed scream about, the state of the nation. The flight attendants set in motion a process of self-reflection and self-analysis that leads to positive changes in behaviour. 'Yo no tengo secretos contigo. Bueno, ni contigo ni con nadie' [I've got no secrets from you. Well, from you or from anyone], Joserra states cogently to Alex at the end of the film. It is a shame that the political leaders of contemporary Spain show no such appetite for addressing the culture of institutional corruption that has beset the nation.

Notes

1 This chapter expands on an earlier short feature on *Los amantes pasajeros* (Delgado 2013). Andy Medhurst (2009) also examines the deployment of farce in Almodóvar's work as a way of considering both how this unsettles his classification as a European art film director and overlooks the Spanish dimensions of his work.

2 It is beyond the scope of this chapter to look at the presence of Federico García Lorca in Almodóvar's work, and *Los amantes pasajeros* does not feature instances from his work (as in *Todo sobre mi madre/All About My Mother*) or sequences that recall scenic configurations from his best-known plays (as in *Volver*), but in *Los amantes pasajeros*, as with many of his other films, Almodóvar shares with Lorca a predilection for naming characters after salient traits.

3 Tricicle is a Catalan performance company with a significant popular following, especially in Catalonia. Its productions, realised by a trio of performers (Joan Gràcia, Paco Mir and Carles Sans), draw on a gestural tradition of slapstick, mime and innuendo. The company emerged, like Almodóvar, from the euphoric climate that marked the transition to democracy; their work is known for its corrosive edge, engaging with a range of social conventions and bureaucratic regulations, and dramatising the trio's often traumatic relationship with the objects of modernity (see Delgado 2009a: 42–3).

4 While it is beyond the remit of this chapter to examine the 'gay' qualities of the film as compared to *La ley del deseo/Law of Desire* (1987) or *La mala educación*, Almodóvar has characterised it as his 'gayest film ever' (cited in Tremlett 2013).

5 For an exploration of the idea of Marisa as a Sleeping Beauty, see Martín Garzo (2011: 123).

6 The emblematic viaduct features also in Valle-Inclán's *Luces de bohemia*, another *esperpento* reflecting wryly on the state of the nation. Almodóvar has expressed his admiration of Valle-Inclán's aesthetic to me on numerous occasions, and numerous essays comment on the esperpentic qualities of his cinema (see, for example, Kinder 2009: 277–8; Zurián 2009: 420).

7 At the time of completing this chapter (March 2015), Ryanair announced that they would be initiating regular scheduled flights from September 2015 serving Castellón and London Stansted (three times a week), and Bristol (twice a week). The decision to open the route was based on the consequences of *la crisis*, with Ryanair's chief marketing officer identifying youth traffic – 'London is the number one destination for unemployed Spanish youth' (cited in Paris 2015) – as a key reason for the opening of the commercial route.

8 I have written elsewhere on the cultural implications of the pact of silence (see Delgado 2015).

9 This is a relationship that has been effectively prised apart by a series of Almodóvar scholars (see, for example, Epps and Kaudoudaki 2009: 1; Smith 2000: 2).

References

AFP (n/a) (2009) 'Almodóvar defiende la memoria histórica y el derecho de autor de directores', *La Prensa Gráfica*, 19 May, www.laprensagrafica.com/fama/espectaculos/33964-almodovar-defiende-la-memoria-historica-y-el-derecho-de-autor-de-directores, accessed 6 April 2015.

Almodóvar, Pedro (2013a) 'Interview with Maria M. Delgado', 23 April.

Almodóvar, Pedro (2013b) Press notes for *I'm So Excited!* [Pathé] (n.p.).

Boyero, Carlos (2009) '¿Qué he hecho yo para merecer esto?', *El País*, 18 March, http://elpais.com/diario/2009/03/18/cine/1237330802_850215.html, accessed 6 April 2015.

Boyero, Carlos (2013) '¿Qué he hecho yo para merecer esto? (II)', *El País*, 8 March, http://cultura.elpais.com/cultura/2013/03/07/actualidad/1362687999_648669.html, accessed 6 April 2015.

Delgado, Maria M. (2009a) 'Barcelona, Mime, Music and a Return to School', *Western European Stages*, 21.2, 29–43.

Delgado, Maria M. (2009b) 'Sensory Perception: Almodóvar's *Broken Embraces*', *Sight & Sound*, September, 40–4.

Delgado, Maria M. (2013) 'Wings of Desire', *Sight & Sound*, May, 36–40.

Delgado, Maria M. (2015) 'Memory, Silence and Democracy in Spain: Federico García Lorca, the Spanish Civil War and the Law of Historical Memory', *Theatre Journal*, 67.2, May, 177–96.

Delgado, Luisa Elena (2014) *La nación singular: Fantasías de la normalidad democrática española (1996–2011)*, Madrid: Siglo XXI.

Denby, David (2012) 'The Artists: Notes on a Lost Style of Acting', *New Yorker*, 21 February, www.newyorker.com/magazine/2012/02/27/the-artists, accessed 6 April 2015.

Dickson, Andrew (2014) 'Women on the Verge of Song and Dance: Why Almodóvar's World is Pure Theatre', *Guardian*, 10 December, www.theguardian.com/stage/2014/dec/10/women-on-the-verge-on-stage-theatre-almodovar, accessed 6 April 2015.

Epps, Brad and Despina Kaudoudaki (2009) 'Introduction', in Epps and Kaudoudaki (eds), *All About Almodóvar: A Passion for Cinema*, Minneapolis: University of Minnesota Press, pp. 1–34.

Evans, Peter W. (1996) *Women on the Verge of a Nervous Breakdown*, BFI Modern Classics, London: British Film Institute.

Gómez, Lourdes (2015) 'Almodóvar planea una película sobre las víctimas del Franquismo', *El Mundo*, 31 January, www.elmundo.es/cultura/2015/01/13/54b3f8b122601d4a488b4592.html, accessed 6 April 2015.

Jordan, Barry (2003) 'Revisiting the "comedia sexy ibérica": *No desearás al vecino del quinto*', *International Journal of Iberian Studies*, 15.3, 167–86.

Kinder, Marsha (2009) 'All about the Brothers: Retroseriality in Almodóvar's Cinema', in Epps and Kaudoudaki (eds), *All About Almodóvar: A Passion for Cinema*, Minneapolis: University of Minnesota Press, pp. 267–94.

Llopart, Salvador (2013) '*Los amantes pasajeros*: perdido en su propia voz', *La Vanguardia*, 8 March, www.lavanguardia.com/cine/20130308/54368149290/los-amantes-pasajeros-critica-de-cine.html, accessed 6 April 2015.

Losilla, Carlos (2013) 'I'm So Excited!', *Sight & Sound*, May, 96–7.

Martín Garzo, Gustavo (2011) 'Lo que pasó en el arca', in Pedro Almodóvar *et al.*, *Los archivos de Pedro Almodóvar*, ed. Paul Duncan in collaboration with Bárbara Peiró, Köln: Taschen, 120–3.

Martínez, Luis (2013) 'Refutación y éxtasis del buen gusto', *El Mundo*, 3 March, www.elmundo.es/elmundo/2013/03/07/cultura/1362681334.html, accessed 6 April 2015.

Medhurst, Andy (2009) 'Heart of Farce: Almodóvar's Comic Complexities', in Brad Epps and Kaudoudaki (eds), *All About Almodóvar: A Passion for Cinema*, Minneapolis: University of Minnesota Press, pp. 118–38.

Muñoz Molina, Antonio (2013) *Todo lo que era sólido*, Madrid: Seix Barral.

Ordóñez, Marcos (2008) *Alfredo el Grande. Vida de un cómico. Landa lo cuenta todo*. Madrid: Aguilar.

Paris, Natalie (2015) 'Ryanair Flying to "Ghost Airport" Partly to Serve Spanish Migrants', *Daily Telegraph*, 17 March, www.telegraph.co.uk/travel/travel-news/ryanair/11477679/Ryanair-flying-to-ghost-airport-partly-to-serve-Spanish-migrants.html, accessed 16 April 2015.

Portalatín, Beatriz G. (2013) 'El landismo fue toda una escuela sexual en España', *El Mundo*, 10 May, www.elmundo.es/elmundo/2013/05/09/cultura/1368130262.html, accessed 6 April 2015.

Rodríguez Marchante, Oti (2013) 'Crítica de *Los amantes pasajeros*: El marinero que perdió la gracia del mar', *ABC*, 8 March, http://hoycinema.abc.es/noticias-cine/20130308/critica-amantes-pasajeros-marinero-571468.html, accessed 6 April 2015.

Sánchez Carbonell, X. and, P. Colomera (2003) 'Consumo de drogas en el cine de Pedro Almodóvar', *Adicciones*, 15: 23–30, www.adicciones.es/files/4.Drogas%20Almodovar.pdf, accessed 6 April 2015.

Smith, Paul Julian (2000) *Desire Unlimited: The Cinema of Pedro Almodóvar*, rev. ed., London: Verso.

Smith, Paul Julian (2006) *Spanish Visual Culture: Cinema, Television, Internet*, Manchester: Manchester University Press.

Strauss, Frédéric (1994) *Almodóvar on Almodóvar*, trans. Yves Baignères, additional material trans. Sam Richard, London: Faber and Faber.

Strauss, Frédéric (2007) *Almodóvar on Almodóvar*, 2nd ed., London: Faber and Faber.

Tremlett, Giles (2013) 'Pedro Almodóvar: "It's My Gayest Film Ever"', *Observer*, 27 April, www.theguardian.com/film/2013/apr/28/almodovar-my-gayest-film-ever, accessed 6 April 2015.

Triana-Toribio, Núria (2003) *Spanish National Cinema*, London: Routledge.

Zurián, Francisco A. (2009) 'Pepi, Patty, and Beyond: Cinema and Literature in Almodóvar', in Brad Epps and Despina Kaudoudaki (eds), *All About Almodóvar: A Passion for Cinema*, Minneapolis: University of Minnesota Press, pp. 408–28.

Index